Reaping the Whirlwind

The Taliban Movement in Afghanistan

Michael Griffin

LONDON • STERLING, VIRGINIA

First published 2001 by Pluto Press
345 Archway Road, London N6 5AA
and 22883 Quicksilver Drive,
Sterling, VA 20166–2012, USA

www.plutobooks.com

British Library Cataloguing in Publication Data
A catalogue record for this book is available from the British Library

Library of Congress Cataloging in Publication Data
Griffin, Michael.
Reaping the whirlwind : Afghanistan's Taliban movement / Michael Griffin.
p. cm.
Includes index.
ISBN 0–7453–1274–8 (hbk)
1. Afghanistan—History—1973– 2. Taliban. 3. Islamic fundamentalism—Afghanistan. 4. Islam and state—Afghanistan. 5. Islam and politics—Afghanistan. I. Title.
DS371.2 .G74 2001b
958.104—dc21

2001000249
Rev.

ISBN 0 7453 1274 8 hardback

10 09 08 07 06 05 04 03 02 01
10 9 8 7 6 5 4 3

Designed and produced for Pluto Press by
Chase Publishing Services, Fortescue, Sidmouth EX10 9QG
Typeset from disk by Stanford DTP Services, Northampton
Printed in the United States of America

Contents

For Liam,
navigating his own route through the Silk Gorge,
and born, happily,
on 25 September 1996,
while all of Kabul held its breath.

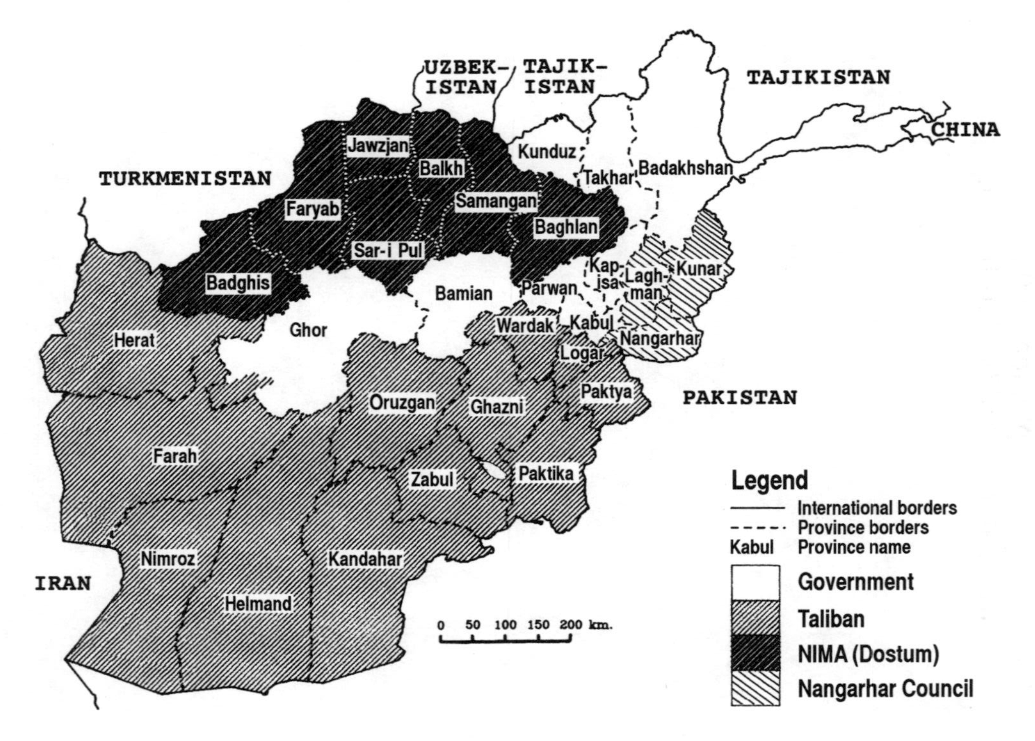

Territorial control of Afghanistan (January 1996)

List of Abbreviations

ACBAR	Agency Coordinating Body for Afghan Relief
ACF	Action Contre la Faim
AIG	Afghan Interim Government
b/d	Barrel per day
BJP	Bharatiya Janata Party
BP	British Petroleum
CDA	Council for the Defence of Afghanistan
CIS	Commonwealth of Independent States
DEA	Drug Enforcement Agency
ECHO	European Community Humanitarian Office
ECU	European Currency Unit
FM	Feminist Majority
GDD	Geopolitical Drugs Despatch
GIA	French acronym for Algeria's Armed Islamic Group
HUA	Harakat ul-Ansar
HUM	Harakat ul-Mujahedin
IB	Intelligence Bureau
ICRC	International Committee of the Red Cross
IRP	Islamic Revival Party
ISI	Inter Services Intelligence
JI	Jamaat-i Islami
JUI	Jamiat ul-Ulama-i Islami
MSF	Médecins Sans Frontières
NGOs	Non-governmental organisations
NWFB	North West Frontier Province
OMON	Russian acronym for Special-Purpose Militia Detachment
OPEC	Organisation of Petroleum Exporting Countries
PDPA	People's Democratic Republic of Afghanistan
PEACE	Poverty Eradication and Community Empowerment
PFLP	Popular Front for the Liberation of Palestine
PKK	Kurdish acronym for Kurdistan Workers Party
PPP	Pakistan People's Party
SCF	Save the Children Fund
SLORC	State Law and Order Restoration Council

SP	*Strategic Policy* magazine
TAP	Turkmenistan-Afghanistan-Pakistan gas pipeline
TTA	Transit Trade Agreement
UAE	United Arab Emirates
UIFLA	United Islamic Front for the Liberation of Afghanistan
UNDCP	United Nations Drug Control Programme
UNICEF	United Nations Children's Emergency Fund
UNHCR	United Nations High Commission for Refugees
UNITA	Portuguese acronym for National Union for the Total Independence of Angola
UNOCHA	UN Office for the Coordination of Humanitarian Assistance to Afghanistan
WFP	World Food Programme
YWCA	Young Women's Christian Association

Chronology

17 July 1973 – King Zahir Shah is overthrown by his cousin, former Prime Minister Mohammad Daoud, with Soviet backing. Afghanistan is proclaimed a republic.

27 April 1978 – President Daoud is killed in a Marxist coup by the People's Democratic Party of Afghanistan (PDPA). Attempts by the new president, Noor Mohammad Taraki, to impose land reform and compulsory education for women spark a nationwide *jihad*.

September 1979 – President Taraki is murdered by his deputy, Hafizullah Amin. Amin is executed three months later.

24 December 1979 – Red Army units seize Kabul airport as four Soviet motorised divisions roll across the northern border. Babrak Karmal, exiled PDPA leader in Moscow, returns as president.

24 December 1979–February 1989 – The Soviet-Afghan War. Seven *mujahedin* parties, based in Peshawar, are selected by Pakistan's President Zia ul-Haq to receive the military supplies pouring in from western countries and the Islamic world.

February–April 1985 – Mikhail Gorbachev assumes power in Moscow. Occupation forces rise to 140,000 men but entire regions, such as the Hazarajat and Kunar valley, are virtual no-go areas to Soviet and government troops. The US supplies the *mujahedin* with Stinger missiles, tipping the balance of power.

4 May 1986 – At Moscow's behest, Maj-Gen Mohammad Najibullah replaces Karmal as president. As Soviet casualties mount, Gorbachev describes the Afghan imbroglio as 'a bleeding wound', but continues to press for a military solution.

February 1988 – Gorbachev announces a 10-month phased withdrawal of Soviet troops, beginning mid-May. The Geneva Accords, signed on 14 April, allow both superpowers to continue to supply arms to the combatants.

14 February 1989 – In Peshawar, the 'Seven-Party Alliance of Afghan *Mujahedin*' announces the establishment of an 'Afghan Interim Government' (AIG), with Sibghatullah Mojadeddi as president. Shia resistance groups and many key field commanders are excluded.

March-September 1989– Battle of Jalalabad. *Mujahedin* forces fail to capture key eastern city after a siege claiming 10,000 lives.

29 August 1989 – Foreign Minister Gulbuddin Hekmatyar, head of the radical *Hizb-i Islami,* breaks with the AIG.

6–7 February 1990 – The US and the Soviet Union agree that President Najibullah will remain in power until internationally-supervised elections can be held.

29 May 1990 – Najibullah announces the introduction of a multiparty system.

25 July 1990 – Refugees begin to return home under the UN's Voluntary Repatriation Scheme.

February–March 1991 – US discontinues military aid to the AIG and announces it cannot guarantee humanitarian assistance for 1992.

21 May 1991 – UN Secretary-General Perez de Cuellar calls for an end to arms supplies to all sides, a cessation of hostilities and elections for a broadly-based democratic government. The AIG rejects any compromise with the Najibullah government.

April 1992 – As *mujahedin* forces converge on Kabul, Najibullah is removed by military officers and takes refuge in a UN compound. *Mujahedin* leaders sign the Peshawar Accord, agreeing to a power-sharing period of transitional rule leading to elections. Hekmatyar is not a signatory.

24 June 1992 – Prof Burhanuddin Rabbani is declared transitional president of the 'Islamic State of Afghanistan' for six months. Hekmatyar's forces fire missiles and rockets into Kabul.

July–August 1992 – Fighting erupts between rival *mujahedin* factions in Kabul. The UN evacuates staff from the city and relocates its offices to Islamabad.

30 December 1992 – In defiance of the Peshawar Accord, Rabbani is confirmed as president for a further two years by a 'Council of Wise Men'. Five of the nine key party leaders boycott the council.

19 January 1993 – Government launches an offensive against Hekmatyar, who responds with a month-long rocket bombardment of the capital. Thousands of civilians perish.

February 1993 – Four UN staff are assassinated in Nangarhar Province on the road to the Khyber Pass.

7 March 1993 – Under the Islamabad Accord, Rabbani's term is reduced to 18 months and Hekmatyar is brought in as prime minister. Fighting resumes two days later over the unresolved status of both Defence Minister Ahmad Shah Massoud and General Dostum, the former communist who controls northern Afghanistan.

16 June 1993 – Hekmatyar is sworn in as prime minister, Massoud resigns.

1 January 1994 – The Battle for Kabul intensifies as General Dostum forms an alliance with Hekmatyar. Fighting continues throughout the year but no clear winner emerges. A blockade halts the delivery of relief food and medicine.

14 February 1994 – Ambassador Mahmoud Mestiri is named head of a Special UN Mission with a mandate to restart the peace process. He tables proposals for a ceasefire, the creation of a neutral security force and the summoning of a *Loya Jirga*, or representative council, to oversee the formation of a transitional government.

October 1994 – Kandahar falls to an obscure militia of religious students, or *taliban*, led by Mullah Mohammad Omar, who calls for 4,000 volunteers from Pakistan.

11 November 1994 – The UN appeals for $106.4 million to meet the humanitarian requirements of Afghanistan for the next twelve months. Fighting during the year has killed 7,000, injured around 100,000 and made more than half a million people homeless, according to the International Committee of the Red Cross.

24 December 1994 – The fifteenth anniversary of the Soviet invasion passes unremarked.

February 1995 – Taliban force Hekmatyar to abandon his rocket bases at Charasyab and Maidanshahr, ending the first siege of Kabul.

20 March 1995 – Following the killing of Abdul-Ali Mazari, leader of the Shia *Hizb-i Wahdat,* Taliban forces are expelled from Kabul by government forces.

5 September 1995 – After fierce fighting in western Afghanistan, Herat falls to the Taliban. Local warlord Ismail Khan flees with 8,000 followers to Iran.

6 September 1995 – Pakistan's embassy in Kabul is set ablaze by rioting Afghans.

October 1995 – Second siege begins as the Taliban rocket the capital and tighten the blockade.

4 October 1995 – At the UN General Assembly in New York, Deputy Foreign Minister Abdul Rahim Ghafoorzai accuses Pakistan of orchestrating and supplying the Taliban movement.

10 November 1995 – UNICEF suspends assistance to education in Taliban-controlled regions.

3 April 1996 – 1,000 Muslim clergymen elect Mullah Mohammad Omar as *Amir ul-Momineen,* or Leader of the Faithful.

26 June 1996 – After a peace deal between Rabbani and Hekmatyar, the latter re-assumes his title as prime minister. Islamic dress code is enforced for women in Kabul.

5 September 1996 – Taliban launch offensive in eastern Afghanistan, capturing Jalalabad.

26 September 1996 – Massoud abandons Kabul.

27 September 1996 – Taliban take control of Kabul, hang Najibullah and declare Afghanistan a 'completely Islamic state'.

7 October 1996 – Rabbani, Dostum and Karim Khalili, leader of *Hizb-i Wahdat*, announce formation of an anti-Taliban alliance called the Council for the Defence of Afghanistan.

13 May 1997 – Afghan opposition forms new government under Rabbani in Mazar-i Sharif.

19 May 1997 – General Abdul Malik, governor of Faryab, mutinies and allies with the Taliban. Dostum flees to Turkey

24 May 1997 – Taliban forces enter Mazar-i Sharif.

25 May 1997 – Pakistan recognises the Taliban government, followed by Saudi Arabia and the United Arab Emirates.

28 May 1997 – General Malik, in alliance with *Hizb-i Wahdat*, turns on Taliban. Hundreds killed and 2,000 captured as fierce fighting drives them from the city.

10 June 1997 – Mullah Mohammad Omar makes his first public visit to Kabul to rally morale.

August 1997 – Taliban blockade the Hazarajat.

September 1997 – Taliban arrest EU Commissioner Emma Bonino in Kabul.

October 1997 – UNOCAL announces trans-Afghanistan pipeline consortium.

November 1997 – General Malik and his brothers flee into exile.

18 November 1997 – US Secretary of State Madeleine Albright condemns Taliban treatment of women.

23 February 1998 – Osama bin-Ladin calls on Muslims to 'kill the Americans and their allies – civilian and military'.

25 March 1998 – UN withdraws staff from Kandahar.

17 April 1998 – US ambassador to UN Bill Richardson holds peace talks with the Taliban.

3 May 1998 – Peace talks collapse.

13 July 1998 – Two UN staff murdered in Jalalabad.

21 July 1998 – Foreign NGOs leave Kabul.

7 August 1998 – US embassies in Kenya and Tanzania are attacked with grievous loss of life.

8 August 1998 – 4–5,000 people, including nine Iranian diplomats, are killed as Mazar-i Sharif falls to the Taliban.

20 August 1998 – US cruise missiles attack four training camps near Khost.

21 August 1998 – After UN observer is murdered in Kabul, the UN and the International Committee of the Red Cross withdraw all foreign staff.

September 1998 – Saudi Arabia withdraws diplomats; Taliban capture Bamian.

21 October 1998 – UN defers decision on recognition.

8 November 1998 – US posts $5 million reward for information leading to the capture of bin-Ladin: Taliban respond with offer to try bin-Ladin in Afghanistan, finding him 'innocent' of wrongdoing by the end of the month.

6 December 1998 – UNOCAL announces its withdrawal from the pipeline consortium.

12 February 1999 – Taliban announce the 'disappearance' of bin-Ladin. UN staff return to Kabul.

21 April 1999 – Taliban recapture Bamian.

May 1999 – Pakistan-backed fighters transgress the 'Line of Control' in Kashmir, provoking an international incident with India.

4 July 1999 – Bin-Ladin discovered near Jalalabad.

4 July 1999 – Prime Minister Nawaz Sharif of Pakistan signs Washington Agreement.

6 July 1999 – US imposes trade sanctions on Afghanistan.

28 July 1999 – Taliban launch three-pronged offensive against Massoud, capturing Bagram air base.

4 August 1999 – Ethnic cleansing of Shomali Plain; Massoud launches successful counter-offensive.

24 August 1999 – Attempted assassination of Mullah Mohammad Omar.

20 September 1999 – US warns Pakistan's military command against a coup d'état.

7 October 1999 – ISI chief Lt-Gen. Khawaja Ziauddin flies to Kandahar to denounce the presence of 'terrorist training camps' on Afghan soil.

12 October 1999 – Nawaz Sharif dismisses army chief Gen. Parvez Musharraf, replacing him with Ziauddin.

12 October 1999 – Troops loyal to Gen. Musharraf seize TV centre and arrest Sharif.

13 October 1999 – Gen. Musharraf pronounces himself 'Chief Executive' in an early morning broadcast.

15 November 1999 – UN imposes sanctions on Afghanistan.

24 December 1999 – 20th anniversary of the Soviet invasion.

February 2000 – Hijacking of Ariana Airways flight to Stansted, London.

March 2000 – Ismail Khan, former ruler of Herat, escapes from Kandahar after three years in chains.

26 March 2000 – President Bill Clinton makes a five-hour stopover in Islamabad to urge a swift return to democracy.

20 July 2000 – US Assistant Secretary Karl Inderfurth tells Senate Foreign Relations Committee the Taliban will be forced out of Kabul by November.

5 September 2000 – After 33 days fighting, Massoud's northern capital, Taloqan, falls to a combined Taliban/Pakistani/Arab force. Thousands of refugees head for the Tajik and Pakistani borders.

12 October 2000 – Washington warns it will attack Afghanistan if bin-Ladin is found responsible for the bomb attack on the USS *Cole* in Yemen, which kills 17 sailors.

November 2000 – UN leaves the Afghanistan seat with President Rabbani. Taliban and opposition agree to peace talks.

7 December 2000 – US and Russia ask the UN Security Council to strengthen sanctions.

10–19 December 2000 – UN and NGO foreign staff withdraw amid fear of reprisals.

19 December 2000 – UN tightens sanctions, imposing an arms embargo, closing Taliban offices abroad and forbidding Taliban officials to leave Afghanistan.

3 January 2001 – The trial, *in absentia,* of Osama bin-Ladin, and scores of others allegedly implicated in the East African embassy bombings commences in a Manhattan court.

Preface

The fall of Kabul to the Taliban in September 1996 focused attention upon Afghanistan in a manner not seen since the 1980s, when a very different kind of Islamist rebellion successfully defied the Red Army only to come to grief upon the contradictions of race and sect imbedded in the Afghan national character. What intrigued western newspaper-readers at the time was less the movement's lightning seizure of the Afghan capital: the city had been under rocket and artillery siege for more than four years without quickening any strong response from the general public. It was more the Taliban's atavistic charisma, and the mysterious ambitions of its reclusive leader, Mullah Mohammad Omar, which appeared to reawaken inklings of a global moral crusade even in *infidel* commuters.

In the West, they disdained the Taliban's policies on women and criminals, and tut-tutted that Muslim peasants could cause such ferment in international capitals. But there was something splendid in the movement's infallible sense of direction while its rejection of all things Western touched some deep chord even in these remote spectators who, while holding opinions on every conceivable aspect of human behaviour, still did not know how to act. The Taliban were the stuff of *Kim,* that other tale from beyond the Khyber Pass. They tapped both a romance with the esoteric and an equally widespread phobia of the hypnotised warriors of the Mahdist uprising which, in the nineteenth century, had sent a supra-personal dust devil careering through Britain's colonial ambitions in the Sudan.

Comparisons between the two recent 'salvationist' interludes in Afghan history – both avowedly nationalist, anti-communist but, above all, 'Islamist' – go little further than that initial description: the 15 *mujahedin* parties – seven Sunni, eight Shia – which fought the Soviet Union from 1979–89 tended toward fragmentation from the outset, while the Taliban, borne aloft by a gust of divine inspiration, have displayed no such Icarian tendencies – beyond their erratic talents on the battlefield. What the two movements do have in common, however, in spite of all protestations to the contrary, is that the Afghan resistance to Soviet rule and the Taliban's crusade against the *mujahedeen*'s subsequent lawlessness were both orchestrated by foreign powers whose interests lay less in the fate of ordinary Afghans, than Afghanistan's role in a grander geopolitical design.

As the story moved on after the fall of Kabul – and events move swiftly, or not at all, in Afghanistan – it took on more suggestive dimensions as journalists discovered how the satellite mysteries of regional energy politics, the heroin trade, international Islamic terrorism and modern Great Game politics appeared to wheel seamlessly around the turbans of this millenarial army of religious students. The Taliban's fortuitous progress scattered hints of light – in a region not noted for transparency – and all pointed to an ultimate objective of far greater sophistication than the ramshackle vehicle which had been hired to arrive at it.

With three, two-month Afghan visits to my credit and no background as a historian or scholar of Islam, I was badly qualified to embark on an academic analysis of the Taliban or the authenticity of its spiritual mission. Nor could I hope to produce more than an outsider's version of events, compromised as I am by cultural prejudice and a pronounced taste for the more lurid aspects of Afghan history. Nevertheless, it seemed that someone should attempt to collate the hundreds of local and international reports that had briefly made that day's news and been promptly consigned to the archives; to sift them for whatever fragments of the Taliban mosaic had actually appeared in the public domain. That task might not solve the riddle of which powers had fomented and supplied the Taliban movement, or for what specific purposes, but it would provide hard and fast sources for speculations which, through the pressure of deadlines and the journalist's tendency to simplify and dramatise, have now become part of the assumptive culture. At the least, such a book might serve as an *aide memoire* for a future generation of Afghan historians.

If Afghans have learned anything over the last 30 years, it has been how to suffer, and to suffer again, for which God grant them swift relief. The accession in the US of President George W. Bush, a man with a strong political interest in disinterring the secrets of his predecessor, may shed yet fresh light on at least two of the central mysteries of the Taliban which this book attempts to address. The first is the extent to which the administration of Bill Clinton actively encouraged its former Cold War allies, Pakistan and Saudi Arabia, to assemble and finance a tribal military force to end the misrule of the *mujahedeen* in the post-Soviet years. The second – of greater sensitivity – is to provide a coherent explanation for the studied incompetence of the FBI, CIA and other American intelligence agencies in addressing the alleged threats posed to the US by Osama bin-Ladin and his network. Bush's links with the US energy industry, most notably UNOCAL, are, regrettably, more likely to restrict the current state of knowledge about US policy in Afghanistan in the late 1990s, than to enlarge it.

Reaping the Whirlwind was plotted as a whodunnit, though neither the motive nor the identity of the perpetrator are revealed in the final chapter. The period under study stretches from October 1994, when the Taliban first appeared in Kandahar, through their defiance of the US over Osama bin-Ladin and the military coup in Pakistan, to the imposition of US and UN sanctions in late 2000. It is not a purely chronological record, but a interpretative history that explores the political and military milestones in the Taliban's progress from a series of varied lines of investigation. Sometimes the Taliban are centre-stage in this account, but more often they appear as a remote will-o'-the-wisp, shrouded in unknowability, far to the left of the frame.

I would like to extend my warmest thanks to Anthony Fitzherbert, for my first introduction to the echoes in the Afghan political landscape; and to Syra Morley.

Michael Griffin
25 February 2001

1 The Killing of Najibullah

'But Najib knows full well his days are numbered. He is like a suspended tear drop, about to fall.' Professor Burhanuddin Rabbani, 20 March 1992[1]

The picture, which went around the world on 28 September 1996, would never be erased, whatever good ultimately emerged from the Taliban's capture of the Afghan capital of Kabul the day before.

Two men had been strung up by their necks from an elevated traffic island outside the Argh, the presidential palace, in Ariana Square. The taller one is drenched in blood from his face to the knees of his *shalwar kamees*, but the location of the wound is not immediately apparent. His throat and upper torso are bound in a cat's cradle of ropes, his fingers sculpted into a still-life of what looks like his last throes. The other man, dressed casually in jeans and trainers, had been executed more dispassionately. The pockets of his suede coat and his mouth and hands are stuffed with *afghanis*, the country's much-debased currency, and a token of his executioners' contempt.

Reporters said the crowd cheered at the sight of the bodies of former President Mohammad Najibullah and his brother, Shahpur Ahmadzai, his security chief until the fall of Afghanistan's communist-backed government in April 1992. But the only jubilation is in the faces of two Taliban fighters, frozen in one another's arms and laughing before the corpses with the euphoria of some vendetta that has finally been settled. The bystanders – mostly teenage boys or old men – look with uncertainty around as if shell-shocked, although the Taliban victory spells an end to the random rocket and artillery sieges that have plagued their lives since Najibullah's fall from power. There are no women in the frame.

Afghans had every reason to detest 'Najib', as he was known to friend and foe alike. As director of Khad, the secret police network set up after the Soviet invasion on Christmas Eve 1979, he is said to have ordered the deaths of 80,000 enemies of the state and orchestrated scores of terrorist acts in the tribal trust areas of Pakistan, whence the *mujahedin* launched their operations, and in the city of Peshawar, their logistical headquarters. In 1986, when Mikhail Gorbachev decided to withdraw the Red Army from a war that he had called 'a bleeding wound', Najib replaced Babrak Karmal as Afghanistan's president, going on to defy Western security prognoses by holding the country together for three years after the last Soviet soldier pulled out in February 1989.

But his subsequent efforts with the UN to negotiate a transfer of power in exchange for his own resignation foundered as the US and the Pakistan-backed *mujahedin*, scenting total victory, pressed for a military solution. Najib had sought to shore up his regime by buying the support of disaffected groups among the Tajik, Uzbek, Turkmen, Hazara and Ismaili minorities, turning them into ethnic militias to fight against their former resistance comrades. When the formidable Uzbek militia, commanded by General Rashid Dostum in the northern city of Mazar-i Sharif, mutinied in January 1992 and then formed an alliance with Ahmad Shah Massoud, *mujahedin* commander of the Tajik-dominated *Jamiat-i Islami* party, Najib's government was doomed. The scene was set for the final disintegration of the anomaly known as the Afghan state.

On the night of 15 April, the president tried – with UN help – to slip out through Kabul airport to seek political asylum in India, but he was recognised by *Jamiat* troops who had flown in from the north a few hours earlier. He took shelter in the UN compound where, for the next four and a half years, he lived in pampered imprisonment, pumping iron to keep his weight down, watching satellite TV and fretting over his kidney stones.[2] According to one visitor, Najib had been making a Pashtu translation of Peter Hopkirk's book, *The Great Game*, a study of the imperial intrigues between Britain and Russia which led to Afghanistan's birth as a buffer state in the nineteenth century. 'Afghans keep making the same mistake,' he told the visitor, 'they ought to learn.'[3]

For only the second time in 250 years, Afghanistan was to be governed by its Tajik minority, with Burhanuddin Rabbani as president and Massoud as his military commander. Najibullah posed this supposedly interim administration with a curious dilemma. Publicly, Rabbani demanded that Najib stand trial for crimes committed during the Soviet occupation, a process that might rally support for his beleagured regime, but he could not physically take the ex-president into custody. Najib's abduction from UN property would infringe international law and alienate the diplomatic community on whose recognition and aid the Rabbani regime sorely relied.

In the limbo which ensued, a peculiar symbiosis evolved between the fallen commissar, with 15 years of Cold War intrigue to his credit, and the inexperienced ex-*mujahedin*, who had not only taken the reins of power but, in many cases, were riding the same horses as the communists they had deposed. Among the many members of Rabbani's regime who regularly consulted Najib at the fortified UN house in Wazir Akhbar Khan, Kabul's most prestigious district, was the minister of security, General Fahim, who had taken over Najib's old job as the head of Khad.[4]

As the Taliban entered Kabul's eastern suburbs on 26 September 1996, General Fahim offered to take the former president north with Massoud's retreating forces to Jabal Saraj at the head of the Salang Tunnel, the only route through the palisade of the Hindu Kush.[5] But Najib feared for his life outside the capital and determined to remain with his brother in what he believed to be the inviolable sanctuary of the UN compound. Early on Friday 27 September, the Afghan *chowkidars* – the night-watchmen who guarded him – disappeared and he began frantically calling the UN for more security. But the senior UN staff had already evacuated the capital, abandoning him to his fate.[6]

By some accounts, he went willingly with the squad of Taliban sent to fetch him and, as a fellow-Pashtun, may have even harboured some hope of negotiating for his life.[7] By others, he and his brother were dragged from the compound and taken to the Argh, where Najib was tortured, shot and hung in public view. A doctor who examined his body said that there was bruising on his upper torso – probably from rifle butts – a bullet injury in the upper abdomen, his fingers had been broken and his brains blown out at close range. Reports that he had been castrated were not confirmed.[8]

'We killed him because he was the murderer of our people,' the Taliban leader, Mullah Mohammad Omar, said later from his base in the southern city of Kandahar.[9] But as the photograph and circumstances of Najib's fate flashed around the world, there was a feeling of revulsion against the new rulers of Kabul and a trickle of sympathy for a man who had enjoyed remarkably little of it during his lifetime. Less than a week after his execution, the Taliban attempted to counteract what had turned into a public relations disaster, re-categorising his murder as a crime of passion, rather than justifiable homicide. On 1 October – day six of Taliban rule – the new deputy foreign minister, Sher Mohammad Stanakzai, told journalists: 'Under his leadership, our country was destroyed. It was the anger of our people which killed him.' He pledged that Najib's killers would be brought to justice.[10]

They never were. Kabulis, born weavers of unverifiable theories, recollected that the father and two brothers of Mullah Mohammad Rabbani, a former resistance fighter and head of the Taliban's new governing council in the capital, had been pushed out of a helicopter on Najibullah's orders when they were captured after a *mujahedin* raid in Kandahar.[11] Nor, it was suggested, could the United States or Pakistan, the Taliban's widely-rumoured sponsors, permit the still influential ex-president to go on living, for fear he would rally the more liberal elements in Afghanistan's political diaspora. With the death of Babrak Karmal, Najib's predecessor, from liver cancer in a Moscow hospital three months after the fall of Kabul, it seemed the last links with the communist past had finally been broken.

In truth, Afghans had never really bayed for Najib's blood, not even in the rural areas. They had borne the brunt of the 10-year war of resistance against Soviet rule, a conflict in which an estimated 1.5 million died and a third of the country's 20 million people were driven into exile. Known either as the Butcher of Kabul, for his professional proclivities, or The Ox, because of his wrestler's build, Najib was, above all, an arch-survivor, manipulating political ideology, ethnic divisions, religion or the nationalist card, as and when necessity required. This – and a ruthless pragmatism – were fundamental requirements for any putative ruler of the whole of Afghanistan, a country whose thin veneer of modernity was being constantly tested by far more solidly anchored ethnic and social divisons. But Najib's roots in the Amadzhai clan of the Pashtun, Afghanistan's largest tribe and its rulers for over two centuries, added an undeniable legitimacy to his claim to rule, in spite of the history of Soviet collaboration. He was, in short, the devil that was known.

If it was grudging, it was a kind of respect and it deepened as the struggle to fill the vacuum caused by his fall from power devastated the capital and reduced its people to a penury they had never experienced during ten years of Soviet occupation. Little wonder that most Kabulis began to associate Najib with the rule of law, efficient administration, good salaries, higher education, full bellies on subsidised food, heat, light and entertainment. But if his continued survival at UN expense seemed the consummate act of this shrewd, political beast, he had unwittingly come to represent all that had befallen Afghanistan since the end of the Cold War: a hostage from an inconvenient piece of history relegated to a long-drawn-out wait on death row. On the holiest day of the Muslim week, the executioners arrived.

A month before his enforced seclusion, Najibullah had given one of his last interviews to a US reporter.

> We have a common task – Afghanistan, the USA and the civilised world – to launch a joint struggle against fundamentalism. If fundamentalism comes to Afghanistan, war will continue for many years. Afghanistan will turn into a centre of world smuggling for narcotic drugs. Afghanistan will be turned into a centre for terrorism.[12]

Najib may have been up to his chameleon tricks again, playing on America's growing awareness that President Bush's much-trumpeted 'New World Order' – the outcome of a secret war waged in the mountains of Afghanistan – had simply ushered in a different set of geopolitical threats and riddles. Mazar-i Sharif had joined the rebels two months earlier, however, and the president may have already begun to write the resignation speech he delivered on television a week after the interview.

In the light of what was later to transpire, the comments had the ring of real insight.

As Massoud's forces withdrew to his stronghold in the Panjshir valley, creating a 20 km tailback on the road to Jabal Saraj, the Taliban set about imposing their idiosyncratic vision of Islamic propriety upon Kabul's cowed population. As in Herat, another mainly Tajik city conquered by the movement one year earlier, the first official edicts focused on the rights of females and the Taliban concepts of what constituted public decency.

These had been moulded in the Pashtun regions of the south, where women are traditionally excluded from public life and girls' attendance at schools is regarded as 'un-Islamic' and a sure path to family dishonour. It was a philosophy with fewer converts in Kabul whose culture, after 35 years of Western tourism, US influence and Soviet occupation, had more in common with the secular republics of Central Asia than with Kandahar, the origin of the Taliban movement and the source, for those who lived in the capital, of an almost agorophobic fear of the ways of the Afghan wilderness.

'All those sisters who are working in government offices are hereby informed to stay at home until further notice,' Radio Kabul – renamed the Voice of *Sharia* – announced on 27 September. 'Since *satar* (the

Islamic dress code for women) is of great importance in Islam,' the radio continued, 'all sisters are seriously asked ... to cover their faces and the whole of their body when going out.' Programming at the station, once a comparatively urbane mix of international news, Asian pop, health advice and topical soap operas, was immediately replaced with bulletins of Taliban victories, religious homilies or fresh directives on how citizens should comport themselves.

Tens of thousands of working women, from social workers and secretaries to office cleaners and engineers, were sent home, paralysing a government in which 25 per cent of the staff were female and seriously compromising the efficiency of whatever form of administration the Taliban proposed to introduce afterwards. The decision affected 7,790 female teachers, the backbone of the educational system in Afghanistan, as well as 8,000 women undergraduates at the recently-rebuilt Kabul University, the country's most important seat of learning. The Taliban ban on education was exclusively directed at girls, but many more boys than girls were affected as 63 of the city's schools promptly closed for want of teachers.[13]

Women who did not put on the all-enveloping *burkha*, which covers the body from head to foot and leaves only a narrow grille of lace to look through, risked being beaten by the kohl-eyed Taliban warriors stalking the streets. The glimpse of an uncovered ankle was enough to arouse their righteous fury, with the result that many women preferred to remain at home, rather than expose themselves – or the male relatives forced to chaperone them – to the frightening mood-swings of what quickly came to be seen as an army of occupation.

In 1959, the French writer Frantz Fanon had described the hallucinogenic experience of female Algerian revolutionaries who had unveiled in order to penetrate the European quarters unnoticed. '... She has the impression of being cut into bits, put adrift; the limbs seem to lengthen indefinitely ... for a long time she commits errors of judgement as to the exact distance to be negotiated.'[14] In Kabul, women who had gone unveiled throughout their lives found their scope of vision reduced from 90° – without turning the head – to a 30° tunnel of claustrophobic mesh which, added to their muffled hearing, posed the constant threat of being run down by traffic or the fleets of silent bicycles which throng the capital. For those who tripped, whether through unfamiliarity with the tent-like covering or on the icy pavements, there was the further danger of exposing skin or under-garment.

For those who could not afford the $30 *burkha,* like the estimated 30,000 war widows in Kabul alone, the enforcement of *satar* was tantamount to a formal sentence of house arrest and slow starvation. Denied the right to work, women without a *burkha* could neither shop nor collect water without fear, while those with one could only go out and beg. Dr Sidiqa Sidiq, a professor at the Kabul Polytechnic Institute and one of the few women to publicly challenge the Taliban's impositions, warned them: 'If you deprive (women) from holding solid and decent jobs and stop them getting education, they will be compelled to resort to immoral activity to rescue their children from poverty.' Dr Sidiq told Afghan women to expect no help from abroad. She subsequently disappeared but, like many dissidents, may have gone underground or secretly travelled abroad.[15]

The only exemptions to the new gender decrees were female doctors and other health workers. They were permitted to continue, but pretexts for harassment were abundant in an occupation with a purely diagnostic approach to differences between the sexes. Women doctors were restricted to treating women patients only, but they faced insuperable difficulties both in communicating with their male hospital colleagues and in getting to work on the newly-segregated bus service. The few who remained active did so to prevent the total elimination of the paediatric and gynaecological services needed by their patients, the logical consequence of a Taliban-regulated, all-male, medical establishment.

Women undoubtedly bore the brunt of this new puritanism, but men were also forced to conform – replacing their Western clothing with the *shalwar kamees*; growing long beards; being forced to go to the mosque five times a day to worship; and abandoning toothpaste in favour of the natural root which the Prophet favoured for dental hygiene.[16] TV, kite-flying, the possession of homing pigeons, dancing, music, singing, chess, marbles and cigarettes were all proscribed in a series of radio edicts, whose growing surrealism was crystallised for many in a ban on traders using paper as a wrapper, in case it was printed with extracts from the Koran and was later defiled by being thrown away. None of this legislation was new. The people of Kandahar and Herat had been subjected to the same dour medicine when they fell to the Taliban. But in Kabul, a city with a far more clearly-defined liberal class and a closer identification with the social policies of the 17-year communist experience, the impact seemed all the more shocking, in spite of the ousted government's record of shattered suburbs, human rights abuses and insincere peace efforts.

The focus of the world's press was inevitably the Taliban's brutal eccentricities, but quantifiable benefits did accrue from the first day of their rule in Kabul. After four years of bombardment, fighting became a thing of the past; food and fuel prices plummeted as roads were re-opened to districts previously in enemy hands; and the few *sharia* judgements carried out in the capital transformed the security climate overnight – even as they inflamed human rights activists abroad. What frightened civilians more were the summary punishments, whether against women for breaking *satar* or alleged sympathisers with the Rabbani regime. As many as 1,000 civilians were detained during Taliban house-to-house searches within the first few days, according to Amnesty International, while the International Committee of the Red Cross reportedly put the figure as high as 1,800.[17] Scores of men and young boys were press-ganged from mosques into serving at the frontline, with some relatives fearing they would be deployed as human mine-clearers.[18] An atmosphere of terror, created by one faction or another, invaded the city following the successive discovery of 16 headless – and unidentifiable – corpses dumped in ruins.[19]

If this was vigilantism in action, perhaps the loss of personal freedom was a small price to pay in a city which had known nothing but destruction and siege since the *mujahedin* takeover in 1992. Human rights abuses by the Taliban were fewer in number than those perpetrated by General Dostum's Uzbek militia and the other armed factions. And while several hundred women were severely beaten by the Taliban, not a single rape was reported during their first nine months in power. Perhaps there was substance to the leadership's claim that its rigorous enforcement of restrictions on Kabuli women was dictated by the need to prevent their mainly rural forces from being tempted in unruly directions.[20]

Diplomats spoke of a trade-off between peace and security on the one hand and human rights on the other. That, at least, was the response of John Holtzman, deputy chief of mission at the US embassy in Pakistan. He told reporters in early October that the Taliban could play a useful role in restoring strong, centralised government to Afghanistan, a position echoed privately by relief veterans who, after two years of fruitless negotiations by the UN Special Mission, saw in the Taliban with all of their prejudices a peculiarly Afghan solution to a problem that had defied international peacemaking mechanisms for four years. Robin Raphel, the US assistant secretary of state for South Asian Affairs, by contrast, had described the Taliban in the previous May as 'highly factionalised' and lacking in strong, consistent central leadership, and she had met the leaders on two occasions.[21]

Such contradictory readings of the same phenomenon were not only due to under-research, for the Pentagon had been equally at sea after the Soviet invasion in distinguishing between the main *mujahedin* parties, split as they were along finely-calibrated ethnic, social and sectarian lines. The newest confusion was more a measure of the Taliban's inherent opaqueness as a political and religious force, even after two years in the relative limelight ignited by its success in battle. As Kabul yielded, nothing was known for certain of its military organisation or long-term agenda, while the Taliban leader, Mullah Mohammad Omar, had never been photographed or interviewed. This information gap provided a fertile ground for speculation regarding covert military support from Pakistan, Saudi Arabia and the United States, the troika which had sustained the *mujahedin* during the Soviet war, only to despair of their endless disputes once victory had been achieved. How else, it was reasoned, could so homespun a movement have made such spectacular advances in a strategic landscape that had been largely quagmired since 1992?

If the West was puzzled by the Taliban, so too was the Muslim world, which had initially applauded its prime objective of establishing an Islamic state in Afghanistan. Taliban officials employed the rhetoric of Islamist revolution, but their points of reference seemed light-years removed from the militant struggles being waged elsewhere in the world, struggles which married the legitimising principles of traditional *sharia* law with concepts of social justice which had their roots in the canons of dialectical materialism. The Taliban could not be criticised for their want of grassroots support – at least in Pashtun districts. But the society which they envisioned, and had begun to build in southern Afghanistan, went so far beyond comparable movements of spiritual revival that it made the ayatollahs look like liberal progressives. Their gender policies, meanwhile, bore an unmistakeable odour of state-endorsed misogyny, given sanction by a questionable parsing of religious texts. Regional guardians of Islamic correctness, such as Iran, Egypt's Muslim Brotherhood and Pakistan's *Jamiat-i Islami* party – all of which had political ties with the outgoing regime – were fiercely critical of the movement's social experiments, which they condemned for 'giving Islam a bad name'. The *Jamiat-ul Ulama-i Islam,* a small but strategic partner in Prime Minister Benazir Bhutto's soon-to-founder government and a vocal supporter of the Taliban, said that it would approve the same penalties for blasphemy and theft, when it finally came to power in Pakistan.[22]

Whether intended or not, the execution of Najib sent a stark message to all who had served in the communist or Rabbani régimes: the Taliban would take its vengeance where it willed and would not be bound by the niceties of international law. By December 1996, according to preliminary UN figures, some 150,000 people had fled the city, heading north to Mazar-i Sharif, or across the border into Pakistan, in spite of the fact that Massoud had shown no real intention of investing Kabul during the bitter winter season. The figure was later adjusted to 50,000. University staff carried out a straw poll in eight 48-flat housing blocks at Microrayon, a vast middle-income residential project built by the Soviet Union which had been on the frontline during the faction struggles of 1994. It revealed that 50 per cent of families had left during 1992–96, while 50 per cent of those remaining had vacated by the end of the first 100 days of Taliban rule.[23]

Without women, or the many technocrats who had gained their experience during the occupation but fled as the Taliban approached, an administration that had always functioned on one cylinder only ground swiftly to a halt. Ministerial positions were parcelled out to Taliban fellow-travellers, some eager to learn, but others scarcely out of their 20s, ignorant of the Dari dialect of Persian spoken in the capital and more anxious about sartorial detail, than coordinating the management of a city of 1.2 million people.

While Kabulis suffered their stern directives, aid personnel in daily contact conveyed reports of Taliban officials so out of touch with modern priorities and protocols that it was like conversing with a group suffering from a specialised form of autism, one that permitted an awareness of an outside world, without allowing it entry. This was especially galling to the UN which, since the Taliban takeover of Herat in September 1995, had counted upon the Taliban modifying its restrictions on female employment and mobility, as it matured from a popular uprising into a responsible government with linkages to the donor community. This would have removed the need for any more forthright condemnation of the Taliban's gender policies in a year which had already witnessed a controversial world women's conference in Beijing and the emergence of what was seen as an unholy alliance between the Vatican and radical Islamic states to prevent the right to abortion being included in the final declaration.

But the Taliban refused to bend their ideology to international norms, meeting any warning that aid might, as a consequence, be suspended not with alarm, but with passive acceptance and vague assurances that such matters would be dealt with in the course of time and when all of Afghanistan was under the movement's control.

UNICEF had announced in November 1995 the suspension of all assistance to education in Taliban-controlled regions of the country, arguing that the ban on female attendance at schools and colleges constituted a breach of the Convention of the Rights of the Child. Save the Children (UK) followed suit four months later, giving the additional reason that the prohibition on female employment made it impossible for the agency to communicate with women, the main carers for children. Oxfam went further after the fall of Kabul, suspending its entire programme of development until female nationals working with the agency were free again to resume their duties.

If the furore over women's rights initially took the new leaders by surprise, it did not stay their hands. Nor did it elicit a more robust reaction from the UN. In New York, the Security Council was prevented from issuing a condemnation of the abuses due to opposition from China and Indonesia – both of which systematically block what they regard as interference in domestic matters – and through the curious abstention of the United States, only one month away from presidential elections. UN agencies stressed the need for a 'non-confrontational' approach, in the hope that the Taliban's desire for international recognition would induce a softening in its stance before the momentum of protest at the abuse of women's rights built to such a point that the organisation would be forced to the brink of the unthinkable: a unilateral break on ethical grounds with a *de facto* government whose every pronouncement on gender made a mockery of the Convention on the Elimination of All Forms of Discrimination Against Women. Afghanistan had ratified that document one year after the Soviet invasion.

They need not have worried. What remained of the international women's movement was more preoccupied with Indian women stepping into bikinis at the Miss World contest, taking place that winter in New Delhi for the first time, than the beatings handed out for dress code violations a thousand kilometres to the northwest.

Even as the *pax Talibana* settled over Kabul, it appeared that this was a government with which nobody could do business.

* * *

Backwoods zealots they may have been, but the fall of Kabul shattered whatever doubts may have lingered about the movement's military and logistical capabilities. In the first six months after the Taliban emerged in Kandahar in October 1994, it had taken control of one-third of the country, disarming local populations and imposing an interpretation of Islamic law that was both harsh in the extreme, but comfortingly familiar to the Pashtun clans living in the east and south of Afghanistan and in the adjacent tribal trust territories of Pakistan.

The largest tribalised society in the world, the Pashtun, share an ethos which combines customary law with an austere form of Sunni Islam. After more than a decade in the refugee squalor of Pakistan, it had hardened into an amalgam of piety and vendetta which found its highest expression in the defence of women's honour and the common call to arms. The movement was born when a former *mojahed*, Mohammad Omar, mobilised a group of *taliban*, or religious students, and killed a local commander who had raped two village women.[24] Whether true or not, the story struck just the right note to capture the spirit of the times and to spark off what, in the early months, had the tenor of a genuine 'victims' revolt.

For the best part of four years, the south had been in the grip of a species of Islamic samurai, gallant fighters once but fallen upon hard times since the end of the *jihad* and determined to fall no further. Their fiefdoms had been carved out as Najib's rule teetered towards its conclusion, sometimes by force of arms but, more generally, through opportunistic alliances between resistance commanders and officers in the government's frightened forces. In exchange for their lives or a role in the postwar dispensation, the latter delivered entire garrisons into *mujahedin* hands, along with their weapons, ammunition, heavy artillery, tanks and jet fighters. These private ceasefires were often made between members of the same clan or family, profiting from both sides of the Cold War divide, but attached to one another by ties more adamant than ideology.

The outcome was a patchwork of rival warlords, each with his ramshackle facsimile of the Soviet war machine. The loyalty of their fighters, whose numbers fluctuated according to season and military need, was assured through a mixture of patronage, loot and salary, often supplemented by a supply of wheat for their families. If the warlord was allied with the government of President Rabbani – and that depended upon the strategic value of the assets he controlled – a few sacks of newly-printed *afghanis* might be delivered every few months to pay the troops and to keep up the appearance of a functioning civil service. Most commanders lacked this influence and had resorted to racketeering, opium-growing, the trade in Cold War arms and outright banditry to shore up their volatile enclaves. It was the *jihad* which had spawned these gangs and it would take another to sweep them away.

As the legend of the Taliban's invincibility spread in late 1994, the impression grew that the long-suffering Pashtun peasantry had finally overcome their innate rivalries of clan and valley in order to impose through their own efforts the peace which had eluded Afghanistan since 1979. The movement was hailed as a living embodiment of the tide of popular rejectionism, but the rejection went far beyond the *mujahedin* and their communist predecessors to embrace the UN's flagging peace initiative, the perfidious United States and a monarchy which, since 1929, had done everything in its power to modernise Afghanistan – and to undermine the foundations of its authentic social and spiritual harmony. As the clock ticked backwards in the towns captured by the Taliban, it seemed that Mohammad Omar's army, like some nineteenth-century millenarian movement, was taking on history itself.

Even while the Taliban scythed northwards towards Kabul, scooping up fresh recruits and arms, the suspicion remained that its core supporters were still 'unblooded' and that the militia had acquired its victories only through a skilful manipulation of spiritual intoxication, shared ethnicity and the occasional, token skirmish. The students rarely met sustained resistance from local commanders who, like the garrison officers before them, preferred to submit to fellow Pashtuns on favourable terms, rather than confront a superior force riding upon the crest of popular acclaim. It was a textbook case of the Afghan art of knowing precisely when to change sides.

Few analysts believed the Taliban could use the same bluff on the government's brigades, seasoned by four years of siege and an attritional mode of combat which, far from the hit-and-run tactics that dislodged the Red Army, had degenerated into a dogged trench warfare more reminiscent of the Iran–Iraq conflict. Ahmad Shah Massoud, President Rabbani's charismatic commander, had been regarded as a wily military strategist in the *jihad*, when he was elevated to near-star status in the western media as the 'Lion of Panjshir', surviving eleven blistering campaigns by the Soviet-led forces. In the defence of Kabul, he had displayed a talent for planning fast-moving, multi-phased operations that was exceptional in a conflict which, since the capture of Soviet weaponry in 1992, had been characterised more by brute force than tactical subtlety.

His reputation may have been tarnished for failing to protect Kabul from the rockets of the Pakistan-backed *Hizb-i Islami* faction, led by the Pashtun warlord Gulbuddin Hekmatyar, or to oust his siege forces from vantage points to the south and southwest of the city. But as a fellow Tajik, he retained the reluctant support of Kabul's citizens who, though desperate for an end to the fighting, expected little improvement in their circumstances from forces whose indiscrimate pummelling suggested they recognised no significant distinction between troops and civilians.

All the evidence suggests that Massoud regarded the Taliban more as a relief than a threat, when they first approached the capital in February 1995.[25] By advancing on Hekmatyar's positions from the south, they divided his forces, allowing Massoud time to concentrate on his other main enemy, the Shia *Hizb-i Wahdat*, then occupying the Karta Se district in southwest Kabul. The Tajik leader reportedly met the Taliban commanders on two occasions during this phase of the conflict, supplying mechanics to repair a helicopter abandoned by *Hizb-i Islami* forces as they abandoned their positions.[26] Massoud had sworn on the Koran during one of these meetings that, if the Taliban took Charasyab, he would give them 'the golden key of Kabul' and withdraw to prevent more civilian deaths.[27] Once the Taliban dislodged Hekmatyar, Massoud attacked *Wahdat*, triggering a two-week government offensive which culminated in the expulsion of the Taliban from all the positions they had won. By 19 March, the first siege of Kabul was over – only to resume six months later, when the Taliban reoccupied Hekmatyar's positions overlooking the city.

Massoud's military position, however, had improved immeasurably since the loss of Herat in September 1995, an event which rang alarm bells from Moscow to New Delhi. After a lengthy period in the wilderness, the Rabbani government was suddenly surrounded by friendly nations, worried by the Taliban's rapid advance and what was perceived as Pakistan's more aggressive policy in Afghanistan. Shipments of fresh arms began to arrive from Iran, Russia, Bulgaria and Albania, while Ukraine reportedly supplied 30 second-hand fighter-bombers and India despatched technicians and a team of trainers.[28] A counter-attack on Herat was considered imminent – Iran underwriting the cost – to push the Sunni militia away from the western border. In May 1996, after a lengthy round of diplomacy, a humbled Hekmatyar finally ended his longstanding feud with Massoud and joined the government's alliance, adding several thousand fighters to the Kabul garrison and reinforcing Rabbani's claims to represent Pashtun as well as minority interests. The reconciliation ended the *Hizb-i Islami* road blockade of the capital from Sorobi, 75 km to the east, at the entrance of the Silk Gorge on the Kabul-Jalalabad road.

Sorobi is the key not just to Kabul but, through an old mountain road that begins there and winds through the Tagab valley, to the Bagram military airbase, 65 km north of the capital and the main supply route of the Rabbani government. Whoever controls Sorobi is free to advance on the capital both from the east and north, while simultaneously blocking the only feasible road of retreat. Hekmatyar had tried on several occasions to punch his troops through the Tagab defile, forcing Massoud to race his brigades across the mountains to deflect them. Frustrated, *Hizb-i Islami* had settled in for a siege, interdicting relief convoys and cutting off the nearby hydro station, the sole supplier of power to the city. But the Silk Gorge was also an equivocal position to hold. You might interdict it, but you could never really overcome it. It runs for 25 km between cumuli of coppery rocks that rise sheer to a thousand feet on either side. At intervals, the road dives into man-made tunnels through the cliffs, making it the easiest position in the world to defend. One stick of Semtex would do it.

Hekmatyar's 'defection' to the government played a crucial role in the success of the Taliban's final putsch, for it pitted Pashtun against Pashtun. This was a risky gamble at the best of times, but particularly when those within the *Hizb-i Islami* rank and file who differed with the leadership's position had, at different times, shared the identical goal with the Taliban of overthrowing the Tajik interloper – as well as common ethnicity. On 8 September, reports suggested that Zardad Khan, *Hizb*'s notoriously rapacious commander at Sorobi, had flipped his coin. A financial understanding in the region of $50–100,000, was in the air and there was every chance that he would surrender the position without a fight.[29]

The likelihood increased three days later with the ambush and killing of 70 of the key commanders of the Nangarhar *shura*, a coalition of factions led by Governor Haji Qadir which controlled the Khyber customs post, the three eastern provinces and showed a preference for peace, commerce and the export of opium over the tedious complexities of governing Afghanistan. The *shura* had been travelling in convoy to Torkham Gate for talks with the Taliban when their vehicles where rocketed at Dakka by a renegade commander, Shah Wali.[30] Haji Qadir, his son Jamal and commander Zaman Gham, allegedly a key link in the province's narcotics trade, escaped over the Pakistani border while Taliban forces, chanting *Allahu Akbar*, stormed Jalalabad a few hours later, hoisting their white banner over the Governor's House.[31]

Without pausing, they pressed on to Sorobi, where Massoud's forces had taken up positions alongside the *Hizb-i Islami* garrison. What happened at the entrance of the Silk Gorge is not altogether clear. By some accounts, Massoud had already decided to quit the capital and had begun detonating ammunition which could not be carried away to the north. This convinced *Jamiat* forces, most of whom were at Sorobi for the first time, that the Taliban had already moved around to their rear, cutting off the escape route to Kabul. Whether through panic or treachery, the result was a shambles. The Taliban stormed through the pass on 24 September and the road was clear to the capital. After two more days of fighting in the eastern suburbs, Massoud decided to abandon the capital, undertaking an organised retreat in darkness towards Jabal Saraj while still in contact with the enemy. Even as his forces withdrew, Rabbani's foreign minister, Abdul Rahim Ghafoorzai, told a Western military analyst by satellite phone that retreat was out of the question.[32]

'Had we not made an alliance with Hekmatyar,' Massoud told journalists in December, 'Kabul would still be in our hands.'[33] His version of events was that the *Hizb-i Islami* leader had refused to deploy his troops against the enemy at Sorobi, doubting their loyalty, while the *Jamiat* forces had been unfamiliar with the terrain. But the truth was that Massoud had been out-generalled. The Taliban had captured 200 miles of contested territory in less than three weeks, displaying a sophistication of command and communication that military analysts found hard to square with the militia's humble origins.

And the Lion of Panjshir was back where he had started a quarter of a century before: the leader of a demoralised guerrilla force in an unassailable valley far from the seat of power.

2 City of Night

The roots of the hatred between Massoud and Hekmatyar went deeper than the Soviet invasion, yet the two men, in many ways, were as similar as siblings. Both had been engineering students in Kabul, gravitating to the radical circles which, in the early 1970s, gathered around the theology professor, Burhanuddin Rabbani, founder of *Jamiat-i Islami* (Society of Islam), Afghanistan's first truly Islamist party.

Both fled to Peshawar, along with their mentor, shortly after the 1973 overthrow of King Zahir Shah by his cousin, Mohammad Daoud, a coup supported by the Afghan army, the Afghan communist party and, covertly, by Moscow. As Zahir Shah's prime minister, Daoud had been an active advocate of 'Pashtunistan', the hypothetical homeland that would reunite the Pashtun communities divided by Britain's arbitrary drawing of the Durand Line. This 1893 declaration had fixed the border between an indomitable Afghanistan and British India, establishing the tribal trust territories in Pakistan – where Pashtun customary laws still hold sway – as a turbulent buffer between them.

With Britain's withdrawal from the sub-continent in 1947, the 'Pashtunistan' grievance rose swiftly to the surface. Pakistan, taking its first steps into independence, immediately found its 1,500-kilometre western borders disputed by the better-equipped and Pashtun-dominated army in Afghanistan. The issue poisoned Afghan relations with Pakistan, and also the United States, which was moving tenuously into the Cold War vacuum created by Britain's abdication of its imperial role. Afghanistan, as a result, drifted closer to Moscow and, by 1970, some 7,000 officers in the armed forces had received training in the USSR.[1]

In Pakistan, Massoud and Hekmatyar were patronised by President Zulfikar Ali Bhutto, father of Benazir Bhutto, as tools to combat Mohammad Daoud's growing irredentism. From 1974 onwards, they and 5,000 of their comrades underwent military training in a programme coordinated by Brigadier Naseerullah Babar, inspector-general of Pakistan's 2nd Frontier Corps and soon to emerge as President Bhutto's chief advisor on Afghan policy.[2] The training culminated in a series of Pakistani-backed incursions into eastern

Afghanistan in mid-1975, which provoked harsh retaliation against domestic opponents.

The violence of the government's response had the effect of splitting the exiled rebels between those, like Rabbani and Massoud, who sought to develop an indigenous movement capable of sustaining a revolt on a national scale, and others, led by Hekmatyar, who wanted to launch an immediate *jihad* with whatever outside support was available. Hekmatyar broke away from *Jamiat-i Islami* to form *Hizb-i Islami* (Party of Islam), a disciplined political organisation with friends in the Pakistani army and the influential Pakistani party, *Jamaat-i Islami*. It then split in two itself, when Yunus Khalis, a Pashtun religious leader, established his own faction, known as *Hizb-i Islami (Khalis)*.

Rabbani's *Jamiat-i Islami* had been formed as a broad-based alliance to counter the strength of the Soviet-backed Afghan communist party – the People's Democratic Party of Afghanistan (PDPA) – which had helped Daoud to power and, in April 1978, would overthrow him. *Jamiat*'s split into gradualist and radical elements uncannily echoed a schism in the PDPA between the moderate *Parcham* and hardline *Khalq* wings. The animosity between *Parcham* and *Khalq* reflected Afghanistan's fierce distinctions of tribe, language and class and was tantamount to a civil war in embryo.

Founded in 1965, the PDPA had suffered its first falling-out four years later as Noor Mohammad Taraki and Babrak Karmal disputed the leadership of the party. Taraki was a Ghilzai Pashtun from the east, where the Pashtunistan question had always been a more vexatious issue. His *Khalq*, or 'People', faction dominated the officer corps, the police force and was more purely Pashtun, with a particular accent on its rural, more 'proletarian' origins. By contrast, Karmal, a Kabuli, was related by marriage to the royal Mohammadzai branch of the Durrani clan which had ruled Afghanistan for the previous 200 years. The *Parcham*, or 'Banner', faction, which he led and to which Najibullah also belonged, was more broad-based, embracing Dari-speaking, non-Pashtun interests, as well as those of the urban elite.

Both factions were ideologically oriented towards Moscow but, while *Parcham* favoured a gradualist approach – allowing, for example, Prince Daoud to remain at the helm after the bloodless coup of 1973, as a symbol of dynastic continuity – *Khalq* aimed for the termination of the Mohammadzai rule altogether and a social revolution along the lines adopted by the Soviet Union in Central

Asia. The rivalry between the two communist wings intensified after 1978 when, with support from Moscow, Taraki had Daoud and his family murdered and declared himself president of the 'Democratic Republic of Afghanistan'.

As a Ghilzai, Taraki's right to hold high office in Afghanistan was nugatory, while the reform programme unleashed after the so-called 'Saur Revolution', aimed at redistributing land, the secularisation of education and unveiling women, sparked off *jihad* in every one of Afghanistan's provinces a full year before the Soviet Union's invasion. And when it invaded, it was to restore the *Parcham* moderate tendency, in the shape of Babrak Karmal, and to prevent a Soviet satellite from being engulfed by the same unstable fervour that had toppled the Shah of Iran that same year. *Parcham* would control the reins of power throughout the 10-year occupation, while *Khalq* military officers – under close Soviet supervision – directed the war effort.

The quarrel between *Khalq* and *Parcham* is crucial to understanding Afghanistan's present situation, and not solely because of the parallel it offers with developments within the emerging Islamist resistance. So entrenched were the prejudices of Afghan society – between Pashtun and non-Pashtun, Ghilzai and Durrani, town and country, traditional and modern – that it is evident that they would not fade away with the Red Army or the PDPA, but only reassert themselves in a different guise in whatever political framework was cast up by post-communist balance of powers.

After Najibullah's fall, *Khalq* elements would be attracted towards Hekmatyar, *Parcham* to Massoud and the Rabbani government while, in the north, the two existed in an uneasy equilibrium in General Rashid Dostum's fiefdom, the least reconstructed of all the remnants of the former PDPA state apparatus.[3] When the UN, in the course of its attempts to secure an end to the faction fighting, proposed a role for the Rome-based ex-King Zahir Shah, it was fumbling in the dark towards a pre-communist era when royal government, at least, had enjoyed cultural and tribal legitimacy. In so doing, arguably, it was straying perilously close to *Parcham* territory, cancelling out whatever benefits might otherwise have accrued.

In 1977, General Zia ul-Haq, commander-in-chief of the Pakistani army, had toppled Zulfikar Ali Bhutto, executing him two years later. When the Soviet invasion compelled President Jimmy Carter first to consider, and then to approve the clandestine supply of weapons and cash to what would evolve into the *mujahedin* resistance, it was to General Zia and the Inter-Services Intelligence agency (ISI) that he delegated the vetting process and monitoring.

Of the seven parties identified and ultimately funded by the ISI, the only non-Pashtun group was *Jamiat-i Islami* which, after the splits in the mid-70s, had taken on the ethnic character of Rabbani and Massoud, Tajiks from Badakhshan and the Panjshir valley respectively. The Dari-speaking Tajiks comprised some 25 per cent of the population, but were a majority in the administrative and commercial centres of Kabul and Herat. All the remaining six hailed from the eastern Ghilzai or 'minority' Pashtun clans, an indication that the ISI was not solely addressing the Soviet menace as it drew up its plans for the resistance, but the danger to its own borders of arming an alliance that included the 'royal' Durranis of the south. As in Bhutto's time, this was to be avoided at all costs if the tribal trust territory of Northwest Frontier Province were to remain in Pakistani hands.

Hekmatyar himself is a de-tribalised Kharufi from Kunduz, one of the northern pockets settled in a period of Pashtun expansionism under the nineteenth-century ruler, Amir Abdul Rahman. He could never play the Pashtun card with great confidence: in fact, it is unlikely that he wanted to at a time when what would evolve as the *mujahedin* parties were stressing Islamist credentials over ethnic affiliations to win sponsorship from General Zia, a devout believer, and other potential sources of funding in Saudi Arabia, Kuwait and Egypt.

Khalis, a Ghilzai from Nangarhar Province, had a better pedigree but his hostility to two 'traditionalist' resistance groups, the National Islamic Front for the Liberation of Afghanistan, led by Pir Sayed Ahmad Gailani, and the Afghanistan National Liberation Front, under Sibghatullah Mojadeddi, precluded the creation of a pan-Pashtun political front. Abdul Rasul Sayyaf, leader of *Ittehad-i Islami*, was another Pashtun, but while his adherence to Wahhabi rites won him backing from Saudi Arabia, where they are widely practised, they were not representative of the religious rituals of his fellow tribesmen.

Each of the seven Peshawar-based *mujahedin* parties professed Islamist ambitions: they could not have claimed otherwise to represent the will of the Afghan people at a time when Islam was under direct attack from communist values – or to have taken a share of the military assistance channelled to the struggle through the ISI. But it was, in the main, an Islam which had been stripped of its local associations of custom and tradition, as it moved into global revolutionary mode. The earliest proponents of this new radicalised

Islam, Hekmatyar and Massoud, had as little in common with the Afghan peasant, with his beliefs in spirits and saints, as the PDPA cadres whom they were defying.

Hekmatyar remained the undisputed champion of Pakistan's interests in Afghanistan until 1994. Through supporters in the ISI, which channelled aid from the CIA, and Pakistan's *Jamiat-i Islami*, which performed the same service for *jihad* sympathisers in the Gulf, *Hizb-i Islami* was allocated more than half of the $6 billion in armaments and cash that were siphoned into the anti-Soviet cause.[4] Some of these resources were devoted to building up a structure appropriate to a revolutionary party, complete with posters, portraits, T-shirts and a smooth propaganda machine. All seven parties maintained offices in Peshawar, but Hekmatyar's privileged standing enabled him to exploit what, during the occupation, emerged as the most valuable outward token of legitimacy – the three million 'captive' population of mainly Pashtun refugees living in camps in Pakistan.

On arrival, all males were expected to register as members of one of the seven exiled parties – whatever their political or religious views. *Hizb-i Islami* established an overpowering presence both in the camps and the aid distribution network, and it was soon understood by incoming refugees that joining the party was a fast-track route to relief. In the eyes of one UN refugee worker, this amounted to a 'reign of terror' but, if so, it was not confined to the camps alone.[5] Throughout the 1980s, a number of noted liberals, including the Mina Keshwar Kamal, founder of the Revolutionary Association of the Women of Afghanistan, and Professor Sayed Bahauddin Majrooh, an independent publisher and journalist, were assassinated in circumstances which implicated *Hizb-i Islami.*[6] As was Mir Wais Jalil, a journalist with the BBC World Service, who was killed on 29 July 1994.[7]

The bad blood with Massoud dated back to 1976 when, with the backing of the ISI, Hekmatyar had the Tajik commander arrested on charges of spying for the Daoud government, along with his close friend Jan Mahmad, who was tortured and murdered.[8] Massoud left Peshawar three years later to raise the revolt against the Taraki regime in the Panjshir valley, not to return for a decade. The enmity erupted anew in 1982, after Massoud agreed a temporary ceasefire with the Soviets in the Panjshir valley to allow time for his fighters to regroup. That winter, *Hizb* forces turned their weapons on *Jamiat* groups in the provinces of Takhar, Badakhshan and Baghlan, where 13 of Massoud's commanders were ambushed and killed.[9]

But their quarrel went beyond personalities or tribal differences to encapsulate wholly contradictory visions of Afghanistan's post-Soviet future. While General Zia held the purse-strings of the *jihad*, Pakistan's Afghan policy would always reflect its own priorities. These were to exploit the tribal factor to protect its western borders and to prevent the survival of a strong, unified Afghanistan with its military muscle – boosted by Soviet training and aid – fully intact. Dismemberment, in that sense, was always on the cards. Pakistan could not dispense with its Pashtun proxies: they constituted 40 per cent, and perhaps more, of the Afghan population and had historically lorded it over the minorities which, on the battlefield, had experienced in the war against the Red Army their first taste of self-determination.

Fostering 'upstart' elements within the Pashtun pantheon, such as Hekmatyar, ensured that Afghanistan would pose no further threat after the Soviets were beaten. But removing the Durrani from a central role in the Peshawar-based resistance was a recipe for postwar anarchy, when Tajik, Uzbek and Hazara had been primed by combat for a greater share of power after centuries of Pashtun hegemony. While Hekmatyar was consolidating his political position in Peshawar, however, Massoud had been trying a more grassroots approach to Afghan power-broking, travelling from valley to valley to unite the disparate ingredients of the northern *jihad* into a workable coalition.

Starved of military supplies, due to his alienation from the ISI and his distance from the Pakistan border, Massoud could still claim with some honesty that he had never been anybody's stooge, merely an Afghan nationalist with Islamist convictions. By 1988, *Jamiat* had established an alliance of commanders from Herat to Badakhshan, which cut across ethnic differences and was known as *Shura-i Nazar Shomal*, the Supervisory Council of the North. Prominent among its members was Ismail Khan, the former army officer from Herat who had led the 1979 mutiny against Taraki's reforms which prompted Moscow's decision to intervene. Massoud had considered the formation of an 'Islamic Army', integrating units from different factions into a single force, a project he would take up again in 1992 following the collapse of the Najibullah regime in Kabul.[10] By 1991, his strength was reportedly up to 12,000 trained men, backed with medium artillery.[11]

The hand of Pakistan and, to a lesser extent, the US and Saudi Arabia in the formation of the first post-Soviet government was, in effect, to guarantee that it would fold. In February 1988, Moscow announced it would evacuate its 100,000 troops by the end of March 1989, a decision which was interpreted as denoting the fall of Najibullah's regime shortly thereafter. In spite of ten years of planning, there was no effective government-in-waiting to replace the PDPA.

It had to be created from scratch, under the supervision of the ISI, the CIA and the Saudi intelligence service, the *Mukhabarat*, from elements of the political spectrum whose primary criterion for selection had been that they served the interests of Pakistan, and not Afghanistan. The Afghan Interim Government (AIG), under the presidency of Sibghatollah Mojadeddi, was announced in February 1989, but its composition ignored the eight Shia factions which, with Iranian coaxing, had coalesced into *Hizb-i Wahdat Islami* (Party of Islamic Unity). No other minority group and – most significantly – none of the senior field commanders, except for those with offices in Peshawar, was considered for office in the new coalition.

The estrangement between commanders and politicians culminated at Jalalabad in 1989. In a showcase operation, designed both to secure an eastern capital for the AIG and to demonstrate that the *mujahedin* were more than a match for the government's supposedly demoralised forces, ISI and Pakistani army strategists planned a full-frontal assault on one of Afghanistan's best-defended cities. Some 10,000 *mujahedin* died in the attempt, the single most crippling loss of the war and a devastating exposure of the resistance's weakness when confronted with the challenge of a pitched battle, instead of guerrilla warfare. On 29 August, hours before the six-month attack was called off, Hekmatyar, the foreign minister in exile, quit the AIG.

In February 1990, the US and USSR agreed that Najibullah should remain in power until internationally-supervised elections could be held. This was a breakthrough in the peace negotiations, although the two superpowers continued to supply their proteges with arms and munitions for two more years. The change in Washington's stance reflected, in part, the resurgence of the *Khalq* faction, a consequence both of Moscow's dwindling interest in its former colony and the *Parcham*, and Najibullah's more accomodating attitude to the non-Pashtun elements among the *mujahedin*.

One month later, in March, the Afghan defence minister, General Shahnawaz Tanai, attempted to overthrow Naijibullah, in collaboration with *Khalq* elements in the military and with the active collusion of Hekmatyar and the ISI.[12] Though serious damage was inflicted on the Argh and other prominent buildings, the coup attempt failed and Tanai fled to Pakistan, while his sympathisers merged with the *Hizb* forces in the field. Tanai's name would be mentioned four years later in rumours that, from the army barracks at Rawalpindi, he had rallied the *Khalq* diaspora to supply the nascent Taliban with the military and air force skills that its troops had, certainly, never acquired in religious school.[13]

In April 1992, Massoud, in alliance with Dostum's Uzbek militia, occupied Bagram airbase 65 km to the north of the capital. Despite requests from *Parcham* sympathisers to declare himself head of state, Massoud called on the leaders of the seven Peshawar-based parties to agree on the formation of an interim *mujahedin* government.[14] It took 10 days of debate before the Peshawar Accord was finally announced on 26 April, and the complexity of the terms reflected the prevailing mood of mutual suspicion. Sibghatollah Mojadeddi would be interim president for two months, followed by Rabbani for four months, followed by a grand assembly, or *shura*, to select an 18-month interim government, followed by the first democratic elections in Afghan history.

It came too late to prevent the clash between Massoud and Hekmatyar which had long been inevitable. On 25 April, the combined forces of Massoud and Dostum entered Kabul to pre-empt a military takeover by Hekmatyar, camped on the outskirts of the city with his *Khalq* allies. The army swifly disintegrated along the ethnic lines which had underpinned, but been camouflaged by, the faultline running through the PDPA. The 1st Division at Kargah, the 2nd Division at Jabal Saraj, the 99th Rocket Brigade and the 40th Division at Bagram sided with Massoud, while the 5th Division *Sarandoi*, a paramilitary police force, joined Hekmatyar, along with officers from the Interior Ministry. The Shia *Hizb-i Wahdat* was also a major beneficiary, scooping up the 95th and 96th Tribal Divisions, garrisoned in south and western Kabul.[15]

In accordance with the Peshawar Accord, Rabbani assumed the presidency in June 1992 and was immediately challenged by Hekmatyar who demanded the withdrawal from Kabul of Dostum's militia and what he called the 'communist elements' which had merged with Rabbani's government and army. In August, the city came under a massive rocket attack from *Hizb-i Islami* forces, which claimed some 2,000 civilian lives. Hundreds of bodies lined the streets, whole districts were razed to the ground and the homeless sought refuge in the notorious Pul-i Charki prison, a Khad complex which had housed 12–15,000 political prisoners.[16]

The first siege of Kabul had begun.

* * *

Four roads snake into Kabul from four cardinal points, bisecting the city octagonally and then dividing it into 16 municipal districts. Set in an amphitheatre of mountains, snow-capped in winter, the city tilts, geographically, towards the Khyber Pass to which it is linked by the thin umbilical of the Silk Gorge, shadowing the Kabul river as it flows downstream to fall on the Indus at Attack. To the north lie the foothills of the Hindu Kush and the folds of the Panjshir valley, Massoud's green and narrow country. Sayyaf held the western access in 1992, congregating his force at the spa town of Paghman, where King Amanullah used to race elephants. Hekmatyar's men had taken up position in the villages of Charasyab and Maidanshahr, a few miles to the southwest.

Kabul had expanded in that direction in the 1920s, along what the traveller Robert Byron called 'one of the most beautiful avenues in the world', to Darulaman Palace, which housed the Ministry of Defence.[17] Overlooked by the 2,000 metres of Television Hill, the neighbouring districts of Karta Se and Qalaye Shada would never entirely be part of Kabul, in spite of the proliferation of new embassies and faculties. Their inhabitants were Shias from the Hazarajat massif, which gave them birth and then promptly expelled them, because there was not enough land to go round. In Kabul, they made a living in service: as *chowkidars* and domestics, barrow wallahs and labourers. The Shia destiny in Afghanistan had always been to slave.

Kabul, generally, had had a satisfactory war. After the Soviets left, Najibullah's Afghanistan wallowed for a period on $3 billion a year in subsidies – on food, fuel, jobs, housing, but mainly on defence to prevent the rip-tide of Islamic extremism, represented by the *mujahedin* victory, from lapping against the then USSR's southern borders. The residential project of Microrayon in east Kabul, built to house 140,000 people, gives some indication of the lengths to which

Soviet planners would go in their efforts to create, and then to recruit, an Afghan political class.

Life in those apartments encapsulated some of the worst civic experiences that were available in the post-Cold War world. Weapons once wielded by a superpower that had mortally overreached itself were now directed at a city that consisted chiefly of mud, medieval wells and wood-burning stoves, however ambitious the outward symbols of nationhood built by the former kings and communists in Afghanistan. In the four years that elapsed after Najibullah's fall, the slaughter in Kabul became so unrelenting that Afghans would ponder, amid the desolation and the international solitude, whether or not it mattered that there was no enemy there apart from the pallid, post-Soviet citizen and the domestics he had never quite managed to shake off.

The point, it seemed, was to kill off the city and all of its attitudes and skills; to wipe the slate clean; to quell government itself, in fact, the source of all the communist murder in the rural areas. What Genghis had achieved at Balkh, near Mazar-i Sharif, Hekmatyar attempted at this other historic junction. It was, probably, never consciously in his mind as his forces hammered away at the fabric of Kabul, but 45,000 Kabulis would testify to the thesis posthumously, and several hundred thousand more would depart the scene, too broken to remain.

Nearly 300,000 Kabulis had fled to Jalalabad by the end of 1994, while 1,000 more escaped from the capital every day to join them.[18] The refugee population of Sar Shahi, the largest camp, was so highly qualified that it was referred to as the 'University of Kabul in exile'. There were 500 experienced secondary school teachers, along with scores of doctors, laboratory technicians, health workers, senior civil servants, former army officers and engineers, the product of decades of Soviet investment in Afghanistan's human resources.

No city since the end of the Second World War – except Sarajevo – had suffered the same ferocity of jugular violence as Kabul from 1992 to 1996. Sarajevo was almost a side-show by comparison and, at least, it wasn't forgotten. An official of the International Committee of the Red Cross, one of only three foreign organisations to remain after the rocketing of January 1994, said: 'Afghanistan seems to have disappeared off the face of the earth.' This was true both figuratively and literally, as first 50 per cent – rising to 80 per cent in 1996 – of the built-up areas of Kabul were turned into a rubble resembling Dresden after the fire-bombing.

There would be clusters of worshippers in a mosque on Friday, or passengers in a minibus, children gathering wood or women in a bread queue. They would explode, to step forward in a bromide report in the back pages of the Pakistani press. These vignettes of daily violence took place against the backdrop of a general meltdown of the life support systems of a city of 1.2 million which, while never modern at heart, had come to depend upon the utilities of urban life. First, the lights went out, and then the water stopped running. The sewer system, rubbish disposal, revenue collection, salaries, free medicine, the postal service, the comfort of fire and the law gradually faded from memory, while food and fuel had to run blockades in the east, south and the north that were only intermittently relaxed to permit the transit of relief goods.

The city's ability to function was further undermined by the flight of the 50,000-strong Sikh and Hindu minorities, who had been at the centre of the money market and the commercial system in Najibullah's Kabul.[19] Despite the absence of bullion or other reserves, the *afghani* remained broadly stable throughout the *mujahedin* interregnum, responding more to the food blockades than the fact that the Rabbani government simply had more cash printed up whenever the treasury was empty. One finance minister, Karim Khalili, admitted that Afghanistan's entire budget of $200 million had been financed by new notes printed in Russia, under a contract awarded to Germany's Giesecke und Devrient in 1994.[20]

This was just one of the mysteries of surviving Kabul under siege. By winter 1995, the cost of fuel-wood was so high that it cost a dollar a night to light a fire, forcing families to choose between keeping warm or cooking a meal – if they could afford the food. In a household survey one year later, it was learned that it cost around one million *afghani* a month for a family of six to survive but average wages were equivalent to one tenth of that amount.[21] A UNICEF survey of 1,100 war widows found that they all lived on nothing more than green tea, *naan* bread and a little yoghurt.

Were the figures flawed? How could they have been, unless the Kabulis had a parallel life support system that still defied detection?

* * *

There were two flies – excluding Hekmatyar – in the bloody ointment that would be smeared over Kabul before it fell to the Taliban in September 1996. The first was Rashid Dostum, the mutinous general from Mazar-i Sharif whose alliance with Massoud had closed off the Salang Tunnel supply route, making Najibullah's downfall inevitable. The nearest the factions ever came to unanimity was on the need to exclude Dostum from any future power-sharing formula. He had served the communists – until it proved wiser not to – while the 20,000-strong Jawzjani militia, which he had personally raised under Najibullah, had fought mercilessly against the *mujahedin* at the sieges of Jalalabad, Khost and Gardez. These Uzbek fighters inspired even greater fear among civilians, who named them *galamjam* – or 'carpet-thieves' – a term that Afghans diversified to embrace anyone with bad intentions. But Dostum controlled the Bagram military airbase and his combined force of 40,000 well-trained regulars, backed by tanks and squadrons of fighter and bomber aircraft, was a threat which Massoud could neither dispense with nor ignore.

The second factor in the post-Soviet equation was the ethnic question. Exacerbated by the alienation of the field commanders from the parties in Peshawar, this underpinned the failure of the *mujahedin* to devise a viable transitional government, bringing down, in September 1996, Massoud whose instincts, finely attuned as they were in battle, exhibited a tendency to betray him in politics. His inability – or that of his figurehead president, the pious Rabbani – to deliver a working alliance of Tajik, Uzbek and Hazara to counter Hekmatyar's claim to represent the traditional Pashtun hegemony ensured four years of unremitting conflict.

This outcome was all but implicit under the terms of the Peshawar Accord which glossed over the all-important detail of who should be represented in the Grand Assembly, called to select the 18-month transitional government, when Rabbani's four-month term of office expired. A traditional *Loya Jirga,* composed of the 'great and the good', was certain to call for the return of Zahir Shah, a move that would be contested by the new military poles cast up by the war. A more democratic approach, based upon district representatives and proportional representation for the minorities, was outside Afghan experience and, anyway, raised the thorny question of Dostum and his Uzbeks, still tainted by their communist past. With no real power base to call his own, Hekmatyar – who had not signed the Peshawar Accord – played the Islamic card by insisting on an assembly of religious scholars.

Despite his image as a beatific, slightly doddery old man of the cloth, Rabbani behaved with estimable rapacity. He summoned his own 'Council of Wise Men' on 30 December, flying in many of its 1,335 delegates from Peshawar, and was confirmed as president for a further two years – to the outrage of five of the seven *mujahedin* leaders. Dostum was not even invited while Hekmatyar declared that this constitutional coup was an act of war. The fiction of peaceful power-sharing had, however, been exhausted even before Sibghat-ollah Mojadeddi – with a reluctance that verges on genetic in Afghanistan – had handed power to Rabbani.

Law and order broke down immediately after the *mujahedin* takeover in April 1992, with rival factions setting up roadblocks every hundred or so metres and indulging in a spree of looting. After Hekmatyar's initial rocketing in April, fighting broke out between *Hizb-i Wahdat*, which was strong in southwestern Kabul, and the Saudi-backed forces of Sayyaf's *Ittehad-i Islami* over the exclusion of the Shia from government and amid rumours that the new constitution must stress Afghanistan's Sunni values. The thriving commercial quarter of Khote Sange went up in smoke.

But the first real onslaught was Hekmatyar's rocket bombardment in early August from Charasyab and Maidanshahr. A single attack on 13 August, using a cluster device, killed at least 80 people and wounded a further 150. Hekmatyar appeared to be targeting the city's communications, for the TV station, the main printing press, an $8 million airport control tower and Ariana Airlines' domestic fleet were all destroyed, while the radio station and presidential palace took hits.[22] A ceasefire was drawn up through the mediation of Haji Qadir, leader of the Nangarhar *shura*, under which a 5,000-strong buffer force of neutral *mujahedin* fighters would stand between the warring factions.[23]

Hekmatyar's insistence – and the ostensible motive for his attack – that the Jawzjani militia be withdrawn was not met immediately. Massoud could not dismiss the *galamjam*, however distasteful their behaviour, while simultaneously trying to defend the city and impose some order on the factions within it. Dostum's forces outnumbered his own and held the strategic positions of Kabul airport, Maranjan Hill and Bala Hissar fort. But, by November 1992, most of the Uzbeks were on their way north and Massoud had begun to create an integrated garrison, merging former government troops with the forces of the *Shura-i Nazar* under *mujahedin* generals.

Rabbani's hijacking of the presidency won the support of only Sayyaf, a breakaway Shi'a group, *Harakat-i Islami*, and members of the old regime. After some initial skirmishes, Dostum also fell in with the arrangement and, while other faction leaders expressed their disapproval, they generally remained neutral in the fighting that followed. Hekmatyar would stand alone, at least until the end of January when Mazari's *Hizb-i Wahdat* entered into alliance with *Hizb-i Islami*. Massoud struck first, bombing Hekmayar's southern bases and the artillery depot at Bagram, 16 km east of Kabul. There followed four weeks of fighting, reaching a peak on 8 February in the worst rocketing since August, with missiles randomly falling into civilian areas. When *Hizb-i Wahdat* attacked from the west, Massoud and Sayyaf joined forces to carry out a combined attack on southwestern Kabul on 11 and 12 February. It was one of Massoud's worst mistakes.

The Hazara had always lived on the defensive. Driven by the Pashtun to the infertile Hazarajat in the nineteenth century, their *mujadehin* descendants had been fighting both for freedom from Soviet rule and greater political representation for a minority that accounted for up to 20 per cent of the population. Pitting the sabre-toting fanatics of Sayyaf's *Ittehad-i Islami* – another sectarian minority – against a population which would have made better allies than enemies, extended the battle for Karta Se over three wasted years and earned Massoud a place in the Shia chronicle of horrors. On 11 February, government forces and their allies entered the Hazara suburb of Afshar, killing – by local accounts – 'up to 1,000 civilians', beheading old men, women, children and and even their dogs, and stuffing their bodies down the wells, '60 at a time'.[24] Local descriptions differ significantly from those of Amnesty International, but are indicative of the event's continuing power to haunt.

Amnesty cited a young nurse who witnessed the incident: 'There were 12 of them. They broke down the door, then they made advances towards my sister and me. My father tried to stop them, but they hit him and then tortured him. They cut off one of his feet and both his hands in the courtyard. One of them threw my father's hands to a dog belonging to one of his commanders.'[25] Such naked massacres were relatively rare, although the rocketing took a different and more consistent toll, killing over 1,000 in February 1993 alone. But the rape or abduction of young women, particularly among minorities, was practised by members of each of the factions, reaching its nadir during the *galamjam* occupation. The Pashtun, it should be noted, counted among Kabul's minorities.

With the exception of Kunduz, Kandahar and Baghlan, the rest of Afghanistan remained peaceful throughout 1992, stimulating a massive return of refugees from Pakistan. Nearly one million had arrived by the end of the year, attracted by the food for work, seed multiplication and irrigation repair projects established by the UN and other foreign donors.[26] That figure plummeted following the signing of the Islamabad Accord in March 1993, which confirmed Rabbani in office, gave the premiership to Hekmatyar but threw a reckless veil over the status of Massoud, his bitterest rival. Fighting broke out two days later and, while Hekmatyar accepted his post and a desultory peace was restored, he chose to remain at Charasyab, only meeting the president in the presence of armed guards. The fighting came and went during the remainder of 1993, as did the refugee population, dragging their belongings between the capital and the displaced camp or Pakistan and the village.

Dostum, however, had had enough. He had spent most of 1993 in disdain of events in the capital, consolidating his mini-state in the north through a round of diplomatic visits to Pakistan, Uzbekistan, Saudi Arabia, Turkey and Russia. Since 1992, he had been excluded from every inter-party discussion about the formation of a new Afghan government, despite his military strength and preponderant role in bringing down Najibullah. As dawn broke on 1 January 1994, Kabul awoke to the sound of heavy artillery. Microrayon was ablaze. Allying themselves with troops loyal to Prime Minister Hekmatyar, Dostum's forces attempted to capture the Argh and the Ministry of Defence, attacks which were repulsed. The factions took up positions on either side of the Kabul river, which runs through what used to be old Kabul, creating a 20-mile-long front which divided the city into a mosaic of conflicting territories.

After two months of intensive rocketing and shelling, some 4,000 people had been killed, 21,000 injured and 200,000 more had left the city.[27] On 14 February, UN Secretary-General Boutros Boutros-Ghali appointed Tunisia's Mahmoud Mestiri head of a special mission to restart the peace process, after two years in which the UN role had been limited to monitoring the transfer of power. After months of meetings with the faction leaders, Afghan intellectuals and religious leaders, he tabled proposals for a ceasefire, the creation of a neutral security force and the summoning of a *Loya Jirga* to oversee the formation of a transitional government. But he stressed that there was no question of dispatching a UN peacekeeping force.

Meanwhile, the battle lines began to shift. In mid-June, clashes broke out between *Hizb-i Islami* and the pro-Rabbani, Shia group *Harakat-i Islami* near Darulaman Palace, inflicting serious damage on the National Museum and its priceless collection of Bagram and

Ghandaran antiquities. Two weeks later, Massoud's forces dislodged Uzbek militiamen from Bala Hissar fort and Maranjan Hill to the southeast, capturing Microrayon and the National Sports Stadium. There followed a spate of revenge rocketings by Hekmatyar. On 17 July, 360 rockets landed on the central districts of Shahr-i Nau gardens, Wazir Akhbar Khan and Khair Khana to the northeast.[28] On 13 August, rockets completely destroyed the city's central medical stores and three hospitals received direct hits, killing over 30 patients. Several people were killed and many others injured when a building housing 5,000 homeless people was hit.[29]

With no end to the fighting in sight, the director of the International Committee of the Red Cross, Peter Stocker, announced on 7 October that the ICRC would airlift emergency medical supplies into Kabul, adding that, although the operation would relieve pressure on the hospitals, it could not possibly meet Kabul's other humanitarian needs. No relief food had been delivered to the city since June. 'Living in some areas of Kabul,' Stocker said, 'is now like living in hell.'[30] The prospect of the coming winter, he admitted, was 'terrifying'.

In the south, meanwhile, a white banner was unfurled on the 15th anniversary of the Soviet invasion.

3 Warriors of God

It began as a faint susurrous, stirring the palms and leaves, the subtlest alteration in a balance of powers whose nervous bursts of violence had terrorised Kandahar since April 1992. Upon the fall of Najibullah, a trio of commanders from different factions, dominated by the *Jamiat-i Islami* warlord Naqibullah and fuelled by profits of the burgeoning opium trade, had seized control of the city of the Cloak of the Prophet, Afghanistan's holiest shrine, dividing it into three well-armed and hostile camps.

If Kabul was Afghanistan's Sarajevo in early 1994, Kandahar could lay reasonable claim to being its South Bronx. This was certainly the view of local merchants trying to revive the border trade with Pakistan, and to capitalise on Kandahar's promising position astride the land route from Central Asia. The factions had established roadblocks willy-nilly throughout the southern countryside, levying taxes from passing vehicles and their hapless passengers. Protection was available to those who could afford it, but most of the population could not, having only recently returned from Pakistan to repair their homes and sow their fields.

With no overlord powerful enough to impose a lasting security, Kandaharis were trapped in a crossfire of killing, extortion and rape from members of all three factions, while owing allegiance to none of them. In one notable incident, two rival commanders in the city held a tank duel over a homosexual lover, killing dozens of people in the local bazaar[1] and, in another, 31 wedding guests died when a heroin addict went on the rampage.[2] The sense of grievance aroused by such episodes, fortified by the promise of a return to social relationships rooted in Koranic law, fanned the first whispers of resistance to *mujahedin* rule into a movement that would ultimately attain cyclonic proportions.

Afghanistan was split into four autonomous mini-states and scores of loosely-affiliated enclaves in early 1994. Kabul remained the cockpit of civil war but, in spite of Hekmatyar's bombardments, the disposition of territory across the country had varied little. *Jamiat* continued to control the northeast, a thin conduit along Massoud's Panjshir valley and the central provinces of Baghlan, Parwan and Kabul.

Hekmatyar held the province of Logar, to the south of Kabul, the Kabul-Jalalabad road and strategic pockets along the eastern border.

Jamiat-i Islami's most significant ally was a former military officer, Ismail Khan, the self-appointed emir of Herat, whose prospering domain in the west, at the crossroads of the Middle East and Central Asian trade, stretched east and south to include Badghis, Ghor, Farah and parts of Nimroz under its sway. The absence of guns in Herat's crowded streets testified to its stability while the mechanisms of government functioned much as they had in Soviet times, in spite of its isolation from international aid channels. General Dostum, in the north, was equally secure, ruling a belt of seven provinces which were all but immune to attack thanks to his control of the Salang Tunnel, the only all-weather route through the Hindu Kush.

The Pashtun regions enjoyed no comparable cohesion. This was partly due to the divisive temperament of Pashtun society, in which a fierce adherence to *pashtunwali,* a tribal code of honour and revenge, placed individual freedom and an eagle-eyed attention to matters of family dignity far above what few prospects existed for dialogue between clans that had historically been unifiable only through *jihad* or the strength of a rare personality. Pakistan's selective seeding of the resistance, moreover, had encouraged this fractiousness by favouring Hekmatyar's radical Islamism over the more conservative – though hybridised – variety practised in the south, where *sharia* law took second place to the *pashtunwali,* and revolution of any description came in a distant third.

In Jalalabad, military commanders and tribal leaders had managed to sink their differences in a provincial *shura,* or council, but its durability was due less to real consensus than the ample profits from the Khyber Pass trade and international relief, both of which would have collapsed on any upsurge of hostilities. Similar alliances existed in Khost, Ghazni and other eastern enclaves but, further south, postwar authority had become thoroughly atomised. *Jamiat-i Islami* and *Hizb-i Islami* held some territory but, being at each other's throats in the capital made for poor neighbours in the provinces.

The party which most closely matched the southern profile was *Harakat-i Inqilab-i Islami,* a traditionalist group led by Mohammad Nabi Mohammadi, which drew its core fighters from the network of countryside *madrassa,* or Koranic schools, and their religious students, or *taliban.* After three years instruction, a *talib* qualified as a village *mullah,* officiating at births, marriages, deaths and providing religious instruction to boys, in exchange for cash contributions or gifts in kind. In rural Afghanistan, religion was the only vocation which required any kind of formal education, but it did not necessarily entail literacy.

Mohammadi was an *alim*, or Koranic scholar, from the Amadzhai – the same clan as Najibullah – and briefly served as vice-president in the Rabbani government, although his forces had stayed out of the subsequent fighting in Kabul. This lent him both a spiritual and ethnic legitimacy, a vital combination in any candidacy for Afghan leadership. One internal UN document went so far as to suggest that Mohammadi was the personality most acceptable to Rabbani as successor in the unlikely event of his stepping down.[3]

Denied any significant funding during the Soviet war, *Harakat* was largely dormant by the time the Taliban made their debut. But the political naivety that the latter went on to display and the quantity of *Harakat* commanders drawn to their ranks would fuel speculation that the movement was not seeking power solely for itself, but was more of an inspirational police force, clearing the path so that a more learned and experienced leader could later walk into office. Who that might be, none could fathom, but the notion that behind the *eminence grise* at the head of the movement there was yet another *eminence grise* waiting to emerge and be identified added another dimension to the Taliban's undeniable air of mystery.

The avalanche that fell upon the factions started in the spring of 1994. Two teenage girls from the Kandahari village of Sang Hesar were abducted by *mujahedin* and repeatedly raped at the local checkpoint. Mohammad Omar, a former *Harakat* commander who had retired to become a *talib* in the nearby village of Maiwand, heard of their plight and summoned 30 of his fellow *taliban* to mount a rescue. After a brief gunfight, the girls were freed and the *mujahedin* commander hung from a slowly-ascending tank-barrel. Appeals for help soon came pouring in from all over the district and, thus, the movement of *taliban* was born.[4]

'We were fighting against Muslims who had gone wrong,' Mullah Mohammad Omar reminisced to Rahimullah Yusufzai, one of only two journalists to whom he had accorded a face-to-face interview by mid-1997. 'How could we remain quiet when we could see crimes being committed against women and the poor?'[5] The righting of wrongs and the punishment of the guilty were the students' first public manifesto, emerging some time before the Taliban developed into a force with sufficient military strength to insist upon the creation of a pure Islamic state. This 'Robin Hood' quality would never vanish from the movement's legend, and even expanded, as it moved east, to embrace the restitution of private property appropriated by the *mujahedin*.

News of the movement did not filter through to the outside world until mid-1995, long after Pakistani journalists had confirmed for themselves that extraordinary changes were underway in the south. Between the Sang Hesar incident – which was recounted by a Taliban spokesman – and October 1994, when what evolved into the Taliban emerged from a curious period of gestation, it had acquired a command structure, skilled manpower, weapons, a strategic plan and funding. Responsibility for this transmutation would quickly fall upon Pakistan, then seeking to build road and rail links through the 'bad lands' of Afghanistan in an effort to compete with Iran for the export trade with Central Asia.

In the absence of any reliable testimony – and contrary to Taliban claims – what is certain is that the Sang Hesar incident did not immediately spark a popular revolt against the Kandahari *mujahedin*. What seems most probable is that, like generations of outlaws before them – and the killing of the Sang Hesar commander certainly qualified them as that – the 30 original *taliban* promptly fled across the border into Baluchistan. On 9 October 1994, Mullah Mohammad Omar, still an unknown figure beyond the confines of his home district, reappeared to announce that a force of 1,500 *taliban* would be deployed to man new checkpoints on the road from the Pakistani border to Girishk, a town 90 km northwest of Kandahar.[6] Their immediate purpose was to provide security for a Pakistani convoy to Turkmenistan which Islamabad intended as the first step towards re-establishing the overland trade route. The *taliban* were reportedly funded by local merchants and relying on the hospitality of the surrounding villages, but there was no indication from where they had come.

The convoy crossed the Afghan border post of Spin Boldak in mid-October, assured of its welcome by a cash advance to the local warlord from Naseerullah Babar, a close confidant of Prime Minister Benazir Bhutto and Pakistan's elderly interior minister. He had traversed the convoy's proposed route through Kandahar and Herat to the Turkmen border in September to gain permission for the journey from local commanders. It was too rich an opportunity for any self-respecting bandit to renounce. Between Spin Boldak and Kandahar, the trucks were allegedly waylaid and their cargoes of food, clothes, medicine and soap were seized. According to the Pakistani press, the *taliban* stood boldly up to the *mujahedin,* capturing their weapons and, after three days of fighting, Kandahar fell.

It was a fine frontier tale, soon to become the stuff of legend, but there were enough discrepancies from the official account that the hand of the strategist could also be detected. Islamabad denied a press report that Urdu-speaking members of the paramilitary Frontier Constabulary and the ISI were seen fighting alongside the Taliban – by now conferred with the capital letter appropriate to their rising political star.[7] One reliable source had an ex-ISI agent and veteran of the Afghan war, 'Colonel Imam', coordinating the rebellion from the safety of the Pakistani consulate in Kandahar[8] while another, less objective, claimed that the Taliban's attack at Spin Boldak had been supported by artillery fire from across the Pakistani border.[9]

The trucks, it transpired, belonged to the National Logistics Cell, the transport arm of the Pakistani army, which had ferried materiel to the *mujahedin* during the *jihad.*[10] We have Babar's word that they contained a goodwill cargo for the people of Central Asia, but they may have transported regular troops, disguised as *taliban,* or the crates of Kalashnikovs, mortars and other assorted firepower needed to capture a city bristling with hard-bitten fighters. The whole story sounded like a whimsy, but traces of any more solid evidence to prove it were swiftly blown away by the euphoria that began to sweep through the south.

If the caravan were not a fifth column, it was certainly an *agent provocateur.* Upon its uncertain fate hung the dignity of Pakistani diplomacy and Mrs Bhutto's bold new strategy in Central Asia. To attack it would be a direct challenge to the powerful eastern neighbour which had stood by Afghanistan throughout the Soviet occupation. If the warlords resisted such a temptation, another ambush would have to be counterfeited. An incident near Kandahar was obligatory in the scenario that Babar had devised.

Naqibullah, Kandahar's most powerful commander, did not resist the new rulers, but the corpses of two other commanders were paraded through the streets suspended from the barrels of their tanks.[11] A six-man *shura,* appointed to run the city, announced the dismantling of roadblocks, the confiscation of all weapons, a crackdown on crime and drug abuse, and the strict seclusion of women. The Taliban declared that their intention was to purge Afghanistan of all *mujahedin* and communists – blurred into the same seamless piece of historical fabric – 'who have become killers, thieves and drug traffickers in the name of Islam' – and to end the looting and lawlessness which characterised the post-Soviet regime.

Such measures were welcomed after years of anarchy and the opening of the roads led to an immediate drop in the price of food. If the prohibition of video, football and girls' education was strict even by the standards of Kandaharis, whose orthodoxy had been moderated through contact with Pakistan's more heterogeneous culture, the loss was a small price to pay for the restoration of stability, and few were heard to complain. These were luxuries that could be done without and asserting that the Taliban might have erred in their assessment of *mujahedin* rule was a thankless task, better left to commanders begging for their lives than to citizens, who felt no particular loyalty to either the conqueror or the vanquished.

It is tempting to interpret what happened next – the transformation of the Taliban from a disciplined cadre into a force for national redemption – as a wholly supernatural process, a spontaneous combustion of spiritual zeal and mass hysteria which forged an army that thundered over all the opposition towards a remote utopia. From a distance, the Taliban forces did bear an uncanny resemblance to a horde – the military equivalent of the swarm – and, like a horde, they obeyed no obvious pattern, penetrating into every vent and orifice, hoovering up the vestiges of randomised power and garnering them into a humming storehouse of invincible legitimacy.

There was no defined hierarchy in this army, no goal beyond the creation of a new spiritual order and the rank-and-file, initially, at least, were acolytes, eyes dilated by faith, antimony and the dream in the far distance. Rumours spread of their purity, their ripeness for martyrdom. Indeed, among the Afghan combatants, the Taliban alone seemed aware of precisely what they were fighting for as they flung themselves down the road to the capital, waving the white flag of *jihad* and chanting *Allahu Akbar* at a superstitious and demoralised enemy.

But that was the army – or part of it – and a surface description at best: the supposition of popular involvement is moot. The enforcement of law and order, including execution for murder and amputation against highwaymen, won immediate acclamation, as did the public humiliation of local warlords. The establishment of a pure Islamic state, moreover, was an unarguable proposition for a people reared upon the irreducible truths of the Koran. To extrapolate from that fundamental convergence of views, however, that the public wholeheartedly endorsed the Taliban's national ambitions, throwing their hearts and souls behind the endeavour, is to underestimate the Afghan's sharp sense of his own individuality and to caricature the range of responses possible in a society unusually dominated by prayer and the rifle.

One of the paradoxes of Afghanistan is that, although made up of over 50 ethnic groups often locked in combat, no minority has ever sought to secede and most fully identify with their common nationality. This was signally brought home during the 1994 fact-finding tour by UN peace envoy, Mahmoud Mestiri, who received over 300 proposals on ways of settling the post-Najibullah conflict, none of which raised the question of partition.[12] But another paradox is that whatever happens in Kabul only matters in the provinces to the extent that it undermines – or not – the foundations of local power or custom.

This had occurred under both monarchical and communist rule and *jihad* quickly followed, religion being the only language in which such absolutes as justice, solidarity and duty could be expressed simultaneously and with pressing urgency. The preferred Kabul was sickly, riven by internal divisions and forced to pay in cash or patronage for influence at the extemities of its domain. This Kabul already existed under President Rabbani and, as wretched as life had become for its mainly Tajik and Hazara inhabitants, it was not, fundamentally, a Pashtun concern unless it attempted to impose its will locally.

The Durrani clans of the south, it is true, resented their exclusion from government and the rise of the Tajik warlord, Massoud, but this was an unfocused rankling, more than a popular call to arms. The Mohammadzai, Afghanistan's traditional rulers, had all but extinguished their claim to legitimacy, first by exchanging their Kandahari roots for the town-houses of Kabul and then, after the overthrow of King Zahir Shah, by taking prominent positions in the communist hierarchy which succeeded the republic and later became the target of Taliban denunciations. Parochial considerations were of far greater concern in the south than distant gunfire in the capital.

In actual fact, the spectre of what amounted to strong government had slipped into Kandahar by the back door, offering peace and a pardon in exchange for obedience and the surrender of the weapons which Pashtun men regard as their God-given right to bear. If, therefore, the arrival of the Taliban was a deliverance from *mujahedin* misrule, it was also an invasion of the Pashtun conception of personal liberty. It was certainly an outright challenge to an economy in which the hiring of guns provided several thousand families with regular income and food.

There are no contemporary accounts of the weapons-collection programme carried out in the weeks after the southern city fell, but it must have been a tense period. The Taliban, ostensibly numbering only 1,500 recruits, had no immediate need of arms, having captured a *Hizb-i Islami* cache at Shin Naray, close to the Pakistani border, on their march to Kandahar in October.[13] This ISI-built store housed an estimated 800 truckloads of arms and ammunition by one account – 15,000 truckloads of ammunition by another – and its fall provided yet another clue to Pakistan's support to the religious students.[14] By February 1995 – four months later – the movement was estimated to have swollen to 20–25,000 men, backed by 200 tanks, artillery, six Mil-17 helicopter transports and a dozen MiG-23 jet fighters.[15] Even if the Taliban's strength was exaggerated, it is unlikely that many weapons had been actually taken out of circulation: their owners had merely changed sides, for the guarantee of continuing possession.

The circular, woollen *kolas,* which had been the *mujahedin* trademark head-gear for 15 years, was tossed aside – along with the old loyalties – in favour of the pure white or black, striped turbans, which identified the warriors of God.

* * *

There was no mistaking the Taliban as merely the latest in a series of Afghan armed factions. Unlike the *mujahedin,* who fought for food or the government's counterfeit currency, its forces were orderly, mirroring the discipline and obedience drummed into students from an early age by the *madrassa* system. They appeared to know what they were fighting for or, more accurately, what they were fighting against. There was no rape, no individual looting and little indication of the intolerance that would emerge later as they moved out of Pashtun districts of the south and east and into Tajik country.

It was, moreover, an army which advanced, a rare characteristic among the groups which had fought each other since the Soviet occupation. The Japanese four-wheel drive pick-ups, which the Taliban seemed to have in abundance, transformed the static military landscape, by allowing squads of eight to ten commandos, armed with machine gun, grenade and rocket launchers, to move at speed through the least-accessible parts of the countryside. Teams of vehicles, linked by radio or satellite phone – of which the movement had a plentiful supply – engaged in offensive actions, mopping-up operations and hot pursuit simultaneously, leap-frogging one another along a chosen line of advance.[16]

This high-speed command and control, far more than sheer weight of numbers, led to the collapse of Kabul in September 1996, leading some observers to speculate that there were, in fact, not one but two distinctive Taliban armies. The first, composed of just 3–5,000 crack infantry, was the force that raced into the capital and pursued Massoud's retreating men into the Panjshir valley, prompting military analysts to doubt that it could have originated unaided in the Pashtun outback.[17] The second, far larger, was made up of ill-trained volunteers from the *madrassa*, turncoat *mujahedin* and other camp followers. This – the avalanche made palpable – was reserved for use as battle fodder in the grim set-piece battles on the western front, or to enforce security in the non-Pashtun cities which fell to the movement.

As they proceeded through the south, resistance weakened, as if commanders had fallen into the grip of a virulent disease which sapped their courage and uncocked their weapons. Military boroughs came tumbling down, whether through the infectious power of Taliban piety or the threat of Pakistani reprisal if they failed to concede. For few southerners doubted Pakistan's support for the movement and the majority of Pashtuns welcomed it. Quantifying the effect on *mujahedin* morale was a different matter in a country where everyone simply adored a brand-new faction. There were chances to shuffle the old pecking order, opportunities for new business and jobs for unemployed fighters. The fact that the south was one huge power vacuum undoubtedly helped, although tales of *mujahedin* atrocities had been much magnified in the Pakistani press to buttress the legitimacy of the Taliban crusade. They were all Muslims in the final analysis, and all relied on the goodwill of the surrounding villages.

In November 1994, Mullah Mohammad Omar called for 4,000 volunteers from Pakistan to help the movement break out from its Kandahar bridgehead.[18] The commanders in Uruzgan and Zabul provinces caved in without a shot in November and December, respectively. There was a brief and bloody skirmish in Helmand, the opium-growing capital of the south, but that province was secured in January 1995. Ghazni fell after one-day's fighting and Paktika's formidable Mullah Abdul Salam Rocketi, named for his mastery of Scud and Stinger missiles, surrendered his weapons and territory in February without a shot.

Such capitulations were the product of negotiation as much as intimidation. A Taliban advance on a town or stronghold would be preceded by the infiltration by night of a *mullah* or another notable, laden with offers, seeking out commanders willing to defect. If the presence of a victorious army not many miles away did not undermine morale, the disappearance of dollars and rupees from the local money market, the guarantor of both business confidence and a comfortable exile across the border, usually did the trick. The struggle against the factions was won through an artful blend of currency speculation and outright bribery. This was no novelty in Afghanistan. Selling out to the highest bidder was a pragmatic choice for commanders concerned for the loyalty of their supporters and the security of their fiefs. And what occurred at the provincial level had its international dimension. Russia sustained Rabbani by printing *afghanis* to pay his troops and Hekmatyar's cash was, reportedly, forged in Pakistan for the same purpose. When Hekmatyar cleaved to the government's side in early 1996, Massoud is reported to have given him $2 million in cash to recruit more *Hizb-i Islami* fighters in Pakistan.[19]

But the Taliban had deeper pockets. In addition to the hundreds of commanders who succumbed to their offers of cash or rank, it was rich enough to sow wholesale panic by soaking up all the foreign currency in the local money markets. This occurred in Kabul, shortly before it fell, and, even more dramatically, in February 1997 when the northern *afghani*, valid only in Dostum's territory, plummeted from 15,000 to 100,000 against the dollar in the space of a few days.[20] Common ethnicity was definitely to the Taliban's advantage in specific transactions, particularly when their spreading fame had nourished whatever desire for change already festered in the community of the ruled. The double jeopardy presented by a restive population, willing to rise and fight alongside the Taliban, and right-hand-men, who may have already agreed in secret to mutiny, was sufficient to convince most Pashtun commanders to sue for terms.

But Uruzgan and Ghazni also contained large communities of Hazara Shias and, though opposed to the government, they had greater grounds for suspicion of the religious students. Rumours were rife that the Taliban, so rigorous in reinforcing dress codes and religious attendance, would impose Sunni rituals upon a minority whose preliminary invocation mentions the fourth caliph, Ali, with the same reverence as the Prophet Mohammad. Forced conversion had never formed a specific part of the Taliban's religious policy: indeed, in an agenda characterised by a return to first principles, it was almost conspicuous by its absence. But there was no guarantee that it would not, one day, become the clarion call of another *jihad*.

In an effort to stem these fears as much as to broaden their ethnic base of support, the Taliban took the unusual step of allowing the Shia *mujahedin* to retain their weapons and operate as an independent, but allied force.[21] This rapport looked as if might deepen in February 1995 as the Taliban forces, commanded by Mullah Mohammad Ghaus, the future foreign minister, stormed Hekmatyar's positions at Charasyab and Maidanshahr, outside Kabul. Again, defection played a part in the rout of Hekmatyar's siege engine. *Hizb-i Islami* forces reportedly refused to fire on the Taliban, but 600 of their Uzbek allies also gave way.[22]

Winter was turning into spring, campaigning season in the central provinces. Mullah Mohammad Omar announced from Kandahar that the Taliban were a neutral, peacekeeping force, appointed by God and popular acclaim to interpose between the factions, disarm them and restore the Islamic law of *sharia* to the country. The assertion had a political precedent in the buffer force of neutral *mujahedin*, assembled by the Nangarhar *shura* in August 1993 to separate Massoud and Hekmatyar's forces in Kabul. It was broadly in line with UN thinking as well, although Mohammad Omar steadfastly refused to be seen to participate in any peace negotiations which involved *mujahedin* or communists.

In mid-1994, Mestiri tabled proposals for an immediate ceasefire, the collection of weapons and the creation of a neutral security force, as a prelude to elections within two years. An international peacekeeping force was categorically ruled out, on grounds of cost and the public's general distrust of foreign troops on Afghan soil. The Taliban appeared eminently suited to the role of neutral security force in early 1995: they were disciplined, popular, imbued with moral conviction and had displayed a rare preference for negotiation over combat during their five-month campaign. Their defeat of *Hizb-i Islami* had brought a welcome pause in a conflict that had claimed 20,000 deaths and 100,000 casualties while the movement's leaders had established lines of communication with the two remaining combatants in the capital, Massoud and Abdul Ali Mazari, head of the Shia *Hizb-i Wahdat*.

The prospects for moving the peace process forward had seldom looked more promising but, within 40 days of their arrival at the entrance to the capital, the Taliban were in headlong retreat, their budding alliance with the Shia in ruins and *Hizb-i Wahdat* finished as a military player in Kabul. The party's tactical strength in the suburbs of Karta Se and Qalaye Shada had always relied upon the rocket and artillery support that could be targeted against government offensives from its ally Hekmatyar's bases out to the southwest. After the capture of these positions by the Taliban, still undecided on what stance to adopt towards Massoud, *Wahdat* was vulnerable to the full panoply of the latter's military power in an attack which was launched on 6 March.

Mazari offered to surrender *Wahdat*'s crumbling positions and its arsenal to the Taliban whom, it was suspected, he also hoped to lure into a direct confrontation with the Kabul commander. But the first promise he could not deliver. *Wahdat* units turned their weapons on the Taliban's troops and Mazari, a hostage against the value of his own bargain, was taken away by helicopter to Charasyab, where he died in dark circumstances. His facial skeleton, a witness said, had been dislocated from the skull, a condition often seen in the victims of high-speed road crashes. There were multiple bullet wounds in the abdomen, inflicted after the first wound but, probably, while he was still alive.[23] The details tended to confirm a popular belief that he had been pushed out of the helicopter, although the Taliban insisted that Mazari, a burly man, had attempted to overpower his guards while airborne. The killing brought the Shia honeymoon with the movement to an abrupt and dismal end.

Wahdat cancelled, Massoud turned on the Taliban, who were expelled from Charasyab and Maidanshahr by 20 March. The defeat exposed their lack of prowess when pitted against a determined force, but may also have helped to shed some of the complacency which had undoubtedly set in during their snowballing advance through the Pashtun lands in the previous half-year. Exhilarated by conquest and the flood of weapons flowing in their direction, the Taliban had begun to believe that providence really was with them, at least in the east. Further west, where a second front had opened in February 1995, a different story had been played out, far from the media's mythologising eyes.

Most of Nimroz province, bordering Iran, surrendered without a fight but the Taliban met much stiffer resistance in March from Ismail Khan's forces, nominally loyal to Rabbani, at Delaram, 340 km northwest of Kandahar on the Herat road. The Taliban pushed through Farah, thanks to the defection of Khan's local Pashtun allies, forcing the government to airlift thousands of troops from the Kabul garrison to Shindand, 95 km south of Herat, in a bid to hold the line. One analyst called the clash over the former Soviet airbase 'the heaviest fighting ... since the battle for Jalalabad in 1989'. The Taliban were finally pushed back to Helmand by late May, thanks partly to the fuel and ammunition provided by Iran which was alarmed by the commotion so close to the frontier.[24]

A 10-day truce in early June relieved tension in the west, but fighting erupted the same month in the north between the government and Dostum, following the breakdown of peace negotiations and amid accusations by Mazar-i Sharif that Massoud was planning an offensive along the Salang Highway. On 20 June, government forces captured Bamian province from *Hizb-i Wahdat,* gaining an alternative route across the Hindu Kush to Dostum's provinces of Samangan and Baghlan, a manoeuvre which the Taliban would imitate some two years later. For the moment, however, the Taliban and Dostum gave every indication of working hand in glove, taking it in turns to harry Massoud, in spite of their pronouncements of mutual detestation.

In August 1995, Ismail Khan launched a major offensive against the Taliban line at Delaram, pushing them as far back as Girishk, where they unexpectedly rallied to inflict an almighty defeat upon the government's allies. Khan's forces fled north in disarray to Shindand and, after a half-hearted resistance before the airbase, Herat fell to the Taliban on 5 September. Ismail Khan, and what forces he could still muster, fled across the Iranian border to Mashad. The capture of Herat increased the number of provinces under Taliban control to nine, or nearly a quarter of the country's 32. The movement, its leaders made clear, would no longer be satisfied until all of Afghanistan were united under their command and, for the first time, it became apparent precisely what that regime would look like. What, from a distance, had seemed a sensational flourish of Afghan esoterica was revealed, in the law-abiding alleys of this cosmopolitan city, as a Pashtun aberration, which used religious purism as a form of terror and hired bullies to implement it.

Women were prohibited from working, girls' schools shut down and beatings liberally handed out for 'abuses' of the strict dress code. In late 1995, working women who demonstrated against their exclusion were attacked and beaten by Taliban soldiers.[25] Amputations, the blackening of faces as a form of public humiliation and the extra-judicial execution of Ismail Khan's erstwhile fighters were all reported, while a systematic house-to-house search for weapons forced young men to flee to the mountains. Gone, it appeared, were the days of pious reconciliation. In early 1996, a suspected murderer was inexpertly hung from a crane: he took several hours to die.[26]

The last hope that the Taliban were the peacekeeping force they claimed to be evaporated for Kabulis in October 1995, when their forces reoccupied Hekmatyar's former bases at Charasyab and Maidanshahr and relaunched the siege of the capital after the six-month lull which had followed their defeat the previous May. On 11 November, 170 rockets landed on the city, killing 37 civilians and injuring 52. Massoud launched offensives to drive them out of range in November but failed to dislodge them. In a counter-offensive on 21 November, the Taliban advanced 10 km to Pul-i Charki, cutting the eastern supply route.

That winter was the most cheerless in Kabul's memory. The city had been without electricity since 1993. Amid daily bombardments and sporadic air strikes, the Taliban set up fresh blockades in the south and west. With the Silk Gorge closed by *Hizb-i Islami* and the Salang Tunnel sealed by Dostum's troops, food and fuel-wood became more scarce, while the *afghani* lost half its value against the dollar. When temperatures fell below -20° Centigrade, most of Kabul's orchards and ornamental trees were felled. On 28 January, the World Food Programme persuaded Hekmatyar to open the road for a convoy of 200 relief trucks and, some days later, the ICRC announced an emergency airlift lasting 25 days.

On 9 March, the *Hizb-i Islami* leader, Hekmatyar, announced a new alliance with Rabbani and the formation of a Joint Military High Council with Massoud. *Hizb-i Wahdat*, under its new leader, Karim Khalili, said it, too, would join the new configuration in Kabul, but then began a round of negotiations with the Taliban. Earlier in the month, Rabbani had signed agreements in Tehran, under which Iran pledged training for army officers, the repatriation of all military-age Afghan refugees for service in Kabul, the repair of the airport and the provision of funds to win over other factions.

Meanwhile, the violence continued. On 15 February, an explosion ripped through an ammunition dump in the Argh, killing 60 outright while hundreds of civilians shopping for the coming *Eid* were cut by the shattered glass from the the nearby Kabul Hotel.[27] Accident or sabotage? Clashes were reported between the Taliban and Ismail Khan's forces in Farah, and a bomb exploded in Herat's Pul-i Ragina quarter, causing even fiercer repression of civilians. In Kabul, rocketing claimed 180 lives and 550 injured in April, peaking on 26 June – the day Gulbuddin Hekmatyar entered the city as prime minister – when 220 Katyusha rockets were fired from Taliban positions.[28] Massoud and Hekmatyar launched joint offensives in Ghor Province, in a bid to retake Herat, and against Taliban positions south of Kabul. In late August, Mullah Mohammad Omar ordered the advance which would see the Taliban sweep through the remaining provinces of eastern Afghanistan and end with their possession of the capital.

* * *

Kabul was lost not by force of arms, but through a strategic checkmate. As the Taliban embarked on their spectacular campaign through Paktya to Jalalabad, their positions at Charasyab and Maidanshahr fell silent. *Jamiat* reinforcements were dispatched to Sorobi to strengthen Hekmatyar's forces, whose loyalty had been severely tested, first by his recent alliance with his old enemy, Massoud, but also by the terrifying momentum of the Taliban advance. Waves of martyrs reportedly cleared the minefields laid in the Silk Gorge, a wholly unsporting approach to the Afghan's traditional conduct of war.

The Taliban's bloodless capture of the capital drew a gasp of astonishment from a world that thought it was inured to the tangled politics of Afghanistan. There was little praise for Massoud's retreat, an organised withdrawal under darkness while in contact with an advancing enemy and, no doubt, accompanied by a high quotient of panic. If Massoud were to survive politically, it was vital that he move his heavily-laden column of men and baggage to Jabal Saraj, 77 km north of Kabul, before the Taliban could cut him off with flying jeeps along the Tagab valley. The order to pullout was given at 3 p.m. on 26 September, nearly two days after Sorobi was overrun and was still continuing in the early hours of the 27th, as the Taliban mopped up the last time-gaining resistance at Microrayon estate.[29]

Massoud claimed that he withdrew to avoid further loss of civilian life in the house-to-house fighting that would have otherwise ensued. This was propaganda. As so often in Afghanistan, there was a distinct air that history was about to repeat itself, this time in a return to the state of military affairs that existed throughout 1994. Some 12,000 *Hizb-i Islami* soldiers of questionable loyalty were now inside the city, along with an unknown number of Pashtun *Ittehad*.[30] If Massoud remained, he would lose Bagram airbase, his only source of supply, to the Taliban, who only had to reactivate the rocket positions at Charasyab and Maidanshahr to close the circle. Massoud's capitulation was inevitable, his execution just as probable.

Jabal Saraj is reached by the Soviet-built New Road, which leads north through the district capital of Charikar, the nearest town to Bagram, en route to the Salang Tunnel and the Amu Darya river. To the east, stretches the Panjshir valley and Khawak Pass, which Alexander the Great had crossed in 328 BC while marching south to Kandahar. Seventy miles long and 7,000 feet high, the Panjshir contains dozens of side valleys, sprinkled with stone villages and their fields of wheat, grapes and apples. Massoud had conducted guerrilla campaigns in the valley for a decade and knew it intimately. In 1982, his Tajiks withstood a 12,000-strong invasion force of mainly Soviet troops, supported by tanks, MiGs and helicopter gunships, at the cost of just 180 *mujahedin* lives. The Taliban would be hard-pressed to fare better.

Massoud had always understood the importance of securing his rear and contingency plans had been laid for just such a setback, when he first entered Kabul in 1992. Rockets, small arms, ammunition, rations, fuel and cash were stored at sites around the valley and, more recently, a supply trail had been opened to Taloqan in Takhar province, where an airport had been upgraded to provide an air bridge from Russia, Iran and Tajikistan, Massoud's major foreign backers. But it was a highly demoralised force that entered the Panjshir in late September. 'I told them: "If you stay with me, consider yourselves to be as good as dead,"' he recalled in February 1997. 'The commanders talked it over with their families. Then they all came back.'[31] His strength had whittled down from 15,000 to a hard core of 8,000 stalwarts, many of whom had served in the Soviet war. The remainder had defected or fled.[32]

The Taliban's impetus carried them to the mouth of the Salang Tunnel where, in a classic guerrilla manoeuvre, Massoud turned and struck at their flanks. Basir Solangi, a key Tajik commander, led his men along the mountain ridges at night and ambushed the enemy, dug in on the road, killing 150 men and pushing the main force back to Jabal Saraj.[33] A bid to break into the Panjshir was blocked by dynamiting the entry, but Taliban pressure continued with rocketing and flanking forays over its icy ridges. On 9 October, Massoud launched a two-pronged attack on Gulbahar, at the mouth of the

Panjshir, and, after five days of intensive combat, the Taliban abandoned first Jabal Saraj, and then Charikar, 14 km further south. It was the first Taliban defeat since Ismail Khan's short-lived victory at Delaram in August 1995, and it brought Massoud to within 10 km of the capital.

The fighting, in the first three months after the city fell, focused on control of Bagram airbase and Jabal Saraj, which commanded the approach to the Salang and Panjshir valleys, and the old road north through the Ghorband valley and Shia-held Bamian province. Dostum had made doubly sure the Salang Tunnel was sealed against any sudden Taliban thrust by blowing up the rocky hillsides on the northern side, but he remained chronically undecided about which side he should ultimately back in the struggle. Pakistan was pressing him to a Taliban alliance to finish off Massoud, but it was equally evident that, with the latter out of the way, the road would be clear for the Taliban to advance on the north. Pakistan's proposal was an invitation to suicide: Dostum was everything that the Taliban despised.

His 'empire' was an uneasy mixture of former communists and *mujahedin*, predominantly Uzbek, but with large Tajik, Hazara and Pashtun minorities. Though stable on the surface, what was essentially a loose coalition of provincial, ethnic warlords would rise to a fever pitch of tension with every alteration in Dostum's pattern of external alliances. Abdul Momen, a Tajik commander of the vital Hairatan river-port on the Amu Darya, had died in mysterious circumstances when Dostum switched sides from Massoud to Hekmatyar in January 1994.[34] Lieutenant-General Rasool Pehlawan, his most important deputy and the strongman of Faryab province, was gunned down in Maimana on 24 June 1996 at a moment when Dostum's reopening of the Salang Tunnel was being construed as the signal of an imminent realignment with the Rabbani government.[35] Sayed Mansur Naderi was one of the few original conspirators to have survived since the mutiny which brought down Najibullah in 1992 and shot Dostum to pre-eminence. The son of the spiritual leader of the Ismaili Hazara – a minority within a minority – Naderi commanded the 80th Division in Pul-i Khumri and was responsible for security along the vital Salang Highway.

Rabbani, Massoud and Hekmatyar all visited Dostum in the first week of October, the *Hizb* leader going on to Tajikistan and Uzbekistan to drum up support for his flagging cause. Delegations from Dostum and Karim Khalili were in Kabul at the same time for talks with the Taliban foreign minister, Mullah Mohammad Ghaus, who publicly invited Dostum to join the new administration 'to prepare the ground for strong central government'. Similar overtures were made on 7 October to Massoud, who 'can have a share in the future government which will be chosen by the people'.[36] But trust was in short supply.

Rabbani's meeting with the northern supremo, the first since January 1994, was more productive. One day later, Dostum, Massoud, Khalili and Pir Gailani, head of the Jalalabad-based National Islamic Front, announced a defensive alliance, the Council for the Defence of Afghanistan(CDA), but Hekmatyar did not join. In November, he said haughtily he would wage an independent struggle against the Taliban, but many of his men were known to have defected and Zardad Khan, his Sorobi commander, along with three other *Hizb* chieftains, threw in their lot with Dostum in late October. With few resources and less support, the consensus was that Hekmatyar's role in Afghan history had come to a end.

The CDA was no less vulnerable. Massoud spoke optimistically of carrying the war into the Taliban's rear but the three main protagonists had been enemies since 1994, using every possible guile to kill one another, or the comrades closest to them. Alliance in Afghanistan differed from enmity in name only, and each member of this one had grounds for suspecting the other of seeking a separate peace with the Taliban. Massoud's men remained in the centre of the CDA's defensive line as a buffer force, but every Tajik death vouchsafed a slightly longer life for the Uzbek and Hazara, shortening the chances for mutiny or defection among Massoud's commanders.

Khalili's fear of betrayal – or of reducing his own opportunities to betray – extended as far as refusing to allow other alliance members to send reinforcements into his territory in the Hazarajat. Dostum, facing rampant inflation at home and the threat of insurrection by his own disgruntled commanders, was still a leading favourite for a coalition with the Taliban, however temporary that might turn out to be. His contribution to CDA joint operations would, in the short term, remain cosmetic – the odd bombing run over Kabul, declarations of spurious solidarity – while the ceaseless intriguing continued in a bid to keep his options open.

The defence coalition finally crystallised on 25 October when the Taliban announced that Qala-i Nau, capital of Dostum's westernmost province of Badghis, had fallen to a force led by Mullah Yar

Mohammad, governor of Herat. The opening of this second front, and the declaration of a *jihad* against Dostum four days later, marked the end of a period of shadow-boxing which had been dictated as much by the diplomacy of Pakistan, eager to prevent an enlargement of the war, than Taliban qualms over Dostum's military strength which, on paper at least, was awesome.

Dostum responded by airlifting troops loyal to the *Jamiat* leader, Ismail Khan, from their Iranian bases to Maimana in Faryab, where they joined with the forces of Gul Mohammad Pehlawan, the younger brother of the murdered Rasool, whom he had replaced as governor. In the face of stiff resistance, the combined force advanced to the Murghab river in central Badghis where, along a 10-mile front, they managed to hold the Taliban advance until winter came. Some 50,000 people were displaced in three months of fighting, many of them Koochi nomads. By January, an unconfirmed UN report stated that up to four children were dying daily in the nearby hills from a combination of hunger and the -10° weather.[37]

North of Kabul, the fighting came and went over the familiar prizes of Bagram and Jabal Saraj. After a desultory month, the Taliban launched an offensive on 24 November which drove Massoud back from the city to Bagram. Tens of thousands of civilians were forced to abandon their homes in the intervening towns of Kalakan, Karabagh and Istalif, not because of the hostilities but because they were Tajik and the Taliban suspected them of providing comfort to the enemy. In an unguarded moment, Mestiri's succcessor as UN peace envoy, Dr Norbert Holl, described the exodus as 'ethnic cleansing', but the Taliban did permit inhabitants some access to their homes by daylight and worse atrocities were being witnessed in Pashtun areas of provinces under Dostum's total or partial control.[38]

Mestiri had resigned on 27 May on health grounds, but his exasperation was obvious in a final report which said that no peace formula was possible with the current heads of the factions. His successor was Norbert Holl, the former head of the South Asia department in Germany's Foreign Ministry. By the time he took up his post in July, he was in a position to benefit from the flurry of alarm that the ultra-orthodox religious movement had provoked among the UN's traditional paymasters, the US and the European Union, as well as the regional powers. This did not result in any concrete progress, partly through Holl's inability to gain access to the Taliban leader, Mullah Mohammad Omar, but also due to the

UN's continued recognition of Rabbani as head of the Afghan government. Holl was not entirely innocent, however: by February 1997, he had won a reputation for arrogance that even the Taliban found difficult to swallow.[39]

The first snow fell in early December, making the roads all but impassable, but bringing a welcome respite to the frozen combatants. The trophies of victory, so bitterly contested since the fall of Kabul, resumed their usual ordinariness under the white light of winter when Afghan fighters traditionally pause for three months of tea-drinking and the resumption of family life. Clashes continued around Karabagh and Bagram, which fell to the Taliban at the end of December. Massoud blamed the loss on a commander who had defected with 2,000 men, but his explanation could not detract from the end-of-term feeling in the air.[40]

Blocked by snow and mud, neither side could advance until the spring thaw, particularly the Taliban, whose southern troops were ill-suited to the climate of the Hindu Kush. Dostum filled the vacuum with random bombing raids on Herat and Kabul, dropping 25 tonnes on the capital in January when his pilots also hit the sprawling but abandoned US embassy in Wazir Akbar Khan. There was further fighting in Karabagh, but Massoud's men had largely gone to ground in the Panjshir, leaving open the approaches to the Ghorband valley to the west of Jabal Saraj. This was the back door to Dostum's country. Prone to landslide and avalanche, the narrow valley ascended to the gleaming heights of the Shibar Pass which, at 4,300 metres, made the Silk Gorge look like a freeway. The Pashtun farmers of Shinwar and Siagard welcomed the Taliban, pledging 1,000 guns to the crusade, but the pass still loomed like the high-water mark of the movement's morale.[41] They had seen Kabul's gilded ruins and the decadence at the extremities of a new Pashtun state, whose heart lay in the oases around Kandahar. Why proceed into the sea of alien steppe, visible from the summit and which rolled inconsolably into the horizons of Central Asia?

The war paused, but the snow went on falling.

4 Mission to Cleanse

Who was – or is – the one-eyed mullah, Mohammad Omar, and what is the nature of his calling? So little is known of his real existence – or so much had been purposefully discounted as a distraction from his value as a symbol – that all that we are left with are a few fogged impressions and a handful of conjecture. But this shadowy figure remains crucial to gauging the essence and trajectory of the Taliban movement. He is its presiding genius; the saint on the satellite phone.

Where would his mission end? At the Shibar Pass? The Oxus river? Is he a second Mahdi, conjuring up the elemental 'swarm-life' of Central Asia's Muslims in an ever-expanding *jihad* that must constantly break new ground, or risk implosion? Or simply a modest, local hero who shows his face only to admirers, lest the charm which overthrew a brutal interregnum and brought about a badly-needed peace will somehow be broken? How much of the plot had God revealed to the Leader of the Faithful?

Seven years after the movement was founded, the Mullah's physical features are unknown outside the city of Kandahar, where he lives simply with his wife and children. He has been described as 40 years of age, 'unusually tall' for an Afghan, alternatively 'heavy-set' or 'distinguished' and, according to one journalist, a speaker of Dari with an Iranian accent – despite being a Pashtun from Maiwand in Kandahar province.[1] His right eye is stitched shut, the result of an encounter with Soviet soldiers when he was a *mujahedin* commander with *Harakat-i Inqilab-i Islami*. The left, his few visitors allow, has a 'hawk-like, unrelenting' gaze.[2]

He assiduously cultivates this air of enigma, in a refusal to be photographed or interviewed and by delegating all but the most crucial encounters with non-Afghans to colleagues or underlings. Dr Norbert Holl, the UN envoy charged with coordinating peace efforts in Afghanistan, cooled his heels for six months after the fall of Kabul before being granted a meeting with the *de facto* head of the new government. What scant media access the Mullah permits has tended to reinforce his image as a sphinx-like visitor from another plane of being. In a bizarrely-constructed exchange with David Loyn, the BBC's South Asia correspondent, Mohammad Omar explained, from behind a curtain and via a third party seated inches away, that his reluctance to hold face-to-face interviews was because he did not wish to meet anybody who was not 'helpful' to his cause.[3] While this put the UN and the BBC firmly in their places, it hinted at a fear of contamination, even an element of *noli me tangere*, that was either strikingly authentic or knowingly theatrical.

The atmosphere in his immediate court, by contrast, is relaxed and informal. Commanders come and go, dipping their fingers into the communal pot and contributing at liberty to whatever discussion is going on. The Mullah keeps a strongbox by his side and hands out expenses, as and when required.[4] But this is no more than is expected under the code of *pashtunwali*, in which relations between men are seldom hierarchical. An established leader extends his influence by keeping 'open house' in his *hujra*, the communal room in which men meet, eat and sleep. The provision of credit is an intrinsic part of a relationship which, fundamentally, remains contractual.

There is nothing remarkable, then, about the Mullah's accessibility to his followers, but the deference which they show to him is unique in an Afghan context. 'Whatever our rank,' explained his liaison officer, Mullah Hashim, 'when we come before him, we consider ourselves as just a simple *mujahid*.'[5] At one level of interpretation, the comment confirms his followers' willingness to discard their rank and prostrate themselves at the feet of their master but, at another, it shines a light into a non-threatening relationship in which the ultimate *mujahid* categorically refuses to adopt the authority and trappings of the prince.

Afghan kings and the *khan*, who made up the traditional baronial class, maintained power through hospitality and political horse-trading, but descent was a more crucial ingredient in their legitimacy.[6] This is particularly true among the Durrani, who trace their genealogy back to Qais Abdul Rashid, a companion of the Prophet. Even poor Durranis regard themselves as *brahmin* in the informal system of clan caste which prevails among the Pashtun, and they are fastidious observers of the four pillars of Islam – prayer, fasting, alms and pilgrimage. But a fifth, invisible pillar exists under *pashtunwali* in the co-dependancy of ancestral virtue and perceived piety.

The generational continuity of rural Afghanistan was interrupted first by the overthrow of King Zahir Shah in 1973 and then by the Soviet war which, in sweeping into exile several million Pashtun, opened the door for the commander to assume the prerogatives of the *khan*. In some cases, a commander would have been chosen to lead the community's resistance to communist rule precisely because he was the son of the local *khan*. After the war, these tended to adopt a more consensual approach to governing. But more often, he was an interloper, whose legitimacy during the *jihad* had expired with the withdrawal of the Red Army. It was this usurpation which estranged the surrounding community, not the abuses which were actually committed. In the logic both of the *pashtunwali* and Islam, abuse was the natural consequence of dynastic disruption.

Mohammad Omar is neither of the *khan* class nor a member of the Mohammadzai branch of the Durrani, which had provided Afghanistan with its kings since 1747.[7] This lent a neutrality to his seemingly accidental role in the orchestration – or re-design – of local power relations after October 1994, for which he has, anyway, demonstrated a studied disregard. But he could lay claim to a pedigree of a different type – the *talib* – one that married the Pashtun martial tradition with the high ideals of selflessness and piety, which are interwoven with tribal concepts of leadership. And religious legitimacy in Afghanistan has the privilege of superceding temporal power during times of emergency, as exemplified by the all-inclusive appeal of *jihad*, which does not jeopardise local authority unless it opposes the tide of 'faith'.

No *mujahedin* group was without its band of *taliban* during the Soviet war.[8] Young, unmarried and with a tolerance for *shahadat*, or martyrdom, higher than their comrades, they maintained a distinct and separate identity during operations, even eating and sleeping apart. At the war's end, they had resumed their studies, only to watch with mounting disgust the behaviour of the same political order which they had helped to install. The *talib* retained the original dignity of the *mujahid*, without the taint which acrued after the Soviet withdrawal; he was, therefore, qualified to embody the spiritual and moral harmonies which are intrinsic to the Pashtun concept of society but which had lapsed under *mujahedin* rule.

The Mullah's first public explanation of the Taliban's mission was that it had arisen to restore peace, to provide security to the wayfarer and to protect the honour of women and the poor. Although the implication was there, no explicit mention was made of *jihad* and, indeed, it could not have been until the Taliban had acquired the critical mass needed to present themslves as a popular force for change. But *jihad* had become something of a hackneyed concept even to Afghans after the events of 1992, when a government of blood-stained communists which, nevertheless, possessed some of the legitimacy required in the traditional leadership equation, was replaced by home-grown Islamists with talents for little more than libertinism.

The impulse had been hijacked once by the West in the war against the Soviet Union which entailed over a million Afghan deaths. But for all its violence, the Soviet invasion was a footnote in the history of Afghan *jihad*, confirmation merely that the countryside's worst fears of urban politicians had been true. Holy war had been declared one year prior to Moscow's involvement, when the *Khalq* faction of the Afghan communist party tried to subdue the three Omegas of rural Pashtun society – *zan* (women), *zar* (gold) and *zamin* (land)[9] – by stripping women of the veil and imposing literacy and land reform. The response was *jihad*, the countryside's sole intervention in the civil war which smouldered between *Khalq* and *Parcham* and the nearest thing, in Afghan terms, to a referendum.

To invoke the word after 1992 was to risk scepticism or the stink of blasphemy. *Jamiat* fighters, slain during the siege of Kabul, were eulogised by the Rabbani government as having embraced *shahadat* but, in truth, their body parts had simply been blown away. Even Hekmatyar exploited the word: he declared a *jihad* against the Taliban after his resumption of prime ministerial powers in mid-1996, vindicating the claim with the short-lived crackdown on women's rights and secular amusements which preceded the fall of Kabul.[10] Mohammad Omar used the term more cautiously. He did not resort to calling a *jihad* until October 1996, and it was not against Rabbani's retreating forces, but General Rashid Dostum, whose dyed-in-the-wool post-communism marked him as a less ambiguous theological adversary.[11]

The Mullah's protestations that the Taliban was a wholly indigenous movement, free from Pakistani influence, formed part of the political shorthand which had arisen following the disillusionment of 1992. Any *jihad* with proven foreign support was condemned, in Afghan eyes, to the fate of its predecessor. All parties to the denouement of the Rabbani episode enjoyed the backing of outside powers, but none could own to it for fear of the legitimacy principle which dictated that an Afghan problem could only be solved by Afghans. It was the Catch-22 in a country of minorities artificially concocted by foreign powers and, hence, the popular suspicion of a UN peacekeeping force on Afghan soil. In the absence of accord, between Pashtun and Tajik or Durrani and Ghilzai, on the meaning of 'Afghan', however, consensus was only possible through an invidious search engine called 'Islam'.

The scramble for spiritual legitimacy was more complex than its portrayal in the Western media. Far from restoring pre-communist virtue in a frenzy of populist iconoclasm, the Taliban were a cultural revolution in their own right, one that hit at the very traditions which the students purported to uphold. The forces which had fought the *jihad* against the Soviets had been assembled in the name of great scholars or the descendants of Sufi saints: men like Professor Rabbani, a poet and postgraduate of Egypt's prestigious Al-Azhar University; or Pir Sayed Gailani and Sibghatollah Mojadeddi, the heads, respectively, of the Qadiriyya and Naqshbandi Sufi orders.

These were eminent greybeards at the summit of an ecclesiastical ladder which had extended since the 1970s to embrace the dynamic radicalism of Gulbuddin Hekmatyar and Ahmad Shah Massoud, both of whom learned their politics at the feet of Professor Rabbani. Behind these two key figures in what would later become the Afghan resistance loomed the silhouette of the Ayatollah Khomeini, whose example had inspired a generation of revolutionaries. Hekmatyar had chosen the high road of an Islamic purism, then reaching into every corner of the Muslim world; Massoud, a rearguard nationalism in which the unifying issue of shared faith was tempered by a greater tolerance of Western modernism. The ultimate collision between the two manifestos on ethnic grounds spelled the end of a discourse on Islamic revolution in Afghanistan which had begun to unravel when they fled to Peshawar in 1973.

The culture of the commander was a degeneration of the old *khan* system but the rise of the *mullah*, under the Taliban, proved to be less a return to the elusive values cherished in pre-communist times than the stupefying of a tradition which once traced its origins back to the footsteps of the Prophet. Lineage was more crucial in matters of Afghan religion than in temporal affairs. The *sayed*, the *pir* and the *alim* – Afghanistan's spiritual aristocracy – comprised a legacy that wove together 'High Church' trends in Islamic thought with a popular belief in spirits and anchored them both in the everyday life of the Afghan village. The Taliban buried them all and summoned the *mullah*, who was a cross between a country parson and a Shakespearian clown, to recite the funeral rights.

It is moot to speculate whether the Taliban's rapid ascent reflected disenchantment in the community at large with the customary channels for the transmission of spiritual values. Force of arms, supported by scripture, would always remain the trump among a people who viewed their prosperity as the product of a successful accommodation with impersonal and transient powers. The standing of some *sayed* – direct descendants of the Prophet – and *pir* – the reincarnation of the virtue, if not the person, of Sufi saints – had undoubtedly been harmed in the aftermath of *jihad,* as their followers embarked on a spree of freebooting, while the *ulama* – plural of *alim,* or religious scholar – had seen their collective authority as Afghanistan's law-givers consistently undermined by a string of modernising kings and the communist party.[12]

The authority of the *sayed* and *alim* was, moreover, received and largely remote from an illiterate peasantry which, when fate proved intolerable, took its complaints and ailments to the nearest Sufi shrine, where the Pashtun's customary sangfroid was swept away in an orgy of spirit possession. Yet it is far from conclusive that the *mullah* was the institution capable of reviving the Afghan's frustrated religious instincts – or bringing them back to the straight and narrow – or even whether *sharia,* the integrated code of justice revealed through Koranic study, fully chimed with the concepts of social equilibrium common among tribal Pashtun.

The *mullah* was not, on the whole, revered for his religious insight. He was a community servant who earned a crust through bone-setting and the selling of religious amulets to protect against the evil eye or the myriad *jinn,* which live in the air and visit illness upon children and women. This was surplus to what he might raise through *zakat,* the variable tithe on local farm produce which was rendered for his services in the mosque, the *madrassa* and at the graveside. In thin seasons, vilifying the *mullah,* a man who worked with his wit more than his hands, came a close second to cursing the landlord, for most Pashtun are sharecroppers forced to make a punitive reckoning at the end of a hard year's graft. In fat, they could make a handsome income from trading in opium, the premier crop in Helmand, Zabul and to a lesser extent, in Kandahar.

Nor did ordinary Pashtun thirst for *sharia,* having already in the *pashtunwali* a system of conflict resolution which favoured arbitration and the adjustment of claims over the draconian punishments meted out under Koranic law.[13] The more extreme *sharia* penalties of *hadud* (amputation) and *qisas,* in which an identical harm was inflicted by the victim's family upon the perpetrator of a crime, tended to further inflame tensions in a society with an already striking susceptibility for blood-feuds. Pashtun courts, supervised by *ulama,* preferred the payment of blood-money for the crime of murder and restitution in the case of theft. The suppression of tribal law had preoccupied Kabul since the nineteenth century, when Amir Abdul-Rahman sought to undermine local autonomy, and it was resumed by the *mujahedin* government, which introduced *sharia* law in 1993 without being able to enforce its use outside the towns.

Despite the the weight placed by the Taliban on law and order, their judicial procedure was summary and non-consultative. Courts, often supervised by illiterate *mullah*, might try a dozen cases in a day in sessions where no provision was made for legal council and where the presumption of innocence was absent.[14] The gravest sentences, moreover, were carried out in public with a clear view to impressing spectators with the terror of the court. In February 1996 in Khost, two Afghans accused of murder were riddled with bullets in front of 20,000 people by the fathers of their victims in accordance with *qisas*.[15] In Herat, a young man was publicly hung from a crane, having confessed to killing two Taliban. Spectators said that he had been clearly beaten 'close to death' before arriving at the execution spot. In several of the 20 or so reported *hadud* cases, hands or feet were summarily axed by Taliban guards without the benefit of a court appearance.[16]

Determining whether the rise of the *mullah* was tantamount to the 'dumbing down' of a richer spiritual – and legal – tradition is hampered by the opacity of the Taliban movement and the convergence of its religious and military agendas. The young *taliban,* who rallied to the cause, and many of their leaders were the product of the Deoband school of Sunni thought, founded 130 years earlier in Uttar Pradesh, India which, in the absence of any domestic school of theological studies, had exerted an influence on Afghanistan's spiritual leadership equal to that of Egypt's Al-Azhar University, the *alma mater* of both Rabbani and Abdul-Rasul Sayyaf, head of the *Ittehad-i Islami* party.

The Soviet interlude tilted that balance in favour of Deoband, first by blocking state subsidies to finance religious studies farther afield and, secondly, by driving millions of Afghans into the border provinces of Pakistan, where the *madrassa* system, dominated by the north Indian school, provided one of the few sources of education. Speculation about the nature of that education is vulnerable to Western prejudice because of general concern at the effects of religious tuition on the very young but, more specifically, because of the suspicion that Islam's highly prescriptive character makes it more susceptible than other faiths to programmes of ideological regimentation.

The Deobandis represent the extreme of such attempts to regulate personal behaviour, having issued nearly a quarter of a million *fatwa* on the minutiae of everyday life since the beginning of the century.[17] There is eyewitness testimony to children, chained to their lecterns, rocking back and forth as they learn by rote a Koran written not in Pashtun, but in Arabic. Boys enter the system as wards, exchanging life in a poor family for bed, board and an austere catechism that will one day lead to life as a *mullah*. It is tempting to identify in this early separation from female relatives the origins of the extreme misogyny which, even more than the objective of a pure Islamic state, lent cohesion to the Taliban as they marched into, and subdued, non-Pashtun lands. Western countries, ironically, contributed to the rise of Deoband influence in Pakistan's tribal trust territories by providing *madrassa* with aid during the *jihad* to foster a new generation of cadets to fight the Soviets.[18]

But *taliban* misogyny went so beyond what is normally intended by that word that it qualified as a kind of 'gynaeophobia', one so broad that the merest sight of stockinged foot or varnished finger was taken as a seductive invitation to personal damnation. Official Taliban policy, in a very immediate sense, stigmatised females as the the evil eye made omnipresent – and a cause for real fear – within the communities which the rank-and-file occupied. They had to be covered, closeted and, where necessary, beaten to prevent more sin from being spewed into society. The Taliban penalty for women showing their face in public was set by the Office for the Propagation of Virtue and the Prevention of Vice, a religious police established in Kabul to enforce such restrictions, at 29 lashes.[19]

Part of this anxiety was sexual and could be attributed to the highly-charged tribal rules of *pashtunwali,* by which girls embark on the perilous road to puberty at seven, when they are first sequestered from boys and men.[20] From then, until marriage, youths have no licit contact with the opposite sex beyond the members of their immediate family. In Kandahar, the custom of seclusion had given rise to a rich and colourful tradition of homosexual passion, celebrated in poetry, dance and the practice of male prostitution. Heterosexual romance, by contrast, was freighted with the fear of broken honour, the threat of vendetta and, ultimately, death by stoning, if the heart were found out. In Pashtun society, man-woman love was the one that dared not speak its name: boy-courtesans conducted their affairs openly.

Under *pashtunwali*, stoning or burial alive are the customary penalties for adultery, a crime which is seen as threatening the peace of the entire community. Unlike *sharia*, which requires four witnesses to the sexual act, the merest whisper of impropriety among the Pashtun is sufficient to ruin a woman's honour and put her life in jeopardy. The most widely-reported sentence of stoning under the Taliban occurred in Kandahar in August 1996, when a married man and his widowed mother-in-law were found *in flagrante* and taken out and killed before the local mosque.[21] A second confirmed instance took place in Laghman in March 1997 when a married woman was convicted in a *sharia* court of attempting to flee the district with a man who was not her husband.[22]

Homosexual liaisons were criminalised by the Taliban but, compared with adultery, the punishments were token. 'We have a dilemma on this,' explained Mullah Mohammad Hassan, governor of Kandahar. 'One group of scholars believes you should take these people to the highest building in the city and hurl them to their deaths. [The other] recommends you dig a pit near a wall somewhere, put these people in it, then topple the wall so that they are buried alive.'[23] In the event, couples had their faces blackened and were paraded around the streets. One can hear the Mullah chuckling in his beard as he outlined the theological impasse.

The *talib* grew to maturity on the gruel of orthodoxy, estranged from the mitigating influence of women, family and village. This ensured that early recruits to the movement were disciplined and biddable. If their gynaeophobia appeared the product of a repressed homosexuality on the march, *taliban* cohorts also conjured up echoes of a medieval children's crusade, with its associated elements of self-flagellation and an innocent trust in the immanence of paradise. This second impression would be strengthened following the Taliban's military debacle in Mazar-i Sharif in May 1997.

It was logical that trainee *taliban* should regard the graduates of their course – the *mullah* – as the natural officer class in the movement's subsequent military career. Among the dozen or so Taliban leaders to achieve public prominence, only Sher Mohammad Stanakzai, acting foreign minister and the main point of contact with the outside world after the fall of Kabul, eschewed a title that was invoked to stress seniority and became inseparable from the movement's corporatist image. Well-travelled and fluent in English and Urdu, Stanakzai was, perhaps, too worldly, too 'un-Afghan' to qualify for the newly-empowered honorific of *mullah*. He had, moreover, spent the *jihad* heading the military committee of Sayyaf's *Ittehad-i Islami* in Quetta and was, arguably, on probation for his former association with Wahhabi rites and Saudi money.[24]

But it is not safe to assume that the Taliban's other leaders, compared with Stanakzai, were more authentic, religious spokesmen. Despite his near-messianic status, Mullah Mohammad Omar 'has not too much religious knowledge', according to Mullah Mohammad Hassan, governor of Kandahar, who added: 'A lot of scholars know more than he does.'[25] The versatility of the Taliban elite, who alternated as military chiefs, governors, ministers, as well as *mullah*, combined with the engrained Afghan practice of adopting *noms de guerre* – Ahmad Shah Massoud is not his given name – argues in favour of the thesis that the movement merely clothed its membership in ecclesiastical titles to disguise their origins.

This process of clericalisation similarly transformed each enemy defection into a Damascene conversion, just as the enforcement of *sharia*-based edicts in non-Pashtun regions added a patina of religion to what was essentially the imposition of martial law. It also veiled a coat-rack of skeletons. 'Mullah' Mohammad Hassan of Kandahar had nothing to do with the religious world before his emergence as the Taliban's number three, while 'Mullah' Borjan, the movement's Rommel, was a former Afghan army officer who had served under King Zahir Shah. A number of other key military appointments – Shah Sawar, the artillery commander north of Kabul, and General Mohammad Gilani, the Taliban air commodore – were *Khalq* members of the Afghan national army until 1992, making a mockery of Mullah Mohammad Omar's claim that his goal was to rid Afghanistan of 'time-serving communists'.[26] The title 'mullah' had as much connection with spiritual integrity, as the term 'comrade' with solidarity.

Mullah Mohammad Omar's closest intimate in these early years was Mullah Borjan, another *Harakat* veteran and a former student of the Kabul military academy. Under his real name, Touran Abdul-Rahman, he was allegedly involved in the palace revolution which led to the death of President Hafizullah Amin in 1979, paving the way for the Soviet invasion. Mullah Borjan was commander-in-chief of the Taliban forces, as they progressed from Helmand to the first siege of Kabul in 1995, where he was wounded at Charasyab, before returning to the fray in Jalalabad in late 1996.

Why Mohammad Omar decided to remain in Kandahar, directing operations by satellite telephone, is open to speculation, if he really were the brilliant *jihad* commander that the Taliban so widely claimed. Perhaps, he was already too valuable a commodity to risk in a mode of combat where field commanders stood roughly the same chance of dying as foot-soldiers. Mullah Borjan perished, along with eight other fighters, after the pick-up they were driving hit a land mine in the Silk Gorge during the final advance on Kabul. A simple roadside epitaph commemorates him, along with a copse of the green and white flags which denote martyrdom.

Some Afghans murmured treachery, claiming that, unlike Mohammad Omar, Borjan had harboured pro-monarchical sympathies to the last. Mullah Mohammad Rabbani was commonly regarded as the Mullah's deputy until his mysterious disappearance from the political scene, shortly after the fall of Kabul. A 38-year-old from Arghastan district of Kandahar, Rabbani fought with *Hizb-i Islami (Khalis)* during the Soviet war, studying at a *madrassa* in Zabul, Kandahar and Quetta, before taking command of the Taliban forces in Logar in March 1995.[27]

On 27 September 1996, he was appointed head of the six-man *shura* in charge of the capital. He also sat on Mohammad Omar's inner cabinet in Kandahar, which included Mullah Mohammad Hassan, the governor of Kandahar; Mullah Mohammad Ghaus, the foreign minister; Mullah Sayed Ghayasuddin Agha, a Tajik from Badakhshan and the only non-Pashtun; Mullah Fazil Mohammad from Uruzgan, the new security commander for Kabul; and Mullah Abdul Razzak, another Khalis veteran and Mullah Borjan's deputy commander-in-chief.[28] A third *shura*, composed of the chief of security, the chief of the armed forces and the chief of police, also met regularly in Kabul to determine policies relating to the maintenance of law and order.

In November 1996, Mullah Rabbani vanished from view amidst a rictus of speculation that he might have been brought down by internal disagreements. As a Durrani descended from the royal branch, he, too, may have had mixed feelings about what appear to have been Mohammad Omar's growing imperial ambitions, while his rumoured involvement in the revenge killing of Najibullah created additional grounds for suspicion.[29] Sher Mohammad Stanakzai, then acting foreign minister, said in January 1997 that Rabbani had merely been suffering from 'mental problems' and had travelled to Saudi Arabia and Kuwait for treatment.[30] He returned to his post that month. Stanakzai was subsequently replaced as acting foreign minister by Mullah Ghaus, one of the Taliban's better-educated leaders, and drifted away from the public scene.

Mullah Abdul Razzak remained the lone soldier on Mohammad Omar's ruling council, an indication of the subordination of the Taliban military to its political or religious wing. Following a demonstration by 150 women against the closure of bath-houses in Herat in December 1996, Mullah Razzak replaced another Taliban stalwart, Mullah Yar Mohammad, as governor of Herat, allegedly because he had been too 'soft'.[32] From there, he opened the western front in Faryab against General Dostum in October 1996, leading the Taliban forces into Mazar-i Sharif in May 1997 where he met his death.

Discernible changes in ideological presentation took place during the first year of the Taliban's emergence, notably after its first defeat at the gates of Kabul. These reflected the growing confidence of a movement which had never been strong on consistent policy statements beyond the objectives of ridding Afghanistan of corrupt leaders, the confiscation of weapons and the introduction of *sharia* law. But they also suggested the development within the Taliban leadership of a far harder line on a range of topics, from the value of the UN peace initiative and the future of ex-king Zahir Shah to Mohammad Omar's perception of himself within the Islamic tradition of warrior-priest and the Prophet's promise that a descendant would some day arise to reanimate the faith.

Despite his four-score years – 20 of them spent in Rome – the king over the water remains a live political issue a quarter century after the overthrow of the Afghan monarchy. As a direct descendant of the Mohammadzai rulers, his legitimacy is beyond question while the tragedies which subsequently befell his country, from the rise of the communist party and the Soviet invasion to the *mujahedin* struggle for power, could all – with a large dose of nostalgia – be blamed upon the disruption of his reign. His last decade on the throne had seen the introduction of a constitutional monarchy, general elections, partial press freedom and a build-up of foreign aid, which had transformed Afghanistan's infrastructure. President Najibullah offered to hand over power to Zahir Shah during the negotiations for a transitional government which preceded his downfall and, after 1994, the UN peace mission consistently returned to the option as the one on which the majority of *mujahedin* factions appeared most likely to sink their differences.

Though refusing to be drawn into the UN-sponsored peace talks, the Taliban remained vaguely positive about Zahir Shah's future status during 1995. But, on 4 April 1996, Mullah Mohammad Omar was publicly anointed as *Amir Ul-Momineen*, or Leader of the Faithful, by 1,000 *ulama* in Kandahar, a sign which was interpreted as a challenge to all Muslims in the region, most notably the Shia minority.[33] The following November, the Mullah entered the great mosque in Kandahar, removing its holiest relic and a symbol of monarchical legitimacy, the Cloak of Mohammad, and displaying it to the excited crowd. He issued instructions by radio that mosques should no longer end their prayers with the customary invocation for long life of the old king. The Taliban's previous offers of a warm welcome home to Zahir Shah were modified to include the description of him as a 'criminal', who would be answerable for the crimes of the past 40 years.[34]

'Many people in Pashtun areas were thinking of Zahir Shah in the beginning,' said Massoud in February 1997. 'They thought the US was behind the Taliban and that the US would support Zahir Shah. They saw the Taliban as a temporary phenomenon. But when the Taliban declared its enmity for Zahir Shah, there was a lot of disappointment among educated people.'[35]

While it presented a veneer of unprecedented Pashtun unity, divisions were not far from the surface, as might be expected from a movement in which a sizeable proportion of its manpower had already changed sides, while others had only donned the turban for the sake of convenience. An early analysis of friction within the Taliban identified three distinct groups: the more devout, waiting for guidance from Allah; those seeking an accommodation with Massoud's *Jamiat,* in exchange for the implementation of *sharia* law; and a *Khalq*-influenced element which sought to re-impose Pashtun hegemony in the guise of Islamic reaction.[36]

The first defections only became apparent in early 1996 when two Taliban commanders, fearing loss of authority in their personal fiefdoms, joined the *Ittehad* forces in Paghman, west of Kabul.[37] Similar disaffection was reported from Logar, Gardez, Maidanshar and Paktya in the run-up to the capture of Kabul, usually over Taliban heavy-handedness towards local customs or the refusal by civilians engaged in blood feuds to hand over their weapons.[38] By December 1996, aid workers in Kabul said that the Taliban were no longer sure of who was actually in their ranks and that their harshness to the Kabuli population was a symptom of that uncertainty.[39] This tended to confirm the contention of Robin Raphel, the US assistant secretary of state for south Asian affairs, that, for all its success, the Taliban remained a highly factionalised movement, held together chiefly by the charisma and vision of Mullah Mohammad Omar.[40]

The Mullah's continued residence in Kandahar after the fall of Kabul was similarly scoured for symbolic content. All other Afghan faction leaders had attempted to maintain a presence near, or inside, the capital as the first crucial step towards winning international recognition for the legitimacy of their claim to power. This, much more than popular acclaim, had been a vital factor for Afghan rulers since the Third Afghan War which, after 80 years of British rule, won Kabul the right to deal as equals with the West and its neighbours. Mohammad Omar, by contrast, gave every indication that he disdained such worldly endorsement. Kabul was not even worth a flying visit from its new conqueror. He remained in Kandahar, rejecting the advances of a stream of foreign dignitaries until June 1997 when the sapping defeat at Mazar finally prised him from his reclusion.[41]

He appeared, anyway, to have an able deputy in Kabul in the shape of Maulvi Rafiullah Muazin, general president of the *Amr Bil Marof Wa Nai An Munkir* – Office for the Propagation of Virtue and the Prevention of Vice or, more demotically, the Department of What is Right and What Is Wrong. Edicts were issued by Maulvi Raffiullah with great diligence to prevent: sedition and 'female uncovers'; idolatry; the British and American hair style; interest charges on loans; the washing of clothes by young ladies in the streams of the city; music and dancing at wedding parties; the playing of the drum; the taking of female body measurements by tailors; and sorcery.[42] His deputy, Maulvi Inayatullah Baligh, a former career bureaucrat with the Rabbani regime, commanded a team of 100 religious inspectors to enforce this flood of *fatwa*, which would mount to include the shaving of male pubic hair, the white-washing of windows to prevent the accidental sight of women residents and the outlawing of 'squeaky shoes'.

Rafiullah appeared to have the ear of Mohammad Omar but there were a multitude of signs that, by virtue of his position at the head of *Amr Bil Marof Wa Nai An Munkir*, he had a tendency to exceed his instructions. Baligh, at least, was an enthusiastic lieutenant, telling one journalist: 'Whenever we catch them doing immoral things, we can do anything we want. We can execute them, we can kill them.'[43] When Radio *Sharia* announced in December 1996 that 225 Kabul women had been beaten in a single day for violating the department's dress codes, Mohammad Omar was persuaded by Afghans to issue a restraining order which was circulated to the Ministry of Information and police stations around Kabul.

The text of the Taliban leader's 'advice' was illuminating since it demonstrated two facts: that the Taliban were certainly not above the law and that Kandaharis, at least, had begun to take steps to curb the excesses of the rank-and-file. Two innocent women had been killed in Kandahar in December by the guardians of public morality but, when two alleged robbers were beaten to death by the Taliban at Qishla Jadid military base in Kandahar, the movement was finally fined around $13,500 ('two thousand *lakh afghani*') by the local *sharia* court.[44] Mohammad Omar's letter also revealed that cases had been reported of people being beaten with electric cables. 'Don't be cruel and don't be dishonest with the Islamic government treasury,' it began, before describing the specific case. 'Such kinds of punishment and beating,' it continued, 'need the permission of the Imam and Emir, otherwise the doer of such actions will be punished under *qisas* (those who make a great sin).' Radio *Sharia* immediately ceased publicising the punishments.

By late October 1996, a new organogram of power began to take shape in Kabul as fresh, generally capable Taliban 'technocrats' were appointed to replace the ministers of the ousted regime. In spite of Mohammad Omar's avowed intention to purge the government of its communist elements – many of whom were undoubtedly fighting alongside the Taliban forces – it was evident that this project had been deferred, perhaps indefinitely, due to the difficulty it presented to the creation of a functioning administration. Nevertheless, appeals were made to expatriate communities in Germany, Norway and the United Kingdom for the well-educated to return and help develop the Islamic state.

Some Taliban-watchers put the share of former *Harakat* members in the ministerial line-up as high as 60 per cent, with Pashtuns wholly predominating.[45] Warming to their new roles and the interaction they afforded with representatives of foreign donors or the aid community, many Taliban bureaucrats spoke *sotto voce* of the need to reopen girls' schools, desegregate health care and create income opportunities for widows. Such attempts at compromise, however, failed to result in any significant change in the existing status quo, possibly out of deference to more conservative opinions within the largely rural infantry, then laying down their lives on the northern fronts.

'The three-man *shura,'* rationalised one aid worker, 'is more powerful than the six-man *shura*. But then there is the one-man *shura*, which is Raffiullah. He is more powerful than either of them. As a result, though ministers are saying: "Alright. You can let women work, so long as they are properly covered," Raffiullah is saying: "I don't care who said what. It is not allowed".'[46] With few or no Tajiks, Uzbeks and Hazaras represented at any one of the concentric rings of power which emanated from Mullah Mohammad Omar, the prospects of achieving a lasting peace without maintaining an apparatus of repression and conditions of martial law remained slight.

As late as October 1996, the movement appeared at odds at the highest levels about its ultimate purpose and the role of its inspirational leader. On 6 October, Foreign Minister Mullah Mohammad Ghaus stated categorically that the Taliban were only a 'caretaker administration', which would take measures towards the establishment of a broad-based elected government in Afghanistan, once security had been assured throughout the country.[47] This was, in a sense, a return to policies outlined early on in the movement's career when the Mullah announced his intention to disarm the factions and to introduce *sharia* law. It even left a window open for the return of Zahir Shah, in one role or other. But Mullah Ghaus was contradicted just two weeks later in a published interview with Mullah Wakil Ahmad, Mohammad Omar's private secretary. 'For us,' he said, 'consultation is not necessary ... We abide by the Emir's views, even if he alone takes this view ... There will not be a head of state. Instead, there will be an *Amir Ul-Momineen*.'[48]

At that late stage, it was not wholly clear – even to the Taliban – whether it was a movement of liberation or of tyranny.

5 Burning Down the House

'This is the work of the Lawrences of Arabia of the ISI,' a journalist was told in November 1995 by Abdul Rahim Khan Mandokhel, an opposition senator for Baluchistan, the province from which the Taliban launched their crusade.[1] It was a colourful comment, satirising the way in which operatives of the Pakistani intelligence service had come to view their part in the Afghan war and even more clandestine exploits across the Oxus river to destabilise Soviet Central Asia.[2] But it is not entirely borne out by the evidence and Mandokhel's use of the plural was all the more appropriate. Pakistan's power structure had radically altered since the mysterious air crash in December 1988 which cost the lives of General Zia ul-Haq and the cream of the officer class that had planned and implemented Pakistan's Afghan policy during the Soviet occupation. New powers and personalities had emerged to challenge the ISI's authority. If there were 'Lawrences of Arabia' out there in the Afghan *dasht*, they were working for different masters and, possibly, at cross-purposes.

By the end of 1991, the geopolitical world was spinning so fast that countries unable to escape from the shivering ranks of former Cold War clients and into the club of the New World Order were in danger of falling off altogether. Former enemies were greeted as long-lost friends, while tried and tested alliances turned into crumbling treaty documents. After a decade transfixed by the Soviet threat, the US swivelled its sensors elsewhere in the world: the Gulf, Somalia, China and the East European republics.

Pakistan was among the first to experience the acuteness of US ingratitude. Washington cut aid from around $660 million a year in the war, to zero in 1990 and then launched an avid courtship of India, Pakistan's historic nemesis, which had previously been aligned with the Soviet Union. Seen from New Delhi, America's former sweetheart looked more and more like a serial home-wrecker. Having turned a blind eye to Pakistan's nuclear programme throughout the Afghan war, Washington awoke to the reality of a turbulent Islamic state, dominated by the military and with a first-strike potential trained on India. Islamabad's assistance to rebels in Kashmir, meanwhile, had so escalated that, in 1991, the US threatened to declare it a 'terrorist' state, along with such outcasts as Libya, Iraq, Iran, North Korea and Cuba. The special relationship was over.

It had been showing strain since 1989, chiefly over the ISI's handling of Afghan policy. To protect Pakistani interests, the ISI had used US and Gulf resources to foster a resistance which excluded the Durrani Pashtuns in favour of the Ghilzai and was dominated by Hekmatyar, the most anti-Western of all seven parties in Peshawar. As the Red Army's phased withdrawal, agreed under the Geneva Accords of 14 April 1988, reached its conclusion, the State Department tried to correct the imbalance by channelling aid directly to the commanders in the field, particularly to Massoud. The ISI blocked this tactic by drawing on Saudi funding, estimated at $400 million in 1989, most of which ended up with *Hizb-i Islami*.[3]

The intelligence agency remained loyal to its protege throughout the post-Soviet years, conniving at Hekmatyar's attempted coup with the former defence minister, General Shahnawaz Tanai, in March 1990; the putsch of April 1992; the siege of 1992–3; the alliance with Dostum which led to the joint assault of January 1994; and, arguably, the reconciliation with Massoud in March 1996, Hekmatyar's last, desperate gamble to stay in the game. An uninterrupted supply of weapons and fuel crossed the Pakistani border at Spina Shaga in Paktya, *Hizb-i Islami*'s strongest military base, which fell to the Taliban only in August 1996.[4] Depleted of resources and political muscle as it was after the death of Zia and the end of US funding, could the ISI have also created the force which was to drive its long-standing ally in Afghanistan from the field?

Not only the geopolitical world had tilted since the collapse of the Soviet Union. The return to power in 1993 of Benazir Bhutto coincided with a relaxation of the army's grasp on power, the result of a decision in 1989 by the then chief of staff, General Aslam Beg, to try to bridge the gulf between civil and military that had opened with the execution of Benazir's father 10 years earlier. Bhutto rode to office on the appeal of her personality cult and a popular rejection of Prime Minister Balak Sher Mazari's efforts to create an Islamic state in Pakistan, replete with proposals for the abolition of interest rates, a mandatory death penalty for defiling the name of the Prophet and the compulsory wearing of veils.

Spores from the anti-Soviet war had by then drifted back across the border to take root in Baluchistan, Malakand, Swat and Bhutto's home province of Sind, where a campaign of urban terrorism by the *Mujahir Qaumi Movement*, an ally of Bhutto's Pakistan People's Party

(PPP) in her aborted 1989 government, had turned whole districts in the commercial hub of Karachi into no-go zones. One of her first acts as prime minister was to appoint her late father's Afghan adviser, Naseerullah Babar, to the all-important post of interior minister. A Pashtun and former governor of North West Frontier Province (NWFP), Babar was a brusque, retired general who boasted in private that 'having made Hekmatyar, he could break him just as easily'.[5] It might have been bravado. Border politics had been transformed since Babar was last in office.

The 100-year treaty marking the Durand Line lapsed in 1993, but the Pashtunistan issue had all but died out with the demise of a strong and unified Afghanistan. To make sure it remained buried, Bhutto and Babar spent the next three years trying to drive military roads into the more inaccessible valleys and bringing the tribal trust areas into the federal system by creating a NWFP assembly. But if the fear of separatism which had been the motor of Pakistan policy in Afghanistan since 1947 was finally silenced, what was left to replace it?

Another key Bhutto appointee was the foreign minister, Sardar Asif Ali, who attempted to open a new page in Islamabad's external relations. A decade of war and military rule had ended with Pakistan diplomatically isolated, with the exception of China, its ally against India, and Saudi Arabia, which maintained close ties to contain Iran from the east. Much of the responsibility for that isolation lay with the ISI and its activities in Afghanistan, Kashmir and the Indian Punjab. Asif Ali took pains to moderate the Islamic rhetoric, that had repelled the Americans, and to develop relations with landlocked Central Asia, where the world's energy future was believed to lie. Though interior minister, Babar was so close a confidant of Bhutto that it was he who was entrusted with the foreign policy task of turning the dream of a Central Asian hinterland into reality. In June 1994, Pakistan announced its intention of building rail and road links with Turkmenistan, a project that the World Bank endorsed with a $1.5 million commitment to a feasibility study. On 14 September, Babar declared that he would travel the length of the Quetta to Torghundi road, to negotiate safe passage for a convoy of 30 trucks bearing gifts for the peoples of Turkmenistan and Uzbekistan.

It was a reckless and improbable journey, worthy of the grand old man of Pakistan's Afghan policymaking. The convoy was timed to arrive in Ashgabat in late October, when Prime Minister Bhutto and a troop of Pakistani journalists were due to celebrate Turkmenistan's independence day. As poor as the Turkmens undoubtedly were, they did not, perhaps, need to be reminded of it on that particular day and 30 dusty trucks hardly amounted to a Marshall Plan. There was some indication that Babar's diplomatic odyssey across war-torn Afghanistan was frowned upon in senior government circles and only went ahead because of his position as Bhutto's 'favourite uncle'.

The 1993 elections held another surprise. The mainstream Islamist party, *Jamaat-i Islami* (JI), which had channelled Gulf funding to Hekmatyar and enjoyed close ties with General Zia and the ISI, saw its share of the national vote collapse from 11 to 7 per cent. Qazi Hussain Ahmad, the JI leader, lost his constituency and was forced to resign the leadership. In August 1996 – under investigation herself – Bhutto would accuse the Qazi of 'minting money' during the *jihad*.[6] The JI appeared, however, to have retained its ties with the military and intelligence services: in May 1996, Qazi Hussain Ahmad spent 10 days shuttling between Hekmatyar and Massoud in a last-ditch bid to sew up an alliance to fend off the swiftly-advancing Taliban.[7] The ISI appeared to be sticking to the old script.

The place of Islamist party closest to the seat of civilian power passed to *Jamiat ul-Ulama-i Islam* (JUI) a Deoband-influenced grouping with a power base in Baluchistan and, to a lesser degree, in NWFP, where Bhutto had never mustered much support. It was an odd alliance: the Oxford-educated, female prime minister with a fine line in saris, and Maulana Fazl ul-Rahman, the JUI's firebrand leader, who took even extremism to extremes. Out of the need for a patina of Islamic respectability, Mrs Bhutto had taken what, in retrospect, was the momentous decision of appointing Fazl ul-Rahman to the sensitive post of chairman of the standing committee on foreign affairs in the National Assembly. In October 1996, one month after the fall of Kabul, he told a public meeting in Peshawar that the JUI would create an 'Afghanistan-like situation' in Pakistan, if 'anti-Islamic and nationalist' elements in the government did not revise their opinion of the Taliban. 'For the first time in 50 years,' he said, 'Afghanistan was able to have a pro-Pakistan government in Kabul.' All the others, he added, had been pro-Indian.[8]

The rise of such a loose cannon into the decision-making heartland of Pakistan's foreign relations was another outcome of the Afghan war. Saddled with a sophisticated war machine designed to project Western interests into Central Asia, Pakistan was spending around 35 per cent of its budget on defence in 1993 and still could not stand down its forces, due to the perceived threat from India. Investment in education, as a result, had crumbled to 2.3 per cent of the gross national product – almost half the average for developing countries. The JUI, like many fringe Islamic parties, flourished by offering country boys a free Koranic schooling and board in a network of *madrassa*, sprinkled in villages, orphanages and refugee camps across Pakistan's poorest states. Many were financed by the United States, Britain and Saudi Arabia, as part of their humanitarian programmes. In a political climate marred by shameless corruption, this was a constituency ripe for the plucking. Once the JUI had attained a position of influence in the National Assembly, it could expand its local power base with *ex gratia* payments from the PPP and through the access the party provided to wealthy patrons in Pakistan or overseas.

Many first-generation Taliban had confirmed ties with the JUI's *madrassa* system and Mullah Mohammad Omar's appeal to the organisation's lawyers for help to prepare a Taliban constitution suggests that he had been one of its students at some time or another.[9] But the JUI's support for the movement was displayed in more practical ways: in September 1996, regular examinations were postponed to allow some 2,000 students to cross the frontier to gain practical experience in *jihad* and the *madrassa* remained a reservoir of Taliban manpower throughout the war.[10] In a flip comment on 27 September – which suggested that his relationship with Maulana Fazl ul-Rahman was not all it might have been – Babar said that the Taliban conquest of Kabul was 'only a change of guard, from JI to JUI'.[11] Another change of guard had occurred in Islamabad.

For 45 years, Afghan policy had been determined by the Pashtun and Baluchi commanders-in-chief of the Pakistani army, operating for the most part on the east-west axis that connects Peshawar with Kabul and passes through Ghilzai lands. Under Bhutto, it shifted to the vertical, linking Karachi with Central Asia through Quetta and Kandahar. That policy was controlled by Punjabis and Sinds, passed through Durrani country and it now needed stability, not desolation, in Kabul. The end would be the same: a Pashtun-dominated government sympathetic to Pakistani interests. But it would arise from a policy of uniting the disparate clans of the Pashtun nation, rather than dividing them and that posed conundrums that had not really been addressed since before the Soviet invasion. How long would an Afghanistan, united through Pakistani devices, remain loyal to Islamabad when both Iran and India were certain to dangle glittering alternatives, if it were to behave contrarily? And how long would it take a movement of soaring national rebirth to rediscover its place on the map, and set a new course for fabled Pashtunistan? 'You cannot buy an Afghan,' people say, 'but you can rent one at a very high price.'

Despite the secrecy surrounding the *madrassa* syllabus, JUI schools were ill-equipped to provide more than the spiritual ethos and *esprit de corps* of the Taliban movement. The military know-how came from elsewhere. The 26 Pakistani Taliban, captured by Massoud in late October 1996 and presented to *Time* magazine, admitted to a 40-day training period, under ISI supervision, where they learned to use Kalashnikovs.[12] Pakistan's Frontier Constabulary, over which Babar, as interior minister, had command, was also cited as a source of the Urdu-speaking fighters who were frequently sighted in the Taliban ranks.[13]

But these were foot-soldiers, not the tank drivers, mechanics, fighter pilots, supply clerks, rocketeers, radio operators, munitions experts and other specialists that constitute even an uncoventional modern army and which were undoubtedly in the Taliban van as it moved northwards from Kandahar. Afghan gossip – again, the only available information resource – would implicate General Tanai, a *Khalq* sympathiser who, after the failed ISI-backed coup attempt of 1990, had taken refuge in the ISI barracks at Chaklala, near Rawalpindi.[14] Tanai's influence among former army professionals, sources say, allied with elements of the Pakistani military and what remained of the *Harakat Inqilab-i Islami* of Mohammad Nabi Mohammadi, provided the skilled steel which underlay the raw populism of the Taliban. The movement's battle captains, according to one Western military analyst, used the 'same tactics as Pakistan's trained strategists, which had nothing to do with the hit-and-run tactics of guerrilla movements'.[15]

But a fifth party – in addition to Babar, the JUI, the Pakistani army and General Tanai – is credited with playing a role in the rise of the movement. This was the Intelligence Bureau (IB), another mysterious tentacle of the military establishment, and one whose funds Babar was accused of siphoning off in 1990 to help defeat a no-confidence motion against Mrs Bhutto. He denied the charge in September 1996.[16] Bhutto could never wholly trust the ISI, because it had been instrumental in killing her father and was constantly poised to unseat her or any other civilian chief executive. The existence of a 'dirty tricks' alternative is credible at a time when her administration was seeking to devise an Afghan strategy, independent of the conventional channels and, quite feasibly, in direct opposition to long-established ISI policy. Nevertheless, the strength and composition of the IB has never been confidently assessed.

'If their numbers are about 30,000, as they claim, and each of them would require $100 for daily and military expenses then, Mr President, a very important question should be asked: who is paying more than $88 million a month for their expenses?' Abdul Rahim Ghafoorzai, Rabbani's deputy minister of foreign affairs, was addressing the UN General Assembly in New York on 4 October 1995.[17] These were not numbers plucked from the air: he had been briefed by somebody with a grasp of military budgeting. 'As far as logistical support,' he continued, 'according to calculations, in order for the Taliban to have their transport vehicles, tanks and other armoured vehicles running, they need more than 15,000 gallons of fuel each day. This is aside from almost the same amount of fuel they require as reserve. Again, who is providing them with such huge logistical support?'

The Rabbani government had much to gain from painting the Taliban as another foreign-backed adventure into Afghan territory. It stripped away some of the legitimacy the movement had justifiably earned by imposing peace and stability in the lawless south. By contrast, Rabbani had always allowed that Hekmatyar had an authentic constituency, even though he transparently enjoyed Pakistan's support. Mahmoud Mestiri, the UN special envoy, was in two minds about it. Shortly after the fall of Herat in September 1995, he said: 'The power of the Taliban is mysterious. I think that they are getting money and help maybe from Pakistan.' But he disavowed the charge three months later, claiming that, in spite of evidence that the Taliban knew how to fly MiGs and helicopters, there was no proof of Pakistani support.[18] By then, he was, arguably, a man broken by the nightmarish complexities of Afghan peacemaking.

Testimony to Pakistani aid, prior to the final advance on Kabul, was rarely more than anecdotal. Fuel, munitions and trained fighters undoubtedly did cross the border, both from Quetta and across the porous NWFP border, and the government was swift to open consulates and even banking branches in cities conquered by the movement. But there is little to indicate a systemic programme of assistance, such as accompanied the operations aganst the Soviet Union. It is even dubious whether Islamabad possessed the kind of disposable income to which Ghafoorzai referred in New York, particularly if the ISI were simultaneously backing Hekmatyar, as appeared to be the case throughout 1995 and until mid-1996. The evidence suggests that support for the Taliban was less a central plank of Pakistani foreign policy, which remained the prerogative of the military, and more a rogue project, triggered by Babar and his friends, to win Afghan policy back to the civilian side in the ongoing tension within Pakistan's administration. The funds, at least, had to have come from elsewhere.

Bhutto's second term of office, like those of her predecessors, would be cut short by Zia's constitutional legacy, the Eighth Amendment, which enabled the president, always beholden to the military nexus, to dismiss a government when it 'erred', or strayed too far from the narrow freedoms permitted it by an overmighty army. The charge of corruption was the Damocles sword hanging over every civilian government in Pakistan, and it usually stuck.

'Those who would ignite the fire in our country,' Ghafoorzai told the UN, 'will burn themselves.' It is a metaphor so commonly used by ordinary Afghans when talking about Britain, the Soviet Union and Pakistan that it has achieved the resonance of a proverb.

* * *

Hekmatyar had begun to look like history in the middle of 1994, when Bhutto and Babar took the decision to concentrate on opening trade links with Central Asia. The Islamabad Accord of 7 March 1993, which had brought him into government as prime minister, had collapsed several days afterwards. It was the last occasion when representatives from Pakistan, Iran and Saudi Arabia sat down together with the faction leaders to hammer out an Afghan settlement that suited all their interests.

Further talks between the *mujahedin* were held in Jalalabad in a bid to resolve the problem of Massoud's position as defence minister, the main issue still dividing the factions. On 20 May 1993, they proudly announced the birth of another unworkable agreement and a further round of blood-letting ensued. Hekmatyar's last bid for power began on 1 January 1994, with a searing attack on the capital, in alliance with Rashid Dostum. That, too, failed to dislodge the Tajik commander. By June, Dostum's troops had been evicted from the city and *Hizb-i Wahdat* was forced out of the wreckage of Kabul University. Hekmatyar settled in for an attritional blockade at Sorobi. The bombardments continued, the civilian hardship intensified but the international community began to denounce the killing with a little more vim. Hekmatyar's momentum was well and truly lost.

If Pakistani politicians were growing disenchanted with Hekmatyar's progress, so too were Saudi princes. Islamabad's Afghan policy had been entrusted to the military but Riyadh's remained squarely in the hands of the external intelligence service, the *Mukhabarat*, headed by Prince Turki bin-Faisal, a nephew of the ailing King Fahd. Hekmatyar's open support of Saddam Hussein during the Gulf War had done little for their relations and Saudi Arabia was further antagonised by his growing terrorist associations and the 1994 alliance with the *Hizb-i Wahdat.* Despite the opportunist nature of all Afghan coalitions, the latter guaranteed – on the surface – a Shia presence in a post-Rabbani government. This was anathema to the Saudis who had, anyway, hedged their Afghan bets by maintaining support to the Wahhabi *Ittehad-i Islami*, an ally of Massoud. But the more Rabbani moved towards Shia Tehran, after the fall of Herat, the more Riyadh would support his chief adversary. This came to look increasingly like the purist Taliban, rather than the radical Hekmatyar, in the light of the defeat at Charasyab and his more promiscuous alliances. In late 1995, envoys from Saudi Arabia, Bahrain and Qatar were separately sighted in Kandahar, a favoured location for the princely sport of falconry. The question of money might then have raised its head – but it may have been partridge breaking cover.[19]

Babar's wheeze had had a domino effect, transforming the balance of Afghan power in the south and southwest. But the Taliban, like every renegade Afghan force that Britain, the Soviet Union or Pakistan had concocted, were not, ultimately, the interior minister's creatures. Asking whose creatures they truly were may, in fact, be a futile errand when religious vision, clan rivalry, Saudi dollars and geopolitical ambition are woven together on such an impetuous loom as the nature of Pashtun leadership. The movement's success had surprised its own leaders as much as their enemies, heightening expectations of what more might be attained in a conflict that, experience suggested, was conducted against bullies and the ghosts of old reputations. Instead of turning left at Kandahar to unlock the Central Asian road, the Taliban veered right, toward the Tower of Victory at Ghazni, which led through Shia country and the apple-growing oases of Wardak.

Such an unbridled rampage would have critical consequences in a region so sensitive that the slightest blip in the political ionosphere could shut down diplomatic relations altogether. Repulsed at Kabul in March 1995, the Taliban pressed on to Herat. If Pakistan regarded Kabul as its strategic backyard in the endlessly recycled quarrel with India, Tehran felt the same possessiveness toward Herat, a city which had once been Persian and still exuded that culture's supple love of poetry, perfume and gardens. The remains of the five filigreed minarets of the *madrassa*, built by Shah Rukh in the 16th century and demolished by the British three centuries later, sneered at the simplistic absolutes of the Pashtun invaders.

'The Taliban,' spluttered the state-controlled newspaper *Jomhour-i Islami* on 16 October 1995, 'are an American hand-fed group, which is fed, equipped, guided and supported by Saudi petrol dollars through Pakistan's 2nd Division. ... Pakistan, since long, is not cutting its coat according to its cloth and has crossed the red line, the criterion of which is Iran's national security limits.'[20] The loss of Shindand airbase, 160 km south of Herat, had graver consequences for it denied Iran the air bridge it had used to arm *Hizb-i Wahdat* and repose a protective arm around the Shia communities of the Hazarajat. This had always formed part of a *quid pro quo* with the Herat boss, Ismail Khan, which included the provision of fuel, ammunition and other backup during his unsuccessful bid to repel the Taliban advance in the second half of 1995.[21] To maintain supplies to the region, Tehran would have to rely on Bagram airbase and Massoud, who had fought *Wahdat* since 1994. New trade-offs had to be contracted with old enemies.

The loss of Herat on 5 September 1995 brought the Taliban within 125 km of the Iranian border. Tehran went ballistic, but evidence of US and Saudi backing remained circumstantial in late 1995 – and it would remain so throughout 1996. Even Pakistani control was beginning to look shaky after January 1995 when the Taliban broke their cables to advance on Kabul. That decision may have been taken to prevent Massoud reinforcing Ismail Khan's forces, then fighting hard to defend the road through Farah to Shindand, but *Jamiat* was pinned down by *Hizb* and *Wahdat* in Kabul and the Taliban intervention had a totally opposite result. The siege of Kabul was lifted, ushering in an unusual period of calm for its inhabitants and unprecedented respectability for the Rabbani regime.

Ghafoorzai's speech to the UN that October was the culmination of a long-sought, diplomatic honeymoon. It was brought about, in part, by a more widespread appreciation of one of the more fundamental principles underlying Afghan governance: the preceding regime is always preferable to the one that comes after it. The yearning for times past had embraced Zahir Shah, Najibullah and, with the Taliban's entry on the scene, it had finally come to claim Rabbani. His coalition of moderate Islamists and former communists appeared the lesser evil in mid-1995, especially when seen against the vandalism visited upon the capital by the Pakistan-backed *Hizb-i Islami*.

After the Taliban defeat at Kabul, it also looked like a contender, badly mauled perhaps but still on its feet. Delegations from the US, the EU states, the Central Asian republics and Saudi Arabia and Iran paid court to a president who, with an enthusiasm verging on hubris, accepted an invitation to mediate between the government and Islamic rebels in Tajikistan, a civil war which Massoud and Hekmatyar had fostered from its infancy. It was a role which the old prelate had long coveted: in the six-month hiatus in the siege, Rabbani took great strides towards seeming statesmanlike. Schools were reopened, plans laid for rebuilding Kabul University, embassies flew in and a multitude of humanitarian organisations galloped diligently back into town.

Echoes of Great Game history had begun to ripple through Kabul with the fall of Herat in September 1995. Blessed with the memory of more humiliating setbacks – particularly the mob-killing of resident Alexander Burnes in 1841 – Britain had pulled out its diplomats in February 1989, leaving a skeleton staff in charge of the embassy mansion in Parwan Mena. The cellars were drunk, the chandeliers extinguished and a dust-cover thrown over the 19th century *pianoforte*. Under an agreement reached in 1947 over the division of imperial assets, the building was finally transferred to Pakistan in early 1995. Whatever else Islamabad was up to, it retained its diplomatic presence in Kabul until September that same year.

The day after the surrender of Herat, tens of thousands of demonstrators forced their way through the mansion's wrought-iron gates, egged on, Pakistani diplomats reported, by Massoud's own security troops. One of the staff is alleged to have shot a high school student from an upper window, driving the crowd into a frenzy. The embassy was torched, one of its employees killed – along with five Afghan soldiers, Ghafoorzai claimed – and several others, including the delegation's military attache, Brigadier Ashraf Afridi, were seriously injured. Pakistan promptly withdrew its delegation and Afghan diplomats were expelled from Islamabad, Peshawar and Quetta. The trace elements of a more coherent Pakistani conspiracy may have coalesced at this juncture. There was no direct diplomatic contact between Islamabad and Kabul for eight months after the embassy's sacking. All calls – and they were few – would be re-routed through Tehran and Iran's Afghan troubleshooter, Deputy Foreign Minister Alauddin Broujerdi. It was a unique and perilous estrangement.

Babar's primary goal had been achieved – the road was clear from Chaman to Torghundi – but the cost had been enormous. The ISI's man, Hekmatyar, was roundly beaten, abandoning his heavy weapons and documents as he scampered away from Charasyab, but the limits of the Taliban had also been exposed. Setting aside what little was known of the movement's organisational weaknesses, it clearly lacked the military skills to take on Massoud's battle machine. The ISI, headed by Lieutenant-General Javed Ashraf, may have decided then to change horses and throw in its lot with Babar's unpredictable proteges.

The Taliban success, however, had rattled diplomats' windows from Ankara to Beijing. Instead of installing a friendly government in Kabul, Islamabad had driven Rabbani right into the arms of Saudi Arabia's worst enemy and their shared competitor in the race for influence in Central Asia. Dostum was under pressure from Russia, Uzbekistan and Iran to bolster Rabbani or, at the very least, to open the Salang route to allow fuel and military supplies to pass. India, a discreet tactical ally of Iran, was reported to be providing assistance to strengthen Massoud's air power.[22] China, which tacitly backed Islamabad's sparring exercises against the common enemy of India, announced plans for an air link with Kabul and the reopening of its embassy.[23] Tensions soared as word spread that Iran might lend armour and other resources to Ismail Khan, whose bid to recapture western Afghanistan was considered imminent. At the end of October, Washington dispatched Robin Raphel, assistant secretary of state for south Asia, to the region to find out what the hell was going on. The entire neighbourhood was overheating.

The winter of 1995 was characterised by a burning desire for political reconciliation. Bhutto visited Tehran in November to calm things down, while Iran's Broujerdi shuttled between Kabul, Mazar, Bamian and Kandahar in a bid to stitch up a domestic consensus. In January 1996, Iran's foreign minister, Ali Akbar Velayati, flew to Islamabad for talks with Bhutto and his counterpart, Sardar Asif Ali. From Washington, the US said it was pressuring Islamabad to show more commitment to the UN peace effort, a disingenuous claim in view of its own lack of solidarity. Proximity talks between Pakistan and Afghanistan, under Iranian mediation, were held in Tehran in mid-February. On the face of it, this was a region struggling to restore dialogue and the status quo, rather than press for further advantage. By April, one analyst sunnily reported that Pakistani support to the Taliban had 'petered out', in exchange for a commitment by Iran not to back an attack by Ismail Khan in the west.[24]

The factions had been no less frantic, though their objective was not containment but to evolve new political configurations for the next campaigning season. Rabbani was in contact with Hekmatyar, Dostum and the Nangarhar *shura* and he also sent a delegation to Torkham Gate to confer with the ISI.[25] Taliban representatives, meanwhile, flew to Islamabad to meet Dostum and Hekmatyar, allegedly at the behest of Pakistan. In mid-February 1996, Afghanistan's consul-general in Peshawar announced that, if all the parties could agree to a mechanism for a transfer of power to an interim government, Rabbani would step down and Massoud withdraw his forces from the capital. The president had promised as much before, counting on the factions' inevitable inability to agree on terms as his excuse for not resigning. He should have left office at the end of the previous March.

But now it was different. Hekmatyar was no longer harrying the capital and had adopted a more conciliatory approach to his former enemies. With ISI support either ruptured or waning, he was in danger of being wholly marginalised, as was Pakistan's *Jamaat-i Islami*, Hekmatyar's main political backer. Viewed in another light, the ISI had witnessed over 20 years of investment in Afghanistan's future governance flushed away in the two short years since Bhutto had come to power. The Pashtun leader continued to profess unanimity with Dostum and *Hizb-i Wahdat,* but put out feelers for a mutual defence pact with the Taliban, which Mohammad Omar rejected. On 9 March, the *Hizb-i Islami* leader announced a new alliance with Rabbani and the formation of a Joint Military High Council with Massoud. Electricity was restored to the capital for the first time in three years. *Hizb-i Wahdat*, under its new leader Karim Khalili, said it would also join the new configuration in Kabul. Earlier in the month, Rabbani had signed a military cooperation pact with Tehran, under which Iran pledged training for army officers, the repatriation of all military-age Afghan refugees for service in Kabul, the repair of the airport and the provision of funds to win over other factions.[26]

This was the second juncture at which a more considered meeting of minds may have taken place between the cliques in the Pakistan government and military, the United States and Saudi Arabia. Rabbani, Massoud and Hekmatyar had become intimately bound up with Washington, and Riyadh's fear of Iranian expansionism. But the involvement of *Jamaat*'s Qazi Hussain Ahmad in the mediation between the three leaders, added to Islamabad's subsequent diplomacy toward Kabul, argued against a consistent and unified Pakistani policy either to the Kabul government or the Taliban. Amid a flurry of top-level meetings by the 'Afghan cell', Islamabad's policy-making unit for Afghanistan, the Pakistani press speculated that a major strategy review was underway, with Bhutto and Babar looking for a face-saving way out of the embassy dispute and the normalisation of bilateral relations.[27] That was obtained before the month was out: Kabul apologised, agreeing to pay millions of dollars in compensation and to assist in the repair of the building. Two months later, in May 1996, Islamabad welcomed the Afghan transport minister, Abdul Ghaffar, who flew in to discuss the construction of a gas pipeline and road and rail links to Turkmenistan. The energy theme had reached a crescendo in October 1995 with the signing of an accord in Ashgabat between the Turkmen government and a US-Saudi joint venture to build a $2 billion gas pipeline across Afghanistan to Pakistan. It coincided with a revival of US interest, demonstrated by Robin Raphel's visit to Mazar, Kabul, Jalalabad and Islamabad in the same month.

She, pointedly, did not pay calls on the Taliban in Kandahar or Herat, the preferred route for the pipeline but would, when she returned in mid-April. But Senator Hank Brown, who sat on the US Senate Intelligence Committee, had met with them one month earlier, inviting the Taliban to send delegates to a conference on Afghanistan in the US timed for July. Again, pointedly, neither Hekmatyar nor Sayyaf were included on the guest list.[28] On his return to the US, Brown was so disappointed with the drift of the UN peace mission that he urged President Bill Clinton in writing to insist on Mestiri's replacement as peace envoy, arguing that he had 'squandered' whatever influence he may once have had with the factions. Mestiri, understandably, was 'very disturbed' by the letter.[29]

Raphel remained pessimistic about the prospects of peace and even less impressed by the Taliban's cohesion. 'These weaknesses,' she said in a press briefing in May 1996, 'combined with Ahmad Shah Massoud's growing strength, appear to be shifting the balance against (the Taliban) somewhat and will prevent them from achieving their stated goal of taking Kabul.' She concluded that they had 'reached the limit of their expansion'. It was an intriguingly downbeat assessment from a country that was widely assumed to be the movement's clandestine sponsor.[30]

The Taliban responded to the new alliance in Kabul with their own initiative: a congress of *ulama*, drawn from the 15 provinces under their control, whose decisions would be binding on the movement's *shura*. Whether this was out of fear for a combined Massoud-Hekmatyar force or the suspicion that the moral high ground of a peace settlement was slipping away from their grasp, it had a distinctly defensive air. Having consistently rejected Mestiri's peace proposals on the grounds that they favoured Rabbani, or involved *mujahedin* and communists, a Taliban spokesman relented: 'If we are satisfied that Rabbani would establish Islamic rule in Afghanistan, we have no quarrel with individuals.'

By May, the movement appeared to have sewn up an agreement with *Hizb-i Wahdat* but Khalili, Mazari's successor, thought better of it and, on 22 May, announced it would join a coalition government with Rabbani and Hekmatyar. The merger was approved by Hekmatyar's former colleagues in the Supreme Coordination Council, but it rankled badly. Five days later, Mestiri threw up his hands in exasperation and resigned, declaring it was impossible to come up with a workable peace formula. Whether that was due to the intransigence of the faction leaders or the absence of US commitment was unclear, but it effectively signalled the end of UN initiatives until after Kabul fell on 27 September. By the time his successor, Dr Norbert Holl, took up his post at the end of July, Dostum had reopened the Salang Tunnel for supplies from Russia and Uzbekistan. But the Taliban were moving so swiftly through the east, mopping up former *Hizb-i Islami* outposts, that the most Holl could muster were vain appeals for a ceasefire.

This was a different, more assured Taliban, which sliced through the last rotten boroughs like a knife. Weapons had never been a problem, but fuel and high-speed transport undoubtedly had. This revitalised Taliban had an abundance of both, and the palm-greasing of local *mujahedin* was more frequently bruited. Rumours persisted that Pakistani professionals were directing operations, with 1,000 fighters entering Afghanistan in the month prior to the fall of the capital.[31] All attempts by Rabbani and Hekmatyar to arrange a power-sharing agreement with the Taliban were rebuffed. But the links between the movement and its alleged sponsors remained deeply tenuous, implied more than confirmed, and the shape of Pakistani diplomacy, yet again, belied the thrust of the general accusations.

On 12 August, Pakistan announced that it would reopen its embassy in Kabul and allow the purchase of food and fuel to relieve the Afghan capital.[32] On the 27th – a month before the government was routed – *Jamaat-i Islami* said it would open a Kabul office to facilitate the alliance that it had been instrumental in moulding.[33] But, on the 24th, Kabul had reported the defection to Bagram airbase of a Taliban transport plane with seven Pakistani military officers on board. They were never paraded for public inspection.[34] Were these diplomatic feints, disinformation, or evidence of a profound rift in relations between Pakistan's military, interior and foreign policy institutions?

The fall of the capital produced mixed feelings in Islamabad. Mrs Bhutto, only 39 days away from her own dismissal, called it a 'welcome development', qualifying that approval with the hope that the Taliban would moderate their gender policies. Nawaz Sharif, her future successor as prime minister, said her Afghan policy had been a total shambles, which had 'turned friends into enemies'. *Jamaat-i Islami* called it a US-sponsored plot to divide Afghanistan along ethnic and linguistic lines. Being so closely identified with the movement's origins, Babar had no other choice than to express unadulterated joy at their conquest. 'The rise of the Taliban,' he declared, 'is of great advantage to Pakistan. This is the first time there is a government which has no links with India, or anybody else.'[35]

But Afghan history had shown time and again that a government without external links is a government without a future. And the thousands of volunteers from Pakistan, who had flocked to the Taliban standards, were now at liberty to return to North West Frontier Province to sow their own individual whirlwinds. Babar may have been putting on a brave face, but Ghafoorzai's prediction looked certain to come to pass.

6 The Zahir Option

The Zahir question had floated to the surface of Afghanistan's narrowing options in the year before the Rabbani regime capsized – though not necessarily with any more buoyancy than in the past. *Mujahedin* leaders routinely gave their approval to wistful, but untenable peace propositions as a way of gaining time and shifting the blame onto their rivals when the project, predictably, guttered.

It was a ritual of Afghan diplomacy, a theatre which pitched wildly between histrionic defiance and abject lullaby and which meshed impeccably with the Mobius strip of a moral dictum attributed to General Zia: 'Muslims have the right to lie in a good cause'.[1] But it was not without its grace notes: dragging out negotiations allowed UN mediators to return to Islamabad with the dim notion that, with just a little more consultation, a little more time, some path to peace might ultimately emerge from the savage Afghan labyrinth. Everyone's face, in short, was saved.

The UN peace initiative in Afghanistan was only two years younger than the Soviet war itself, harking back to 1981 when Secretary-General Kurt Waldheim appointed Perez de Cuellar to mediate between Moscow and the main sponsors of the *mujahedin*, the United States and Pakistan. One year after the Soviet withdrawal, on 14 February 1990, the Office of the Secretary-General in Afghanistan and Pakistan was created, with Bevan Sevan at its helm, to supervise the transfer of power from President Najibullah to a transitional coalition of *mujahedin* parties and the non-communist old guard. When that transfer skidded off the rails in April 1992, leaving Najib a prisoner in the UN's Kabul office and Massoud in command of the capital, the UN hastily withdrew from the affray, as had the United States one year earlier.

Sevan's successor was the former Tunisian foreign minister, Mahmoud Mestiri, a smooth-shaven, stooped figure with snow-white hair and piercing blue eyes. From his appointment by Boutros Boutros-Ghali on St Valentine's Day 1994 to his resignation a little over two years later, he shuttled between the faction leaders and regional capitals at the helm of a peace mission which, by comparison with the $3 billion lavished upon the UN's Transitional Authority in Cambodia, looked distinctly down-at-heel. With the air of a harassed schoolmaster and just a handful of helpers, Mestiri, in the view of close observers, was little more than a sacrificial offering by an international community which, if it did not actively wish his failure, stood poised to blame it upon the indecipherable rivalries of the leaders with whom he was supposed to negotiate – rather than its own lack of political will.

That some of these leaders continued to receive armaments from the country upon which Mestiri depended for office space and the UN for its relief effort was not lost upon his *mujahedin* interlocutors who had scant respect for an organisation which had retained an unbroken presence in Kabul throughout the Soviet occupation, only to evacuate it in August 1992 after the first upsurge in intra-*mujahedin* hostilities. In February 1993, four UN staff were assassinated in Nangarhar on the road to the Khyber Pass, an indication that one faction at least had begun to regard the organisation as fair game.

The UN's failure to denounce Pakistan's covert assistance to Hekmatyar, before Mestiri arrived on the scene, in addition to his own reluctance to incriminate Islamabad in the subsequent rise of the Taliban, branded the peace mission as *parti pris,* at worst, and pusillanimous, at best. From the Afghan point of view, the charade was quite transparent: while the mission publicly deplored the violence wreaked upon Kabul by *Hizb-i Islami,* it was precisely upon an escalation of the siege – which, in turn, could only occur by turning a blind eye to Pakistan's support – that the UN appeared likely to achieve its own objectives. And that entailed forcing Rabbani into such a desperate position that he would have to step down.

In that sense, Hekmatyar was serving two masters and blood would have more blood, however plaintive the would-be peacemaker. It remains significant that, during his entire 27-month mission, Mestiri was never able to rig up even a symbolic pledge by the regional powers to observe an embargo of arms to the factions. The *Jamiat* government, reasonably enough in the circumstances, portrayed any political solution which had Pakistani support as contrary to the true interests of sovereign Afghanistan, of which it was, tortuously, still the UN-recognised representative.

'Everyone blames Mestiri,' said the Afghan intellectual Homayoun Assefy after the former's resignation in May 1996, 'but nobody helps him. Everybody criticises him, but everybody also puts obstacles in his way.'[2] Not least the factions who saw in the UN special negotiator a dunce who could be summoned or sent on mendicant circles of mediation secure in the knowledge that there could be no reward for his wanderings without Pakistan's approval – and that would never be forthcoming without US pressure. Bereft of the mandate to send in a peacekeeping force, because of the UN's fear of becoming as hopelessly mired in Afghanistan as the Soviet Union had been before it, he entered this lion's den with neither stick nor carrot, a silvery after-image of the might which the United States had once deployed to 'liberate' Afghanistan from the Soviets, but could not spare to curb the ravages of its proteges.

The first Mestiri mission, nevertheless, triggered a surge of expectation among ordinary Afghans which belied the cynicism elsewhere apparent. Between 27 March and 29 April 1994, the UN envoy talked with hundreds of people from all walks of life – governors, tribal and religious leaders, commanders, students and women's representatives, intellectuals as well as peasant farmers and refugees – while receiving the Afghan equivalent of ticker-tape receptions in Mazar-i Sharif, Herat and Kandahar. They 'implored' the UN 'not to abandon or fail them and that it be involved at every stage of the political process', Mestiri noted in his progress report.[3]

His welcome from Rabbani, soon to break his oath to step down in June, and from Hekmatyar, whose bombardment of Kabul continued unabashed, were somewhat less affable, in view of an unguarded remark by the envoy early in his travels that the two men were no more than the 'leaders of armed gangs'. Mestiri wrote:

> The impression that one gets is that many of the soldiers fighting for either side are reluctant to risk their lives in this struggle. Most of the combatants appear to be young men and adolescents, many of whom may be illiterate. Over and over, the Mission was told that the majority of those fighting were doing so for the money, since this was one of the only ways to make a living, especially in Kabul.[4]

In May, Mestiri took his roadshow to the other key players in the Afghan imbroglio – Iran, Saudi Arabia, Russia, Turkey and the United States. All pledged whatever assistance the UN considered necessary to bring about a ceasefire – without interrupting the support they were clandestinely providing to one or other of the factions. The mission concluded with the publication of a set of proposals which, in retrospect, were a triumph of wishful thinking. In tune with its mandate to conveyance, rather than to impose, a peace agreement, the UN undertook to help create a transitional authority which would oversee a ceasefire, implement the collection of weapons, create a neutral security force and summon a *Loya Jirga*, or representative council, to prepare for democratic elections within two years.

The *Loya Jirga* was a doubtful mechanism, but was the closest Afghan power-broking had ever come to a consultative exercise. Last employed by Najib to rubber-stamp the 1988 constitution, which was written by the Soviets prior to the withdrawal of their forces, it dated back to 1747 when Ahmad Shah was 'elected' king of the Afghans by a selective process of acclamation. The *jirga* was seductive in historical and customary terms but, as an institution, it failed to represent the comparatively urbane, Kabul middle class, which did not ride to *bushkashi* matches on thoroughbred stallions or dress in the robes of the *ulama*. Legitimacy was, sketchily, observed but not the broader diversity of Afghan opinion which Mestiri had specifically solicited during his first trip. Dissent, anyway, had always played a walk-off role in Afghan king-making.

This was particularly the case with the modern version, tainted as it was by Afghan communism. But Afghanistan lacked any variant through which less polarised voices could be heard, so it was to a *Loya Jirga* of faction heads, commanders and spiritual leaders that the UN mission leaned when it contemplated the means of achieving a ceasefire. And to Zahir Shah, a hazy paradigm of national unity and fledgling democracy, whose personal bodyguard in the 1950s had dressed in cast-off SS uniforms, until a notorious encounter between one of their number, the then-US ambassador and a Kabul swimming pool.[5] Zahir's credentials were impeccable, but his purpose, amid the gunfire, remained cloudy.

He had ascended the throne in 1933 on the assassination of his father, Nadir Shah, at a school prize-giving. But, over the next 30 years, two regent uncles ruled in his stead, to be succeeded – apparently with his approval – by the king's cousin, Mohammad Daoud, who honed the Pashtunistan issue into a razor-sharp threat to regional peace. Zahir Shah was that rarest of Afghan phenomena, a reluctant ruler. It was only in 1963 that he finally came into his kingdom, to preside over a decade-long dismantling of the monarchy's autocratic powers until his overthrow by Daoud and the army in 1973. It is probable that he survived the murderous politics of Afghanistan thanks only to this intervention – unlike its perpetrator who was slaughtered, along with his family, during the pro-communist coup of 1978.

Zahir's potential as head of an interim government of reconciliation had been recognised by Najib during his negotiations with the UN's Bevan Sevan in 1991–92. Support for his return was particularly strong in the the refugee camps of North West Frontier Province and Baluchistan where, two years later, Mestiri would be handed a petition for his restoration by tribal leaders who claimed to represent over one million Afghans.[6] But in Islamabad Zahir Shah was still regarded as a threat. Enfeebled by 80 years of history and the conflagration in his kingdom, the old man living on *gnocchi* in Rome nevertheless summoned up the ghost of Pashtunistan, a bleared memory in Afghan eyes, but an abiding menace to Pakistan's elusive sense of wellbeing.

Lacking any tradition of legitimacy at home, Islamabad tended to become overwrought at the slightest hint of its existence beyond the Khyber Pass – and the influence it could exert upon Pakistan's half-tamed Pashtun population. The military nexus, in particular, was bent on preventing Zahir's return. Benazir Bhutto attempted to arrange the ex-king's restoration in her first government of 1988–90, only to be thwarted by Hamid Gul, head of the ISI, and Aslam Beg, chief of the army.[7] Pakistan's interests were better served by a continuation of strife and the meltdown of Afghanistan's military capability, than a government of national reconciliation. Islamabad paid attentive lip service to the need for peace in Kabul, but resorted to shabby tactics whenever asked to facilitate Zahir Shah's return: visa denied.

Against all the odds, the tide was running with Mestiri in late 1994 and early 1995. The conquest of Kandahar by the Taliban in October 1994 failed to dent the peace initiative and may possibly have given it a fillip by setting in motion a process of consolidating the south under a single overlord, whose origin and appeal to traditional values appeared, on the surface, to guarantee a more conciliatory approach and wider support for the ex-king's cause. But this could only become 'bankable' in the peace account if the Taliban were, as Bhutto and its own leaders insisted, a truly indigenous phenomenon rather than a subterfuge which used religion and local grievance to effect a virtual annexation of the south.

On 26 December 1994, Rabbani had announced that he would step down, in line with UN planning, but two days later he extended his term to June 1995. Mestiri extracted a compromise whereby Rabbani would hand over power to an interim council on 21 March. Discussions then moved on to the 'modalities': a council, composed of two representatives from each of the provinces, along with 15–20 'eminent' Afghans, would constitute the 'mechanism council' or interim authority, while a committee of 30 military officers would be charged with the recruitment and training of a 'neutral' security force. Afghan advisers assured the mission that, in spite of the factions, a neutral force was still feasible because of the popular surge for peace.

The Taliban's arrival at the gates of Kabul in February 1995 effectively stopped that process in its tracks. Whether it was their intention – or that of their sponsors – is impossible to confirm, given the movement's shadowy motives and the *mujahedin*'s justified reputation for making ephemeral pledges for short-term gain. The voluntary renunciation of power by an Afghan warlord was, indeed, unprecedented – with the sole exception of Zahir Shah – and Rabbani's agreement to step down, however faint-hearted, had certainly been extracted under duress. But if the Taliban's subsequent humiliation by Massoud proved beyond doubt that it was incapable of taking the capital by force, it also killed the Zahir option by relieving the pressure on Rabbani to continue negotiations with the UN and his besiegers. The noose, which had tightened around Kabul since the siege began in 1992, became the rope with which the Rabbani regime would hang itself.

In that light, the Taliban's first bid for the capital can be seen either as a simple military miscalculation or an outflanking tactic of Machiavellian cunning. It might, conceivably, have been both for the process of negotiation tends ineluctably toward convergence, however unwilling the participants to concede. And for all his political weakness at the outset, Mestiri was definitely on a roll in late 1994, urged on by thousands of Afghans and the scores of local interests not directly implicated in the battle for Kabul, but alarmed at the speed with which Afghanistan and its people were vanishing from the international map of the world.

In defeating Hekmatyar, the Taliban ushered in the regime's halcyon days which were to last until the fall of Herat in September 1995, a loss which Rabbani later said had been far more grievous than his expulsion from the capital.[8] Trapped between a hostile Pakistan to the east and an army in the west that gave every indication of behaving in conformity with Islamabad's larger strategy, the collapse of the *Jamiat* government became a matter only of time and tighter logistics. An earlier capture of Kabul might have yielded a wholly opposite outcome, given the scope for an extended war of resistance from the Panjshir valley and the better-supplied western provinces. If, indeed, there were method to the Taliban's manoeuvres, it was governed by an intelligence of considerable psychological, as well as strategic, insight.

The Zahir question was mooted with undimmed seriousness after the Taliban defeat but, as *Jamiat* strengthened its control of the capital and briefly succumbed to hubris, it was evident that control of the peace initiative had passed from the UN to Pakistan and its military. On 28 May, US Under-Secretary Robin Raphel re-entered the diplomatic fray after a protracted absence from the Afghan scene, urging an arms embargo, without setting very much store by it. In late June, Zahir's cousin, General Abdul Wali Khan flew for the first time from Rome to Islamabad where he told Mrs Bhutto and Foreign Minister Aslef Ali that, while the king was willing to join a transitional government, he would not seek to resume the crown.[9] Analysts viewed the apparent reconciliation as theatre, intended either to placate Washington but, more probably, to taint the king's cause through association with its fiercest opponent. By late 1995, Raphel was herself in Rome to talk to the ageing heir apparent.

Mestiri was less sanguine. In a blunt presentation to the UN Development Programme's donor conference in Stockholm in June 1995, he admitted that the peace mission had failed, that a new formula was needed and that the ethnic war so widely feared was now looming. 'The Pashtuns, Uzbeks and Hazaras,' he said, 'have been alienated ... There is either a national solution in which all segments of society participate freely, or there is continued conflict, leading to a possible ethnic war and the break-up of the country.'[10] Attempts to revive the negotiations by involving the Taliban failed and, in November, Mestiri publicly condemned the Taliban's refusal to cease rocketing Kabul.[11]

Six months later, on 27 May 1996, Mestiri asked to be relieved of his post because of ill-health. He said that peace had become impossible and that he could see none of the faction heads – his unwilling collocutors for over two years – as potential future leaders of the country. 'Afghanistan needs somebody much stronger, much more famous, more healthy and younger,' observed one Islamabad-based diplomat. As if a course of aerobics in California were, somehow, a more suitable training for bringing the mullahs and the *mujahedin* to terms.

* * *

Four months to the day after Mesteri resigned, ex-President Najibullah was dragged out of the UN compound by Taliban, tortured and lynched on the traffic-control island in front of the Argh. Mestiri's successor as peace envoy, Dr Norbert Holl, a career diplomat from the German Foreign Ministry's south Asia department, had taken up his post in July. The steep learning curve and rapid pace of military developments in late 1996 combined to sideline any further UN initiatives, while Mullah Mohammad Omar's refusal even to meet Dr Noll underlined that, if the Taliban were indeed to seek a ceasefire, they would not be looking to the international community to deliver it.

Snatches of the Zahir refrain lingered in the air as the Taliban closed in on their prey. On 30 August, during a visit to Islamabad by a member of the US Congress, Dana Rohrabacher, Pakistan conceded it was not averse to the king playing some role in a settlement and, four days later, General Dostum fell in line, on condition that Uzbek rights and interests were protected. Even *Hizb-i Wahdat*, a Hazara faction with no love, retrospective or otherwise, for the traditions of Pashtun monarchy, declared its support for the Zahir plan on 4 September – though no such plan existed on paper. Rabbani, characteristically, remained aloof from the subject, while appearing to ponder a five-point proposal for joint government, offered by the Taliban. These were the gestures of drowning, not waving.

Pakistan's interior minister, Brigadier Naseerullah Babar, the suspected mastermind behind the Taliban's seizure of the capital, had no such difficulty gaining access to the mullahs in Kandahar. He persistently denied direct involvement – in spite of the embarrassment of Pakistani professional and irregular soldiers identified in the Taliban ranks – but it was evident from Islamabad's dispatch of a diplomatic delegation to the new government the day after Kabul fell that Pakistan had taken upon itself the role of the movement's public relations adviser. On 1 October, the Taliban drove the last nail into the king's cause with the taunt that he was welcome to return 'as a private citizen, as king, as president, or as criminal.'[12]

More pressing negotiations were in hand. The Taliban's grasp of Kabul was by no means secure: the city had been surrendered without a fight to volunteers high on bravado, by a general whose ability to convert rout into victory was legendary. Massoud gave a vivid demonstration of this talent in the first week of October when he turned on the pursuing Taliban at Jabal Saraj, sending them packing to within 10 km of the capital. Massoud could not be defeated, Babar and his advisers concluded, but he could be cooped up in the Panjshir valley and stripped of his supply line to Taloqan if only General Dostum could be won over.

Hekmatyar's ally in the first siege of Kabul, Dostum had been groomed for years by Islamabad. It had extended to him all the honours due a visiting head of state and he was regarded as an integral part of Pakistan's historic project of opening trade and energy links with landlocked Central Asia. His relations with Massoud, moreover, were raddled with political and personal animosities although, as the leaders of ethnic minorities, both had received cash and arms from members of the Commonwealth of Independent States to withstand the advance of the Taliban's dervish army. Alliance, however, was anathema to Kandahar, which had never once seriously contemplated a power-sharing agreement with the main factions, and the movement was unlikely to start with a former communist mercenary.

Yet Babar's advice prevailed. Ostensibly to prevent the war from widening, he embarked on a five-day peace mission in mid-October, flying between Kandahar and Mazar-i Sharif. Dostum expressed concern about the security of his forces in the west, where the Taliban had launched an offensive from Herat earlier that month. Babar proposed a twelve-man commission, divided equally between the Taliban and the northern warlord, which would rule the country under the supervision of the UN and the international Muslim forum, the Organisation of the Islamic Conferences.[13] But building the structures for peace in Afghanistan rarely produced more than the micro-structures of war. Talks were expanded to include Massoud and *Hizb-i Wahdat*, but they collapsed when the Tajik commander and Dostum insisted that the Taliban must first withdraw from Kabul before a ceasefire could be agreed. The dismissal of the Bhutto government on 5 November ended any further attempts to mediate.

Babar's media-friendly attempt to seduce the north ran parallel with a secret operation by the ISI whose purpose was to impose the Taliban stamp over all Afghanistan. A small ISI station had reportedly been established, under Brigadier Ashraf Afridi, at the Taliban's base of Charasyab in mid-1996 to coordinate the second siege and orchestrate the final assault on the capital.[14] A Pashtun in his early 50s, Afridi had been involved in training Hekmatyar's guerrillas during the Soviet occupation but he had more recent cause to resent Rabbani. As military attache, he was injured and seriously humiliated during the sacking of the Pakistani embassy in September 1995.

After the capture of Kabul, Afridi moved his headquarters into the city where, aided by a large support staff, it supervised the transport of arms and other supplies from depots in Peshawar and Rawalpindi. Pakistani officers and NCOs, disguised as Afghans, allegedly accompanied the weapons to the Taliban front-line positions, where they assumed direct control for training their undisciplined charges. By mid-April 1997, Dostum's deputy, Mohammad Mohaqiq, reported the presence of 5,000 Pakistani troops in the Kabul area.[15] Dostum still refused to play ball with Islamabad, so a new game was about to be devised.

* * *

With the rounding-out of the year, the Taliban offensive resumed. An early *Eid al-Fitr* was observed in a frozen but snow-free Kabul with 85 mm artillery and a stream of celebratory tracer fire: clusters of crimson jewels, alternating velocity and formation, like shifting patterns of hot wax dripping upwards toward a glimmer of high-altitude moon. The city had seen worse, but the carnival atmosphere that traditionally accompanied the end of *Ramadan*, even under *mujahedin* rule, had thoroughly vanished.

Jabal Saraj fell to the movement on 21 January 1997, compelling Massoud to move his headquarters across the Hindu Kush to Andarab, east of the town of Doshi. On the 25th, Dostum's southernmost troops blew up a vital bridge and avalanche protector north of the Salang Tunnel, rupturing a link between north and south Afghanistan that had lasted for 30 years. Three weeks later, an auxiliary tunnel, 10 km south of the main structure, was sabotaged. This blocked the road from Jabal Saraj to the Salang, delaying any further northward advance, but it prevented Massoud from opening a second front to the rear of the Taliban, then grappling in sub-zero temperatures with *Hizb-i Wahdat* over the Shibar Pass at the head of the Ghorband valley.

Were Shibar to fall, the Taliban would stream into *Wahdat*'s capital in the Buddhist temple complex of Bamian and the Shia heartlands of the Hazarajat, while a second force switched north along the old royal road to Doshi and thence to Pul-i Khumri, the key to Dostum's defences. The latter was held by Sayed Jaffer Naderi, son of the spiritual leader of the Shia Ismailis, a significant and tenacious minority in the northern provinces. Naderi was a Birmingham-educated, former Hell's Angel with a taste for hashish, heavy metal rock and Pekinese dogs.[16] These interesting traits were unlikely to save his skin were the Taliban to induce a crisis of conscience among his followers.

On paper, Dostum looked impregnable. He boasted an air force of 28 fighters and bombers while his army of 25–40,000 men retained the surface discipline of regular uniforms and professional officers, many of whom had joined up during the Soviet occupation.[17] After the loss of Kabul, its confidence had been bolstered with the promise of 500 nearly-new tanks from Moscow and the Central Asian republics, of which 50 T-62s and 72s had arrived in the New Year.[18] With their flat, semi-desert terrain, Dostum's seven provinces appeared tailor-made for the kind of tank warfare for which his forces had been specifically trained. His supply lines across the Amu Darya or Oxus river, meanwhile, grew daily more secure.

In practice, the anti-Taliban alliance, the CDA, had never looked more tenuous. 'We are not united,' said one of Naderi's troops in the ghost-town of Khinjan, just north of Salang, 'and so we will break.'[19] Though it comprised over 153 *mujahedin* and militia commanders – a 'Who's Who of the *jihad*' – the CDA was held together less by common interest than common fear – and the seasonal freeze in military activity which, in turn, had reduced the opportunities for treachery.[20] As the spring melt set in, the incompatibilities of the CDA's mercurial parts soon began to appear.

The same could be said of the ruling *Junbish-i Milli-i Islami*, Dostum's National Islamic Movement. Its existence lent a patina of political coherence to what was fundamentally a coterie of clan chieftains, whose richly-braided uniforms could not disguise that the roots of their power lay in the tribal militias created by Najibullah and the vicious blood-letting which followed Dostum's mutiny in 1992. Mazar was, by Afghan standards, a wealthy, secular town with a sumptuous mosque at its heart, a university admired throughout Central Asia and 16 accessible TV channels. But it was held together by aid, whether Western or Russian, a fictitious currency printed in Uzbekistan and a personality cult of ruthless *braggadocio* in which, from hoarding to hoarding, Dostum's moustachioed face boomed out, now a carbon copy of the president he had betrayed, now a backwater Saddam Hussein. It was all paper.

And it was highly flammable. Exchange rates in the Kefayat money market in central Mazar oscillated wildly as the warring season drew near and Dostum's commanders, sniffing defeat in the wind, leached out whatever hard currency was available to feather a future for their wives across the Amu Darya. In January, the northern *afghani* plummeted to 100,000 against the US dollar, compared with 20,000 in Kabul, causing rice prices to triple and cooking oil to appreciate five-fold.[21] In February, the incipient panic was temporarily shelved when the currency recovered to 26,000 in a single 24-hour period, a revival which many attributed to a secret transfusion of dollars from Russia or Iran, the countries with most to lose should Dostum's line turn to marshmallow before the Taliban showed their faces.

The jitteriness in Mazar was transmitted as pre-shock to the men dug in at the Taliban's expected points of impact. Ill-fed, cold, demotivated and often abandoned by their officers, there was nothing left but to wait and listen to the rumours or the radio. Control of the airwaves was to prove a far more effective weapon than control of the air. Radio *Sharia*'s bulletins of captured towns and trophy defections – though far from the truth – fuelled front-line misgivings that the path of resistance was futile, while appeals for reconciliation under Islam or withering attacks upon the morality of their fleeing commanders sedated fears that the Taliban intended any harm to their homes or families.

Marooned in the ice of the Shibar Pass, Khalili's *Hizb-i Wahdat* would prove the only group impervious to Taliban bribery or disinformation during the extraordinary turn of events in early 1997. One can only guess whether this was due to Iran's iron hand or the unifying fear of Sunni supremacism, but the line continued to hold against fierce tank and artillery attacks, and in spite of Taliban claims that *Wahdat* commanders had been bribed to stand aside. The breakthrough came instead in the west where Governor Abdul Malik Pehlawan, Dostum's foreign minister, later joined by the ousted emir of Herat, Ismail Khan, had spent several months resisting incursions by forces commanded by the new governor of Herat and Mullah Borjan's former second-in-command, Mullah Abdul Razzaq.

On Tuesday 20 May, Taliban radio announced that its troops had captured the Shibar Pass and were within 5 km of Bamian. This was never confirmed but, on the same day, General Abdul Malik Pehlawan and his brother, Gul Mohammad Pehlawan, commander of 511th Division, mutinied, carrying 4,000 troops with them and leaving the western flank undefended.[22] A third Taliban force was claimed to be attacking the city of Kunduz on Dostum's east. The motives given out for Malik's rebellion were his conviction that Dostum had ordered the assassination of his elder brother, Rasool, in Maimana in June 1996 and the subsequent murder of another close companion, Mullah Abdul Rahman Haqqani, over afternoon tea in Mazar-i Sharif two weeks prior to the defection.[23]

But Dostum's security bodies had allegedly discovered a plot by Malik to shoot down his helicopter in February and other sources suggested that Malik had simply surrendered to the atavistic temptations of wealth and power.[24] Brigadier Ashraf Afridi reportedly visited Maimana with a delegation of ISI brass in mid-May to persuade Malik to rebel in exchange for Dostum's throne,[25] while General Shahnawaz Tanai, Najibullah's former defence minister and the suspected sponsor of the Taliban, had attended a 1996 memorial service for Rasool in Peshawar, testimony to his close personal links with what can only be regarded as the Pehlawan mafia.[26]

Massoud airlifted troops to the airbase at Shiberghan, the Dostum fiefdom 130 miles west of Mazar along the Silk Route, in a bid to shore up the line but, by the night of Tuesday 20 May, Malik had added the provinces of Sar-i Pul and Jawzjan to his growing collection. As late as Friday, three days after the mutiny, reporters in Mazar were still describing a city going about its normal chores. That initial restraint, however, turned to panic one day later as news arrived that Shiburghan had fallen without a fight to Malik's forces on Saturday morning, followed shortly after by the arrival of the first of Dostum's frightened rabble.

The general had fled by then, along with 135 of his commanders, to the border crossing at Termez where, beneath a giant portrait of himself, he was forced to jettison his vehicles, all of his cash and more of his pride before the guards allowed him to walk across Friendship Bridge out of the north and into Uzbekistan.[27] In the few hours that remained before Malik reached Mazar at dusk on Saturday, citizens availed themselves of the hiatus to go on a looting spree of aid workers' property that was as frenzied as it was indiscriminate. The following day, a convoy of 12 UN vehicles departed for the bridge at Termez.

Sunday 25 May 1997 was a red letter day, marking the apogee of the ambitions of both the Taliban and Pakistan. Malik's euphoric troops had announced their arrival the previous nightfall with a fanfare of gunfire in the western suburbs which provoked not the slightest retaliation. The next morning, fleets of pick-ups, packed with Taliban, roared into the city after a headlong drive from Herat through the night, while additional forces were airlifted from Kabul and Kandahar, along with a delegation of Taliban leaders, which included the foreign minister, Mullah Mohammad Ghaus, and Mullah Abdul Razzaq, the governor of Herat.

By the end of the day, between 2,000 and 3,000 Taliban infantry had entered the city, under the command of Qazi Gargari.[28] Further south, it was reported that Basir Solangi, the *Jamiat* commander who played such a vital role in deflecting the Taliban advance into the Panjshir the previous October, had embraced God and ceded the Salang Pass on 27 May, allowing 2,000 Taliban to pass through the tunnel.[29] In Islamabad, Prime Minister Nazir Sharif's new foreign minister, Gohar Ayub Khan, told a press conference that Pakistan had finally decided to recognise the Taliban government which, he added, 'genuinely comprises the various ethnic groups in Afghanistan'. One day later, on 26 May, Saudi Arabia followed suit, a sure sign that everything was about to go haywire.[30]

Whatever agreement General Malik may have made, either with the Taliban or their Pakistani intermediaries, appears to have been set aside once the Pashtun warriors were safely installed within the city. The general and Mullah Razzaq met for talks on Sunday morning, reportedly to discuss a power-sharing arrangement for the north, prior to their both addressing a meeting of 3,000 citizens in the mosque of Hazrat Ali, Mazar's spiritual focal point. Malik attempted to reassure his audience: 'The Taliban came here not to create problems, but to resolve them.' Speaking in Pashtu, which few of his listeners could comprehend, the mullah banned women from work and education, imposed the *burkha* and introduced summary punishments for murder and theft.[31]

None of this fundamentally went against the Uzbek grain – except the language in which it was expressed – but hundreds in the congregation were seen to stalk out. Perhaps, more crucially, the people of Mazar had not experienced random gunfire since Dostum's mutiny in 1992 and the 'silver lining' argument, which had won over potential dissidents in Kabul and elsewhere, carried far less weight in the north, which had been peaceable since April 1992, except at the margins. Ethnic undercurrents, the conqueror's swagger, the fear of Taliban reprisals and the loss of autonomy all played a part in determining what would happen 72 hours later but, when it happened, it was with a speed and ferocity that defied attempts to find evidence of logic or planning. 'This alliance,' said one of the last aid workers in the city on Monday 'is one bullet away from disintegrating.'[32]

Accounts differ as to where that bullet came from. A face-off between Malik's men and a 100-strong band of Taliban on the outskirts early on Monday demonstrated to onlookers that there was absolutely no doubt in the latter's mind as to who was responsible for 'security'.[33] The incident, however, did not lead to violence. Elsewhere, there were reports of the Taliban commandeering General Malik's vehicles and of treating billboard posters of his dead brother, Rasool, with the same disrespect as those of Dostum. The two men's images, in the nature of things, were all but indistinguishable.

But the provocation which carried most resonance, given their unflagging resistance on the slopes of the Shibar Pass, and the one on which most journalists agree, happened in a poor Shia district where a Taliban squad attempted to disarm members of a local *Hizb-i Wahdat* faction that had formerly been allied with Dostum. A fire-fight ensued in which eight Taliban died but, when the Shias agreed to the collection of the bodies by pick-up, the Taliban used the opportunity to launch a second, fatal attack. Within minutes, the warren of alleys to the north and south of the central mosque had turned into a killing ground as Shia and Uzbek, militia and citizen, embarked on a turkey shoot for Pashtun stragglers, few of whom had had any experience of real battle, let alone urban warfare.[34]

An estimated 350 Taliban, little more than *madrassa* freshmen, perished during a terrifying 18-hour street battle which lasted through the night of Tuesday 27 May and into the next morning when 2–3,000 of their comrades surrendered to Malik's forces.[35] Among them was Foreign Minister Mullah Ghaus who only 'escaped' to Kunduz Province in late July, probably in exchange for a large ransom.[36] Mullah Razzaq, the military commander who had become governor of Herat, was reportedly killed in action though, given the fierce personal animosity between Afghan warlords, it is more probable that he was executed.[37] Soon he would be joined by 2,000 of his frightened troops: their remains would be unearthed from eight mass graves in Shiburghan, Dostum's former stronghold, when the old fox returned later in the year from Turkey to reclaim his inheritance from the Pehlawans.[38]

The rump of the Taliban invasion force retreated to Pul-i Khumri, which was captured as their forces advanced into Dostum's territory. But Massoud had retaken Gulbahar and Jabal Saraj on 29 May, cutting off their retreat, and Malik's forces and troops loyal to Sayed Jaffer Naderi harried them from the north and south. In early June the Taliban leader, Mullah Mohammad Omar, made an unprecedented visit to Kabul to rally morale and appeal for a fresh intake of volunteers from Pakistan to replace his losses.[39] Across the Amu Darya, where he was forced to flee after the Mazar débacle, one Pakistani diplomat conceded: 'Recognising the Taliban was a big mistake.'[40]

7 The River Between

On the map, the Amu Darya makes a striking frontier, but it is a sluggish river, more suited to black market smuggling than the transmission of spiritual riot. Rising in the eastern peaks of the Hindu Kush, the waters of the ancient Oxus shadow the boundary from the Rabbani-held province of Badakhshan, on the border with Tajikistan, to Jawzjan in Dostum's latterday khanate. The river strikes out northwest from there, across Uzbekistan to debouch, after 1,400 fatiguing miles, in the dried-up Aral Sea.

In the classical era, merchants kept it company for weeks at a time as they followed the Silk Route on the long road to Rome. Known as the 'river-sea' in Turkic, it flooded five miles across after the annual snow melt, but this epic sprawl has long since been bridled to irrigate the cotton mono-cropped across Central Asia under a series of five-year plans which leached out the skin-deep fertility to feed the factories of the Soviet economy. When Moscow tore off its colonial crown in 1991 and stormed off the Central Asian stage, the surly flow in the Amu Darya struck an easy parallel with the seepage of faith and identity that had overtaken the Muslim marches in almost 70 years of Soviet rule and which came back to haunt them in the last decade of the century.

That irrecoverable stamina – both of the river and the Soviet project even in its twilight years – was as nebulously mourned by the newly-impoverished in the abandoned republics, as it was feared by the totalitarian leaders who had commandeered the post-Soviet harness. President Islam Karimov of Uzbekistan – in spite of his name – dreaded Islamic revival like a long-suppressed genetic trait. Once awakened, it could plunge the region's most populous state into the type of suicidal civil war which devastated Tajikistan in 1992, sweeping away all confidence in the shabby imperial forms upon which the post-Soviet rulers relied. The resulting slaughter, moreover, provided Russia with an unassailable pretext to reassert its authority through direct military intervention to protect its borders against the forces of 'rampant Islam'.

Uzbekistan, as a 'front-line' state, had had plenty of time to ponder the surprises hurled up by history south of the Amu Darya. In the 1980s, Moscow introduced a policy of conscripting Central

Asians to fight the Afghan war, both for their linguistic fluency and to reduce the impact on the Russian public of 'white' Soviet casualties. The measure had backfired – but still lay smoking – by fostering a mutual sense of grievance between Uzbeks, Turkmens and Tajiks serving under both flags in the Cold War. Shared ethnicity, subordinated to the latent community of Islam, challenged the post-Soviet order only in Tajikistan. But beneath the remainder it had hollowed out an explosive network of tunnels and galleries which, despite the vigilance of the intelligence services, amplified the faintest rumour of discord, Islamic or otherwise, into a security siren that wailed as far away as Moscow.

Russia's regret at Gorbachev's shedding of the southern empire crystallised in 1992 with the establishment of the Commonwealth of Independent States (CIS), a collective security organisation which Turkmenistan, alone among the Central Asian republics, refused to join, pleading neutrality. Both decisions were dictated by the headlong rush for influence in the new republics which followed the formal dismantling of the Soviet entity in 1991. Iran, Turkey, Saudi Arabia, Western corporations and China had all begun to muscle into what, in the space of a few brief years, had metamorphosed from an economic sump of unpredictable stability into the next oil frontier, dripping with the promise of Caspian profit.

The richest of the republics, Turkmenistan, was in no mind to institutionalise its defence accords, sharing a border with Iran and anticipating investment, rather than aggression, from its more sophisticated neighbour. But, if Moscow was apprehensive at losing its monopoly over Central Asian energy supplies, it was more exercised by the dangers to national security. Russia's sovereign territory had collapsed in on itself since Gorbachev's abolition of the Union, but the tripwire of its defence instincts remained as far-flung as a decade earlier. This was partly due to the alarmism of hardliners from the former Red Army, who construed any diminution of its 'historic duty' as a ploy by the executive to further reduce its share of political and budgetary influence. One of the army's best allies in the palace struggles which characterised the presidency of Boris Yeltsin was the one-eyed Mullah Mohammad Omar, the apparent harbinger of a fanatic and merciless pan-Islamism.

But the real shock for post-Soviet Central Asians was less the meteoric rise of the Taliban, than the overthrow in April 1992 of President Mohammad Najibullah. Like Karimov, he had been forced to temporise a post-Soviet order out of the conflicting demands of religion, party and clan, an equation made more frustrating north of the Amu Darya by the patchwork of minorities, some indigenous, but others who had arrived in Tsarist times as settlers or following Stalin's mass deportations in the 1920s and 1940s. Karimov had certainly played a central role in determining the downfall of Najibullah and, subsequently, of Russian influence as a whole in Central Asia. But what would strike him with unerring directness after the fall of Kabul and the execution of the former Afghan president was the realisation that, in some eerie way, he had become Najibullah. It was not an insight he chooses to record on his website.[1]

Karimov smoothed the passage of several billion dollars a year of arms, fuel and food from Hairatan river-port and through the Salang Tunnel to Kabul during the three years following the Soviet retreat from Afghanistan in February 1989. This was a logistical operation which, with hindsight, tied the survival of the USSR to the destiny of an embattled dictator and made the fate of both dependent upon the uneasy alliance of the Uzbek, Pashtun, Tajik, Shia and Ismaili militias which defended Najibullah's northern flank under the command of General Rashid Dostum. In November 1991, under pressure from the US and Pakistan, Moscow announced it would halt the supply of arms and fuel to the Afghan president, a decison which deprived him of the patronage necessary to stamp his authority at the crumbling edges of his domain.

For months, Dostum and Massoud had been secretly negotiating a non-Pashtun alliance for the post-Najibullah era, a process that accelerated following Moscow's decision to withhold aid. But Dostum would not have decided to leap clear of Najib's sinking regime and into a dubious pact with Tajik *mujahedin* without assurances that Soviet support would be swiftly replaced by material aid from a different source. Karimov, in the spring of 1992, provided that assurance when he lent his political support to a century-old Tsarist thesis that the empire's southern flank could best be defended by advancing the then-existing frontier across the Amu Darya and up to the natural barrier of the Hindu Kush.

Britain's concern for the security of its Indian empire had thwarted this ambition in the nineteenth century by establishing the buffer state of Afghanistan exactly a century before the Soviet invasion. But Soviet strategists toyed with the notion of creating a separate, seven-province state in the north in the mid-1980s as the human and financial consequences of occupying the whole of Afghanistan began to tell. Its resuscitation as a bona fide strategy for quarantining Russia from the centrifugal violence of its Afghan escapade reinvented the plan as a set of smaller, interdependent buffers, each ultimately reliant upon the metropolitan power.

A northern khanate, headed by the former communist Dostum, could plug the Soviet-built Salang Tunnel and control supplies to whoever inherited control of Kabul. In view of the budding alliance with Dostum, their common northern origin and ethnic ties to Central Asia, the most likely candidate in early 1992 was Ahmad Shah Massoud, a man with whom Moscow knew it could do business for they had brokered ceasefires in the past over mastery of the Panjshir valley. Karimov, a lifetime party member and commander of Central Asia's most powerful military forces, continued in the logistical role once devised to uphold Najibullah. In late 1991, Moscow relinquished any futher attempts to control the Pashtun east and south, while the new state of Russia concentrated on consolidating its southern defensive ring at the Hindu Kush, using a second generation of proxies, paid generously to absorb casualties. Like other strategies in Afghanistan, however, this failed to take into account the mercurial propensities of the region and its commanders' negotiating enterprise.

Within a month of Massoud's and Dostum's forces entering Kabul in April 1992, a pro-democracy demonstration by 50,000 supporters of Tajikistan's Islamic Revival Party (IRP) and Democratic Party had exploded into a full-blown civil war between the dominant clans of Khojand and Kulyab regions, the Ismailis of Gorno-Badakhshan and the inhabitants of the Garm valley. In the space of four months, between 40,000 and 60,000 Tajiks were killed in internecine fighting, while a further 600,000 fled across the Pamir mountains to refugee camps controlled by either Massoud or Hekmatyar, whose Pashtun forces had taken control of Kunduz shortly after Dostum's mutiny,

In December 1992, at President Karimov's impassioned request, Russia deployed a 20,000-strong peacekeeping force in Tajikistan, composed of KGB troops, OMON special-purpose police detachments and the 201st Motorised Rifle Division, a supposedly crack unit which, three years earlier, had been stationed in Afghanistan.[2] Fighting continued into 1993, as IRP militants made forays against border posts from a reported 14 cross-border training camps, which Russia said were funded by Pakistan and Saudi Arabia.[3] It took two years before a ceasefire was signed in September 1994 but, even with Russian military backing, the new government of President Imomali

Rakhmanov failed to regain control of the Gorno-Badakhshan border region.

The involvement of Pakistan and Saudi Arabia was hard to confirm but, with the 13-year saga of their support for the *mujahedin*, it was a credible explanation of the IRP's energetic resistance, particularly given Hekmatyar's enclave on the Amu Darya. The invention of an international conspiracy on its southeastern frontier, however, suited Moscow's purpose, which was to justify Russia's first, post-Soviet military adventure to a population which, similar to the Serbs, had been breast-fed on the horror of Islamic revenge. The Tajik war, on the one hand, embellished the epidemiological analysis of Afghan 'fundamentalism', but, on the other hand, it cooled the region down by establishing a fire-break between the virus and its most likely victims – the Russian settlers who, symbolically, guarded the passes in the Muslim marches.

Karimov had furnished air power to crush the insurrection out of trepidation at the impact of an IRP victory on the 1.2 million Tajik minority concentrated in the holy cities of Bokhara and Samarkand. But the presence of a permanent Russian garrison across the eastern borders threatened Uzbekistan's own independence and its growing aspirations toward hegemony over Central Asia, a role for which its larger population, industrialised workforce and superior military power patently equipped it. The final bifurcation, between the old and the emergent orders north of the Amu Darya, would not occur for a further 15 months after hostilities ended in Tajikistan. And it would have more to do with the economic, rather than the military, balance of power.

After the fall of the Soviet empire in 1991, Turkey had been seduced into believing that ties of shared culture and language would provide the template of a new imperial dimension to its Central Asian policy. Only Tajikistan, wedged between the Pamir mountains on the Chinese border, dissented from the common Turkic tongue, speaking an eastern dialect of Farsi, the language both of Iran and Massoud. While Turkey worked to deepen its links with a dream hinterland stretching from Azerbaijan to Xinjiang province in China, Iran had also seen its opportunity. As a revolutionary Shia state, Iran had less to commend it in Central Asia, where a lapsed Sunnism was universal after three generations of Soviet rule. Turkey's brash capitalism and its constitutional commitment to secularism held more appeal to Karimov and Saparmyrat Niyazov, the president of Turkmenistan, who combined the Soviet predilection for cults of personality with a wide-eyed hankering for expensive construction contracts. Analysts said Ankara was forwarding US strategy by providing a role model in tune with Central Asia's transition from the Soviet to the modern, but it was Tehran, a wealthier and better-connected player in the region, which actually made the running.

In the west, Iran offered Turkmenistan a path to the Indian Ocean: in the east, it extended to Tashkent and Dostum an archipelago of fresh influence that connected the *Hizb-i Wahdat* enclaves in Mazar, the Hazarajat and the Kabul suburbs with the Tehran-backed client, Ismail Khan, emir of Herat. Tehran opened an embassy in Mazar in the summer of 1992, confirmation that, if not yet overtly allied, they had discovered common ground over *Hizb-i Wahdat*, the Shia alliance which guaranteed Iran a stake in its neighbour's affairs and, at five minutes past midnight, would rescue the northern city from Taliban occupation. The liaison was sealed with dollars and guns, further diversifying Dostum's sources, but it also put him in closer touch with *Hizb-i Wahdat*'s ally, Hekmatyar, who ordered the first rocket salvo on Kabul and its combined garrison of Massoud-Dostum forces in August of the same year.

The persistence of such back channels between the opposing factions bedevilled their foreign sponsors throughout the post-Najibullah period, stymying every attempt to orchestrate events on the ground according to the rules of hard-and-fast alliance. That very notion had only percolated into the Afghan conduct of war prior to the Saur Revolution in April 1978 when the Soviet Union stepped in to intervene between the *Khalq* and *Parcham* factions of the communist party, while the fates of Najibullah and Hekmatyar, in their different fashions, were eloquent testimony to what befell those who believed the promises of outsiders. The universal distrust of non-Afghans, greatly exacerbated after the US turned aside in 1992, reiterated another underlying theme: despite the UN's mounting warnings that Afghanistan was in danger of splitting along ethnic lines, the conflict remained at heart an intensely family quarrel: vicious, unprincipled and short-termist, certainly, but one in which a fratricidal enemy was a more valued asset than a foreign friend, however powerful or close in ethnicity.

To outside observers, the ensuing conflict came increasingly to resemble the eruption of ancient hatreds, whether of race or sect, supercharged by Cold War weaponry and the logic of the post-Soviet vacuum in Central Asia. But, to the participants, it was the celebration by traditional battle rites of an almost mystical sense of national kinship incomprehensible to non-Afghans. Whatever alliances they drew up, neither Dostum nor Hekmatyar truly aspired to control Kabul, knowing full well that to conquer would only transfer to their own heads the fire and loathing which had rained down successively on Massoud, Najibullah and, in his own time, Mohammad Daoud. The warlords played a game so long that it melted into the Olympian. Ultimate victory, they knew, was out of the question, but not temporary advantage: the essence was to survive.

Russia understood this more clearly than most. Having met its nemesis in the valleys of Afghanistan, it was content to let the ensuing conflagration run its course, as was the United States. The resulting power vacuum was a matter of indifference to the latter, swivelling into the more familiar conventions of fighting the Gulf war, and it posed little immediate danger to Russian security until such time as it threatened to spill across the Amu Darya and into Central Asia. Tajikistan notwithstanding, that was unlikely to occur without a radical shake-up in the internal balance of powers and, from 1992 until a few weeks before the fall of Kabul in September 1996, it was still Dostum, Tashkent's Cerberus on the road to Friendship Bridge, who held the casting vote. Tehran, broadly, was of a similar view, so long as the security of its eastern border was assured, but it played a more active role in ensuring that no pan-Afghan consensus could emerge through its consistent aid to *Hizb-i Wahdat*, a militant army of apostates in an internecine Sunni struggle.

Iran and Pakistan had cultivated extensive connections during the *jihad*, networks which deepened and coalesced after the collapse of the Soviet Union and the failure, one year later, of the *mujahedin* peace talks. Tehran's costly reinforcement by air had turned *Hizb-i Wahdat* into a serious contender for a power-sharing role in the post-Najibullah dispensation. The party's subsequent alliance with Hekmatyar in August 1992 seemed to place Tehran and Islamabad on a parallel course, in spite of Massoud's Farsi culture and his besiegers' virulent anti-Shiism. To complicate the picture further, Pakistan's paymaster, Saudi Arabia, had placed an each-way bet by continuing to support Massoud's Pashtun ally, *Ittehad-i Islami*, while Iranian diplomacy in Mazar-i Sharif was weevilling away at the interim government's northern ally, Dostum. The only straight bat, it appeared, belonged to Pakistan, which pursued a policy almost unchanged since the dictatorship of General Zia and the ISI, that of installing in Kabul a sympathetic Pashtun government under

Hekmatyar which would uphold Islamabad's claims in the North West Frontier.

For Tashkent, stranded well to the east of Iran's energy and transport corridors, the unofficial alliance with Tehran produced defensive, rather than tangible benefits. It strengthened Dostum through a tangle of contradictory obligations – largely honoured in the omission – but did little to mitigate Karimov's dependence on Russia for revenues. Pakistan, by contrast, was potentially an avid market for raw cotton and gas, but Karimov's undertaking to sustain and supply the Dostum-Massoud alliance on behalf of Russia negated any chance of access through Hekmatyar-controlled country to the Khyber Pass.

The conflict of interest was equally transparent to Massoud: he depended upon the Uzbek *galamjam* for control of Kabul, but despised its pillaging ways; Dostum had always been reluctant to use his superior air power against Hekmatyar, since his own position relied upon a shifting alliance with northern Pashtun warlords; and both Dostum and Hekmatyar during 1992 had been excluded from the flawed Peshawar Accord, one for his communist background, the other by choice.

Dostum's defection to Hekmatyar and Pakistan's side in January 1994 did little to enhance Tashkent's prospects however. The road through Salang to Khyber remained resolutely shut, while Massoud's offensives into Badghis, Bamian and Balkh provinces further taxed Uzbekistan's scant military budget.[4] More crucially still, Tashkent had been lured deeper into the maelstrom of regional diplomacy – a field for which it was desperately ill-equipped – by overtly siding with Pakistan's foreign policy objectives at the expense of Moscows'. Within weeks of the launch of the second siege of Kabul, Moscow had found more direct means of shoring up Massoud and dispensing with Karimov as a go-between, although it still depended on the latter as a buffer.

Tashkent's latest liaison was the first indication that it had abandoned the policy of collective response which underpinned the charter of the CIS. Of the front-line states, Uzbekistan and Tajikistan, under its newly-installed president, Imomali Rakhmanov, had always been compliant with Moscow's intentions, the first due to economic dominance, the latter through military occupation. Turkmenistan's neutrality and its proximity to Iran had earned Ashgabat some discretionary latitude. The alliance between Dostum and Hekmatyar drew Moscow closer to the role of an active participant in the Afghan imbroglio, one it did not relish because of the historic associations. Nevertheless, in the heat of the siege in April 1994, as Massoud's troops failed to break out of Kabul and sieze the Salang Tunnel, a new supply route was breached east of the contested zones of Baghlan and Pul-i Kumri to Sher Khan Bandar on the Tajik border.[5] This can only have been achieved with Moscow's blessing.

Russia's reinforcement of its old enemy proved vital to his survival in 1994 and it increased after the Taliban's abortive first thrust on the capital in spring 1995. Working akimbo, Iran and Pakistan had thrown all they could shift by air and land to their various proxies and still Massoud had held out. From Islamabad, Western diplomats testified to having seen documentation which showed 'massive requisitions of rockets from Pakistan's army munitions depots designated for Hekmatyar', while Massoud's intelligence claimed in August 1994 that Uzbek tanks and troops were fighting alongside Dostum, and Uzbek jets had made bombing sorties over *Jamiat* territory. The scale of Iranian military aid is harder to gauge for the *Hizb-i Wahdat* bases were buried deep in the Hazarajat. However, civilian deaths notwithstanding – an estimated 20,000 had died in Kabul alone by the end of 1994 – the most critical element of external aid was financial: Russia, Uzbekistan, Pakistan and Iran, at various times, were all cyclostyling *afghanis* as fast as the minions of their appointed warlords could spend them.

The appearence of the Taliban in Kandahar in late October 1994 at the head of Brigadier Babar's convoy to Ashgabat barely flickered on the radars of the regional powers. If the movement was acknowledged at all, it was as an obscure, revivalist side-show, a cross-wind of no account in a derelict district marginal to a quarrel of far graver calibre being slugged out in the seat of Afghan power. The presidents of Uzbekistan and Turkmenistan might conceivably have been aware that something was in the offing, either in the summer of the same year, as Mrs Bhutto's state visit to Ashgabat approached, or in September, when Babar and his entourage travelled to Herat and Torghundi to arrange free passage to the Turkmen border. As Bhutto, Karimov, Niyazov and President Rafsanjani of Iran conferred, together or separately, at the Turkmen independence celebrations in October, however, the point at issue was not to change the shape of northern power, for both Dostum and Ismail Khan were also present.[6] Nor was it to discuss a change in tactics around Kabul for Pakistan, Iran and Uzbekistan had no reason to complain of the

Hekmatyar-*Hizb-i Wahdat*-Dostum triangle that was then pounding the capital to dust.

On the surface, the meeting was precisely what it seemed: a regional mini-summit held to discuss the improvement of trade links and, by implication, how best to stabilise the transport corridor through southern Afghanistan without raising hackles in the region. With the Taliban already installed in Kandahar, Bhutto may well have sought her homologues' endorsement of any further Pakistani-assisted efforts to pacify *mujahedin* commanders along the Herat road, but any indication that plans were in progress for attacks upon Herat itself or anywhere else in the north would have triggered an immediate walk-out by one or other participants and a furious denunciation through their official media after the closure of the summit. Not a voice was raised in anger until February, when the Taliban marched against the benign and generally well-liked Ismail Khan. Bhutto and Babar's real purpose in Ashgabat had been to gain time to consolidate the movement and to prepare it militarily and at a command level for a more ambitious role in Afghan politics.

The gloves came off with the advance on Kabul, though there is doubt whether the order came from Kandahar or Islamabad and, if the latter, from which office. With the killing of the *Hizb-i Wahdat* commander, Mazari, and the defeat first of Hekmatyar and, subsequently, *Hizb-i Wahdat* and the Taliban in March, the regional consensus on the Afghan problem that had been agreed in January 1994 and confirmed at Ashgabat the following October was in ruins. The rupture between Islamabad and Tehran became absolute after the fall of Herat in September, forcing the latter to reassess its relations with Massoud, a former foe, and his enemy Dostum, a proxy whose value had demonstrably waned after the collapse of the first siege of Kabul, only to rise again in February 1996, as Taliban rocketeers took over Hekmatyar's former positions at Charasyab. Siding with neither of the two remaining factions in the struggle for power at the centre, Dostum milked his casting vote for all it was worth, as Russia and Iran both pressured him to join with the *Jamiat* commander and reopen the Salang Tunnel.[7]

Only Russian policy remained consistent after the debacle in Kabul. Moscow had stepped up supplies of arms, fuel and currency to Massoud long before the fall of Herat, though it diguised its direct involvement by sub-contracting shipments through private companies and third-party suppliers, a lesson which might have been drawn from the CIA's management of supplies through the ISI to the *mujahedin* more than a decade earlier.[8] On 5 August 1995, an Illyushin-76, owned by the Tatarstan-based freight-handler Aerostan, was intercepted by Taliban jets on its flight path to Bagram airbase and forced to land at Kandahar. On board were 3.4 million rounds of AK47 ammunition and heavy machine guns, originating from Albania but piloted by Russians.[9] The crew remained stranded in Taliban territory for over a year, only to 'escape' to the United Arab Emirates (UAE) following the intercession, ironically, of Hank Brown, the senator from Colorado and a member of the Senate Intelligence Committee (so mortified were the Russians' Taliban guards by the 'subterfuge', they said, that they 'could not eat their lunch').[10] The plane was one of possibly hundreds of Russian-sponsored flights that landed in Bagram during 1995–96.

Russia also provided Massoud with logistical assistance. Denied access through Uzbekistan and the Dostum-held Hairatan river port, Russian engineers were discovered by US satellites to have constructed a new bridge over the Amu Darya, well-upstream from Mazar, so as to furnish an alternative land route to Massoud-held Badakhshan from Tajikistan.[11] Moscow's aid was solicited to upgrade the airport of Taloqan in early 1996, creating an air bridge through friendly airspace to Bagram.[12] If all else failed and Massoud lost Bagram to the Taliban, control of the Panjshir offered his forces an arduous but ultimately incontestable corridor of retreat through to Taloqan and the fastnesses of Badakhshan.

Iran's policy matched Russia's while simultaneously continuing to cooperate with Dostum so as to protect *Hizb-i Wahdat* and laying the groundwork for a counter-attack by Ismail Khan's demoralised troops. After Herat fell, some 8,000 had escaped across the Iranian border to the eastern city of Mashhad where five training camps were constructed to accommodate them. A number of incursions were successfully repulsed by the Taliban in early 1996 but a major redeployment of 1,000, largely Turkmen, fighters occurred in October when they were rearmed and airlifted by Iran to Badghis province to fight alongside troops loyal to Dostum, now finally – if not firmly – in Massoud's camp.[13] Mashad was also the springboard for a massive airlift of fuel and *materiel* to Bagram which, on 22 November 1995 alone, received a reported 13 Iranian cargo planes.[14]

Taliban expansionism caused even India, long a back-seat observer of Afghan affairs, to adopt a more active role in the closing scenes. As a Soviet ally, New Delhi had kept a diplomatic establishment throughout the rule of Najibullah – who chose India as his preferred place of political asylum – and it was retained after Rabbani took power as a means of gathering intelligence about Pakistan's intrigues in Afghanistan, Kashmir and the Punjab, where two separatist wars had been bolstered by *mujahedin* veterans and ISI money. By way of recompense, India permitted the Afghan national carrier, Ariana, to stable the rump of its fleet at New Delhi airport, where they were free from attack but, if on returning home to Kabul, the Boeings were filled with military equipment or spare parts, no word of it has ever come to light. By early 1996, by contrast, 30 Indian technicians were reported by one usually reliable source to be servicing Massoud's few remaining MiGs and Sukhois; artillery instructors had been flown in; and arms were being channelled via Mashad to Bagram.[15]

But money more than weaponry was the key to the scattered fiefdoms which lay between the Taliban and mastery of Kabul. While Pakistan's well-oiled but still dimly-understood guidance of the movement had effectively alienated all governments sharing borders with Afghanistan – threatening to ignite real confrontation with Iran – it was the financial resources of Saudi Arabia and the UAE, which made the capture of the capital possible and emboldened Islamabad to openly vex its neighbours with the threat of an Islamist revival in the region.

No hard evidence has surfaced to link the Saudi government with the Taliban, beyond the mutual exchange of visits that routinely take place between the officials of powers with a similar Islamic mind-set – and the engrained suspicion that some wealthier sponsor must lurk behind the shoulders of an impoverished Pakistan. Nor did the UAE obviously stand to profit from a movement whose hostility to Tehran risked the potentially catastrophic closure of the trans-Iranian land route used by its merchants to access the lucrative markets of Afghanistan, Pakistan and Central Asia. But both countries leaped to recognise the Taliban after their short-lived victory in Mazar in May 1997 and Riyadh's joy had been boundless when *sharia* law was declared after the fall of Kabul to the Taliban eight months earlier. Shared faith alone could not explain why two members of the pro-US Gulf Cooperation Council, set up to isolate Iran, should have lent international respectability to a rabble of religious die-hards whose activities set the teeth of the entire region on edge.

North of the Amu Darya, the Taliban's victory procession into the Afghan capital was greeted with equal portions of alarm and alarmism. Russia's Security Council chief, General Alexander Lebed, promptly warned that the movement intended to swarm across the river and annex parts of Uzbekistan and Tajikistan, a fear exacerbated by Taliban front-line commanders who promised journalists they would not pause until the shrine cities of Bokhara and Samarkand were in their grasp.[16] The sentiment was exploited in a photo-montage in *Krasnaya Zvezda*, a defence ministry journal, which showed a woman in a *burkha* walking down a Moscow street: 'It could come to this,' read the caption, 'if the army continues to be seriously weakened.'[17]

8 The New Emirates

While at one level the Taliban appeared bent upon hurling Afghanistan back into the medieval age from which the Soviet Union had inadvertently rescued it, at another level the movement's successes were curiously well-tailored to the realities of a region, which is forecast to challenge the Middle East as a source of energy in the twenty-first century.

All of the foreign powers suspected of arming the Afghan factions were playing for much higher stakes in the international in-fighting that has permeated the politics of the Caucasus and Central Asia since the dissolution of the Soviet Union in December 1991. Cut off from their natural trading partners to the west or south by over a century of Soviet domination, the new republics found themselves blessed with an astonishing wealth of oil and gas. But there was no way of getting the energy to market, save through the network of pipelines pointing northwards into Russia, a colonial power in sharp decline which had historically milked their resources at bottom-rouble prices.

The struggle to command – or restrict – this energy windfall has embroiled the United States, Russia, Turkey, Iran, Saudi Arabia and Pakistan, winning comparisons with that earlier saga of geopolitical manoeuvring, the Great Game. The first Great Game pitted the military and intelligence services of Tsarist Russia and the British Raj against one another in a bid for ascendancy over the independent khanates and kingdoms that lay between Asia's two most powerful empires in the nineteenth century. It subsided when the two powers reached agreement on a definition of the frontiers of Afghanistan, an artificial state contrived solely to end the friction between their conflicting spheres of interest.

The second has been conducted over a broader geography and by corporations as much as states, but it is no less epic and still far from resolution. In 10 years, the new game has spawned four small but remarkably ugly wars, fired the long-standing Kurdish insurgency in Turkey and dangerously intertwined the flammable worlds of geopolitical rivalry, Islamist revolution and state terrorism on a canvas that stretches from Dagestan to China's Xinjiang province. The tensions in the new Great Game have been exacerbated, like those of its prototype, by the weakness of the states it most concerns, the enormous prize at stake and the fact that none of the participants admits to being in an open state of war.

Recent conflicts in Nagorno-Karabakh, Abkhazia, Turkish Kurdistan and Chechnya are all linked by a single, golden theme: each represented a distinct, tactical move, crucial at the time, in determining which power would ultimately become master of the pipelines which, some time in this century, will transport the oil and gas from the Caspian Basin to an energy-avid world. Global demand – along with its population – will double in the next 25 years and Azerbaijan, Kazakstan and Turkmenistan are sitting on the largest known reserves of unexploited fuel in the planet.[1] These resources offer the West a unique opportunity to break free of its dependence on the Middle East, which furnishes 40 per cent of US demand, and a chance to command a strategic reserve which will stabilise the future price and flow of a scarce commodity. The Gulf has suffered two major wars and the producers deemed most crucial to Western interests – most pointedly Saudi Arabia – are alarmingly susceptible to destabilisation, whether through terrorism, outright invasion or the social pressures building up within their repressive regimes.

From early on, Moscow has insisted that Caspian exports must be transported through the Russian pipeline system to its Novorossiysk terminal on the Black Sea, ensuring handsome transit fees for its treasury and a continuing stranglehold on the region's natural resources and the independence of its constituent republics. Political instability along prospective alternative pipeline routes through the Caucasus to the Black Sea, added to the US's long-standing trade boycott of Iran, which is the cheapest path to the open sea, effectively imposed a blockade on resources whose potential has tied up billions of dollars' worth of Western investment. Western companies were desperate to prevent this new energy supply from falling into the hands of Russia's large, but ill-endowed oil and gas monopolies. After the 1991 disintegration, the US government continued to acknowledge Russian hegemony in the so-called 'near abroad' – the former Soviet republics other than the Baltic States – lest they fall prey to fundamentalist forces from within or outside. But the prospect of Moscow controlling the Caspian's projected 2 million barrels a day (b/d) oil output, in addition to the 7 million b/d flowing west from oilfields in Siberia, raised fears that one crisis-prone energy partner in the Gulf was only being replaced by another, with far greater scope for economic mayhem.

To Saudi Arabia and Iran, divided by military suspicion as much as religious differences, the Caspian represents a further threat to oil revenues already diminished by low prices and an enfeebled OPEC. If they were not in a position to stop the emergence of a new generation of oil-rich emirates to the northeast, they could at least pre-empt the loss of future income by profiting from their development and exploitation – at the expense of their rival where possible. Throughout the 1990s, both states assiduously courted the regimes in the Caucasus and Central Asia with offers of soft credits, technical partnerships – or assistance in rebuilding their religious inheritances after nearly a century of communism.

The other key player was Turkey, which has cultural links with all but one of the five Central Asian republics and was thought to offer an alternative role model of how a modern state could accommodate secular values with Islam. Turkey was Russia's main competitor for the energy transport business, having tabled its own proposals for alternative pipeline itineraries through Georgia or Armenia and into national territory. But the long-running Kurdish insurrection, which sapped the government with no appreciable end in sight, continued to put investors off.

The Taliban's conquest of Kabul followed swiftly upon the Rabbani government's surprise announcement in February 1996 that it had signed an agreement allowing for the construction of a $3 billion pipeline across Afghan territory connecting the newly-discovered Yashlar gas field in Turkmenistan with the Indian Ocean.[2] Having lost Herat and Kandahar to the rebels, the government was in no position to guarantee security along the route proposed for the scheme, but the decision marked a turning point in what had become an acrimonious and dangerous dispute over the routing of Caspian energy. The mooting of a trans-Afghanistan pipeline opened a brand-new chapter in the latterday Great Game and signalled the arrival on the scene of another player, Pakistan. Bleeding $1.5 billion each year in energy imports, Islamabad would be the most obvious beneficiary of whatever transport agreement could ultimately be assembled. After years amid the forgotten rubble of the post-Cold War world, Afghanistan was suddenly propelled from the periphery to the heart of the energy wars in the region.

A trans-Afghanistan route would preserve the boycott of Iran, weaken the Russian monopoly and still emerge geographically closer to the faster-growing energy markets in Asia. It was also ideal in the eyes of the United States and Saudi Arabia, the two countries with the easiest access to oil industry finance and the greatest interest in the continued isolation of Iran. A trans-Afghanistan route could shift the region's centre of gravity well out of its Russian orbit, while remaining far from the attractions of Iran's developed system of pipelines and ports.

Earlier plans for energy routes had presumed the building of west-flowing pipelines beneath the Caspian to funnel oil and gas from Central Asia into infrastructure designed to export production from Azerbaijan to Europe. But the greatest potential in the contemporary energy market lies amongst the increasingly wealthy populations of China and India. By reversing the direction of flow, perhaps, oil and gas from all three new-wave energy producers could travel southeastwards via Afghanistan, whose weakened government would welcome the blandishments of the new global energy order.

By 27 September 1996, the Taliban's solipsistic mullahs controlled the pipeline route, the seat of government and the key to the treasure buried in the Caspian hub. Their success in dislodging Massoud might have been greeted with cheers in energy company boardrooms but, with so much at stake if the Afghan pipeline were to go ahead, it was more intriguing to speculate on the reaction of Russia.

* * *

Afghanistan, oddly enough, is no stranger to the oil and gas industry. Dostum's mini-state in the north prospered since 1992 from bartering crude from Shiburghan Province with Uzbekistan for the refined fuels, arms and the other equipment needed to run his war machine. By contrast with most cities in Afghanistan, Mazar-i Sharif was in a business boom in 1995 with five-storey office blocks going up around the shrine of Hazrat Ali, the Shi'ite caliph, and its markets bursting with produce from Central Asia and the Far East.

Soviet geologists had estimated Shiburghan's potential at around 50,000 tonnes a year, more than sufficient to support a small refinery and to turn Afghanistan into a net exporter.[3] Other promising geological areas had been identified at Karakum in the northwest, the Afghan-Tajik basin in the northeast, Tirpul, to the west of Herat and the Helmand and Kundar-Urgun basins in the southwest. But if the Afghan geology qualified it as a minor province in the new oil empire, it was equally evident that the real wealth lay in natural gas. Non-associated gas was discovered in Sar-i Pul in the 1950s and larger fields in Jawzjan and Faryab came on stream during the 1970s. By

1984, Afghanistan was exporting around 2.4 billion cubic metres a year to the Soviet Union, earning an impressive $315 million, or around half the country's total export revenue.[4]

Before the departure of Soviet forces in February 1989, the gas fields were capped to prevent sabotage, denying the country its main source of export earnings. Efforts by the Najibullah government in the early 1990s to reactivate the industry came to nothing. As the last khanate to fall under Soviet rule, Afghanistan found itself in a predicament identical to the Central Asian republics: they all had potentially vast resources but the energy transport infrastructure pointed north into the former Soviet Union. Russia preferred to sell Siberian on the hard-currency market and sideline Central Asian stocks to poorer customers, such as the Ukraine, Belarus and Armenia. And to underscore its stranglehold, Moscow unilaterally imposed 'gas-for-debt' swaps to pay for earlier weapons deals, as occurred in Afghanistan until 1989, or offered only half of the world price, which Turkmenistan was forced to accept in its 1995 negotiations with Gazprom, the Russian monopoly which controls nearly a quarter of the world's natural gas supply.[5]

No less than during the Soviet era, the interests of Russia's energy companies reflect the foreign policy of the state, in much the same way that the British East India Company was the cat's paw of London's imperial ambitions during the early years of the Raj. So closely were they intertwined, in fact, their respective managements were interchangeable. Prime Minister Viktor Chernomyrdin made a personal fortune as head of Gazprom's board of directors until mid-1996, when he was replaced by another prominent politician, Deputy Prime Minister Alexander Kazakov, in spite of the company's declared intention to introduce foreign participation by selling off part of the government's holding. With little capital to spare, and strategic objectives to pursue as much as profit margins, Gazprom and Lukoil, Russia's largest oil company, were increasingly compelled to turn to political intimidation as a means of ensuring their seat at the feast being prepared around the shores of the Caspian. Whenever the new republics tried to forge genuine political independence from President Boris Yeltsin's Russian Federation, they were swiftly overtaken by destabilisation or civil conflict, usually camouflaged as ethnic insurrection. These mini oil wars served the dual purpose of reasserting Russia's dominance in the 'troubled' Caucasus and undermining the feasibility of alternative pipeline routes which did not pass through Russian territory.

Azerbaijan's so-called 'deal of the century', signed in September 1994, gives some insight into how much is involved in the region. The 30-year production-sharing agreement, between the state oil company Socar and a consortium of nine Western companies, led by British Petroleum (BP), promised to provide the government in Baku with a dazzling $118 billion from the development of just three offshore oilfields – the Azeri, Chirag and Guneshli. The consortium intended to build current production of 160,000 b/d to 700,000 b/d by the end of the century.[6] Some US companies believe there could be four times this amount of oil in the Azerbaijani share of the Caspian Sea. In Kazakstan, Chevron invested $1 billion of a projected $20 billion in the offshore Tengiz field, one of the world's largest with reserves estimated at 1 billion tonnes. Richard Matzke, the company's president, called the stake 'Chevron's biggest and most important project since the opening of Saudi Arabia about 50 years ago'.[7] Turkmenistan contains the world's third largest natural gas reserves and a total of 7.4 billion barrels of oil. But none of this energy has reached Western markets in significant volumes, due to the constant wrangling over the pipeline routes. By the end of 1995, Chevron was reportedly losing tens of millions of dollars every day from its Tengiz gamble, which had yielded only 60,000 b/d out of a total capacity of 700,000 b/d.[8]

The importance of the oil transport issue arose early on. As Boris Yeltsin took power in Moscow in August 1991, the former Soviet general, Dzhokhar Dudayev, declared Chechen independence, with the active encouragement of Turkey and Saudi Arabia. Though Chechnya contains few oil or gas reserves, it is crucial to oil exportation from the new emirates because the Caucasian pipeline system, linking Baku to Novorossiysk, passes through Grozny, the capital. If Moscow lost control of Grozny, it would be disqualified in Baku. Azerbaijan and Georgia had also been trying to break away from Moscow's influence and seek closer economic integration with Turkey, Russia's main regional competitor. Western oil companies interested in the region had proposed two alternative pipeline routes to Turkish territory through Georgia and Armenia, by-passing the Grozny intersection altogether. In 1991, Azerbaijan and Georgia tested the limits of their recent autonomy by refusing to join the CIS, on the grounds that Russia had fomented the Armenian uprising in Nagorno-Karabakh and supplied Abkhazian secessionists in western Georgia with weapons. The then-presidents Abulfaz Elchibei of Azerbaijan and Zviad Gamsakhurdia of Georgia were soon overthrown by armed rebels, to be replaced by politicians more amenable to Moscow's way of thinking.

President Haydar Aliev, a former member of the Brezhnev politburo, was brought to power in Baku while his predecessor, Elchibei, was in London to sign the oil production-sharing agreement with BP. Aliev promptly renounced a budding alliance with Turkey and brought Azerbaijan back into the fold of the CIS. In a bid to appease Russia – and the parallels with racketeering were becoming inescapable – the third field in the 'deal of the century', Guneshli, was unceremoniously detached from BP's original proposal and handed over for exclusive development by Lukoil, which was granted a 10 per cent share of the whole project.[9] In September 1993, President Eduard Sheverdnadze of Georgia agreed to allow Russia's military bases in Georgia and along the frontier with Turkey to remain open.

The message to US and UK companies was uncompromising: Caspian oil and gas will be exploited only with the participation of Russian energy companies and under the protection of the Russian security umbrella. Washington had no particular dispute with that, having a grander ambition in the survival of the Russian Federation under Boris Yeltsin, and the defence of its significant commercial interests in Western Siberia, by far the larger energy supplier. When Chechnya's declaration of independence deteriorated into open war in the winter of 1994, the US never officially queried Moscow's right to dispatch an invasion force, settling instead for expressions of concern over the handling of a crisis that would go on to devastate Grozny and claim 80,000 lives.

When the Chechen invasion backfired so spectacularly – prompting ordinary Russians to draw parallels with the Soviet debacle in Afghanistan – Moscow was finally forced to concede over the pipeline question. Chechnya's successful resistance destroyed for ever the myth that Russia could easily impose its military will within the federation, let alone the broader Caucasus, and this had the consequence of downgrading the security arguments in oil company circles which had favoured the inevitability of using Russia's pipeline network. The Chechen war revealed that it was as vulnerable to sabotage as all of the alternatives.

In October 1995, the BP-led consortium, which includes Exxon, Amoco, Norway's Statoil, UNOCAL, Ramco, McDermott International, the private Saudi concern Delta-Nimir, Turkey's TPAO and Lukoil, agreed to a compromise. From 1996 onward, the 'early oil' from Baku would be transported through both the Russian and Turkish pipeline systems.[10] The agreement satisfied some of Russia's concerns, while broadly meeting US requirements, which were the earliest possible end to the dispute and the provision of a dual-route system to prevent the emergence of a transport monopoly. But it was little more than a face-saving solution, designed to break the logjam in the Caucasus, rather than lay the foundations of a transportation system to last for 30 years, the average life-span of the production contracts. Oil would begin to flow under the arrangement, but up to a ceiling of only 700,000 b/d – a fraction of the capacity currently being developed around the Caspian. More important, the sums the consortium earmarked for upgrading the Russian pipeline ($60 million), and for opening a second export route through Georgia to the eastern Black Sea ($250 million), were paltry by the standards of long-term, oil industry planning.[11]

They underlined the oil giants' general air of caution and suggested that, far from being the looked-for breakthrough, this agreement was just a truce, or breathing space, in the pipeline wars being waged throughout the region.

* * *

Turkmenistan has the best chance, among the Central Asian republics, of becoming the first 'new sheikhdom' of the twenty-first century. With 11 per cent of the world's gas reserves and large tracts of its desert geography still to be explored, it already earns over $1 billion a year from energy exports. Little wonder if the ex-communist president, Saparmyrat Niyazov, has felt confident enough to embark on a spending spree, mortgaging future deliveries of energy and the 1.5 million tonne cotton crop to pay for new railways, presidential pavilions, five-star hotels and a $200 million theme park. The self-styled *Turkmenbashi*, or 'leader of the Turkmens', has promised to turn his four million subjects into the beneficiaries of 'a second Kuwait'. They cannot wait. Turkmenistan suffered the worst poverty levels of the Soviet Union when it was ruled by Moscow, and has entered an irreversible ecological decline with the drying up of the Aral Sea, the lifeblood of the cotton which dominates local farming to the detriment of grain. In the capital, Ashgabat, food shortages are now worse than in Soviet times.

As the only country in the region with significant onshore deposits, Turkmen ambitions were best-placed to avoid being derailed by the bidding quarrel over drilling rights in a divided Caspian Sea. Moscow has threatened legal action over the issue on many occasions as a way of whipping its unruly offspring into line. But Moscow – in the shape of Gazprom – continues to control the export routes for Turkmen gas and oil which, at current volumes and prices, could command over $7 billion in revenues each year. Ashgabat steadily raised its prices after independence in 1991, from 6 roubles per 1,000 m^3 to 870 roubles in 1992, but Turkmen gas remains among the cheapest in the world. Most is still sold to the Ukraine and other CIS members, struggling economies with scant dollars, with the result that Turkmen gas continued to be plundered after independence in the same manner it had before. In a round of negotiations with Gazprom in 1997, Ashgabat won a hike to $42 per 1,000 m^3, but this was still half world levels and there was no guarantee that the user would ever pay.

President Niyazov worked hard to create new trading relations to replace those which existed at the time of the Soviet Union. Turkmenistan was the only state in Central Asia to have developed close ties with Iran, the others having been frightened off by the US boycott, or Russian anger. In May 1992, the two countries agreed to extend the Iranian railway system from Mashad to the Turkmen city of Tedzen, at a cost of $500 million. A $7 billion gas pipeline linking Turkmenistan to Europe through Iran and Turkey was also under consideration, though financing was not easy due to the US boycott. Iran provided Turkmenistan with an alternative supply of cash through swap deals. Under this arrangement, Turkmen gas is trucked or railed to Iran, where it is traded for the equivalent value of Iranian gas on the foreign market.

Alarmed that it was losing out in the Central Asian oil rush, Pakistan launched a vigorous initiative to entice Turkmenistan into its own sphere of influence. In August 1994, President Niyazov visited Islamabad to sign accords on transport and energy and, in October, Prime Minister Bhutto attended the independence celebrations in Ashgabat, rubbing shoulders with President Akbar Rafsanjani of Iran, President Suleyman Demirel of Turkey, General Rashid Dostum and General Ismail Khan. It was the same month that the Taliban were first sighted in Kandahar, liberating from *mujahedin* control a goodwill convoy of Pakistani trade goods destined for the people of Central Asia.

The idea of a gas pipeline from Turkmenistan to Pakistan had been simmering for some years, but it seems to have been seriously discussed in the months leading up to Turkmen independence day. Generals Dostum and Khan sniped at one another through the media of the Pakistani journalists sent to cover Mrs Bhutto's visit but, whatever their political differences, they were in harmony when it came to negotiating the trans-Afghan leg of the proposed route. Energy transport could bring wealth, while the diplomatic and commercial linkages which the work entailed might amount to international recognition for their fragmentary domains.

Pakistan had suggested in 1994 the building of a railway across Afghanistan, connecting Tedzen with Karachi. While this project seemed optimistic, in view of the security situation, Islamabad officials protested that they had received guarantees from the relevant authorities. The independent Argentine company, Bridas, would claim it had received similar assurances, when it unveiled its proposal for a Turkmenistan-Afghanistan-Pakistan (TAP) gas pipeline in July 1995. Bridas had been the only international energy company prepared to take a stake in the infant Turkmen republic, setting up a 70:30 joint venture in 1991 to explore and develop the Yashlar field, situated 450 km east of the capital in the Karakum desert. In January 1995, after three years' work and what it later claimed was close to $1 billion in investment, it found it had a major discovery on its hands. Yashlar contained $20 billion worth of gas, sufficient to feed growing demand in Pakistan and India and to provide a surplus for sale to the Far East.[12]

In March 1995, President Niyazov and Prime Minister Bhutto signed a memorandum of understanding for the construction of a 1,300 km pipeline from Yashlar to Pakistan's largest gas field at Sui, in Baluchistan. Bridas's contract with the Turkmen government stipulated an option to build the transport system to international markets. A feasibility study was carried out by Bridas's technicians under an agreement signed that April, working with representatives from the oil ministries of both countries. Negotiations with Afghan leaders began shortly afterwards. 'Agreements have been reached and signed, that assure us a right of way and the backing of the various groups in the conflict, authorising us to build the gas pipeline through Afghan territory,' Bridas's chairman, Carlos Bulgheroni, declared confidently in March 1996, one month after President Rabbani made his own announcement.[13] The deal awarded Bridas an exclusive right to build, operate and maintain a sub-soil pipeline from the Turkmen border to the Pakistan boundary for the next 30 years.

It was a remarkable concession, even for a war-torn country that had seen no foreign investment in two decades. Bridas's project was an 'open' pipeline, with spur-lines shooting off to supply Kabul, Lahore, Islamabad and Karachi as and when required. Islam Karimov, president of Uzbekistan, had been considering another pipeline to carry Uzbek gas across Afghanistan to Sui. An 'open' line could accommodate both his resources and the capped, but still recoverable stocks lying under Dostum's territory. And Bridas, in principle, had exclusive rights to the business – as well as 70 per cent of the Yashlar strike.

In practice, everything had begun to fall apart before the ink was dry. On 5 September 1995, the Taliban expelled Ismail Khan from Herat, introducing another armed and unknown element into the pipeline equation. Worse developments were to occur in Ashgabat. On 21 October, Turkmenistan signed a contract with two new partners – the Los Angeles-based UNOCAL and Saudi-owned Delta-Nimir – to build a $2 billion pipeline across Afghanistan to the Pakistani coast. That pipeline would be a 'closed' or dedicated line, pumping gas for export only, and from an entirely different source, the Delidibide-Donmes field.[14]

UNOCAL was one of the high-stakes rollers from the western shores of the Caspian, where it controlled 9.5 per cent of the Azeri, Chirag and Guneshli fields in Azerbaijan. With revenues of $8.4 billion in 1995, it is involved at every level of the oil industry from exploration and transport to the development of clean-air petrols to meet California's strict environmental standards. In the last 30 years, it had become a major player in Thailand, Indonesia and in Burma, where a $1 billion joint venture in the Yadana offshore gas field was the single largest foreign investment since the suppression of the democracy movement in 1988.

Its Saudi collaborator consists of a 'strategic partnership' between Delta Oil, owned by a Jeddah-based group of 50 prominent investors close to the royal family,[15] and Nimir Petroleum, dominated by the bin-Mahfouz family, which also owns the National Commercial Bank where King Fahd and other royal household members keep their swollen accounts. In 1989, Khalid bin-Salem bin-Mafouz was made a member of the 'supreme council' of Saudi Aramco, the company that keeps the kingdom more or less afloat. His reputation was tarnished somewhat in 1992 when he was indicted for fraud in a US court in connection with the collapse of the Bank of Commerce and Credit International, though this had scarcely impinged on his banking career in Saudi Arabia.[16] Were the trans-Afghan pipeline to go ahead, UNOCAL and Delta-Nimir would be the only non-Russian energy companies with interests on both sides of the Caspian basin.

In June 1996 – three months before Kabul fell to the Taliban – Bridas filed a suit in Houston, which alleged that it had been prevented from developing its investment in Yashlar because of UNOCAL's interference. Company lawyers claimed $15 billion in damages, equivalent to the company's share of the estimated gas reserves. The Argentinians had succumbed to the curse of Central Asian energy prospecting: they had plenty to sell, but the only customer was now their biggest commercial rival. 'They are not going to put Bridas gas into UNOCAL's pipeline,' said a Bridas lawyer. 'Nobody was interested in this field while it was a wildcat. These guys took the risk and are entitled to the rewards.'[17] In his deposition, the lawyer claimed Bridas had invited UNOCAL into the TAP project in early 1995. The company said it preferred to negotiate directly with the Turkmen government.[18]

Delta-Nimir took responsibility for negotiating the rights of way for UNOCAL's pipeline across Afghanistan, a task made easier following the recruitment of Charles Santos, a former political adviser to the UN peace envoy, Mahmoud Mestiri, and a man well known to all the faction leaders.[19] UNOCAL, meanwhile, hired Robert B. Oakley, the former US ambassador to Zia's Pakistan and a lynchpin in organising the anti-Soviet *jihad,* to advise on its negotiations with the increasingly successful Taliban.[20] The movement initially opposed the project because of what diplomatic sources in Islamabad described as 'Pakistan's insistence on controlling the pipeline in its entirety'.[21] But when Islamabad agreed to share the profits, the project won the mullahs' blessing. Indeed, the faction leaders were all enamoured of pipelines. Whatever the military ramifications, they were seen as conduits for peace, patronage, investment and international recognition. Though anxious at the prospect of transit revenues falling into hostile hands after the fall of Herat, Kabul even overcame its reservations. Rabbani's announcement in February 1996 that it had approved the TAP project, interestingly, coincided with the first hard signs that Washington had revived its interest in Afghanistan.

But Kabul had backed the wrong pipeline: the announcement came four months after the Turkmen government signed the UNOCAL contract, which effectively disqualified Bridas as a valid negotiating partner. At any event, it was unlikely that Kabul would ever be in a position to guarantee security for a project likely to take from two to three years to complete. Its writ ran in just three central provinces, inspiring one Taliban wit to describe President Rabbani as 'the mayor of Kabul'.[22] The Taliban, on the other hand, controlled the preferred route in 1995, and had only been kept out of the capital by the adroit generalship of Massoud, with military assistance from Russia, Iran and India.

The interests of Russia and Iran had been broadly similar in Afghanistan since the rise of the Taliban. Russia was committed to containing the movement, for fear that it would ignite the smouldering Islamist movement across Central Asia. To that end, Moscow had actively begun to bolster the Kabul government from the start of 1995, as well as the Uzbek, Turkmen and Tajik warlords who ruled the intervening lands. Iran conceived the Sunni Taliban as a US-sponsored gambit designed to gnaw at its eastern borders and diminish Tehran's influence both in the Farsi-speaking regions of Afghanistan, and Central Asia as a whole. But there was also symmetry over oil. A trans-Afghan pipeline would undermine Russia's control over energy prices from Central Asia, while Iran risked seeing its eastern rival, Pakistan, regain the rapport it had enjoyed with Washington during the Cold War, this time in the defence of US energy interests. With the Afghan parties to the conflict all endorsing the pipeline idea, it was essential that no faction should accumulate the military power sufficient to dominate the country and so make it a reality. The oil issue had not entirely displaced internal security as Russia's and Iran's primary concern in Afghanistan, but it had become passionately bound up with their geopolitical futures.

By the end of September 1996, the Taliban appeared close to defeating that objective. Marty Miller, UNOCAL's vice-president, announced after the capture of Kabul: 'We have been in negotiations with the Taliban and they have been very supportive of the project.'[23] UNOCAL called the Taliban's success 'a positive development',[24] while the US announced it would send a diplomat to Kabul for talks with the new government. With the US elections barely one month away, Washington swiftly backtracked, stating on 8 October that neither international recognition nor aid would be forthcoming until there was respect for women's rights. Saudi Arabia expressed delight at the imposition of Islamic law, although it did not follow up its moral support of the new regime in Kabul by bestowing it with diplomatic recognition.

As the Taliban advance bogged down outside the Panjshir valley in early October and General Dostum abandoned his neutrality to join Massoud's regrouped forces, it became clear that the loss of the capital was not the knockout blow it was at first thought. The pipeline would have to be shelved, until the shelling ceased. On 4 October, UNOCAL's Robert Todor informed reporters: 'International lenders have told us that the project is not currently financeable,' but he began to actively court the Taliban by establishing a UNOCAL office in Kandahar and inviting Taliban leaders to visit the company's headquarters in Sugarland, Texas.[25]

By early November, the fighting had spread northwest to Badghis and Faryab and expatriate staff evacuated Herat as rumours flew that Ismail Khan's troops were massing for an invasion from Mashad across the Iranian border. On 4 November, Dostum's air force bombed the city. It appeared that the next round in the new Great Game was about to begin.

9 Nest of Vipers

The US and Saudi Arabia had a further motive for venturing back into Afghanistan, one that had nothing to do with the welling of hydrocarbons beyond its northern frontiers, but which impinged no less upon their shared oil and security interests. In the four years that elapsed between Washington abandoning the *mujahedin* to their murderous devices and the resumption in 1994 of what would blossom into a furtively active role in the region, a striking reappraisal had taken place in the State Department and among the US intelligence agencies which inform its decisions.

This reassessment addressed the region's growing instability as a result of the spread of Islamist extremism. It mattered less whether the immediate trigger for the change in US policy were the destabilisation of near-nuclear Pakistan, the hot wars in Kashmir and Tajikistan or even the transformation of India from a derelict command economy into potentially the world's largest middle class constituency. Important as these and other considerations were, they remained secondary to the recognition in the US capital that, far from washing its hands of its Afghan proxy after the termination of direct diplomacy in 1992, it had, in fact, brought the vengeful bastard of its Cold War affair back into the happy home. For a new and far less predictable threat to domestic security was now at large in the shape of a nimble Islamist conspiracy which transcended national and sectarian differences and was quite able to deliver devastating explosions not only in Asia, Africa and the Middle East, but on US territory itself.

The vague spokes of what, in time, would sharpen into a global wheel of terror all appeared to converge on Afghanistan – although the controller was ritually identified as Tehran's intelligence services. In the absence – when the UN peace plan was discounted – of any more committed strategy for bringing the rule of law to a country which had blanked all memory of government in the few short years since Najib's fall, the Taliban, on the face of it, could be viewed as supplying a uniquely eccentric alternative – whatever fears the movement ultimately raised that it would pour yet more petrol on the fire. Arson had rarely been a US qualm in Afghanistan.

From being the Armageddon of the great powers in the 1980s, Afghanistan had become their rubbish tip: a graveyard for peace overtures and reconstruction plans – and a sanctuary for graduates of Islam's most influential *jihad*. What in the West had been seen exclusively as a duel of the Cold War, with both sides using Afghans as proxies, had served in the East as the forcing ground for an entire generation of Islamist freedom fighters, men who had looked in turn at their blue-eyed Soviet or US paymasters and could not, finally, tell the difference. Inspired by their audacity in the clash with the Red Army, they returned to raise insurgencies in their own lands.

The Afghan *jihad* united the Muslim world like no other twentieth-century event until Bosnia, another milestone in the wider conflict between Western secularism and radical Islam – crusader and saracen. For a decade, it was the East's equivalent of the Spanish civil war, a rite of passage, symbolic but still entirely genuine, between absolute values which wrestled over the destiny of the Muslim century. *Jihad*, in Western eyes, had been a worthy rallying call when it was mobilised against the Soviet Union but, as it began to leak out and corrode the governments which sponsored it in Afghanistan – Saudi Arabia, Egypt and Pakistan – it became speedily demonised. That polarisation quickened after the 1991 Gulf War, which split the Muslim world into the rival camps of governments which appeased Western foreign policy and energy priorities, and those which openly defied them.

It culminated in a desecration that was experienced throughout the Islamic world – the garrisoning in 1991 of 'Christian' troops in Saudi Arabia, keeper of the two shrines of Mecca and Medina. But the truly defining moment was the 1993 bombing of the New York World Trade Centre, the first foreign-backed act of aggression on US soil since the Japanese attacked Pearl Harbor in 1942. The tremors from the blast urgently altered the way that the US looked at the post-Soviet and the Muslim worlds. Having manipulated Islam's convoluted, but impotent, quarrels for decades, Washington awoke to the knowledge that, in the two years since the Soviet empire fell, it had replaced Moscow as the only Western power occupying the lands of the *Umma*, or Muslim community, and, therefore, the most politically convenient target of international *jihad*. Even more surprising, perhaps, its global civil and military infrastructure were defenceless in the face of dedicated and well-planned sabotage.

The literature dealing with state-sponsored terrorism at an international level, or *Hizballah* International as it is known, is as suspect as it is sensational, being based on information leaked by one or other intelligence service in the countries most affected by Islamist subversion. It needs to be treated with extreme caution, rather like CIA estimates of the Soviet military capability in the 1980s, particularly at a time when Tehran had largely replaced Moscow as Washington's foremost cause of insecurity. Nonetheless, the conviction had gained ground in the early 1990s that Islamist organisations across the world had begun to pool resources in order to maximise the impact of their operations against mutual enemies – the United States, Israel and pro-Western Arab governments. In the few reports that saw the light, Tehran's *al-Quds* (Jerusalem) organisation was identified as the organising genius of what was characterised, in Washington at least, as a fully-fledged international conspiracy to destroy US installations and take American lives.[1] Afghanistan was identified as its training ground.

No other country in the world offered a better selection of asylum or arms than Afghanistan in the early 1990s. With no effective central government, it was wide open to any renegade who, upon coming to terms with the local military commander over *chai* could lead an unrestricted life by satellite telephone, immune from intruders and cocooned by the Pashtun's traditional hospitality to fugitives from state 'justice'. As for weaponry, the US had shipped hundreds of thousands of tonnes to the *mujahedin* in the previous decade, an armoury that came back to haunt as it surged over the borders and into the local flashpoints – Kashmir, Baluchistan, Karachi, Tajikistan, Swat and China's Xinjiang province – all of which shared an Islamist dimension, tending to confirm the analysis that much of the region was careering towards 'Afghanisation'.

In 1994, Congress had voted an official budget of $18 million for operations to destabilise Iran, a programme which gathered momentum with an outright trade embargo the following year, as President Clinton nominated 'global terrorism', especially from the Moslem world, as 'the most significant threat to the West at the end of the twentieth century'.[2] Washington's relations with Islamabad had also undergone another sea-change between the Soviet withdrawal from Afghanistan in 1989 and 1994 when, after five years of increasingly stony diplomacy, a new south Asia department was created at the State Department, headed by Robin Raphel, former political counsellor at the US Embassy in New Delhi.

US policy since 1991 had nourished a wave of anti-US feeling in a population only too conscious of the sacrifices it had made in a war, originally sold on the basis of a spurious solidarity with embattled Islam. The abrupt cessation of $600 million of aid each year in 1992; the refusal to deliver military aircraft already paid for; efforts to block Pakistan's emergence as a nuclear state; and the threat to blacklist it as an 'exporter of terrorism' had all been interpreted as means of hobbling Islamabad's geopolitical ambitions and, by logical extension, those of the Muslim world. The equally abrupt end of US assistance to Afghanistan in 1992, ostensibly on the grounds that it was a narcotics-producing state, had further rankled, leaving several million Pashtun refugees chasing the same jobs as their Pakistani hosts.

Raphel's first impressions left little doubt as to the motives for what was a timely revival of US engagement. 'Afghanistan,' she told a press conference in 1996, 'has become a conduit for drugs, crime and terrorism that can undermine Pakistan, the neighbouring Central Asian states and have an impact beyond Europe and Russia.' Terrorist incidents in the Middle East, she said, had been definitively linked to training camps on Afghan territory.[3] Her warning was almost a word-for-word echo of Najibullah's prediction four years earlier.[4]

Afghanistan's links with what would evolve into an international Islamist movement of terror had two distinct phases. From 1985 onwards, when Saudi Arabia increased its financial aid to the anti-Soviet *jihad*, some 14–25,000 Arab volunteers had made their way to the front to join up with the *mujahedin*, predominantly with the ISI protege, Gulbuddin Hekmatyar, or Abdul Rasul Sayyaf, leader of *Ittehad-i Islami* and a Riyadh favourite for sectarian reasons.[5] Neither Hekmatyar nor Sayyaf made any secret of their anti-Western stance, in spite of the aid they also received from the US and Europe. Hekmatyar, whose political ardour was modelled on that of revolutionary Iran – from which he also extracted funding[6] – had long been identified with extreme Islamist movements from around the world, a trait which endeared him to the pan-Islamist President Zia and private sympathisers in the Gulf. In 1991, both Hekmatyar and Sayyaf had denounced Washington's declaration of war against Iraq, refusing to send even a token force to support the Gulf alliance in spite of their debts both to the US and Saudi Arabia.[7]

The majority of Arab volunteers came from the non-oil world – Sudan, Chad, Mauritania, Somalia and Yemen – but as many as 5,000 Saudis, 2,000 Egyptians and 2,800 Algerians were also reported to be in their ranks.[8] Among the Pashtun, Arab 'Afghans' gained a reputation for enforced marriages, excessive brutality and an intolerance of the local Hanafi ritual, though they fought with conspicuous courage in the border areas adjacent to North West Frontier Province.[9] Arab 'Afghans' continued to be visibly active in Khost, Kunar and Jalalabad until at least 1993, and another force was based in Kunduz, close to the frontier with Tajikistan, another scene of Islamist insurrection.[10]

With the demobilisation that followed the Soviet withdrawal, Arab 'Afghans' were sighted further afield. Two thousand veterans reportedly joined the Groupe Islamique Armée (GIA) in Algeria when the military seized power after the Islamist victory in the elections of January 1992, while other contingents surfaced in Kashmir, Somalia, Yemen, Azerbaijan, Bosnia-Herzegovina, Chechnya, Tajikistan and even the Philippines, where they were identified fighting alongside the Moro Liberation Front.[11] With little to offer but fighting skills, it was inevitable that a large proportion of the 'international brigade' would graduate to mercenary status – 'rent-a-*jihad*', to use one journalist's phrase – particularly after March 1993 when, under US pressure, Pakistan issued a deadline for all 'Arabs' to leave the country. Less predictable was that a core in their ranks would go on to instil panic in the mind of the world's last superpower.

Nangarhar had developed into a sanctuary for absconding terrorists by 1993. Mohammad Shawky al-Isambouli, brother of the Afghan veteran who led the organisation responsible for assassinating President Anwar Sadat in 1981, had sought shelter there after being sentenced to death *in absentia* in 1992.[12] Aimal Khansi, number-one on the FBI's 'most wanted' list for the murder of two CIA employees on the doorstep of the agency's Fort Langley headquarters on 25 January 1993, had enjoyed Afghan hospitality for four years until he was finally lured to a Peshawar hotel in mid-1997 following an operation which cost $3.2 million and, reportedly, starred special agents, disguised in *burkha*.[13] On 31 July 1993, Hekmatyar – in his capacity as prime minister – offered asylum to Sheikh Omar Abdel Rahman, then about to stand trial for the World Trade Centre bombing.[14] Another famous fugitive was Ibrahim al-Mekkawi, who fled to Pakistan after Sadat's murder and was reportedly running training camps in Nangarhar. By March 1997, when Islamabad finally signed an extradition agreement with Cairo – once a major weapons-supplier for the Afghan *jihad* – some 1,200 Egyptian militants were thought to be loitering with intent in the tribal trust territories, or over the Afghan border.[15]

Most Arab 'Afghans' entered Pakistan with the help of the *Jamaat-i Islami*, the Pakistani branch of the Muslim Brotherhood and the main conduit for the ISI's aid from the Arab world. But the largest private recruitment organisation was Qa'ida (The Base), located in Peshawar, and financed by Prince Turki bin-Faisal, a nephew of King Faisal and head of the Saudi external intelligence service, the *Mukhabarat*.[16] The agency was administered by Osama bin-Ladin, the scion of a family construction business, close to the Saud dynasty, which had its roots in Yemen's Hadramaut but had since diversified around the world as the Saudi Investment Co. (SICO), with offices in London, Geneva, Curaçao, the Cayman Islands and the US.[17] In 1992, the head of the bin-Ladin family had established two fellowships in Islamic studies in Harvard University.[18]

Born in 1957, bin-Ladin flew into Peshawar days after the Soviet invasion, but he stayed long enough in the nerve centre of *jihad* to build enduring contacts, based on faith and funding, not just with the *mujahedin* chiefs, but the ISI and the Arab 'Afghans' – as well as to break irrevocably with the rulers of his own country. When Saudi Arabia suspended its support to the Arab 'Afghan' cause in 1990, bin-Ladin went rogue, setting up a private base near Jalalabad and activating links with Saudi exiles in Iran and Syria. Two years later, he was in Sudan, where diplomatic isolation of the military junta had led to an almost last-resort alliance with Iran in exchange for oil. He lived in Omdurman under the protection of Prime Minister Hassan al-Turabi, a spiritual leader of the Muslim Brotherhood and Tehran's closest friend in Africa. While there, his wealth was identified as a primary source of finance for Egypt's *Gamaat al-Islamiya*, headed by Ayman al-Zawahiri. In 1994, Riyadh froze bin-Ladin's assets and cancelled his passport, effectively declaring him a public enemy.[19]

The details of bin-Ladin's life have since passed out of the personal and into the realm of legend, a process he encourages in interviews which gild his image as a blend of the then Khartoum-based assassin, Carlos the Jackal, the Great Gatsby and a latterday Old Man of the Mountains. Estimates of his wealth varied madly from £100 million to $7 billion, a figure allegedly supplemented by a heroin-trafficking operation run jointly with commanders from Hekmatyar's *Hizb-i Islami*.[20] On the one hand, he is the equal of princelings and presents a model of spiritual gallantry for the young Turks within the lower reaches of the Saud family tree: on the other, the intellectual consistency of his graduation from a minor engineer in the Afghan *jihad* to the outlaw symbol of a defiant Islam has won him an unassailable status throughout the Muslim world. By his own account, Riyadh had offered to pay two billion Saudi riyals (£339m)[21] if he would call off the *jihad* he declared against his motherland in late 1996, while one reputable news magazine claimed that he gave the Taliban $3 million to buy the defections which opened the road to Kabul in September 1996.[22]

The allegation that Riyadh had tried to buy back bin-Ladin's loyalty was curious, for it implied that Saudi Arabia had found common cause with a nemesis described by the State Department as 'one of the most significant financial sponsors of Islamic terrorist activities in the world today'.[23] Bin-Ladin's name had been variously linked – sometimes, one suspects, almost willy-nilly – to terrorist operations in Egypt, Yemen, Somalia, Saudi Arabia and the US, although his cloak of mystery was of a kind to which rumours naturally clung. With King Fahd gravely ill by the mid-1990s and his quarrelling sons casting round for a way of securing the succession of his dynasty, there can be no doubt that the rebel bin-Ladin had become an enemy with which to reckon – and, perhaps, do business. The riddle of whether he had been definitively recruited as the *Mukhabarat*'s Taliban controller or, conversely, that the Taliban had received financial wings from Riyadh to hasten the terrorist's capture may never be solved. But, like the Taliban, bin-Ladin was master of the back channel, the art of bribery and, at least, he spoke the same spiritual language.

Bin-Ladin had epitomised Afghanistan's transition from an accidental to a mature terrorist 'state'. After his expulsion from Sudan in 1993, he transferred to Nangarhar where, according to Saudi intelligence, he ran the camp which trained three of the four men arrested for the November 1995 bombing of a US military facility in Riyadh.[24] He was also implicated in the June 1996 bombing of a US air force housing estate at Khobar Towers, Dahran, which claimed 19 American lives and injured hundreds more – as was his family business, which won the $150 million tender for refurbishment. Sheikh Omar Abdul Rahman, perpetrator of the World Trade Centre bombing in 1993, was also a colleague: Abdul Rahman's two sons had fought in the *jihad* and he had bin-Ladin's Peshawar address in his pocket when arrested.[25]

Investigations after the Khobar bombing revealed traces of an organisation which, far from the standard media description of a rabble of ill-disciplined proto-martyrs, was truly global in coordina-

tion and reach. Preparations for the explosion at the King Abdul-Aziz air base had been made at least six months earlier and required extensive reconnaissance, the smuggling of explosives from the Middle East and the infiltration into Saudia Arabia of terrorists whose names were already well-known to the *Mukhabarat* and US intelligence. Some were Tehran-based Saudi Shias, like Ahmad Mughasil, but the Iranian intelligence officers held responsible for masterminding the bombing had allegedly been impressed by the strength and commitment of the Saudi Islamist opposition within the country.[26] This was an undoubted tribute to bin-Ladin's example and his far-flung influence.

Bin-Ladin's significance went even further, if US intelligence sources are to be credited. According to a scrupulous account in the journal *Strategic Policy* (SP), the shadowy financier had become an integral part of *Hizballah* International, a pan-Islamic terrorist conglomerate conceived by the new Iranian chief of external intelligence, Mehdi Chamran, and designed to carry out precision attacks into the heart of US, Saudi and Egyptian power.[27] Several of these operations, including the Khobar bombing and the assassination of a female US diplomat in Egypt, were sufficiently well-advanced to be incorporated in Chamran's new strategy, formally unveiled by Iran's spiritual leader, Ayatollah Ali Khameini at his Friday sermon of 7 June 1996, and described as carrying the *jihad* into 'all continents and countries'.[28]

A two-day 'terrorist' summit was reportedly held in Tehran two weeks later which attracted delegates from Islamic groups from around the world. Senior commanders from nine well-established organisations, including Palestine's Islamic *Jihad* and the PFLP, the Lebanese *Hizballah*, the Egyptian *Jihad, Hamas*, the Kurdish PKK and the Islamic Change Movement in the Gulf agreed at the conference to unify their financial resources and standardise combat training in some 30 states in order to establish 'inter-operability'.[29] A committee of three, composed of bin-Ladin, Imad Mughaniya of the Lebanese *Hizballah*'s special operations command and Ahmad Salah of the Egyptian *Jihad*, was appointed to meet every month, under Chamran's chairmanship, to vet and coordinate terrorist 'works in progress'.[30]

SP's senior editor Yossef Bodansky, later appointed director of the US House of Representatives' Task Force on Terrorism and Unconventional Warfare, claimed that a second summit of key leaders was held the following month, July, in the 'biggest training camp for

Arab "Afghans", quite close to the Pakistani border town of Konli' – a town that does not appear on any detailed map. Among those present were bin-Ladin; Ayman al-Zawahiri, the leader of Egypt's main terrorist group; Abdul-Rasul Sayyaf; commanders from *Hizb-i Islami, Hamas, Hizballah* and Algeria's GIA; as well as senior officers from the Iranian and Pakistani intelligence services.[31] Bodansky's detailed account of that meeting suggested that he had somehow gained access to its minutes, but, however compromised that may make it appear, it also raised a number of intriguing queries.

Was it possible that a Shia Iran could successfully bridge the sectarian divide and command the loyalty of revolutionary Sunni factions. Certainly, yes: *Hamas* and *Hizballah* both had Iranian support in efforts to derail the Arab-Israeli peace process in the Middle East and, since the rise of the Taliban, Tehran had swung its influence behind Rabbani, a decision which, in Washington, probably amounted to the kiss of death for the regime. Secondly, could officers from the Iranian and Pakistani intelligence services, as Bodansky claims, have discovered ground so mutual that they were prepared to contemplate what amounted to treachery? Even this proposition is credible, for there were known to be powerful elements within the ISI still committed to President Zia's Islamist mission, despite Mrs Bhutto's policy of disproving US accusations that Pakistan was actively sponsoring international terrorism.

As a token of good faith, she had handed over Ramzi Ahmad Yusuf, the alleged mastermind of the World Trade Centre operation, to the US authorities in February 1995, a gesture quickly followed by the assassination of two US diplomats in Karachi one month later. Mrs Bhutto's apparent realignment with the pro-Western bloc of Arab states prompted a flurry of unclaimed terrorist operations in Pakistan. In December 1995, a suicide attack on the Egyptian Embassy in Islamabad left 16 dead, and 31 people were killed after a bomb was planted in one of the busiest shopping areas of Peshawar shortly after.

Despite Bhutto's more conciliatory approach, Pakistan was identified in 1997 as the 'world's leader in hosting international terrorist organisations', with 63 separate camps for Sikh and Kashmiri separatists, and others training militants for cross-border operations inside India.[32] Pabi refugee camp near Jallozai, 40 km east of Peshawar, was the main operational base for the Arab 'Afghans', but others were situated on Pakistani soil at Warsak, Miram shar and Sa'ada refugee camps.[33] In May 1997, some 3,000 Arab 'Afghan'

families were said to be living in all four camps which were reportedly supervised by representatives of Hekmatyar, Sayyaf and the Taliban.[34] Such proliferation, indicative both of Pakistan's lack of control over the border territories and the ISI's continuing tendency to make policy at odds with the government's stated objectives, was matched only in Afghanistan where bin-Ladin's camps, Badr-1 and Badr-2 near the town of Khost, hosted between 1,000 and 2,500 trainees from the Gulf, Palestine, Tajikistan, Egypt, the Philippines and China's Muslim and oil-rich province of Xinjiang.[35]

Mindful of his own security, bin-Ladin then lived three hours' drive to the north of Jalalabad, surrounded by 350 personal bodyguards.[36] Even allowing for journalistic licence, his eyrie was as impressive as it was vertiginous. Situated at 2,500 metres, at the head of a road he had personally built to facilitate the anti-Soviet war in the Kunar valley, the camp is defended by anti-aircraft guns, tanks, armoured vehicles, rocket launchers and Stinger missiles and equipped with generators, computers and a 'huge' database.[37] Bin-Ladin, like his men – who are all 'doctors, engineers, teachers' – lived in a cave which

> resembles a room, six metres long and four metres wide. In the middle, there is a library full of heritage and interpretation books, such as Ibn-Taymiyah's *Fatwas*, the *Prophet's Biography* by Ibn-Hisham and so on. There are five beds made of very hard wood. They look like those platforms used in vegetable markets. As for the walls, they are decorated with Kalashnikovs.[38]

Tall, slight and dressed in the by-now traditional attire of *shalwar kamees* topped with a camouflage jacket, bin-Ladin had a modesty unusual for a man on the run from the world's most extensive intelligence dragnet. His relationship with the Taliban, however, was possibly more immediately perturbing. When he told the journalist Robert Fisk in late 1997 that he had 'struggled alongside' the Taliban since 1979, he was clearly speaking metaphorically, though his reference to the 'obvious improvement' since they assumed control of Jalalabad should be taken with a pinch of salt.[39] One of his two media visitors around that time had enjoyed a Taliban escort on the the journey from Torkham Gate to Jalalabad.[40] But bin-Ladin's declaration of *jihad* against US soldiers in Saudi Arabia, during a televised interview with the CNN's Peter Arnett in May 1997, appears to have stretched his hosts' patience.[41] Soon after, he was persuaded to move with his three wives from Jalalabad to Kandahar, where he set up home close to the airport. The Kandahar governor, Mullah Mohammad Hassan, told journalists: 'He is a human being and we have to rescue him.'[42]

It was a very different approach from the one publicised shortly after Kabul fell in September 1996. The Taliban were prompt to dissociate themselves from international terrorism, asserting that Afghanistan would be used neither as a training ground nor as a haven for foreign extremists. Shir Mohammad Stanakzai, then acting foreign minister, announced: 'If foreign terrorists fall into the Taliban's hands, we will punish them.'[43] But this, perhaps, was to encrypt an answer to the question posed in the Western mind: in the Afghan equivalent, a terrorist is someone who, first and foremost, damages Islam; all Muslims are brothers; and a foreigner is always non-Muslim. One of the most glowing tributes paid to bin-Ladin in Jalalabad was that he used his own money to hire Haji Qadir's plane to carry Nangarhar notables to Mecca on pilgrimage.[44] Certainly, not the act of a 'terrorist'.

But was he the Taliban's honoured guest or a hostage? Some weeks after the fall of Kabul, bin-Ladin had been seen in the capital, a VIP passenger in an armoured personnel carrier and in the company of 'a retired, high-ranking Pakistani air force officer'.[45] The Saudi had spent half his life with ISI officers and *mujahedin* but, even so, that apparent camaraderie was hard to square with the Islamabad-Riyadh axis, then believed to underpin the Taliban's success and which, logically, might rather have sought his extradition. The sighting naturally led to speculation that he had won a reprieve for his Khost training camps and the base near Jalalabad and hinted at his possible role in financing the Taliban's rise to power. However, it also preceded the 5 November fall of Mrs Bhutto and Brigadier Babar by several weeks. With the new government of Prime Minister Nawaz Sharif safely ensconced at the end of that month, bin-Ladin mused that he might spend a little more time among the Waeela tribe in northern Yemen, a suggestion that Sana'a frostily rejected.[46]

Still he lingered. But the Taliban had begun to explore more confidently the terrorist assets they had inherited since the fall of Kabul. On 10 December, Information Minister Mullah Amir Khan Muttaqi said that, while the movement supported the struggle of the Islamists in Tajikistan, it had no 'special relationship' with them. Nonetheless, the Tajik opposition leader, Abdullah Nouri, flew into Kandahar to meet Mullah Mohammad Omar, who observed 'that the rights of the *mujahedin* should also be given to them.'[47] A more practical ally, however, was Jalaluddin Haqqani, the veteran *Hizb-i Islami (Khalis)* commander in Khost, who led the forces which captured and looted the city in March 1991 and who served, farcically in view of his blood-thirsty reputation, as minister of justice in the first *mujahedin* government of 1992. Haqqani had also controlled access to bin-Ladin's training camps at Badr-1 and Badr-2, which housed some 2,000 terrorist operatives.[48]

According to pro-Rabbani sources, Haqqani had defected to the Taliban sometime in autumn 1996, well before the fall of the capital – but whether under pressure from Pakistan, Saudi Arabia, or at the prompting of bin-Ladin himself remains open to surmise.[49] After the capture of Kabul, he installed his menage in a villa in Wazir Akbar Khan, doing aggressive service as a commander in the winter campaign north of Kabul, where he was accused of 'ethnic-cleansing' the Tajik villages around Istalif and Karabagh. Two years later, in a continuation of the gallows humour which characterised Haqqani's government service, he represented Afghanistan as the Taliban's minister of tribes. Whatever other services he performed, however – and for which of his several patrons – none of the foreign terrorists in his gift were used to reinforce the Taliban as they fought their way northwards through the snow in 1996. Sources claimed they were far too valuable to be wasted as cannon fodder.[50]

The Khost contingent had included several hundred militants from the *Harakat ul-Mujahideen* (HUM), parent of *Harakat ul-Ansar* (HUA), a terrorist group with alleged ISI connections which, in 1993, launched a bloody war of liberation against Indian rule in Kashmir. HUM's secretary-general, Fazi Rahman Khalil, like many other party members, had been blooded in the *jihad* fighting alongside Haqqani's forces, where he also developed ties with Maulana Fazl ul-Rahman, head of the *Jamiat ul-Ulama-i Islam* (JUI), a political ally of Mrs Bhutto and the supplier, via his network of *madrassa* in the tribal trust areas, of much of the Taliban manpower.[51] The alliance between the JUI and HUM was so close that one Western intelligence analyst described the HUA as 'essentially the armed wing of the JUI'. But only one of them, perhaps: for the HUM also had links to *Al Faran*, the Kashmiri militant group which kidnapped six Western tourists in 1995, decapitating one, a Norwegian, shortly afterwards; as well as to the radical anti-Shia party, *Sipan-i Saheba*, responsible for a wave of sectarian killings in Pakistan, and suspected of involvement in the assassination of several Iranian diplomats in Lahore.[52]

As the root and branch of the Taliban's extended family of terrorist affiliations was made apparent, it also became obvious that Stanakzai's initial commitment to dismantling the training camp network had been revised. In February 1997, Egyptian intelligence announced that bin-Ladin was still training 1,000 fighters in Khost, accusing the Taliban of 'breaking their pledge'.[53] Later that year, BBC journalist Rahimullah Yusufzai reported from Khost that training camps, previously used by *Hizb-i Islami* and Massoud's *Jamiat-i Islami*, also remained open. They had merely been transferred to Haqqani's successor, and local placeman, Sayed Abdullah, who had reallocated them to the HUA, which was then training 50 Arabs and 300 Pakistani or Kashmiri fighters for the armed struggle against India.[54]

Still, bin-Ladin dallied. It was reported in late 1998 that he had married one of his daughters to Mullah Mohammad Omar's son, so tying the Taliban leader with bonds of blood, as well as hospitality. His new accommodation close to Kandahar airport, however, suggested he was prepared to bolt at any moment – though the number of boltholes was fast diminishing. In May 1997, Iranians elected the moderate Mohammad Khatami as president, and he initiated tentative moves towards normalising relations with Washington after 18 years of rancour. This, quite feasibly, closed any immediate prospect of an exile orchestrated by his friends in Iranian intelligence.

But it was mooted he had, by then, become the pawn in a different bargain. Whatever deal the Taliban may have originally undertaken with the *Mukhabarat*, the issue of international aid had since entered the equation. In early 1998, the Taliban were reported to have refused to hand over bin-Ladin unless Riyadh paid $400 million in cash.[55] With the relaunch of the peace effort in April, US ambassador to the UN Bill Richardson paid a one-day visit to Kabul, where he urged Taliban leaders to keep bin-Ladin 'under wraps'. He later told reporters that the Saudi had 'threatened' the mission and become a 'very negative force' in the attempt to draw up a truce between the Taliban and the Northern Alliance. Yet no attempt had been made to secure bin-Ladin's extradition. 'He is a guest,' he explained ruefully, 'and Pashtun traditions do not allow any harm to come to friends and guests.'[56]

Particularly when they are worth more than their weight in gold.

10 Oblivion's Feast

With the capture of Kandahar in October 1994, the Taliban took command of the southern outlet of a smuggling empire which, since the withdrawal of Soviet forces, had expanded deep into Central Asia and beyond, opening a back door into Pakistan's heavily-protected market of 135 million people. In this prototype of the regional trading bloc which Interior Minister Naseerullah Babar was so keen to create, entrepreneurs inside Afghanistan and an 18,000-strong community of expatriates in the port of Karachi played – and continue to play – pivotal roles as middlemen and hauliers.

There had been half-hearted attempts to curb these 'cross-border movements', as the IMF tastefully terms them, but well-established combines continued to swamp Pakistan's economy with impunity. A flood of cut-price manufactures from the CIS, including tyres, vehicle spares and machine parts, along with consumer electronics from the Far East and barrels of Iranian oil, streamed across the two official customs points at Torkham Gate in the Khyber Pass and Chaman in the south.

Border smuggling was not a new phenomenon: in North West Frontier Province and Baluchistan, where Pakistani law does not apply, it had practically become a way of life, along with the trade in arms and narcotics. But smuggling took off as the old political and economic order wilted. A north-south axis grew up to service the Central Asian hinterland. New routes swarmed across the 1,500 kilometre border with Pakistan, following the dirt roads used by the ISI to convoy military supplies to the *mujahedin*.

The value of the genuine Central Asian trade with Pakistan shot up from $100 million in 1993 to $350 million a year later,[1] but the smuggling industry was probably worth much more. Dubai is the main entrepot for trans-Afghan smuggling, with 80 companies dedicated to trading across the narrow Straits of Hormuz to the Iranian port of Bandar Abbas. From there, it is just five days' journey by road to the Pakistani border, at freight prices one-quarter of the alternative routes. When Iran closed the border in June 1997, in response to the Taliban's expulsion of its diplomats in Kabul, some 1,400 containers bound for Afghanistan were stranded in Bandar Abbas after just 10 days.[2]

The breadth and scale of these parallel operations were a tribute to Afghan resourcefulness and the strength of family ties, which had easily outlasted the creation, a century earlier, of the Durand Line. Referred to – only half jokingly – as Pashtunistan's 'Berlin Wall', it was transformed by Afghan merchants into a vast Panama Canal, allowing commercial passage between divided hemispheres and the free circulation of otherwise banned commodities and substances.

The concentricity of the drugs, arms and smuggling rings around a single imploded state created the conditions for the birth of a unique, post-modern phenomenon: an illegal trading empire that defied customs, frontiers and laws, connected New York and Dubai with Osaka and the two Koreas but which, to all intents and purposes, was controlled by scarcely literate warlords living hundreds of miles from the nearest bank or fax. Its capital market was the roadside money booth where, amid the bundles of bills from a coterie of nations, the only real currency was trust – and the fear of reprisal, if it were broken.

Though *Hizb-i Islami*'s stranglehold on the road from Kabul, and General Dostum's control of the Salang Tunnel, ensured there was little transit traffic from the north or west, Torkham Gate was the hub of a booming re-export operation which circumvented Islamabad's high duties on imports. The Transit Trade Agreement (TTA), signed between Pakistan and Afghanistan in 1965, effectively handed private traders a blank cheque once government monitoring mechanisms had broken down, as occurred after 1992.

The TTA entitled Afghan merchants and their Pakistani partners to import through Karachi unlimited quantities of duty-free goods, allegedly for consumption in Afghanistan. Along with food, fuel and other genuine necessities, however, millions of dollars' worth of vehicles, TVs, videos and CDs, with consignment notes duly signed for the penniless inhabitants of Kabul, were daily waived through Torkham by complaisant customs officials. Once inside the territory of the Nangarhar *shura*, these high-value products were openly transferred to camel and mule for the journey back across the Khyber foothills, and reloaded onto trucks bound for the bazaars of Peshawar.

This trade – along with many others – had made Haji Abdul Qadir, the then-governor of Nangarhar province, an extremely wealthy man. His private fleet of ageing Antonovs, flagged Khyber Airlines in an excess of romance, cost $53 million[3] to assemble and flew in regularly from Dubai, loaded with Pancheros, TVs, air conditioners and generators. His mud citadel, at the head of the poppy-growing

Surkhrud valley, was outclassed in splendour only by the fortress in Landi Kotal, on the Pakistan side of the border, owned by Haji Ayub Afridi, the lord of Khyber heroin dealing, who surrendered to the US authorities in 1996. Standing on the pitch-black tarmac that leads 15 kilometres up to the governor's palace, the only newly-paved highway in Afghanistan in over 20 years, it was easy to conceive that the two men saw themselves as the Murdoch and Maxwell of Pashtun commercial *chutzpah*.

Smuggling had always been more crucial to the Kandahar economy, which suffers regular drought, forcing its inhabitants to rely upon imported grain. Cross-border trading provided one of the few hedges against such eventualities, but it was a far riskier investment after 1992, as the three quarrelling *mujahedin* factions in the city ate into fast-depleting profit margins. The 670 km road from Herat, crossroads of the Central Asian and Iranian trades, passed through the checkpoints of a myriad of rival commanders, each loosely affiliated with one or other faction, but of one mind when it came to extorting 'taxes' from passing vehicles.

The importance of this road, Highway One, was to soar in the spring of 1995 when the Pakistani authorities limited duty-free eligibility to just a few categories of basic goods, slashing duty and sales tax on a further 30 items in a bid to cut down abuse of the TTA. The decision, taken by the finance ministry, might have been a response to the IMF's dismay at Pakistan's fiscal chaos, but it coincided with the Taliban's capture of Kandahar and the beginning of their advance upon Herat. On 30 March 1995, Babar unilaterally announced that Pakistan would provide $3 million and workers to repair Highway One. The decision enraged the Rabbani government, which had assumed, quite mistakenly perhaps, that Kabul, and not Islamabad, had suzerainty over the western extremities of its embattled domain. Yet more traffic shifted to the western route.

If, in the eyes of their Pakistani and Afghan sponsors, the Taliban's primary mission had been to clear the Kandahar-Herat road of bandits, that task had largely been accomplished by September 1995, when Herat fell after several months of fighting. But this did not spell an end to one of Kandahar's most profitable lines of business. The Taliban showed not the least sign that they wished to disrupt the trading status quo, which would have indicated, at the very least, that they were serving Pakistani, as opposed to smugglers' interests. They simply streamlined the movement of illicit goods across Afghan territory, by removing the obstacles posed by the predatory *mujahedin* and imposing a single, uniform tax for the benefit of their treasury.

Along with the equipment and vehicles, looted from Herat's ministries but now heading south, there was a surge of trade, as merchants in Iran, the Gulf and Turkmenistan dispatched their goods towards the raucous truck-stop at Chaman. And though an electronic *purdah* had descended upon entertainment for Afghans, with TVs and videos smashed or symbolically lynched, trucks piled to the gunwales with the products of Sony and Toshiba continued to trundle unmolested between the potholes towards the Pakistani border.

Despite tension between the Iranian government and the Taliban, border officials on both sides had been convivial when it came to facilitating trade until the closure of the embassy in Kabul in 1997. Some 80 new or reconditioned vehicles, imported from the United Arab Emirates, crossed the border post at Islam Qilla every day for onward smuggling to Pakistan. There, through the adroit falsification of registration documents, they could be sold at half the local rate.[4]

Among these vehicles were 400 single-cabined Toyota Hilux pickups in mint condition, with smoked glass, exotic decals and plates from the Emirates.[5] They had followed the usual route from Bandar Abbas but would never cross the Pakistani frontier. They were a gift to the Taliban from an unknown, but wealthy, benefactor. The ultimate beneficiary, perhaps, of the Taliban's still obscure mission. The same Toyotas would one day be loaded with troops and quivers of rockets, a white pennant flying from every aerial. If their style suggested that even the Taliban were susceptible to the swagger of fine engineering, like the 'technicals' in Somalia, the loudest message they conveyed was immediate surrender.

Mad Max. Meet the motorised mullahs.

* * *

Behind the warmth which greeted the Taliban during their liberation of the Durrani heartlands, there was more than a tremor of anxiety. In a series of communiques about the movement's goals, its leaders had made a definitive commitment to the eradication of opium, the most crucial element of all in the economy of southern Afghanistan.

Indeed, the Taliban's zeal over the matter tended to reinforce perceptions in many quarters that the movement was receiving covert US support as the only practicable means of stemming the astronomical rise in output from the 'Golden Crescent'. In 1994, production had peaked at 3,270 tonnes of dry opium, pushing Afghanistan past Burma as the world's largest producer, and creating a regional shortage of acetic anhydride, the chemical used to convert morphine base into heroin.[6]

Always a modest grower for domestic use, Afghan opium production rose to around 100 tonnes in the 1960s to satisfy demand in Iran, where a million-strong population of addicts had suffered the pangs of a 16-year ban that was only reversed in 1972. The toppling of the Shah and the Soviet invasion of Afghanistan, cascading one after the other in 1979, overturned not only the balance of power in an energy-producing belt that stretched from the Straits of Hormuz to the Arabian Sea. Combined with the failure of the rains in the Golden Triangle, they created an upheaval in the way that heroin had traditionally been supplied to, and distributed in, the West.

While the Soviet occupation blocked the Silk Route along which southeast Asian heroin was traditionally moved to Turkey, the ayatollahs' ban on narcotics forced many Iranian dealers across the border into Pakistan. Over the next decade, the latter's expertise and capital, wedded to a vast hinterland in which poppy flourished unfettered by authority, won for Pakistan the dominant position in the European market.

By the mid-1980s, the processing and export of heroin had created a black economy in Pakistan of around $8 billion[7] – half the size of the official one – and Pakistan's military administration was showing signs of having evolved into a fully-blown narco-government. Among the high-ranking officials directly incriminated in the trade were Lieutenant-General Fazle Haq, governor of North West Frontier Province and a confidant of General Zia; Hamid Hasnain, another personal friend and vice-president of the state-owned Habib Bank; and Haji Ayub Afridi, the National Assembly member for Khyber agency, an important coordinator of Pakistan's Afghanistan policy and, according to many reports, its largest drugs baron.[8] The number of Pakistani addicts, meanwhile, had spiralled from nil in 1979 to between 1.2 and 1.7 million at the end of 1988.

Such a rapid rate of growth would have been impossible without the protection or active collaboration of the ISI which, empowered by CIA funding and arms deliveries, had grown from a small military department into a modern intelligence network with a staff of 150,000 and hundreds of millions of dollars a year at its disposal.[9]

The links between the narcotics industry in Pakistan and the military were apparent from the start, with 16 officers arrested on drugs charges in 1986 alone. Vehicles of the army's National Logistics Cell were regularly discovered trafficking on their return from supply operations inside Afghanistan.[10]

The US colluded in the development of this new heroin source for fear of undermining the CIA's working alliance with General Zia and the *mujahedin*. From Peshawar, the office of US Drugs Enforcement Agency issued a stream of deflated estimates of cross-border opium production, while failing to obtain from the authorities a single investigation into any of the 40 drugs syndicates then known to be operating in Pakistani territory.[11] It was only after 1989, with the general in his grave – the victim of an unexplained air crash – and the US media again free to consider factors other than the by-then retreating Red Army, that the scale of the ISI's involvement began to emerge.

A decidedly small number of *mujahedin* commanders had actively promoted poppy cultivation during the war but, as US funding tapered off following the Soviet withdrawal and refugees returned to claim their land, its production and export finally became systematic. The process accelerated with the election in 1989 of Benazir Bhutto, whose initial crackdown on poppy-growing in Dir, Bunair, Khyber and Momand tribal agencies and the introduction of the death penalty for trafficking had the effect of switching Pakistan's own opium production over the Afghan border, where it was less vulnerable to enforcement measures.

That was the case in Nangarhar, the province adjacent to North West Frontier Province, which had been virtually depopulated during the Soviet occupation. After 1989, it was rapidly integrated with the heroin laboratories and distribution system established by the Afridi syndicate in Khyber. By 1994 – five years after the war ended – Nangarhar produced close to 1,500 tonnes of opium, or nearly half of Afghanistan's total production. One year later, it had established its own processing facilities.[12]

Even then, some districts in Nangarhar eschewed the crop altogether, usually on the orders of their local commanders. In Kunar, controlled by Wahhabi forces under Jamil ul-Rahman, opium production effectively stopped from 1990 until his murder one year later. But there were more attractive alternatives in the immediate postwar period, such as the barter of military scrap, the trade in weaponry or in illegal timber-felling.

Afghanistan was awash with weapons by the time of the Soviet withdrawal. In addition to the jets, helicopter gunships, tanks and rocket launchers supplied to the Afghan army by Moscow, the US and Saudi Arabia had funnelled an estimated $6 billion in guns and money to the *mujahedin* during the 1980s. From 1987, when Washington stepped up its covert aid programme, annual shipments of arms amounted to 65,000 tonnes. Shin Naray, the massive weapons depot built by the ISI on the border south of Kandahar, housed an estimated 15,000 truckloads of ammunition by 1993, along with 400 of the Stinger heat-seeking missiles, supplied after 1985 and which had turned the tide of the war by destroying Soviet air superiority.[13]

Much of this weaponry ended up in the tribal trust arms bazaars of Dara, Miram Shar and Landi Kotal, where rocket launchers and medium-range mortars were openly displayed for sale, like any less lethal commodity. To prevent the Stingers falling into the hands of undesirables, the CIA launched a 'buy-back' programme in 1989, offering $175,000 for each of the missiles still in *mujahedin* possession. In 1993, Congress allocated $55 million for the programme, but the missiles nevertheless found their way into the armouries of the Kurdistan Workers Party in Turkey, the GIA in Algeria, UNITA in Angola and the Iranian mafia, which deployed them to defend overland drug caravans.[14]

Timber, too, was a booming outlaw industry. Hundreds of acres of primary pine and cedar in Kunar and Paktya were hauled down the mountain sides to be sawn into cheap window frames or furniture in Pakistan for sale to the Gulf. So attractive were the profits, in fact, that their loss provoked the only significant resistance offered to the Taliban in any of the regions which had fallen under their thrall.

After expelling Haji Qadir from Jalalabad, the Taliban imposed a levy of $750 per truck of timber, before banning the trade outright. Haji Qadir, exiled in Peshawar, but aided by two other warlords, Malik Zarin and Haji Kashmir Khan, responded with a well-armed attack into Kunar in February 1997. The offensive appeared to rattle the Taliban leadership which, while denying any losses, demanded – without cracking a smile – that Pakistan desist from supporting groups seeking to destabilise the Afghan government.

Even outside Kunar, Afghans remained ambivalent about growing a crop which brought profit and opprobrium in roughly equal measure, but entailed a massive increase in workload. With no opium appetite of their own, farmers justified switching to poppy on the grounds that its effects were exported beyond the pale of Islam and outside the *pashtunwali*. With the exception of Badakhshan, the Tajik province in the northeast and the only one in Afghanistan with an addiction problem, poppy was almost exclusively a Pashtun trading activity, abetted by clan and family links in the tribal trust areas.

After the Soviet war, poppy-growing acquired the characteristics of a modern agro-business. Farmers required enormous quantities of fertilisers to make a good profit – nearly half a tonne a hectare – but traders had set up operations to supply inputs and to provide the credit with which to buy them. Indeed, opium was the only crop in Afghanistan against which cultivators could expect a cash advance against future delivery. Poppy, in fact, equalled credit and every family returning from Pakistan needed to borrow.

In Helmand and Nangarhar, which account for 80 per cent of total Afghan production, traditional poppy varieties had been replaced by genetically-enhanced seeds, which raise quality and boost yields. In both provinces, irrigated farms formerly owned by the state were set aside by commanders for the cultivation of poppy. The largest of these were in the northern reaches of the Helmand valley, a grain-producing project developed with US assistance in the 1960s, but controlled for much of the war by Mullah Nasim Akhundzada.

The 'King of Heroin', as he was known – apocryphally, perhaps – was a living rebuttal of the thesis that poppy-growing would cease if people could be convinced that it was against Islam. Mullah Nasim controlled most of the 250 tonnes of opium grown in Helmand province in the 1980s, issuing quotas to farmers which he reportedly enforced through threats of murder or castration.[17] This policy detracted not one dot from his religious prestige. Many of Afghanistan's petty drug barons have been mullahs, owing to their right to *zakat*, the 10 per cent tithe levied on all farm produce in kind, including opium. Just as many mullahs had also become commanders.

The only protagonist from the *jihad* repeatedly reported to have been engaged in the downstream end of the opium industry is Gulbuddin Hekmatyar, the ISI's chief protege and, through its influence, recipient of more than half the CIA's assistance to the Afghan resistance. Hekmatyar's commanders established six laboratories in the Koh-i Sultan district of Baluchistan in the mid-1980s to process opium from Helmand before smuggling it through the ports on the Makran coast, or across the nearby Iranian border.[18] This latter vicinity, where the borders of Iran, Pakistan and Afghanistan meet, is known suggestively in enforcement parlance as the 'zero line'.

In 1988–89, heavy fighting had broken out as Hekmatyar's forces tried to wrest control of the Helmand valley from Mullah Nasim. One year later, as deputy defence minister in the transitional Afghan government, Nasim secured an agreement with the US ambassador to Pakistan, Robert B. Oakley, to suppress poppy-growing in exchange for $2 million in 'aid', a deal which may have also contained provisions for the return of Stingers.[19] Oakley was subsequently hired by the US oil company UNOCAL to negotiate a pipeline route with the Taliban.

The ban tripled opium prices in Baluchistan, sparking off another round of fighting with *Hizb-i Islami* over a resource whose value overseas was now being counted in billions. Though the mullah was assassinated, his brother Rasul, a commander in the *Harakat-i Inqilab* party, retained control of the valley. When the US failed to deliver on its promise, opium production resumed with unprecedented vigour.

The ISI could not have been ignorant of Hekmatyar's involvement in the heroin industry: in fact, the evidence indicates that the ISI actively encouraged it after 1990, when a stunned Islamabad was informed that Washington had decided to terminate all economic and military assistance. After a decade of glorious unaccountability, the service faced a funding drought that threatened its operational capacity, while a series of elected – and, summarily, ejected – civilian prime ministers were feeling distinctly queasy about the ISI's determination to continue as Pakistan's secret government.

In an unusually frank interview in September 1994 – which he later denied – the former Pakistani prime minister, Nawaz Sharif, disclosed that General Aslam Beg, the army chief of staff, and the ISI boss, Lieutenant-General Asad Durrani, had proposed raising money for covert foreign operations through large-scale drug deals.[20] The cut in US funding coincided with a precarious escalation in the ISI's 'forward' policy, not just in Afghanistan, where Najibullah defied Western expectations by clinging to power, but in Kashmir and the Indian Punjab, where Pakistan's brazen support for the insurgents caused Washington to threaten to brand it a terrorist state.

The ISI's involvement in the Sikh separatist movement was recognised in a 1993 CIA report on Pakistan's drug trade, which stated the heroin was being used to fund its purchases of arms, adding: 'Heroin is becoming the lifeblood of Pakistan's economy and political system.' The same report named Sohail Zia Butt, a relative of Nawaz Sharif, as a suspected drug smuggler.[21] The connection between drug money and the Kashmiri insurrection was more tenuous, although the ISI, Pakistan's *Jamaat-i Islami* party and *Hizb-i Islami* were also identified as material backers of the pro-Pakistan terrorist group, *Hizb ul-Mujahideen*.

As the nineties wore on, the province of Badakhshan began to figure more prominently in narcotics dispatches. Analysis of raw opium samples showed a morphine content twice as high as anywhere else in the country, in spite of the fact that Badakhshan farmers used neither fertilisers nor irrigation. More alarming still for investigators was the fact that the forgotten province, controlled by President Rabbani and Ahmad Shah Massoud, had become the stepping stone for an entirely new means of conveying opiates to Europe, via Tajikistan, Uzbekistan and Russia's Central Asian railway service.

Another rascal from the gallery of regional grotesques, Aliosha the Hunchback, commanded the flow of opium over the Pamir peaks into the Tajik region of Gorno-Badakhshan, until his alleged murder by Russian border guards in 1996.[22] Since 1992, the region has been controlled by the Islamic Revival Party (IRP), which had prosecuted a bloody civil war against the Russian-backed regime in Dushanbe, using cash gleaned from the heroin trade and IRP supporters in Iran and Pakistan. Both Hekmatyar and Massoud actively supported the Tajik rebels, offering training and sanctuary to fighters in their respective bases of Kunduz and Taloqan. According to the Vienna-based UN Drug Control Programme (UNDCP), the most significant trafficking event in the region since 1995 had been the amount of Heroin No.1 (pure heroin) and Heroin No.3 (crude heroin, or 'brown sugar') transferred from the Makran Coast and the 'zero line' into the new Central Asian corridors.[23]

To conclude that profits from the the world's only 'Islamic drugs cartel' were underwriting acts of terrorism by Islamist groups may be stretching the imagination. Drug Enforcement Agency (DEA) officials deny the linkage but, given the US role in creating the Afghan-Central Asian nexus of drugs, arms and orchestrated destabilisation, it is reasonable to assume that they would. What is certain is that the US had remarkably little influence over a process that its own agencies had, inadvertently or otherwise, set into motion in the 1980s.

Hekmatyar, the only faction leader with an internationalist profile, runs like a golden thread through this otherwise tortuous history of entanglement between the Cold War, the *jihad*, the drugs trade, regional terrorism and the intelligence establishments of two countries. Was he the accidental beneficiary of US opportunism or a kingpin of the narcotics industry, whose ambitions spanned not solely Afghanistan, but the Balkanised heartlands of Muslim Central Asia?

And was he, after the fall of Kabul and his flight into the north, finally vanquished? His former information officer responded to that query with a particularly cryptic Afghan proverb: 'There are always bones around the wolf's lair.'

* * *

It was into this complex web of high finance and low life expectancy that the Taliban ventured in October 1994, with the capture of Kandahar. In November, Uruzgan fell and, one month later, the eastern province of Zabul, with scarcely a shot being fired. In January 1995, the Taliban took control of Helmand, the source of 150 tonnes of Heroin No.1, with a total retail value in the European market of $25.5 billion at 1996 prices. Governor Ghaffar Akhundzada, a relative of the dead mullah, quit the provincial capital, Lashkargah, without a fight but when the Taliban moved into the poppy-growing districts of Musa Qala and Kajaki, his home turf, hostilities finally erupted. The religious students, and the former *mujahedin* who had since rallied to their cause, routed Ghaffar's men, suffering fewer than 50 casualties.

In capturing Helmand, the Taliban could no longer hide behind their image as an ascetic, but, essentially, naive revivalist movement with relevance only to the domestic Afghan scene. Whether by accident or design, they were now in the real world, controlling a commodity upon which vast fortunes rely. Within two years, they would have it all: 2,200 tonnes, with a final street value of $37 billion. It was the ultimate temptation for the self-styled Leader of the Faithful.

If the Taliban takeover of Helmand and, subsequently, Nangarhar and the capital were dictated by the political dynamics of heroin, it is worthwhile exploring the beneficiaries of such a campaign. Afghan gossip had long identified the US and Saudi Arabia as the Taliban's covert financiers and, whatever their ulterior designs, it was clear that the mullahs could play a useful role in stamping out the opium industry. After years of war and fragmentation, Afghanistan's main poppy-growing areas were finally controlled by a single dictatorial authority by the end of 1996. In November of that year, Giovanni Quaglia, director of the UNDCP office in Pakistan stated, somewhat blithely: 'In these circumstances, the problem can be dealt with in ten years.'[24]

And yet the consolidation of opium production under a single individual – just like the Central Asian transit trade – could be of equal advantage to the downstream processors and distributors of heroin as well. Compelled for years to deal with greedy and unpredictable *mujahedin*, a force such as the Taliban could have a 'downsizing' influence on the middle-management rung of the poppy business. It could streamline the industry and help it to fight off the global competition from emerging and more savvy poppy-planters in Colombia and Mexico.

Financial support for the Taliban, at least in the early days, appears to have been forthcoming from Afghan and Pakistani traders, concerned at the high rate of extortion on the transit routes. But parallel backing might have been furnished by heroin cartels to seize control of its supply sources or, at least, to vest them in a caretaker authority which undercut the existing financial arrangements.

Such backers would also benefit from the third strand in this hypothesis. The transfer of the heroin trade from the 'zero line' countries into the hands of the Russian 'Mafia', with its logistical advantages and lower enforcement risk, threatened the very existence of the Pakistani economy, according to CIA accounts. The capture, by a friendly force, of Helmand and Nangarhar would help to anchor these primary suppliers within the Pakistani sphere of influence, and counter-balance the attractions of the rapidly-expanding drug empire in the north.

In short, were the Taliban a genuine movement of national revival or a fifth column, playing on popular grievances, to effect radical shifts in the structure of the world's leading illicit industry? Or had they really strayed into the business by accident, gifted amateurs in pursuit of a *jihad* against corrupt commanders?

The advent of the Taliban in Kandahar immediately halved the acreage allocated for poppy for the 1995 season, a trend that farmers attributed to the fear of reprisals. But wheat prices were also booming that year. There had been a signficant carry-over from the previous bumper opium harvest and this had further depressed prices. Helmand saw its 1995 crop fall by 8 per cent, but again there were external influences at work, apart from the Taliban. Even in remote areas, Afghan poppy farmers are highly responsive to the global laws of supply and demand.

During that first season in Kandahar, the Taliban produced a catechistic booklet outlining what was permitted under religious law, and what not. It was deeply ambivalent. 'The cultivation of, and trading in *chers* (cannabis),' it read, 'is forbidden absolutely.' In Afghanistan, every village has its *chersi*, often referred to with condescending affection, but all were gone by the following season, along with the hundreds of hectares of cannabis that once surrounded Kandahar. Many users of the drug found themselves in prison.

'The consumption of opiates,' the document continued, 'is forbidden, as is the manufacture of heroin, but the production and trading in opium is not forbidden.' The Taliban justified this distinction on the basis that Afghanistan's rural economy had been so shattered by war that to eliminate poppy would push many of the 200,000 families growing the crop to the brink of starvation. But it also reflected the reality that the smoking of opium, unlike cannabis, was not a particular Pashtun vice. One Kandahari farmer put it more succinctly: 'The opium goes to our neighbours, who are our enemies, and to the infidels, who sent the guns here.'

A special envoy of the *Geopolitical Drugs Despatch (GDD)*, which monitors the global narcotics market, visited the Kandahar customs shed in November 1996. He reported:

> Even before the heavy padlock is removed, a strong smell emanates from the room. Inside, five tonnes of opium have spent two years waiting ... for the occasional journalist to pay them a visit. The five tonnes, in 50 kg sacks, ooze a blackish paste. In a corner of the room, there are a few dozen kilograms of coarsely refined brown heroin. The room next door contains hashish: 10 tonnes, the customs officer says ... That is what the Taliban's seizures amount to. They date from the movement's first few months in power.[25]

After that brief interlude, it was business as usual. It was a pragmatic decision, given that the Taliban needed to retain the support not only of the southern Pashtun, but the *mujahedin* commanders who, in most cases, had been absorbed into the movement, rather than deposed by it. To tamper with the economic status quo in the south, while pressing forward to Herat and Kabul, was to risk triggering revolts in their rear and stiffening the opposition up ahead. The Taliban simply could not afford a crusade against everyone.

In more ways than one. The *zakat* on opium, formerly paid to the village mullahs, was redirected to the Taliban treasury, netting the movement an estimated $9 million from the south's regular output of 1,500 tonnes. Apart from that, the *shura* appears to have introduced no interdiction and effected no structural changes in the way that opiates were traded in Taliban-controlled areas over a two-year period.[26]

In Mullah Mohammad Omar's home district of Maiwand, production actually doubled to 24 tonnes in 1996. Laboratories continued to operate in Nimroz, Kandahar and Helmand in spite of the ban on processing, according to the GDD. But whether the Taliban were actively involved in the trafficking end of drugs is more difficult to prove.[27] Taliban-protected drugs convoys set forth from Herat and Iran, which was fighting fierce battles with smugglers in the mountains, sent a delegation to the city in August 1996 to remonstrate with the governor, Mullah Yar Mohammad, over those cross-border movements. Cases of trafficking by air, from Kandahar to Dubai, were also reported.

In Herat, the governor appears to have taken opium's legal status a radical stage further. Customs officials from the regime of the former emir, Ismail Khan, were arrested and beaten until they made restitution to traders, whose opium they had once confiscated when, apparently, it was illegal. One prisoner, a former police officer, was 'beaten for about a week' until he submitted.[28]

Days before the fall of Kabul in September, the deputy speaker of the Organisation for Security and Cooperation in Europe, Willy Wimmer, openly accused the Taliban of smuggling heroin into Hamburg. He added that the Taliban 'clearly enjoyed the support of Russian troops in Afghanistan's border regions with Tajikistan' and demanded that the US and Saudi Arabia explain why they so obviously supported the movement. It was a garbled analysis, but an apposite question.

The US had also been wondering about the mullahs' drug habits. A DEA report in November 1996 said that 'the Taliban had reached a *de facto* agreement with cultivators, and perhaps even traffickers, to limit their attack on opium cultivation and domestic drug abuse'. The report was based on the first contacts between the Taliban leadership, the DEA and the US State Department's narcotics subsidiary, the NAS. The US satellite, usually so forgiving, determined that there were 3,000 tonnes in the fields, rather than the 2,600 tonnes declared by the UNDCP.[29]

On 11 November, shortly after the DEA report was published, the UNDCP received its first formal note that the Taliban had agreed to take the 'necessary measures' to suppress the production, processing and trafficking of narcotics in Afghanistan. The statement, from the foreign minister, Mullah Mohammad Ghaus, proposed a concerted programme of regional and international cooperation, but stressed 'the principle of non-interference in the internal affairs of states'.

The UNDCP had already devised a four-year $16.4 million programme of law enforcement and crop substitution, which offered some chance of restructuring its own crediblity after years of mis-hits in the largest opium-supplying country in the world. There was a general air of optimism, but no shortage of problems. During the DEA's visit to Kandahar, sources claim, Taliban officials were heard to use what, in diplomatic circles, had become known as the 'R-word' – recognition.[30]

Collaboration over poppy eradication would take place after state-to-state relations between Washington and Kabul were established and the Rabbani regime surrendered its seat at the UN General Assembly in New York. For the US, whose policy is to recognise states and not governments, this presented neither difficulty nor attraction. But the UN recognises governments. To sign would mean endorsing the Taliban's gender policies. Female rights in return for drug eradication. An unhappy choice.

The other contention was whether the Taliban, having taken such a *laisser-faire* attitude to local power and trading relations, could actually impose their will upon the opium lords of Helmand and Nangarhar. It is interesting, in this context, to ponder the fate of the Akhundzadas. Wealthy, gifted with dynastic continuity and a talent for killing, they nevertheless appear to have melted quietly from the Helmand scene, shortly after the Taliban takeover. Neither the DEA nor the UNDCP, which maintain a constant watch on the region, could recollect the mullah who had negotiated with the US ambassador, held a portfolio in the first Afghan Interim Government, and whose family had dominated the Helmand poppy trade for more than a decade.

That Rasul Akhundzada, his legatee, had been a commander of *Harakat-i Inqilab*, like Mohammad Omar, is more intriguing since it suggests that what had taken place in Helmand that day was less an act of submission than a gathering of old comrades.[31] But how would Rasul react – and the hundreds of others like him – when the choirboys tried to barter away his patrimony?

11 Hostages

'We've fallen into a black hole, 500 years back in history.' Former communist, reported 8 October 1996.[1]

The bodies of former President Najibullah and his brother Shahpur hung in Ariana Square for 26 hours until, at Pakistan's insistence, they were cut down and released to a Kabuli relative for burial in Paktya.[2] Elders of the Amadzhai clan, to which Najib belonged, threatened to sue the UN for failing to protect its most famous son, but the matter was forgotten amid the brouhaha which followed the loss of the capital.[3] Four days after his death, Kabul's international airport was reopened for the first time in a year to welcome the UN's new envoy to Afghanistan. Dr Holl faced an uphill task.

After an initial spurt of enthusiasm, the US, Pakistan and Saudi Arabia backed away from official recognition, realising that the fugitive Massoud still represented an inescapable threat to a movement whose policies towards women were scandalising newspaper readers in Western capitals and in the Muslim world at large. The Tajik was far from beaten: the Taliban, universally unpalatable. Official relations could wait until the movement proved beyond any doubt that it was the inalienable master of Afghanistan. Such ambiguity cast longer shadows at the UN where President Rabbani continued to occupy the General Assembly chair for Afghanistan, even going to Rome in November to attend a UN Food and Agriculture Organisation conference, although, at that point, he represented no more than the impoverished bleakness of the Little Pamirs.

All three powers besides retained the luxury of back channels to Mullah Mohammad Omar, channels which allowed them to test the military winds from a distance and fine-tune future political relations far from critical eyes. The UN, by contrast, had to take most of its decisions in public, on the hoof and with its hands tied by humanitarian considerations – as well as the real physical risk to its staff. Yet for the next two years, the organisation which had so conspicuously failed to prevent genocide in Rwanda and Bosnia was tasked with presenting a coherent Western response to what would become an unprecedented redefinition of human rights violation:

the institutionalised suppression of women. That, in itself, was tacit admission of how low on the scale of Western priorities women's rights had fallen.

It was not a pretty sight that met the envoy's eyes. Taliban strictures on the participation of females in education affected 106,256 girls, 148,223 boys and the 7,793 women who had taught them.[4] An estimated 150,000 women held jobs in Kabul before Massoud's flight; they had all gone to ground, with the 25–30,000 widows who relied upon relief aid for their survival.[5] Among the former category were Shafiqa Habibi, the country's foremost newscaster, and her 300 female colleagues at Radio Kabul; Sohaila Sidiq, chief surgeon at the 400-bed army hospital; and her sister, Dr Sidiqa Sidiq, director of the Polytechnic Institute and the first eminent Afghan woman to speak out against the Taliban. 'A movement,' she said three months later, 'no matter how strong, is just a movement. It does not last forever.' But since the fall of the city, she had left her house just four times – usually to attend funerals.[6]

Even with the lights on and the rockets sheathed, Kabul was a dark, unpredictable place. Religious observance, once a wishful, but voluntary ideal, had become the benchmark of presumed party loyalty. Men were lashed into the mosque, or the soccer stadium now transmogrified into a theatre of Taliban justice, where squealing ambulances ensured, at least, that anaesthetised thieves received the benefit of post-operative treatment. Women were less fortunate. In October, one woman had the tip of her thumb cut off for wearing nail varnish and another was whipped with a car radio antenna for letting her *burkha* slip – while a curtain fell like a deep depression on the majority who failed to qualify for such exemplary punishments. A man who had chosen not to pray was taken to the street called *Kafir*, or 'godless' and executed.[7] In the first week of October, the Taliban bulldozed 1,400 cans of Heineken and 400 bottles of spirits with a Soviet tank, leaving the UN guesthouse the sole drinking hole in an otherwise dry city: Agence France-Presse reported an 80 per cent drop in weddings.[8] Although the end of the Taliban siege had indisputably improved living conditions in Kabul, 125 Afghan refugees a day shambled across the border to Pakistan in early October, rising to 870 per day by the end of the month.[9]

Under President Rabbani, 200 female staff had worked at Kabul's Mullalai hospital but, even though the Taliban exempted the medical profession from its ban on women's employment, barely 50 would appear regularly for duty, either out of fear of intimidation at work, or for the eminently practical reason that it would have required double the number of vehicles to provide *sharia*-friendly transport to male and female employees alike. The six-man *shura* forbade women from going out without a male relative to chaperone them, but men were prevented by the identical code from travelling in the same bus as unrelated female passengers. As for other means of transport, wheels skidded in the opposite direction every time a *burkha*-clad figure tried to flag down a taxi. The capital was gripped in a religious gridlock.[10]

'It's a confusing situation,' conceded a field officer with the Swiss NGO Terre des Hommes, struggling to tailor a project for street children to the bizarre new norms.

> Afghan statute law says that children cease to be children at the age of 18. *Sharia* law states that girls cease to be children at the age of 14 and boys at the age of 16. The Taliban say that there is no specific age for boys, but girls cease to be children at the age of seven. There should be no mixing of the sexes after that.[11]

He had smuggled in malnourished 10-year-olds, whose wasted frames belied their ages, but at Kabul's largest state-run orphanage, Taskia Maskan, the new regulation could not be ignored. After the female staff were sent home, the 400-odd girls who lived there were locked up for a year without going outside to play. What had been a regular halt for journalists during the siege of Kabul became a powerful – if unvisitable – symbol of the aid community's dumping of its core constituency.[12]

'Even a woman has trouble in examining a woman in Afghanistan,' a doctor with Médecins du Monde had explained in Herat over a year earlier. 'There are still women doctors, but for how long one doesn't know. If the access of females to medical studies is forbidden, there will no longer be any women doctors to assure a service of gynaecology or obstetrics.'[13] The Taliban allowance that women doctors could continue to practise – though women were prevented from studying for a medical career – convinced the UN and NGOs that further windows might, with patience, open. But Taliban concessions were determined less by humanitarian logic – in this case, the condition of poor or pregnant women – or Islamic propriety, and more by diplomatic advantage. Even that trait would prove to have a short attention span. On 19 October, the *shura* banned women from attending the city's 32 *hammam*, or bath-houses, a six-cent, hot-water rite usually enjoyed after sex or menstruation. Combining warmth and opportunities to socialise in the depths of winter, the excursion was proscribed as 'unIslamic'. The UN warned of an imminent surge in scabies and vaginal infections among a population now denied hygiene, as well as easy access to health care.[14]

The Afghan vagina was a murky area for aid worker and Taliban alike for within it were enscribed the viral fingerprints of its proprietor's way of life and, since this was frequently in the cross-border trade, or in killing, there were ample opportunities for outside contact. Medical care for women, as a result, was tantamount to forensic work for, in curing, it also identified the vector and his respectable charade. The spirit of *omerta* which governed Afghan family life ensured that word of rape, adultery or bisexuality rarely leaked out to the wider community, but it hung above the husband at prayer, poisoned the hearth and, when laid bare in the Petri dish, shocked the few professionals to have done hard-core gynaecological research in the village. Afghan women stood a greater chance of dying in childbirth than anyone outside Sierra Leone; and they gave birth on average nine times in their lives. In between parturitions, they withstood a sustained siege from second- and third-generation sexually-transmitted diseases. Access to the vagina, in the shape of basic health care, would become the cockpit of a new cold war in Afghanistan.

The UN's projected role as master of ceremonies in the post-Rabbani era was scarcely mitigated by its humanitarian pretensions, for foreign aid had been viewed by most Afghans as a political, even missionary, tool since the 1950s when Prime Minister Mohammad Daoud first initiated the custom of milking the USSR and US for development loans. The failure to maintain a balance of debt to the rival powers had cost Afghanistan its Islam, and Daoud his life, tainting in the process all subsequent aid initiatives with the suspicion of a hidden, malignant agenda. When the West created 'solidarity committees' during the *jihad* to offset the social impact of the Soviet invasion, aid had also become intertwined with the politics and patronage of military commanders. Even the Swedish Committee for Afghanistan, the respected architect of a seed revolution which swept through the countryside in the early 1990s, had once been branded a 'sister organisation' to *Hizb-i Islami*, for were not its wells built near party headquarters and its clinics, dominated by posters of Hekmatyar, known to deny services to members of other parties?[15] The British NGO Afghan Aid, whose work was in Badakhshan, and the French agency Madera, expelled from Pakistan in late 1996, were similarly at risk of being viewed as 'foreign aid' to the Francophone Massoud, rather than humanitarian aid to Afghans. To help in Afghanistan was, ultimately, to take sides, for aid had a long tradition of tilting the ethnic or military playing field. Neutrality was inconceivable.

This was nowhere more so than in the fields of education and female empowerment, both of which had been prioritised by the Afghan communist party and the Soviet occupier over the wishes of their subjects, only to be taken up by the UN as the apparently humdrum elements of any late twentieth-century programme of social development. But education was religious dynamite in Afghanistan: it was no coincidence that Nadir Shah, Zahir's father, had been murdered at a school prize-giving in 1933. Educational establishments were centres of influence which challenged the authority of the mosque so, while the fruit of school knowledge – a government salary – was undoubtedly prized, the means of acquiring it entailed a scary fraternisation with the demonic.

Teachers had been one of the soft targets of the *jihad*, with some 2,000 assassinated and 15,000 forced to abandon the profession out of fear for their lives. In Nangarhar, one commander admitted to burning down the local primary school and slaughtering its nine teachers, because 'that was where the communists were trained'.[16] Postwar school curricula were painstakingly deconstructed – by mullah and educational consultant alike – for the heresies which were impossible to eradicate from a text which was, at bottom, alien to the very people it was intended to serve. And their suspicions were sometimes well-founded: in 1994, UNICEF and several Norwegian NGOs banned the use of textbooks developed during the *jihad* for use in refugee camps by USAID in association with the University of Nebraska in Omaha, on the grounds that the teaching of basic arithmetic in terms of dead Soviet soldiers or working Kalashnikovs served only to glorify war. Despite the limited information at their disposal, Afghans grasped instinctively the corrosive effect of too much, or the wrong kind of, knowledge on their children. Against such a backdrop, the ascendancy of the Taliban, a movement firmly rooted in the disciplines of the *madrassa*, was a sure sign that the half-century polemic over the place of secular education in society was finally closed.

Widows were doubly victimised under the Taliban. Not only were they denied paid employment, like other Afghan women, but they lost access to food aid which, under the new government, had to be collected by male relatives. The possibility that they had none was inconceivable and Mullah Ghaus, the new acting foreign minister, said he was 'astonished' at the level of international concern for 'such a small percentage of the working population'.[17] The UN estimated the number of widows at around 800,000 after 17 years of war, a statistic which, like most used in Afghanistan, was deeply flawed, but unusually convenient.

Najibullah had institutionalised the widow by establishing women's councils and assistance agencies to liaise between them, the UN and the social services ministry. Prior to that, she would have expected to enter a Levitical marriage with a brother-in-law while her children were cared for by the extended family. Najib's successor, Rabbani, had absorbed the mechanisms into his own administration, swelling the list with *mujahedin* widows and the dependants of the siege victims, which by the middle of 1996 amounted to some 20–30,000 people. They were taken up enthusiastically by donors and with very little scrutiny for the line between an authentic widow and an impoverished, but still married woman became hopelessly blurred as the siege tightened and food and mothering grew scarce.

With no clearer access to females in the more conservative rural areas, projects for widows provided the easiest means for agencies to nail gender credentials – and the equally-important rubric, 'income-generating schemes' – to their fund-raising masts. 'Widows are and remain an emotive issue,' said Jolyon Leslie, the UN's regional coordination officer in Kabul, 'for whom it has been easy to secure support.'[18] In Kabul, widowhood was the next best criterion – after wealth – for exemption from the conventions which prevented women from working or moving around unveiled – long before the rise of the Taliban. And, in a city in which half the two million population lived on relief, widows, at least, had a ticket to eat and that was a tradeable asset in the *bazaar* and an extended familiy similarly beset by bombardment.

Few agencies bothered to make their projects for widows credible outside the narrow context of the siege. The bakery and sewing schemes supported by the World Food Programme, UNICEF and UNOCHA did nothing to instil self-sufficiency or business skills among their illiterate beneficiaries who were granted a 'salary' of relief food, but below-market prices for their bread or quilts, which were distributed elsewhere under the Kabul emergency programme. A similar flavour of *de haut en bas* infected most UN programmes for women, acccording to an evaluation report which emerged after the Taliban takeover, but which referred to projects conducted under the Rabbani government. 'The pressure to reach women has led to a focus on quantities, at the expense of quality of support offered,' said the writer in tones which accented the need to avoid repeating the past. She went on to identify three classic UN responses to the restrictions introduced by the Taliban. One was 'adaptive', and entailed continuing to operate within the dominant political values, and a second was 'defeatist', whereby all decisions were deferred until the political situation had altered. There was little to choose between them. The third, termed 'challenging', treated every violation of gender equity as a violation of human rights, to which the only coherent response was the suspension of social aid.[19]

The arrival of the Taliban heralded a curious transformation in the widow's already anomalous status. Like all working women, she was sent home and denied the right to roam without a *burkha*, but the gaggle of blue-veiled beggars in the streets were a vivid rebuttal of the Taliban's insistent claim that all women had the support of male family members and, therefore, no further need of relief. She owed her political profile to aid and the women's organisations created under the communist regime, which were both anathema to the religious movement. But, while the Taliban's prescriptions on women in general remained non-negotiable, the widow provided the vehicle for the emergence of an embryonic *lingua franca* between the new government and the international community. According to Leslie, writing in February 1998,

> There is a sense here that the current authorities, like others before them, have manipulated the issue of widows for their own ends. For the time being, this seems to work for both sides. The issue of women's rights has been kept safely distinct from the relief needs, both by the international community and the Taliban.[20]

That distinction had a lengthy pedigree. In November 1995, two months after Herat fell to the movement, UNICEF had announced the suspension of all assistance to education in Taliban-controlled regions of the country, arguing that the ban on girls' attendance at schools constituted a breach of the Convention of the Rights of the Child. It was the first apparent attempt to set a policy benchmark in the long shadow of the Beijing women's conference earlier in the year and to strengthen UNICEF's profile as the lead agency in matters pertaining to women and children. SCF (UK) withdrew entirely from Herat the following spring, saying the new ban on employing Afghan female staff made it impossible for the agency to communicate with women, the main carers for children. But these gestures were not entirely of UNICEF's or SCF's making. Pamela Collett of SCF (US), a doyenne of women's literacy programmes in Mazar-i Sharif, had leaked details of what she described as the UN's 'appeasement' of the Taliban's gender policies to the *New York Times* on 10 November after a training visit to Herat, causing a flurry of backtracking.[21] Peter Hansen, then head of the UN's Department of Humanitarian Affairs, admitted that local women aid workers did risk losing their jobs under the new dispensation and talked of the 'terrible dilemma' facing agencies in Taliban-controlled provinces.

Hours later, UNICEF's chief executive, Carol Bellamy, declared a freeze on support to schools projects, but the decision was more an exercise in damage limitation than a coordinated response by the UN to its first challenge over gender equality, a challenge, moreover, that had come not from the Taliban but from one of its own NGO partners. File, therefore, under 'defeatist'. For simple logic dictated that the Taliban's gender policies had tainted every stratum of an aid effort supposedly mandated on equality of access, from the provision of relief food and drinking water to the basic arena of health care, the only sector where women were still permitted to work. Drawing the line at education was sophistry disguised as policy. The UNHCR, under pressure from Pakistan to reduce the number of Afghan refugees, had begun to debate the ethics of repatriating them to a country where basic human rights and access to health or education were denied to half the population. Afghans had drawn their own conclusion: returnees dwindled to 11,000 in the first five months of 1997, compared to 121,000 in the previous year, suggesting that something remained seriously awry in the Taliban's inward investment programme.[22]

In their different fashions, agencies were forced to grapple with the political consequences of what, implicitly, signalled the Taliban's wholesale rejection of any effort to address the structural – read 'religious' – context of women's marginalisation in society, in favour of a bottomless reliance on unconditional relief. The Taliban decreed that you could feed women, but not help them in any more meaningful way. The quintessence of development – which for aid workers anywhere was shorthand for the empowerment of women and girls – had been effectively outlawed. But, with the notable exception of Oxfam, international agencies and NGOs in Kabul believed they still had a job to do saving lives, whatever the human rights environment. 'We are addressing humanitarian needs,' said a spokesman for ECHO, the EU's relief arm. 'Obviously witnessing and human rights need to be addressed too, but that is not the work of a humanitarian organisation. The people of MSF, Solidarité and AMI are not equipped. Their job is to keep people alive.'[23]

Any confrontation over the issue of widows, however, began to recede within days of the Taliban settling into the capital. WFP projects were individually inspected and permitted to continue, so long as men and women were not working together. Female supervisors were appointed – on condition that they had no contact with male staff in the Kabul office. It was an inefficient and costly compromise, for expatriate females would have to be hired to do the tasks usually done by female Afghans, and it drew agencies closer into a collaborative working relationship with the Taliban on worrisome terms. The material needs of widows and their children had been secured, but the remainder of Kabuli women were still locked out from work, school and, by September 1997, all but one of the city's hospitals. Reports of suicide attempts by women who dared not leave their home began to circulate, but no agency felt able to raise the alarm.

In mid-February 1998, the main relief agencies finally began to re-examine the 'widow caseload', with a view to redefining the criteria for selecting beneficiaries. 'It is demographically impossible,' said Leslie, 'for such large numbers of females to have been widowed, even taking into account the scale of loss of life here in recent years. It will be interesting,' he continued, 'to see the response of the authorities to this. In all likelihood, they will choose to view it as another demonstration of the international community's "lack of commitment to Afghan women".'[24]

* * *

The UN Charter, which had allowed the UN to work vicariously with Najibullah, Rabbani, Hekmatyar and General Dostum, hardly equipped the organisation for survival in the treeless prairie of the Taliban's daily discourse, a landscape of utter simplicity dappled only by Manichean shadows. Save the Children's Matthew Bullard gave a succinct account of its climate following the agency's withdrawal from its schools programme in Herat in spring 1996, a trend initiated six months earlier by UNICEF:

> To be fair, the new governor is quite open in his rejection of Western humanitarian aid. He ends each meeting by suggesting that the best thing we could do would be to become Muslims and join the struggle. He specifically offered us our money back. 'All the money you have spent in Herat, you can have it back, and go away'.[25]

Michael Scott, manager of the UN agency Habitat's urban regeneration programme, summarised the communication breakdown: 'The degree of cognitive dissonance and communicative distance we can see and feel now with these new potential partners is unlike anything we may have experienced with previous Afghan factions, authorities or regimes.' He added: 'Neither in the new order does there to be any notion of accountability; the real authorities are to this day a nameless *shura*, who mediate the will of the Supreme Authority.'[26]

The UN was not about to ask for a refund but it was concerned – along with every other agency – about how its money would be spent by the Taliban. Between 1988 and 1992, over $1 billion had streamed into Afghanistan, a 'peace dividend' that turned aid into an industry on a par with heroin and which, in the view of some critics, essentially assisted its transformation into the world's largest opium producer by funding the repair of its myriad irrigation systems. The US pulled out in 1992 for that very reason, citing the Foreign Assistance Act which prohibits aid to narcotic-producing countries. Four years later, the EU had become the UN's largest donor, contributing ECU76 million ($96 million) out of a $134.8 million budget, broadly divided into three main activities: the provision of emergency aid, support to refugees and the displaced, and the supply of relief food. Nearly half this amount, around $41 million, was allocated to Kabul's winter emergency, a programme created to ease the effects of the Hekmatyar and Taliban sieges, and which sustained many of the 38 foreign NGOs working in the city. While the UN waved its arms about in Afghanistan, it was the EU, in principle, which pulled the strings.

On 8 October 1996, after protracted meetings in the UN Guest House, NGOs responded to the Taliban's new gender regime in a position statement which called for a return of the 'status quo of 11 days ago', the end of discrimination between the sexes, the restoration of women's right to work and study, and guarantees for the safety of their staffs.[27] Secretary-General Boutros Boutros-Ghali, three days later, confirmed the UN's commitment to Afghanistan, but only under the terms of its charter, which states that UN activities must be 'for all without distinction, as to race, sex, language or religion'. He acknowledged the importance of local traditions and cultures, but stressed that they could not be used by UN member-states to override international obligations to uphold basic human rights, including those of women to education and employment.

In the first week of October, the UNHCR suspended seven Kabul programmes affecting 8,000 people, when the *Amr Bil Marof Wa Nai An Munkir* issued an edict warning Afghan women not to continue working with foreign agencies, 'otherwise, if they were chased, threatened and investigated by us, the responsibility will be on them'.[28] Former women employees were so frightened by what they had seen of the movement that they asked that agency vehicles should not even park in the vicinity of their homes, lest they be falsely acccused. Oxfam reacted by closing all programmes, including the multi-million dollar Logar water supply project which, when completed, would have supplied clean, running water to half the capital's households. The Oxfam line, defended in the face of intense pressure from donors and its own engineers, was that no effective community water project could be realised without guaranteeing access to its chief users, women. On 24 October, the EU Parliament asked donors and UN members to refrain from signing new cooperation programmes or granting diplomatic recognition. In November, Save the Children (US), which had closed land-mine awareness programmes when girls were barred from schools, reported a 300 per cent increase in casualties, 'due to civilians moving back into front-line areas following the ousting of the Rabbani regime and to Kabulis throwing away weapons and ammunition under a Taliban crackdown on unauthorised arms'.[29]

The one man who stood somewhat aloof from the narrow intransigence of the *shura* in Kabul was acting Foreign Minister Sher Mohammad Stanakzai, the English-speaking, former representative of *Ittehad-i Islami* in Quetta, who became its interface with the world after the fall of the capital. He alone seemed to grasp that the quarrel over women's rights was more than rhetoric and had set the movement, and the international community on which it depended for recognition and its social services budget, on course to inevitable loggerheads, however constitutionally reluctant the UN system was to take offence, impose sanctions or, in a word, 'suspend'.

On 30 September, he sought to mitigate the Taliban's mandatory redundancy of women by insisting that laid-off female staff would continue to receive their wages – though no salaries had been paid to anyone for three months and Massoud had, anyway, made off with the treasury.[30] On 2 October, he reminded journalists that 'according to Islamic rules, education is a must for women' and, on 23 December, he promised that girls' schools would surely reopen in March, at the end of the traditional, three-month winter holiday.[31] It was simply a question of arranging for segregated facilities. In the same month, his superior, Mullah Rafiullah, then head of the *Amr Bil Marof Wa Nai An Munkir*, or religious police, was seemingly reined in by Mullah Mohammad Omar after authorising the whipping of 225 women in a single day for dress code violations.[32]

It was enough to keep the UN relief operation rolling for a further three months, for it chimed with the impression, growing in aid circles, that, while 'you could get nothing at the commanding heights of the régime, you could get a lot locally'.[33] The Taliban were not as monolithic, single-minded or secure in power as was first supposed. Their intransigence in more liberal, non-Pashtun cities was dictated in part by the fear of losing face in front of the troops, but, as the Soviets had found before, the Taliban writ travelled only a short distance beyond the main arteries before meeting the unyielding autonomy of the village. Even when restrictions were categorically announced by radio, private arrangements were still viable in the districts, if they were couched in a dialect which did not directly challenge political or religious allegiances. 'Taliban' authorities in Ghazni and Khost permitted girls' schools to function within a home context; female health workers continued to make house calls in certain districts of Nangarhar; while, for want of any practical alternative, women in Jalalabad freely travelled in buses with men.[34]

Attacks on Western aid workers had begun some time before the apparent difference over conduct of external affairs between Rafiullah and Stanakzai, the one gravely pondering the Koran, the other more attuned to a world outside. In a letter on 18 November, the UN's security chief in Afghanistan, Daniel Bellamy, warned New York that a serious casualty was imminent, citing

> an escalation of insults, threats and harrassment, culminating in the flight of some local staff, explicit threats against international and local staff and the invasion of UN offices and personal residences by armed Taliban fighters including, in one case, the detention of the UN Team Leader in his own home by 16 armed men for five hours.[35]

Bellamy's correspondence was an angry reaction to a UN agency meeting in Islamabad three days earlier held under the auspices of the Department of Humanitarian Affairs in which it was suggested that 'consideration should be given to separating urgent issues related to actions by the Taliban towards the UN from broader issues related to the Taliban policies in the areas of human rights and cooperation with the UN'.[36]

In December, an employee of the International Committee of the Red Cross (ICRC), the agency that had been most stoic during the blitz of 1992–96, was stopped after curfew in the Wazir Akhbar Khan diplomatic quarter, soundly beaten and thrown into a police cell where he was discovered, accidentally, by an ICRC prison visiting team several days later.[37] The incident was blamed on a 'hooligan' element within the rank-and-file, but top Taliban leaders were housed in villas nearby and crossing the boundary between supercilious disdain and outright violence was a decision that could only have been taken at the highest levels. Foreigners interpreted the attack as a conscious attempt to put the aid community in its place.

Other encounters followed. Four elderly nuns in Kabul were given the strap in early January 1997 for some vague infringement of *satar* and, in February, aid workers referred confidentially to another confrontation, 'far more serious', which was brought to the attention of Stanakzai who 'pleaded that it not "go outside"', lest it affect negotiations over recognition.[38] One month later, that approach appeared to have been dropped when French aid workers from Action Contre la Faim (ACF) were raided during a farewell lunch for three expatriate females, attended by male and female Afghan staff. It was not an honest mistake: most aid workers played a conscious game of hide-and-seek with the authorities, either by trying to maintain clandestine contact with their former female staff, or hoarding the videos, CDs and cassettes banned by the *Amr Bil Marof Wa Nai An Munkir*. The force's authority allowed it to recruit spies anywhere – and, with particular ease, among *chowkidar*, or compound watchmen. The Taliban went on to demonstrate that they were not to be teased. On 19 March, a tribunal sentenced the two ACF staff to one month in prison, and the Afghan men to one-and-a-half months and between 9 and 29 lashes each.[39]

But it was Afghan NGOs – of which there were a remarkable 240 at the end of 1994 – which were expected to bear the brunt of the Taliban's anger, and not solely because they were subjects. Their ex-civil service staff had been trained in the Eastern bloc, thrived under Najibullah, consorted with women and yet still found accommodation with the UN and the *mujahedin* commanders in the areas where their projects were situated. In the Taliban's prayer-glazed view, they were the epitome of apostasy, their very own fireside Satan. The first Afghan NGOs had been established during the Soviet war as US-backed relief arms to the seven main resistance parties, but more were formed after the launch in October 1988 of the UN's 'Operation Salam', a cross-border initiative anchored in Peshawar and directed at the return of the 3.3 million Pakistan-based Afghan refugees.

The real mushrooming, however, occurred after 1992, a year which saw both the US withdrawal from development and the outbreak of faction fighting in the capital. 'It seemed that every other Afghan was starting an NGO,' recalled Nancy Dupree, a writer on Afghan affairs employed by ACBAR, one of two bodies in Peshawar set up to coordinate their activities.[40] Afghans brought to the fledgling NGOs the skills of a well-educated elite, and a closer rapport than non-Afghans could ever hope to achieve, while stripping away the formality that interposed between isolated rural communities and well-endowed foreign agencies. Known – both affectionately and derisively – as 'Bongos' (business-oriented NGOs), the most efficient competitively tendered for development 'contracts' put out by the UN or international NGOs. By 1994, their share of funding amounted to $44 million – though nearly half that amount was split between five Afghan-run de-mining agencies – and some 29,000 professional Afghans were believed to be sheltering under the 'NGO system'.[41]

The results had been startling in development terms. 'One of the most positive things about this war,' continued Dupree, 'is that Afghans as well as foreigners, the UN as well as donors, have seen for the first time what they have always talked about in rhetoric: grassroots community participation for community development.'[42] By the mid-1990s, rural Afghanistan was in the throes of the same green revolution that had swept through Indian agriculture more than a generation earlier, and the credit was entirely due to the local NGOs, which were able to tap the same filaments and cells of mass propagation that, essentially, had underpinned the *jihad*. By late 1995, the 'NGO system' had evolved into what amounted to the virtual privatisation of the services normally provided by government. That worried the UN Development Programme (UNDP), which traditionally coordinated UN operations and whose role was hardly to tinker with the administrative mechanics of a member state, however imploded. It also bothered the Rabbani government, too involved in withstanding the siege to register the raft of agencies, but wary of the proliferation of new aid fiefs in its strife-torn territory. In the history of Afghanistan, influence had always shown a tendency to ebb away from the centre.

Hopes that the professional staff of Afghan NGOs, familiar with funding and the protocols which governed it, might fill the skills vacuum and develop into a think-tank for an apparently thought-free Taliban, faded even as Kabul fell. In Jalalabad, where NGOs had multiplied on the back of the displaced emergency, moveable assets such as vehicles and motorbikes were looted and Taliban appointees inserted into the staff to ensure the agency's compliance with the new gender edicts.[43] In May 1997, the US-based international relief and development organisation CARE suspended a food programme for 10,000 widows in Kabul, after Jalalabad Taliban stopped a bus carrying five of its male Afghan employees and beat them with sticks.[44] There were fewer Afghan NGOs in the capital, where government ministries and the presence of foreign NGOs had ensured more orthodox project implementation. But the ones that were there experienced a sequence of lootings, first as Massoud withdrew, then as his pursuers commandeered vehicles to ferry soldiers to the front at Jabal Saraj. As late as February 1997, private vehicles were still to be seen on Jadayi Maiwand, the bombed-out boulevard that once housed Kabul's celebrated carpet *bazaar*, battened to the roof of buses for the long trip to Kandahar 'to have their papers checked'. They rarely returned.

With the gunfire stilled due to the winter recess, agencies met to consider their options at a long-planned donor conference in the Turkmen capital of Ashgabat on 21–22 January which attracted representatives from 250 governments, agencies, development banks and NGOs – as well as scores of dollar prostitutes until an 11p.m. closure was imposed on all bars and discos. The original intent had been to drum up support for the UN's flagging emergency appeal for 1997, but the Taliban victory in Kabul converted the forum into a session devoted to seeking a united response to the movement's gender policies. This was not easy. The resources of some agencies were dedicated exclusively to emergency relief: to close programmes down, it was argued, would penalise the recipients rather than their new, and perhaps unwanted, rulers. Others, including the EU's relief arm, ECHO, maintained that their work was humanitarian in orientation – as opposed to political – while a consultant for UNICEF, the first agency to have withdrawn support in Taliban areas, opined that UN programmes in Afghanistan never had much of a gender perspective in the first place, focusing as they did upon women's biological, rather than social roles.[45] Even education failed to produce consensus. Afghan NGOs and the Swedish Committee for Afghanistan said the total denial of assistance because of the closure of girls' schools would be to 'hold hostage' Afghan boys. Where convergence of views did occur was on the creative working climate in Mazar where, under the former communist Dostum, gender was still no obstacle. As a result, in the following months, UNDP and its sister agencies allocated $35 million to a Poverty Eradication and Community Empowerment (PEACE) programme in Mazar that was more coherent as an acronym than a strategy, since it appeared to lend international support to the Taliban's enemy. Apart from that, the conference produced a list of ten conclusions – in which the Taliban were mentioned second to last – and a resolution to spend $50,000 on a resource centre for gender and human rights issues in Afghanistan.[46]

The deadline was nearing for a more vigorous approach. 'At what point,' enquired UNICEF's regional director Ruth Hayward in an internal memo,

> are we taking orders from a foreign government, let alone jeopardising our success at a local level? ... I urge that criteria for a decision as to when to suspend activities in a field office, based on programme considerations, not only security ones, be made explicit, if not yet done.[47]

As the leading agency in health and education, UNICEF was considered the UN's weathervane on issues of gender rights but, between the baying of the Western press and the prospect that the Taliban might gradually respond to dialogue, it was a hard judgement to call. 'UNICEF discussed non-discrimination as a criterion to guide decisionmaking about the allocation of resources in Afghanistan,' Hayward continued. 'The idea was to apply this systematically, taking into account both security and efficiency concerns. Did we go far enough? I doubt it. Can we now go further? I hope so.'[48]

Over the winter Stanakzai had been replaced by Mullah Ghaus, a more hard-headed player who was in constant contact with Mullah Mohammad Omar in Kandahar. In March, UN representatives met the minister of education, who reportedly agreed to allow girls up to nine years old to return to schools, then due to reopen in April. Days later, the decision was reversed. The Taliban reiterated its promise to reintroduce schooling for girls when the military situation had 'stabilised', adding for good measure, and when 'they have been recognised as a legitimate power base'. UNICEF's Carol Bellamy responded with an irate press release restating her organisation's commitment to non-discrimination.[49]

But the system to which UNICEF belonged had been insufficiently robust in its response to the Taliban and the conduct of 'constructive dialogue' with the mullahs had ended by coining a language of complicity.

12 Ignoble Grave

> Wherever you go, we will catch you. If you go up, we will pull you down by your feet; if you hide below, we will pull you up by your hair. Mullah Manon Niazi, August 1998

The encounter at Mazar in May 1997 cost the lives of at least 2,500 Taliban, but as many civilians were reportedly killed in an anti-Pashtun pogrom in the city later orchestrated by General Abdul Malik and the Hazara Shia leaders.[1] The ethnic war, predicted by Mahmoud Mestiri, flexed its jaws. In December – one month after the first of eight mass Taliban graves came to light in the desolate Dasht-i Leili near Shiburghan – sources claimed that a further 20,000 Pashtun non-combatants had vanished from Faryab, Jawzjan, Balkh, Badghis and Samangan, the provinces abandoned by the Taliban in their desperate escape from the northern bloodbath.[2] The allegation was never confirmed, but nor was it thoroughly investigated either by the UN or Amnesty International, both of which were subsequently castigated by Kabul for their indifference to atrocities committed by the CDA – now renamed the United Islamic Front for the Liberation of Afghanistan (UIFLA) in honour of the uneasy new alliance between Malik, Khalili and Massoud.[3]

The Mazar reversal placed the movement in the same military deadlock it had occupied one year earlier. Massoud blocked any southward retreat by again blowing up the Salang Tunnel, while his troops in the Shommali plain, from which an estimated 200,000 people had fled, prevented any relief force from reaching the besieged Taliban in Pul-i Khumri.[4] The utter collapse of the advance into the north, meanwhile, yet again emphasised the Taliban's insouciant attitude to the fundamental rules of military engagement. Instead of a measured advance, consolidated by securing supply lines and strategic towns en route, they had gambled 5,000 lives on what was assumed at the highest levels to be a mere victory procession. The miscalculation triggered the single worst massacre since the rise of the movement in October 1994 and it would lead to even more copious spillage of blood in the following year. It also raised again the riddle of how, if the Taliban were indeed receiving consistent military guidance from Pakistani experts, their forces could race forwards to such an unmitigated disaster.

The defeat, however briefly, reassured Central Asia that the Taliban was a stoppable phenomenon. Pakistan, Saudi Arabia and the UAE did not retract their diplomatic recognition, although, in a bid to prevent Malik joining Massoud for a counter-assault on the capital, Islamabad announced that Mullah Mohammad Omar had agreed that the north should retain its 'unique culture' and invited its leaders to peace talks.[5] General Malik countered with his own proposal to convene a *Loya Jirga,* along lines so similar to those drawn up by Mestiri in 1994 that the name of Zahir Shah was among the notables called to attend. Against the counsels of his now closest allies, Russia and Iran, Malik sent an emissary to Washington and the UN in New York to drum up support for his plan.[6]

Significant changes had taken place in both the US and the UN administrations since the fall of Kabul nine months earlier. After months of rancorous debate, in which US demands for accelerated budgetary reform at the UN figured prominently, the General Assembly had finally agreed upon Ghana's Kofi Annan as the replacement for the outgoing secretary-general, Boutros Boutros-Ghali. He took up his post on 1 January 1997, the same day that the former US ambassador to the UN, Madeleine Albright, became the nation's first-ever female secretary of state and the executor of President Clinton's second-term pledge that 'concerns related to women will be incorporated into the mainstream of US foreign policy'. Though no radical feminist, the uniqueness of Albright's appointment and remit ensured that gender issues would assume greater weight in the US's ambivalent relations not only with the Taliban, but also with the UN, which still held the key to international recognition. Rabbani's representative continued to occupy Afghanistan's seat in the General Assembly, though that anomaly was due for review at the annual meeting of the UN's Credentials Committee in September 1997.

Recognition was vital if the UNOCAL pipeline to Turkmenistan were to win the $2.5 billion funding needed to get it off the drawing board, but there had also been far-reaching alterations in the energy balance of power since the fall of Kabul and they proliferated at dizzying speed as the Credential Committee meeting drew near. In a bid to pre-empt UNOCAL's plans, Iran had begun work on a 200 km pipeline to link the Turkmen gas field of Korpedzhe to its Caspian port of Kurt-Kui barely one month after the capital succumbed to the movement. Though capable of transporting less than half of UNOCAL's proposed gas volumes, the $190 million line, opened in December 1997, became the first energy export route from Central Asia outside Moscow's direct control and it represented, simultaneously, a major setback to the US policy of containing Iran through the trade boycott.[7] With one international pipeline in place across Iran, the argument for others could only become more compelling and American contractors risked being left out in the cold because of an increasingly obsolete US foreign policy. The election of the moderate Mohammad Khatami as president in May provided further impetus for a review of Washington's Iran policy. UNOCAL was not, however, about to give up. In February, a delegation of Taliban leaders flew to its headquarters at Sugarland, Texas, for a whirlwind of corporate hospitality and, two months later, the company opened a project office in Kandahar, the seat of Taliban power.[8]

In a further change of watch in Washington, Robin Raphel, the assistant secretary of state for south Asia, was replaced in July by Karl Inderfurth, a forthright and ambitious individual with better access to Albright's ear. Neither despaired of ultimately doing business with the Taliban, but it was clear by the end of the year that distinct limits had been formally drawn around the foundations of any future relationship. 'The Taliban will not change their spots,' Inderfurth said, 'but we do believe they can modify their behaviour and take into account certain international standards with respect to women's rights to education and employment.'[9] US policymaking in Afghanistan, hitherto geared to the exigencies of the scramble for Caspian energy, had been rouged, however unwillingly, with a women's rights sensibility.

The death of so many fighters in Mazar did little to dent Taliban morale. Indeed, with the dead removed from the debating floor, there were even grounds for optimism. Mullah Mohammad Omar's appeal on 5 June for more fighters summoned 10,000 willing martyrs from the apparently inexhaustible reservoir across the Pakistani border.[10] Dostum's surprising escape to Turkey – in view of the fact that he owned a home in Tashkent – had critically weakened the northern coalition, for General Malik was neither as ruthless nor as cunning as his former overlord. Herat's Ismail Khan, an early casualty of the May mutiny, had flown to an uncertain fate in Kandahar,[11] while another veteran of the Rabbani government, the Pashtun prime minister, Abdul Rahim Ghafoorzai, died on 21 August in a plane crash at Bamian, the victim not of foul play, but the shortness of the mountain runway.[12] By then, however, the Taliban had launched their bid to secure the north before the Credentials Committee assembled.

On 10 June, two weeks after the Mazar debacle, 2,000 Taliban broke out of Pul-i Khumri and drove northeast on their last fuel to Kunduz, where they were welcomed by Arif Khan, a Pashtun ally of Massoud since 1980.[13] Kunduz, the home area of Hekmatyar, had a large Pashtun population and a functioning runway, but resupplying this depleted expeditionary force by air was an impossible logistical task. Logic dictated an attack on Hairatan port, 30 km north of Mazar-i Sharif on the Amu Darya river, where Uzbek and Russian supplies of fuel and munitions were piled high, alongside UN relief food. In early September, a part of the Taliban force, joined by local Pashtun commanders formerly allied with Hekmatyar, swept out of Kunduz on a 100-mile dash across the north, capturing first Tashkurgan, Hairatan junction and finally Hairatan port. No sooner did they enter the city than they fired a celebratory volley of rockets across the river, killing several Uzbek nationals.[14]

Replenished, they launched a second assault on the northern capital, supported by warplanes and heavy artillery. On 9 and 10 September, Taliban troops lined up and shot 100 Shia civilians in the villages of Qazelabad and Qul Mohammad and, one day afterwards, they took control of the airport, without quite managing to penetrate Mazar.[15] In a routine display of the quality of northern leadership, Malik had abandoned the city for Samangan shortly after the attack began, returning four weeks later, well after it had petered out.[16] Troops took advantage of the resulting disorder to ransack aid agency offices, stealing whatever vehicles, equipment and furniture had been overlooked in the pillage four months previously. Suddenly, out of a clear blue sky, on 12 September, the burly figure of General Rashid Dostum was reported back in the saddle fighting alongside his troops to recapture the supply base at Hairatan.[17]

Dostum said he returned at the request of Massoud, Khalili and Rabbani, although other sources suggest the invitation was issued by the largely autonomous *Hizb-i Wahdat* militia in Mazar.[18] In a classic gesture of Afghan *kow-tow*, however, the two generals met for the first time since Malik's mutiny at Dostum's personal headquarters in Shiburghan on 28 September.[19] The dialogue crackled but, to prevent any further rents appearing in the shredded fabric of the Northern Alliance, a power-sharing formula was agreed whereby Dostum took Jawzjan, Malik retained his pre-mutiny stronghold of Faryab, while his brother, Gul Mohammad Pawlawan, was given command of the north central province of Sar-i Pul.[20] Dostum immediately left for the eastern front, 42 km from the city, where his return was portrayed as having galvanised the rank-and-file – without any reference whatever to his humiliating desertion four months earlier.[21] Hairatan fell to the alliance on 10 October, removing the springboard of the Taliban's second attempt on Mazar-i Sharif.

The assault on Mazar ran in tandem with a Taliban blockade of the *Hizb-i Wahdat* heartland of Bamian in the central Hazarajat, where heavy rains in 1997 had ruined the harvest in what had historically been a chronic food-deficit area. The Taliban first denied aid agencies road access in August, arguing that local commanders had 'taken the civilians hostage' and that relief food would simply prolong the war.[22] The World Food Programme complained that its 2,400 tonne stockpile in Hairatan and a further 1,400 tonnes in Mazar had all been looted, either by Taliban or Northern Alliance forces.[23] By November, almost one million people faced food shortages while women, attempting to smuggle in grain beneath their *burkha*, were being turned back by Taliban guards.[24] Fighting erupted the same month in Mazar between the factions of the Northern Alliance. Dostum's Jawzjan militia swept west out of Shiburghan, capturing Adkhoi and Malik's capital at Maimana on 24 November. Malik, along with Gul Mohammad, fled across the Turkmen border to exile in Iran, leaving their remaining brothers in Mazar dungeons.[25]

Little of these events filtered out in detail for, ever since September 1996, the Taliban had cracked down on foreign journalism, often literally. In a country with no newspapers, no independent radio and only the BBC or Voice of America to provide hard information, media criticism as a rule was immediate and summary. The BBC's Alan Pearce, the only correspondent to witness the fall of the Kabul, was hauled from his Land Rover days later and beaten with rifle butts because of the slants perceived in his coverage.[26] Photographing 'living things' was outlawed early on, although Taliban troops could usually be flattered into making exceptions. But the prohibition on contact between the sexes effectively censored any reporting of the main story in Kabul: how Afghan women were coping under Taliban constraints. Poorly indeed, according to one survey of 160 women which disclosed that 97 per cent showed symptoms of major depression and 71 per cent reported a decline in their physical health status.[27] In September, the foreign ministry further tightened restrictions by banning commentary and analysis. 'News which could hurt people's feelings,' read the statement, 'cause dissension or ethnic, religious and linguistic discrimination, should be seriously avoided. The news and reports which agencies send abroad must conform with the rules ... and traditions of the country.'[28] 'Serious avoidance' was standard Taliban shorthand for imminent physical retribution.

The news blackout, ironically, shielded the UN, whose failure to create a coherent strategy out of its policy of 'constructive engagement' had begun to cause severe embarrassment. Plans to relocate mother-and-children programmes to the north under the hastily-concocted $30 million PEACE programme had, of course, been shelved by the fighting in Mazar, Pul-i Khumri and Maimana, while the lack of progress over both girls' education and the provision of relief to the Hazarajat held out little hope for any meaningful improvement. With no sign of movement within Afghanistan, voices were beginning to be raised abroad. In a confusing double negative on 24 June, Amnesty International called for President Clinton to 'state unequivocally that neither a gas pipeline, or counter-narcotics operation, or simply short-term stability are not more important than confronting human rights violations against women, the majority of Afghans'.[29] Two days later, Kofi Annan announced a categorical ban on UN investment in Afghanistan's crumbling services. 'UN agencies,' he said, 'will not engage in the institution-building efforts of the Afghan authorities as long as their discriminatory practices continue.'[30] Two UN agencies, the World Health Organisation and UNHCR, disregarded the injunction by using their allocation of EU funds to rehabilitate Rabia Balkhi hospital, one of the city's 22 health facilities. Following a Taliban decree in late 1997, it was designated as the sole institution in the capital permitted to accept women patients, despite the fact that it still lacked light, water or adequate surgical facilities.

Emma Bonino, head of the EU's relief arm ECHO, Afghanistan's largest benefactor, flew to Kabul on 28 September in what she admitted later was an attempt to 'use the media to draw international attention to a "forgotten crisis"'.[31] Her entourage of 18 journalists included the CNN's star correspondent, Christiane Amanpour, who gave the order to film women patients as soon as they were inside the controversial hospital. A group of Taliban raced to the scene shortly after, threatened Bonino with a Kalashnikov and clubbed the CNN cameraman and a European aid worker with rifle butts. It took three hours of careful diplomacy to sort out the 'misunderstanding'.[32] The outcry was curiously short-lived, partly because of Bonino's reputation as a Versace-clad radical. This was a politician who could get beaten up anywhere.

A more considered contribution to the belated, but growing, furore over women's rights was taking place in the US, coordinated by the Feminist Majority (FM), an alliance of 30 national women's organisations, including the YWCA, the American Nurses Association and the National Organisation for Women. On 30 July, the FM mounted its first pickets at the Pakistani and Afghani embassies in Washington, and followed these up with a campaign of lobbying at Congress, the State Department, the UN and UNOCAL to prevent recognition being granted to the Taliban.[33] With the Credentials Committee safely out of the way, the FM's 30,000 members focused their attention on a postal campaign to political leaders, winning a public condemnation of the Taliban from First Lady Hillary Clinton.[34] On 5 November, a woman with burns over 80 per cent of her body was turned away from another Kabul hospital on the order of a Taliban and subsequently died untreated.[35] The story was widely editorialised in the US press during the November stand-off with Iraq over UN access to its weapons programme, a period of maximum tension during which Madeleine Albright nevertheless took the time to make a symbolic, one-day stopover in Pakistan. During a visit to the Afghan refugee camp of Nasir Bagh near Peshawar on 18 November, Albright denounced the Taliban's 'despicable treatment of women and children and their lack of respect for human dignity'. She later told a press conference: 'I think it is very clear why we are opposed to the Taliban.'[36] One week later, the authorities agreed to admit women to most hospitals in the first concrete display of a *sharia* decree being overturned through outside pressure.

Albright's signal cut less ice in Sugarland. In September, the Taliban's energy mullahs had flown to Buenos Aires to negotiate with its Argentinian pipeline rival, Bridas which, since the collapse of its own scheme in September 1995, had followed UNOCAL's example of trying to win back the contract by linking up with a Saudi company. Ningharco, its new partner, was no ordinary firm: it led directly back to the head of Saudi intelligence, Prince Turki bin-Faisal, who was widely credited with having financed the Taliban phenomenon in the first place.[37] Notwithstanding, one month later, the formation was announced of the Centgas pipeline consortium, with UNOCAL as lead partner with 54.1 per cent, in association were Delta Oil (15 per cent), Japan's Itochu Corporation (7.2 per cent), Inpex (7.2 per cent), South Korea's Hyundai (5.5 per cent), Crescent Group of Pakistan (3.89 per cent) and the Turkmen government (10 per cent).[38]

Construction was set to begin in 1998. UNOCAL declared it would not move the project forward until the Taliban were recognised internationally, but the company promptly invested $900,000 in the University of Nebraska in Omaha to train 140 Afghans in pipeline construction techniques and Marty Miller, UNOCAL's vice-president, told the Taliban authorities they could confidently expect between $50 and $100 million a year in transit fees when the pipeline became operational.[39] FM stepped up its campaign in late 1997, winning a gestural commitment from UNOCAL to include Afghan women in any future training programme.[40] By the following March, when FM joined up with Emma Bonino to launch the 'Flower for the Women of Kabul' campaign to draw greater international attention to the state of women's rights, the oil and gender issues had virtually osmosed: 'The price of a pipeline must not be the enslavement of women,' said FM President Eleanor Smeal.[41]

By then UNOCAL was again encountering legal difficulties. Bridas's $15 billion damages suit for spoiling its Turkmen investments had been met with demands from UNOCAL that the case should be heard in Turkmenistan or Afghanistan instead. At a preliminary hearing in May 1998, the Texan company's lawyers handed the court a set of over 2,000 separate civil codes from districts along the pipeline route, still in Dari or Pashtu calligraphy, inviting the judge to disentangle the issue of jurisdiction.[42] A decision, understandably, was deferred till later in the year. A more menacing legal threat, however, had begun to arise from its 1995 signing of a $1 billion joint venture with Burma's ruling State Law and Order Restoration Council (SLORC) to build the Yadana pipeline, a project on which the UN Commission on Human Rights and independent activists had scrupulously documented incidents of murder, rape, torture and forced labour. In early 1998, residents of the Tenasserim region in Burma brought a class action suit against UNOCAL under the 1789 Alien Tort Claims Act, the first time the legislation had been targeted against a non-governmental party. The case, heard in the Federal District Court in Los Angeles in March 1998, could ultimately define the legal responsibility of transnational companies for the consequences of their business activities in foreign states. UNOCAL's motion to dismiss was denied by the judge, Richard A. Paez, who ruled that if UNOCAL were proven to have been aware of SLORC's forced labour policies and had financially benefited from them, it would then create liability.[43] If successful, the repercussions of the case on future corporate practice will be revolutionary, and not solely in Afghanistan.

UNOCAL's proposed partner in Afghanistan, meanwhile, was displaying its usual sensitivity to international opinion. In July, the authorities reportedly rounded up 2,000 Tajik and Hazara civilians in Kabul, cramming them into Pul-i Charki political prison in an effort to deter their fellows from joining the anti-Taliban alliance.[44] In the same month, Afghans were banned from changing their faith, and Kabulis were invited to 'introduce' to them any remaining Hindu, Sikh or Jewish residents for a chat.[45] In September, women were banned from wearing 'squeaky' shoes lest they impose an untoward awareness of their wearers' existence upon male citizens.[46] In October, an upsurge in *Sharia* punishments was reported as the religious police cracked down hard on beards and whiskers, which had to be sufficiently long to extend out of the bottom of a fisted hand.[47] Defaulters said they were whipped with steel cables, but not necessarily by the *Amr Bil Marof Wa Nai An Munkir*, for a stricter police force, loyal to Justice Minister Mullah Mohammad Turabi, had since taken to patrolling the streets of Kabul.[48]

On 11 November, two Afghan employees of UNICEF were hauled out of a vehicle in Jalalabad and one was given 10 lashes.[49] A day earlier, the UN's special rapporteur on human rights, Choong-Hyun Paik, released a report which described the 'cries of prisoners being tortured' in Taliban-held Kunduz; a mullah who had raped and killed five women, only to be released 'for being a good "Talib"'; and a remark by a Taliban leader that 'there were only two places for Afghan women: in her husband's house and in the graveyard'.[50] On 12 November, Angela King, the UN assistant secretary-general and special adviser on gender relations, arrived in Kabul but was not received. One day later, a UN cooordinator, Alfred Witschi-Cestari, urged the Taliban to lift the Bamian blockade, describing it as 'among the cruellest things to have happened here this year'.[51] By the New Year, the execution of sentences in the national sports stadium had become the chief source of amusement to crowds of 20–30,000 spectators: after a purge of 'weak men' in the ministries, Mullah Manon Niazi announced that a backlog of 25 alleged murderers and twelve cases of theft were due to be dealt with.[52] In Kandahar, Mullah Mohammad Omar had taken to presiding personally over the execution of sentence.[53] Dispensing with the customary Kalashnikov, the father of Jalil, murdered at Spin Boldak, used a knife on 30 March 1998 to slit the throat of the alleged perpetrator, amid the chanting of religious slogans.[54]

Two months earlier, a man who could expect much shorter shrift in a Taliban court, was publicly accused of serial fellatio in Washington.

* * *

Pakistan had little to show by early 1998, after nearly four years of investment in the Taliban. Saudi Arabia and its Gulf allies may have been underwriting the cost of military operations and the purchase of enemy defectors, but it was Islamabad which paid the full cost in terms of diplomatic isolation. Iran, predictably, was at daggers drawn: after three years probing of its eastern flank by Sunni extremists, the border with Afghanistan was closed and communications between the region's two largest Muslim powers had been reduced to monosyllables. That estrangement, at least, had been implicit from the very first draft of the Taliban plan.

But Pakistan's recognition of the movement in the previous May had put all the governments of Central Asia – with the exception of Turkmenistan – on high alert, while adding a layer of deeper complexity to the Afghan conflict by pre-empting a decision by the UN's Credentials Committee, still the final arbiter on questions of sovereignty. Further attempts to forge the kind of multi-ethnic government once envisaged by UN special envoy Mahmoud Mestiri were, henceforth, doomed first to renegotiating the status of a locally recognised, militarily secure but still Pashtun-dominated, Taliban rather than addressing the unwinnable character of the conflict itself. A string of delegations from the EU, the UN, Turkey, Uzbekistan, China, Iran and other leading Muslim states visited Islamabad in early 1998 to plead with Prime Minister Nawaz Sharif to press the Taliban to peace talks prior to the formation of a government of all the factions.[55]

Sharif's command of foreign policy was arguably as shaky as his military's control of the Taliban. He had been elected by a windfall in February 1997 – albeit on a turnout of less than 30 per cent of the electorate – to clean up the corruption of Benazir Bhutto's second administration, a mission he pursued vigorously through the law courts without ever seriously getting to grips with the economic malaise which had cast her profligacy in such a cynical light. Sharif's influence over foreign affairs, traditionally the realm of the military, was far less assured, except insofar as the cabinet could convert its *de facto* decisions over India, Kashmir, Afghanistan and, ultimately, the nuclear option, to domestic advantage, a vital consideration in a political landscape in which the shrinking centre was under constant pressure from the Islamist tendencies of the street.

For all its reputation as the guarantor of order in an otherwise volatile national chemistry, Pakistan's military tended towards the vainglorious in its conduct of foreign policy, currying flamboyant Islamist expectations and caring little for the cost to a civil administration which it treated no better than pen-pushers. The Taliban project had been indelibly felt at home. Thousands of unemployed young men flocked to the *jihad*, while guns, drugs and a bleak, sectarian ideology were re-imported, fostering violence between Sunnis and Pakistan's large Shia minority, and jeopardising in turn relations with Iran, the US and Saudi Arabia, whose interests demanded far more careful pandering. Sharif might have preferred to hedge support for the Taliban with more diplomatic restraints than Mrs Bhutto or her interior minister, Naseerullah Babar, but he was in no position to impose policy on the generals who had run the 'Afghan Cell' since 1979. One knowledgeable analyst suggests that Sharif, a novice in diplomacy, was kept intentionally in the dark about Afghan policy by Foreign Minister Gohar Ayub, going on to describe a ministry which had 'relegated its broader regional policy aims to a handful of Pashtun and fundamentalist policy makers ... who are the driving force of a pro-Taliban policy at the expense of all other interests'.[56] Even the kingpins of the ISI, however, must have been queasily reminded, after the defeat at Mazar, of their former protege, Hekmatyar, who managed always to draw blood, without ever quite delivering the *coup de grâce*.

The US, considered a sleeping partner in the scheme to impose a Pashtun-led peace – whether to open up Central Asia's energy, or suppress the local opium crop – had found grounds for altering its priorities between the Taliban's defeat and the next *Eid al-Fitr*. Despite his compelling significance in the background, bin-Ladin had not yet made the leap into contemporary demonology that would occur so explosively less than one year later. And, despite the raised voices of Hillary Clinton, Madeleine Albright and Emma

Bonino, the issue of gender rights had not percolated deep enough to cancel the *realpolitik* of gas pipelines. What was to transform perceptions of the region and Afghanistan was the suspicion that, inadvertently, the US had moved from one geological era of foreign policy management to quite another, a transition which would prune the expertise of a generation of Soviet-era advisers and open up an unmapped terrain in which, even as Pakistan teetered on the brink of eruption, Iran had mysteriously simmered down. As if in confirmation, 1998 was a year littered with anniversaries and fresh precedents.

The transition had been set in motion towards the end of 1997 with the creation of the UN's 6+2 Contact Group, a conference of all Afghanistan's immediate neighbours, with the addition of the US and Russia. It was the first successful attempt to assemble in the same room all the surrounding powers – excluding Saudi Arabia – which stoked the Afghan fires with weapons, fuel and money. More historically, the Contact Group provided an opportunity for the first face-to-face discussions between Washington and Tehran officials since the hostage crisis nearly 20 years earlier. They discovered they had more in common than either had realised: mutual concern over Iraq; the fight against drugs; instability in Afghanistan; and the future of Central Asia. This epiphany-strewn new relationship was nurtured for the remainder of 1998: first, through their studied collaboration over Iranian reactions to Taliban provocation – and the survival of Massoud; and then through Washington's assiduous screening of Tehran from any incrimination in the later activities of its former ally, Osman bin-Ladin.

The Afghan warlords spent the winter of 1997 rebuilding their stocks. The Taliban blockade of Bamian remained firm but Iran flew in supplies unmolested until December when the airport was bombed.[57] In the same month, Massoud captured the Tagab valley, east of Kabul, placing his forces in a similar position to the one Hekmatyar had enjoyed three years earlier, though his continued occupation of Bagram assured a continuing air-bridge from Tajikistan and Iran. In the north, the front between Mazar and Kunduz remained tense: on 13 February, Dostum was injured by mortar shrapnel and he retired to Tashkent for treatment.[58] One week later, Massoud advanced into Laghman, either as a prelude to a bid to cut the Jalalabad road or to relieve Taliban pressure on the Hazarajat.[59] Beyond this, there was little evidence of coordination between the components of the UIFLA alliance. In March, faction fighting broke out between Dostum's forces and *Hizb-i Wahdat* in Mazar, forcing the ICRC again to evacuate the northern capital.[60]

Efforts to further a peace internally had largely foundered the previous October, after the resignation of the UN special envoy, Dr Norbert Holl. He had been replaced by Lakhdar Brahimi, an Algerian with a successful history of resolving hostage situations, but he focused on a regional approach from New York, leaving Holl's Ugandan deputy, James Ngobi, in charge of the Islamabad office. On 25 March, UN relations with the Taliban took a more confrontational stance when the organisation suspended operations in Kandahar, after an edict barring foreign female Muslim employees from going out, unless accompanied by a male relative. Since most female staff were recruited from distant Muslim states, the ban was interpreted as a direct challenge from the emir, Mullah Mohammad Omar, himself. The decision to suspend operations followed three physical attacks on personnel: one had a coffee pot thrown at him by a Taliban official; another was slapped across the face; and a third assaulted with a table. Fourteen international staff were evacuated to Pakistan, and 120 local employees sent home.[61]

It was the US, rather than the UN, which set the pace in a bid to head off a return to total war in the spring. On 17 April, America's ambassador to the UN, Bill Richardson, flew to Kabul to meet the Taliban's number two, Mullah Rabbani, becoming the highest ranking US official to visit Afghanistan since Henry Kissinger.[62] 'He must not have with him the idea of imposing the values of Western civilisation under the terms the defence of human rights and women's ... rights,' warned the Taliban's *Shariat* newspaper, indifferent to the unique honour bestowed upon the leadership.[63] But that was precisely the kind of message Richardson had brought from Washington. In exchange for a softening of Taliban social policies in accordance with international norms, the US would use its influence at the UN to confirm international recognition.

That was only the first of his business. Attached to the recognition offer was an urgent codicil concerning bin-Ladin. Over the winter, Saudi intelligence secured the defection of Mohammad bin-Mosalih, one of bin-Ladin's chief accountants, who provided detailed information of the Saudi's extensive network of overseas financial transactions.[64] On 23 February, bin-Ladin issued a communique which announced the formation of the World Islamic Front, or *Qa'ida*, which called on Muslims to 'kill the Americans and their allies – civilian and military'. The release was co-signed by Refai

Ahmad Taha, spiritual leader of Egypt's *Gamaat al-Islamiya*, Ayman al-Zawahiri, head of Egypt's *Jihad*, Fazal ul-Rahman of Pakistan's *Harakat ul-Ansar* and Abdul Salaam Mohammad, chief of Bangladesh's *Jihad*.[65] Bin-Ladin had also been linked by US intelligence to two aborted attempts to assassinate President Clinton in the Philippines and Pakistan. The CIA's Counter-Terrorism Centre had reportedly organised a raid to capture the Saudi in the very month of Richardson's visit, a project that was dropped 'because of the potential for casualties among Americans and innocent Afghanis'.[66]

Richardson flew from Kabul to Shiburghan and Faizabad to meet Dostum and Rabbani, but Massoud was not included in the discussions and Mullah Mohammad Omar did not stir from his Kandahari reclusion. Richardson described his visit as a 'breakthrough' on returning to Islamabad – as if US influence could obtain in a day what had eluded the UN for nine years.[67] The Taliban, he said, had agreed to 'broaden girls' access to education' and allow more foreign female doctors to practise, promises that were neither elaborated in his statement, nor carried through. The peace process that all sides had agreed upon entailed the creation of a steering committee of five Taliban and nine opposition representatives charged with assembling a commission of 40 *ulama* to negotiate terms before 27 April – the 20th anniversary of the Saur Revolution which had brought the communists to power.[68]

Despite inevitable hair-splitting over what constituted an *alim* – and a shortlived Taliban offensive the day before – the commission met in Islamabad at the appointed date, evidence perhaps of a wistful desire on the part of all sides to give the American something concrete to take home. UIFLA demanded a permanent ceasefire, the exchange of prisoners and an end to the blockade of the Hazarajat. In Taloqan, Massoud expressed his weariness at 'resolutions' devised in Islamabad, while hawks in the Taliban had clearly received no firm notice from Pakistan that the military option had been worn out.[69] On 30 April, Mullah Wakil Ahmad Matawakil, head of the Taliban delegation, flew to Kandahar with a progress report for Mullah Mohammad Omar, never to return.[70] The Richardson initiative collapsed three days later and, on 5 May, fighting flared in the north as the Taliban in Kunduz launched an offensive into Massoud's province of Takhar.

Interest in the outcome was swiftly eclipsed by India's detonation of five nuclear devices at the Pokharan test range in Rajasthan during 11–13 May, barely two months after the Hindu extremist BJP took power in New Delhi. The abrupt nuclearisation of the sub-continent, with the increased potential for open war with Pakistan, earned condemnation and an immediate embargo on aid and investment from the US, which demanded that India sign the Comprehensive Test Ban Treaty and agree not to arm or deploy its weapons. New Delhi refused. Fifteen days later, Pakistan responded with six trials of a lesser magnitude in Baluchistan's Chagai Hills but, while the US reaction was muted by the recognition that Islamabad had acted in genuine self-defence, the punishment was identical and cut much deeper. Muslims around the world welcomed the birth of an 'Islamic bomb', but Pakistan suffered the cancellation of a crucial $500 million loan from the IMF, a 30 per cent collapse of the rupee, while food and fuel prices soared by 25 per cent.[71]

At 4.7 on the Richter scale, Pakistan's nuclear debut was 2,000 times less powerful than the earthquake which struck Badakhshan and Takhar on 2 June, killing some 5,000 people across an area of 1,750km^2.[72] Journalists detected a causal connection between the two events, due to Afghanistan's position on a 'tectonic plate border' – as good a way as any to sum up its importance for the political stability of the region. The June shock measured 7.1 on the Richter scale and tore fissures a quarter of a mile long in Dashtaq, close to the epicentre at Shari-i Bazurg, where a small blue lake suddenly appeared.[73] More than 70,000 people lost homes and livelihoods, but heavy summer rains and the tug-of-war between agencies and factions meant that no significant aid reached them till the third week of June. The fiasco was played out in the full glare of the cameras. Troops in Faizabad, mainly aligned with Massoud's *Jamiat-i Islami*, halted all shipments until they were granted their own ration, while companies across the Amu Darya haggled for special war insurance for the use of their helicopters.[74] NGOs condemned the UN's 'obsession' with helicopters, dispatching columns of relief-laden ponies over the passes and into the devastated valleys.[75] The Taliban launched an attack on Bangi, west of Taloqan, which was repulsed. An Israeli offer of 15 tonnes of relief was rejected by Kabul on religious grounds. On 29 June, the US agreed to find the helicopters to break the blockage, but neither Massoud, Pakistan nor the charter companies across the border would relent.[76]

The earthquake in the northeast was a potent reminder of the permanent need for a relief capability, however unwieldly, but it did little for the UN's standing in Kabul. Within days of the earthquake, Mawlawi Qalamuddin, head of the *Amr Bil Marof Wa Nai An Munkir*, ordered the closure of the clandestine schools for girls which had sprung up like mushrooms in Shia neighbourhoods after the Taliban took Kabul in September 1996.[77] 'These schools were operating illegally and in secret,' said a shocked spokesman, 'moving to different locations every day.'[78] In fact, the authorities had winked at the 100 or so 'home schools' for nearly two years, but Mullah Mohammad Omar had finally reached his momentous verdict on the wisdom of teaching the 'Three Rs' to girls under seven, even in a secluded setting. After the intimidation in Kandahar the previous March, and a humiliating climbdown by the UN in late May, it is likely that the Leader of The Faithful, or his deputies, had finally decided to terminate the UN mission in Afghanistan.

On 13 July, two UN Afghan staff, former professors at Jalalabad University, were abducted as they waited for a lift by the road, and their bodies were later found in river beds near the city.[79] Days later – in a not necessarily related move – Mullah Rabbani instructed all 38 NGOs working in the capital to move their quarters from Wazir Akhbar Khan to a group of unheated and unlit faculty buildings at the bombed-out Polytechnic, near the Shia neighbourhood of Karta Se. Relief workers protested that this placed them directly in the line of fire, while $1 million in repairs were still needed to bring the buildings to a habitable condition.[80] Two reasons were given out for the order: it was due to the NGOs' covert support to the home schools in the shape of books and salaries – or because their premises in the diplomatic quarter had so many windows through which to peer at Afghan women.[81]

Efforts by the UN and the EU to strike a compromise came to nothing, as did warnings of what would befall Kabul's 400,000 indigents were the agencies to live up to their threat and shut down programmes altogether. The Taliban insisted that the order had to be obeyed to 'protect our families'.[82] By 21 July, all but one of the NGOs had withdrawn their staff to Peshawar but their vehicles were attached by Taliban troops as they passed through Torkham Gate.[83] 'If we see them on the street,' said the head of security, 'we will take action under our laws.'[84] The UN estimated that the withdrawal would affect 75 per cent of relief projects in Kabul: Health Minister Mohammad Abbas, a former communist who also served under President Rabbani, announced an allocation of $25,000 to meet the immediate needs of the population in the wake of the NGO withdrawal.[85] In what appeared a retort to all who maintained that the Taliban lacked a sense of humour, the authorities ordered the closure of the ECHO office on 23 July, because Emma Bonino had 'used it for the spread of Christianity'.[86] But the Taliban weren't kidding: the 'joke' came closest to defining the true bone of contention between such alien cultures.

North of the Hindu Kush, the Taliban were again on the march. On 10 July, Maimana and Shiburghan succumbed in quick succession and, though Dostum attempted a counter-attack through Faryab, the offensive collapsed and he fled the country a second time.[87] In Maimana, aid workers reported that between 25 and 40 per cent of the conquering army were Urdu-speakers and, a month later, Massoud claimed that there were 1,700 Pakistanis among the 8,000-strong force.[88] When Sar-i Pul fell on 4 August, the UIFLA announced that 9,000 troops had been summoned to reinforce Mazar but, in the event, only 2,000 *Hizb-i Wahdat* fighters arrived from Bamian, Dar-i Suf and Balkhab.[89] So unflustered were the Mazaris by the danger from the west that, when 5,000 'Taliban' entered the city to the sound of gunfire at 9.30 a.m. on 8 August, they assumed it was just another of the frequent fallings-out between the armed factions and simply went about their business.[90]

The force that captured Mazar included Pashtun fighters from nearby Balkh – the 'mother of cities' – under the *Hizb-i Islami* regional commander, Juma Khan Hamdard, who had remained part of UIFLA in spite of the defection to the Taliban of the Kunduz Pashtuns one year before. *Hizb-i Wahdat*, suspecting their loyalty, had attacked their positions some weeks earlier, indulging in widespread rape and driving the Pashtun into the arms of the advancing enemy.[91] But the Taliban had grown wary of gift horses, wanting no repetition of General Malik's treachery in 1997. To prove their mettle and avenge their families, the Pashtuns agreed to circle behind the main line of defence at Qala Zainim in the western suburbs, trapping the entire *Hizb-i Wahdat* garrison of 1,500–3,000 troops, most of whom were picked off on the roads leading north and east out of the city.[92] A contingent of 700 fled south towards the Alborz mountains, along with stragglers from Dostum's and Massoud's forces and thousands of panicked Mazaris. The road was black with people and vehicles. For two days, the Taliban fired Katyusha multiple rockets at the retreating columns, while jets dropped cluster bombs on their heads.[93] Worse befell those who stayed behind.

The Balkhi Pashtuns acted as a shield as the Taliban entered the city, randomly shooting at anybody they met in the narrow streets surrounding the bazaar and in the boulevards which lead to the blue and gold shrine of Hasrat Ali – the so-called 'Noble Grave' – where Abdul-Ali Mazari, the *Hizb-i Wahdat* leader slain by the Taliban in February 1995, had also been interred.[94] They relished their new work. Hundreds of civilians lost their lives in the first hours after the city's capture but the shooting had largely subsided by midday when, again following leads provided by the Balkhis, the Taliban launched a house-to-house search for anyone of fighting age in the Hazara neighbourhoods of Zara'at, Saidabad and Elm Arab and, to a lesser extent, in the Tajik and Uzbek quarters.[95]

Those who spoke Pashtu, or whose faces lacked the Hazaras' characteristic Asiatic physiognomy, sporadically bluffed their way to survival, but most were betrayed by the ultimate *shibboleth* of not being able to pronounce the Sunni prayers. Discovered Hazaras were usually shot on the spot, preferably in the face or testicles, while some had their throats cut and yet more were carted off to the city jails.[96] One man escaped by throwing himself over the side of the truck. 'I landed on the right side of the road where there was a mosque,' he reported. 'I ran in ... and began to wash, as if I was preparing to pray.'[97] His friends landed on the left and were shot, as were most Hazaras upon arriving at their destination. Mazari Pashtuns who attempted to shelter their erstwhile neighbours were warned of a similar fate.[98]

The Balkhis' method of dealing with Hazaras was swiftly endorsed by the new governor of Mazar, Mullah Manon Niazi, a Farsi-speaking Pashtun of a Herati mother and one of a handful of sympathisers from minority groups brought into the leadership after the 1997 massacre to bolster Taliban claims that it was a multi-ethnic coalition, rather than a wholly Pashtun movement.[99] Niazi distinguished himself as governor of Kabul by fast-tracking the programme of public executions and he arrived at his new northern appointment with great enthusiasm.[100] On 9 August – the second day of the takeover – he began a series of speeches on local radio, in mosques and other public spaces in which he denounced the Hazaras for the 1997 massacre – although it was general knowledge that General Malik's Uzbeks had carried out the atrocities in Shiburghan – and threatened reprisals at a rate of three Shia lives for every Taliban slain more than a year earlier.[101] But Niazi went further.

'Hazaras are not Muslim,' he said at one mosque, 'they are Shia. They are *kofr* (infidel).'[102] And, therefore, no better than animals. Seventy men had their throats cut at the tomb of Abdul-Ali Mazari in the *halal* ritual reserved for sheep, while Shia patients were dragged from their beds in hospital and taken outside and shot.[103] Niazi forbade relatives from removing the bodies of the dead from the street for five days or 'until the dogs ate them', a dreadful sacrilege, and Shia mosques were whitewashed, renamed and converted to Sunni places of worship.[104] Of greater moment, however, was the fact that Niazi's official dehumanisation of Shias was understood by the rank-and-file as permission to rape, an event without precedent in the Taliban's four-year career. In one of several recorded instances, a girl from Ali Chopan was among 20–25 girls held for an unspecified time by Taliban and raped every night. 'One Talib told her that now that you are *halal* (sanctified), [she] should go to his parents in Kandahar and wait for him to come and marry her.'[105] From other houses, Hazara girls were taken south to work as *kaniz*, or maids, a fate their great-grandparents might easily have suffered a century earlier when the enslavement of Hazaras was commonplace in Afghanistan.[106]

On their arrival in Mazar, the Taliban had freed Pashtun criminals to make space in the prisons for Hazaras, Tajiks and Uzbeks. As the jails overflowed with the fresh intake, detainees had to be shifted to prisons in Shiburghan, Herat and Kandahar in containers 20–40 feet long, each of which could hold between 100–150 men in asphyxiating conditions. The shipping container has achieved in Afghanistan a status imbued with architectural, historical, but sometimes horrific meaning. Plastered with mud and thatched, boxes that once held Cold War munitions or smuggled cargo were transformed into cool, secure artisans' premises: ordered ranks of them are found outside every town, like so many fast-food outlets at the edge of an American city. They also make excellent prisons. Abdul Rasul Sayyaf, head of the Pashtun faction *Ittehad-i Islami*, killed Hazaras in Kabul by locking them in a container and building a fire around it.[107] Some 35 containers left the prisons of Mazar in the week following the takeover and, in two cases at least, nearly all the prisoners had died from heat or lack of air by the time the metal door was reopened. 'In Shiburghan,' said one witness, 'they brought three containers close to the jail. When they opened the door of one truck, only three persons were alive. About 300 were dead... The Taliban asked [someone I know] and three Turkmen to go with them to the Dasht-i Leili. The Taliban did not want to touch the bodies, so the porters took the bodies out of the containers.'[108]

News of the massacre did not leak abroad until November 1998 when, evading a nationwide dragnet, the first Hazara refugees crossed the border to spill out their sombre tales in Pakistan. Hazaras had to convince the Taliban guards in Zabul, Kandahar and Jalalabad that they were not 'fighters', while, at Spin Boldak, bribery was necessary to cross the border. Human rights organisations later set the toll as high as 4–6,000, with an estimated 4,500 men still under detention as late as October.[109] The Taliban denied all knowledge, but applications by journalists to investigate the killings in Mazar – even from Pakistanis with close links to the Kandahari leadership – were dismissed out-of-hand. 'In the run-up to their bid for international acceptance,' commented a European diplomat, 'imposing this iron curtain is sending very bad signals to the outside world.'[110]

'Bad signals' had already been received in the Hazarajat. Three weeks after the fall of Mazar, the Hazara stronghold of Bamian capitulated but, when the Taliban column streamed into the city which had once boasted 40,000 inhabitants, it found only 50 old men – who were promptly killed.[111] The entire citizenry had fled into the famished highlands, fearing hunger less than a fresh encounter with their now rampant enemies. Some *Hizb-i Wahdat* commanders bowed to Taliban rule without offering resistance, but there was heavy fighting in Yakawlang, the party's main headquarters, before the region finally succumbed. 'The clock has been turned back 100 years to a time when the Hazaras were officially denied the most basic of human rights,' commented one Western analyst.[112]

A further casualty was one of two ancient Buddhas carved 38 metres high in the sandstone cliffs which overlook Bamian and had made it a pilgrimage centre for over 2,000 years. In the whoop of victory, a Taliban tank commander took aim and fired, hitting the figure squarely in the jaw and groin.

13 A Fistful of Dollars

> It's been an amazing run. Hey, every once in a while, we do something right. FBI agent[1]

On 7 August, the day before the Taliban stormed into Mazar-i Sharif, bank worker Jack Omukhai visited his wife Elizabeth at the Ufundi Cooperative Building at the corner of Moi and Haile Selassie Avenues in the heart of Nairobi, Kenya. They spoke of 'little things' and, after sharing a cup of tea, he left. Half an hour later, she was dead, one of 263 people – 12 of them American – who perished in a bomb attack on the nearby US embassy that left a further 5,500 injured.[2] The explosion had been planned to the split second. A lesser device was detonated at the US embassy in Dar es Salaam at the same time, killing 10 Tanzanians. It was eight years to the day since US troops first touched down in Saudi Arabia to take up their positions for the Gulf War in 1990, a date that rankled throughout the radical Islamic world.[3]

The ambassador had warned of poor security at the city centre location well before February, when bin-Ladin's threats against US targets, military and otherwise, were first taken seriously, putting all US facilities in a state of high alert. The Nairobi embassy was especially vulnerable. Since the closure of stations in Khartoum and Mogadishu, both in different ways cauterised by failures in US policy in Muslim Africa, Nairobi had evolved into the CIA's chief listening post for an area reaching from Madagascar to former Zaire and Yemen and encompassing the entire, war-prone Horn of Africa. Jomo Kenyatta Airport, meanwhile, had become the crossroads of a trading empire which once sailed the Indian Ocean and Red Sea and had adapted seamlessly to flying. But lack of resources, Africa's low priority in Washington and the sheer scale of the Nairobi watch had led to a critical deterioration in preparedness. So far gone was regional intelligence in January 1996 that the CIA publicly discounted 100 of its leading reports on Sudan – officially a 'terrorism-exporting' country and a proven ally of both bin-Ladin and Iran – after concluding that their source, not American, was a 'fabricator'.[4]

A posse of CIA and FBI agents descended upon Kenya after the bombings to explore every avenue of enquiry from Nairobi to

Mombasa on the coast, where Kenya's Sunni minority lived. Suspicion, at first, fell on Egyptian *Jihad*, the nearest, active Islamist grouping to Kenya and one that had demonstrated the least qualms when it came to the murder of Western civilians. Secretary of State Madeleine Albright offered a $2 million reward for information leading to the perpetrators, but it was a shot in the dark. A day after the explosion, a US official said: 'We have no suspects. Everything is up for grabs.'[5]

Since the Oklahoma City bombing by white terrorists in 1995, Washington had become wary of ritually pointing the finger of blame at 'Islamists'. Yet, in the reams of editorial copy generated by the Kenyan cataclysm, one thesis is singularly absent. Nowhere is there speculation as to possible involvement in the explosions by Sudan, Libya and, even more particularly, to Iran, states which had all been accused of sponsoring overseas terrorism in the past. Even Saudi Arabia had something to gain from counterfeiting a bin-Ladin operation, in view of the crumbling trade and political embargoes which had characterised recent US policy towards Tehran, hitherto a confirmed backer of the renegade Saudi. Through an apparently silent, but inexorable, process of consensus-building, the Nairobi bloodbath had been turned from a conspiracy of countries, to one of freelance individuals. Days after the explosion, Radio France International was contacted by the unknown Islamic Army for the Liberation of Muslim Holy Places, which claimed responsibility for both bombs.[6] The communique, according to the Lebanese newspaper *Al-Safir*, was the product of a learned mind, free of religious hyberbole, determined upon its enemy and evidently capable of superb planning.

One day after the bombing, the first suspect in the conspiracy, Mohammad Saddiq Odeh, was arrested in Karachi, having travelled from Nairobi on a Yemeni passport whose photo did not quite match his face. Under intensive interrogation, he confessed to working for bin-Ladin's *Qa'ida* and to assembling the Nairobi bomb, though he later recanted, accusing Pakistani intelligence of employing torture.[7] In late August when, according to the FBI, he was 'singing like a canary', Odeh told a Manhattan court that the plotters left Kenya the day before the attack and that they had shaved their beards so as 'not to raise suspicion'.[8] So much for planning. He sullenly refused to repeat his confession to the FBI, to whose custody he was transferred in mid-August, having been first wrung dry by Pakistani and Kenyan intelligence. Odeh, 34, made an unprepossessing holy warrior. A Palestinian from Jordan, he arrived in Kenya in 1994, settling near Mombasa to work as a fishmonger, buying upcountry stock to sell to the city's hotels. In 1997, he moved to the dead-end settlement of Witu near the bandit-ridden Somali border – an ideal conduit for smuggled explosives – where he opened a carpentry shop, living piously but in poverty. His Kenyan wife said he had travelled to Nairobi only once in the previous five months, but that was untrue. He must have caught the plane to Karachi from the capital and Kenyan carpenters, as a rule, do not fly. He could account neither for the fare, nor his income. The FBI charged Odeh with riding to the embassy in a bomb-laden vehicle and tossing a grenade at the guard. He faced charges of murder on 12 counts, all against American dead.

As such evidence emerged – and it remained extraordinarily tenuous until mid-September – bin-Ladin was propelled from a shadowy *eminence grise* into a front-page villain. In the absence of solid leads, however, the press focused upon the Saudi's finely-spun web of financial interests and his back catalogue of alleged confederates – including, during the *jihad*, the CIA – rather than the case in hand and none took the time to enquire whether the indiscriminate slaughter at the Ufundi Cooperative Building actually chimed with the self-styled seer's recent *fatwa*. The first rule in vilification is to strip the target of a human dimension, and then its right to reply. In February 1998, bin-Ladin had issued the ruling that 'to kill the Americans and their allies – civilian and military – is an individual duty for every Muslim who can do it in any country in which it is possible to do it'. But he relied for listeners, then as in the past, upon the moral authority of his pronouncements and the tragedy inflicted upon so many Kenyans – some of them devout Muslims – formed no part of such a persona. When asked, he strenuously denied any direct involvement in the embassy bombings, though he did admit to having 'instigated' them, an equivocation which could have stemmed from bin-Ladin's overweening vanity as America's public enemy number one – or the need to cover up a bungled operation.[9] To admit to incompetence would have detracted from Islamist rapture at outwitting the US war machine. Nevertheless, FBI Director Louis Freeh appeared to side with bin-Ladin, telling a journalist that, personally, he had come to 'no firm conclusions' as to who was responsible for the bombs, and that was some days after the US took its furious revenge.[10]

As Odeh was being questioned in Karachi, other strategic killings were taking place in Mazar. 'At about 12 noon, a group of Taliban came to the door of the consulate-general,' recalled an Iranian diplomat, Allahdad Shahsavan-Qarahosyeni.

> In the mission at the time were all [nine] staff and the [official news agency] IRNA correspondent, Mahmoud Saremi. After asking us to hand over any weapons, they moved us into another room, where they conducted body searches and took our money. One, possibly a Pakistani, asked to use the telephone to call Pakistan. Since Pakistan had undertaken to ensure our safety, he probably wanted to let them know about the state of things at the mission. But the others stepped in and wouldn't allow him to call.
>
> We did not in any way act contrary to their wishes. They asked for the keys to the mission's cars, they asked for fruit juice. We gave it to them. Then they moved us down to the basement, which contained a single desk. Three of their leaders walked in and immediately raised their weapons. They said they were going to kill us and lined us up against the wall. As they fired the first one or two bullets, I decided to throw myself to the ground and it occurred to me that I had to use the only piece of furniture that was there. I dragged the top half of my body under the desk and lay totally flat. All my friends and brothers were falling to the ground and some were martyred in that first instant.
>
> I tried to make not the slightest movement and to control my breathing. I shut my eyes and recited my final prayers. I was, in a way, waiting to witness my own death, but God bestowed his mercy on me. It seems I was destined to live so I could act as an ambassador who could recount the truth, in view of the fact that they wanted to portray events differently. I could see their legs from beneath the desk and I saw them slowly leave. I waited a few moments. The mission was totally silent.[11]

Shahsavan-Qarahosyeni was the only occupant to escape the Mazar consulate and no record exists of how he survived in the city until 12 September when, under open threat of invasion by Iran, the Taliban managed to 'discover' the bodies of his colleagues on a suburban midden. The rattling of Iranian sabres had become deafening in the preceding weeks as spiritual leader Ayatollah Sayed Ali Khameini called the Taliban 'lowly and worthless', former President Akbar Hashemi Rafsanjani vowed revenge and President

Khatami contributed the interesting mantra 'orthodox savages'. Revolutionary Guards rushed to the border after the diplomats' disappearance, building to a strength of nine divisions, or around 200,000 troops, supported by armour and air power. The US urged restraint, but a stream of visceral militarist and sectarian rage flooded through Iranian loudspeakers.

Mahmoud Saremi's reports from the Shibar Pass, Shiburghan, Mazar and other battlegrounds had made him into a well-known media figure and Iranians listened, first gripped but finally horrified, as the Taliban approached the Shia pilgrimage centre and turned it into an abattoir. Now, having captured Massoud's rear base of Taloqan on 11 August after 12 hours of shelling, they were poised to take Bamian, promising slaughter in another populous Shia centre, while the authority of Karim Khalili, the *Hizb-i Wahdat* leader, was faltering and his party threatened to splinter into three factions ahead of a damaging struggle for the leadership of the Hazara cause.[12] Fifty Iranian truckers, meanwhile, remained in Taliban custody, accused of transporting arms to the alliance.

Intervention by Iran was inevitable on a variety of counts; histrionic, in the case of the diplomats, Saremi and the drivers; chauvinist, to repel the Pakistani-backed onslaught against Iranian influence and honour in Afghanistan; religious, to prevent a sectarian massacre in Bamian, similar to the one in Mazar; and military, to divert Taliban troops from the north and so win Massoud and *Hizb-i Wahdat* a breathing space in which to regroup. As the war rhetoric flew, however, there was little interest in how a diplomatic delegation, widely known to have coordinated supplies of weapons to the Northern Alliance, had been allowed to remain at its post even as an enemy, bent on revenge for the murder of Taliban prisoners in May 1997, was hammering at the gates and the frontier lay just 50 km distant. The prospect that the diplomats were purposely sacrificed by elements in the polarised Iranian government to create a foreign policy dilemma for President Khatami, then seeking to mend fences in the world outside, rather than declare a state of war, was far from outlandish.

The hunt for evidence to connect bin-Ladin to the East African bombings galloped parallel – with scarcely a nose between – to Special Prosecutor Kenneth Starr's pursuit of testimony to illuminate the precise nature of President Bill Clinton's relationship with Monica Lewinsky. The former White House intern's secrets had transfixed America since January, when allegations of her sexual relationship with the president were first leaked to the press. The disclosure hurled the US public into a frenzy of prime-time soul-searching, paralysing the proper workings of government and converting the US's highest office into a worldwide object of mirth. Dried semen, in the public eye, had replaced national security as the chief concern of a naked and exposed presidency. It was against this background that National Security Adviser Sandy Berger, Defence Secretary William Cohen, Joint Chiefs of Staff Chairman General Henry Shelton and CIA Director George Tenet met in Washington on 12 August to examine the US's options in response to the East African bombings, amid 'intelligence reports' that there was to be a gathering of the leaders of Islamist militant groups at bin-Ladin's training camp at Al-Badri, near Khost, on 20 August.[13]

US intelligence had been aware of the new functions of Badris 1 and 2 for at least two years, and probably far longer, but it had taken no action for fear of estranging Pakistan and because, a generation earlier, the CIA itself had helped establish the facilities as a means of furthering the *jihad* against the Soviet Union.[14] As revelations of bin-Ladin's alleged activities tumbled forth from the press, quivering at point like a novice gundog, a Senate enquiry appeared way overdue into the indecision displayed by the intelligence services when confronted with a real and present danger, eerily reconstituted from their own past misdemeanours. What precisely had the combined CIA and FBI leadership done to pre-empt bin-Ladin's two aborted assassination bids against President Clinton? What efforts had been made to eliminate the Saudi, or to disrupt his hostile network in the wake of the bombings of the World Trade Centre and Khobar Towers? Very little in the past two years, according to intelligence sources, apart from the defection of one close adviser. The sole attempt to kill or capture bin-Ladin, planned sometime prior to Bill Richardson's visit in April 1998, had been aborted due to the expected number of US and Afghan casualties. Was fear of casualties a convincing enough reason for America's Praetorian Guard to allow a committed assassin to remain on the loose, or was it fear of public exposure, or something more unthinkable? Blame-shirking, it seemed, had become a guiding principle of the CIA and the presidency equally in the days after the Nairobi bombing.

For all their posturing, only the intelligence services could identify targets worthy of American vengeance in its fight against this invisible, Islamist conspiracy. The protocol of terror required a minimum of two US strikes, one for each embassy. Intelligence provided three; one was unanimously fictive, the second, a debateable shot in the foot, while a third, in the form of a postscript, served as a gunboat to the distant, but no less alarming, polemic over nuclearisation in the Indian sub-continent. On 14 August, the four US military and spying chiefs briefed Clinton, who approved their plans and, three days later, US citizens were advised to leave Afghanistan.[15] At 6.30 GMT on 20 August, as Monica Lewinsky lay dreaming of the detail she would reveal to the Grand Jury later that day about oral sex and fondling, 70–100 Tomahawk cruise missiles were launched at targets in Khartoum, Sudan and near Khost. The Afghan-directed missiles contained 166 bomblets each of 3.3lbs and were designed – like Lewinsky's confession, perhaps – to cause maximum damage over a wide area, rather than to take out a single, pinpointable target.

The missiles purred across the Arabian Sea and Pakistani fields before dropping, on a satellite's instructions, into four terrorist training sites in the valleys around Khost. Sources vary as to which groups were targeted, but the more reliable agree that two were administered by *Harakat ul-Mujahideen* (HUM), schooling militants to fight in Kashmir; a third, Al-Farooq, used to train 'Arabs'; while the fourth, situated 16 km west of the city and controlled by bin-Ladin, was Al-Badri, identified by the press at Zhawar Kili Al-Badr.[16] The Saudi had called a Pakistani journalist on his satellite phone just three hours before the bombing, allowing US electronic tracking to confirm his presence in the camp.[17] In September, he passed a message to the London-based *Al-Quds al-Arabi* saying six of his followers had been killed, including three Yemenis, two Egyptians and one Saudi.[18] He himself was unharmed, but rumours of lumbago or kidney trouble circulated for some weeks after as he appeared in Kandahar walking with the aid of a cane.[19]

HUM's casualties were higher. At a rambunctious press conference in Islamabad's Holiday Inn, HUM Secretary-General Fazi Rahman Khalil, whose party has been implicated in the murder of four Western hostages in Kashmir, claimed that 21 of his troops were killed and 40 wounded in a camp that he described as an 'educational institution'.[20] A score of well-armed security men agreed. Post-strike conditions at Al-Farooq, by far the most interesting and least visible of the four targeted camps, were never followed up, unfortunately. But one of the Tomahawks launched that morning landed – but did not explode – at Kharan, close to the nuclear-testing facility in the Chagai Hills in Baluchistan. It exposed, accidentally or intentionally, Islamabad's amateurish vulnerability as a new-wave, nuclear contender.[21]

President Clinton broke the news of the missile strike at a press conference in the resort island of Martha's Vineyard, calling bin-Ladin's network 'as dangerous as any state we face'. Under pressure to deny that US foreign policy had degenerated into a tool of the president's legal team, Defense Secretary William Cohen and George Tenet, director of the CIA, responded with remarks that gave flesh to bin-Ladin's new profile as a psychological mastermind who dwelled in permanent twilight, planning the next urban massacre while hanging on the phone to acquire biological weapons for more nefarious purposes. Evidence for the latter allegation was fast unravelling. The second major target of the 20 August attack had been the Al-Shifa pharmaceutical plant near Khartoum, a factory allegedly constructed with bin-Ladin's financial assistance during his sojourn there in the early 1990s and which, US intelligence insisted, was engaged in the production of VX nerve gas. This assertion was founded upon soil samples collected outside the plant by field agents – some of whose evidence the CIA had found reason to discount in January 1996. According to Washington, Saddam Hussein had evacuated part of his biochemical armoury to Khartoum during the Gulf War and bin-Ladin, increasingly his equal in the annals of Western paranoia, was using the plant to reap the jackpot. In a rare display of the unblinking stare, however, Khartoum categorically reiterated that Al-Shifa was nothing more than what it seemed, a factory in one of the world's poorest countries which produced medicines for children and vaccines for Sudan's multitudinous cattle. The government called on the UN to hold an independent enquiry. The factory's engineers argued that the US allegations were implausible on technical grounds. The US refused to divulge its intelligence. As far as Washington was concerned, the matter was closed.

* * *

In what followed the US failure to bomb bin-Ladin into oblivion in August 1998 there was a resounding echo of the attack three years earlier on the Pakistani embassy after the fall of Herat to the Taliban. In both cases, the mob was summoned to the street and a delegation, which had breezily presumed immunity to events on the ground – even as it appeared to work hand in glove with the aggressor – discovered it had become the focus of orchestrated, public anger. It was the UN's turn, after Al-Badri, to suffer for the ambiguity of its functions. Protests erupted across Afghanistan and Pakistan within hours of the strike becoming known. Thousands marched though the derelict streets of Kabul on 21 August to protest in front of the empty US embassy in Wazir Akhbar Khan and, in Jalalabad, a UN compound was set ablaze. Across the border, UN workers were hastily evacuated from Peshawar to the more sedate capital. In Kabul, staff were left to fend for themselves.

Lieutenant Calo Carmine, a UN military observer from Italy, and the French diplomat Eric Lavertu, were driving to their offices on the morning after the Khost attack, when a pickup loaded with armed men overtook and fired at their clearly-marked jeep. Carmine was hit in the chest, Lavertu in the hand. 'This was not an error, but a reaction to yesterday's American attack,' said the Italian chargé d'affaires in Islamabad.[22] Carmine later died of his wounds in a Red Cross clinic. The authorities promptly arrested two Pakistani suspects, leading in time to the macabre scenario whereby the Italian's grieving mother was invited to Kabul to carry out the execution by Kalashnikov in accordance with Taliban justice. In spite of their outrage at the US missile attack, the Taliban were clearly mortified by what had happened. Armed escorts were provided for the last 20 international staff on their final journey to the Khyber Pass. Afghanistan had joined the small club of states which could no longer guarantee the safety of their foreign 'guests' – except one, that is – and all within weeks of the next UN Credentials Committee meeting.

Pakistan was also rocked by disorder in the wake of the Khost attack and not solely in the streets. Amid rumours of further strikes, Prime Minister Nawaz Sharif was accused of having received advance warning of the raid – painting him as a collaborator with US 'anti-Islamism' – while columnists openly speculated that the country might be so destabilised that its new nuclear capability could fall into the hands of HUM's Fazi Rahman Khalil or Maulana Fazl ul-Rahman, head of the pro-Taliban *Jamiat ul-Ulama-i Islam*, both of whom appeared inclined to wage 'total war' against the US. Islamabad could not be seen to be hindering Washington's pursuit of bin-Ladin, but nor did popular opinion allow it to assist in his capture. 'The possibility of backlash is there,' said former ISI head Hamid Gul, 'if people feel that the government helped Americans in the 'get-Osama' operation.'[23] Whether the government had prior knowledge or otherwise, the Tomahawks exposed Pakistan, at the very least, as a co-sponsor of 'terrorism' simply for allowing such training camps to exist so close to its borders.

The only US voice raised in Pakistan's defence, interestingly, was that of James Woolsey, CIA director in the first Clinton administration. He deplored the attacks on HUM and warned of the dangers of a pro-Indian bias stealing into the US handling of regional politics: 'We do not have a dog in this fight. Depending on who you believe, these people are terrorists or freedom fighters'. He queried the value of the phrase 'states sponsoring terrorism'. In Sudan and Afghanistan, individuals were richer than states, he said: 'it is a case of terrorists sponsoring the state' and 'the state is a victim'.[24] The US attacks were sufficient to tip the prime minister towards a significant concession to the extreme conservatives, a direction he might in time have chosen anyway to strengthen his power base, but one which nonetheless confirmed the fear that Pakistan, a former Cold War satrap, was sliding inexorably towards 'talibanisation'. At the end of August – 10 days after Khost – Sharif committed the government to introducing *sharia* law by the end of the year. 'Today in Afghanistan ...' he elaborated, 'I have heard that one can safely drive a vehicle full of gold at midnight without fear. I want this kind of system in Pakistan.'[25] 'That will doubtless bring peace,' responded the Human Rights Commission of Pakistan, 'the peace of the graveyard.'[26]

If Islamabad was anxious about the loss of Islamist 'face', the Taliban seemed more concerned by the challenge presented by the raids to their sense of sovereign and personal integrity, the *pashtunwali*. Mullah Mohammad Omar, spiritual leader of the Taliban, arguably had no dog in the fight either, preferring to address the immediate problem of recognition by persuading the UN to return to Kabul, to becoming embroiled in an international incident with the US and seeing his aid-dependent economy further martyred for a cause in which Afghanistan had no obvious stake. It was less than two weeks since the conquest of Mazar and Iran was still in a high lather about its diplomats, whose fate would not become clear for three weeks more. Massoud's disorganised forces, meanwhile, were bottled up in the valleys of Parwan, Takhar and Badakhshan provinces, clinging to the arms trade through a single river crossing at Ishkashim in the far-off Wakhan Corridor. Immediate pursuit was vital to prevent their resupply and eventual recuperation. But bin-Ladin was a friend and quite possibly a relative as well and none of the charges made by Washington convinced the Mullah that his friend was guilty of anything. Mohammad Omar was in a typically Afghan trap of hearing ultimata from a superpower and the genetic reaction had been mapped out centuries ago. 'Even if all the countries in the world unite,' he said the morning after the raid, 'we would defend Osama by our blood.'[27]

Halfway through September, another close friend of the Taliban, Saudi Arabia, withdrew its diplomats from Kandahar and cut off the movement's supply of dollars. Riyadh's rupture with the Taliban leader was threatening in the extreme. The national intelligence service, the *Mukhabarat*, cleared bin-Ladin of any involvement in the Khobar Towers bombing in 1997 – much to the disgust of its US counterpart – so the cutting, or 'downgrading' as it was termed, of the Saudi diplomatic link signalled that an influential ally had either been bullied back into some semblance of obedience after the African bombings, or had decided to press more forcefully for bin-Ladin's extradition. With the Credentials Committee meeting approaching, the Taliban's advocates were reduced to two, Pakistan and the UAE; one was tainted after the bombing of Khost, the other generally mute in international fora. By November the collapse in hard currency inflows from both Saudi Arabia and the UN relief effort had the movement teetering on bankruptcy amid a wave of defections by fair-weather friends in the north, not unconnected to the Taliban's precipitous finances.

In spite of the Khost bombing and the disappointment of the Richardson mission the previous April, the US continued with efforts to negotiate the extradition of bin-Ladin in a series of letters to the Afghan ambassador to Pakistan, Mulawi Saeed ur-Rehman Haqqani. He refused to accept delivery of one such letter on 1 September as a result of the attack but, three days later, dispatched a lowly *chowkidar* to take the proffered envelope.[28] It specified the US's willingness to actively expedite the process of international recognition in exchange for bin-Ladin – a remarkable offer in view of other bones of contention with the West. 'This seems to be the only hurdle in winning recognition...,' the Mullah said two months later when the gambit was finally exhausted. 'Other issues, like respect for human and women's rights and control of drug-trafficking, are no longer mentioned as vigorously as in the past.'[29]

Mohammad Omar was prepared to ground the Saudi, but not to surrender him. Surviving Khost, bin-Ladin had also learned an important lesson about the traceability of the satellite phone user and his calls to the press took a steep tumble thereafter. 'We asked him to refrain from military and political activities,' the Mullah told one journalist, using the euphemisms of command. 'Bin-Ladin has accepted our advice and promised to abide by it.'[30] On 14 September, the irrepressible terrorist got word out via an accomplice to the London-based *Al-Quds al-Arabi*, denying that he had been placed under house arrest, although the paper's editor, Abd al-Bari Atwan, later relayed the message that 'they put him up in a house, a safe house and prevented any outside contacts' – which amounted to much the same.[31] Atwan was certain of one thing: 'The man has been attacked by the Americans and usually when he threatens, he delivers. We should take this threat as seriously as we can.'[32] The US had, in the wake of the East African bombings, allocated $10 billion to counter-terrorism activities and shut down all but three of its embassies in Africa, a continent of over 50 nations.

In spite of the Mullah's confidence, evidence against his friend was fast accumulating. On 22 September, bin-Ladin's alleged weapons procurer and accountant, Mahmoud Salim, was arrested in Bavaria while on a mission to buy used cars. Two days later, London police arrested Khalid Fawaz, of the Saudi dissident group Advice and Reform Committee, along with Adel Abdul Mageed Abdul-Abari and five other Egyptians, all known associates of bin-Ladin. Abdul-Abari had been sentenced to death *in absentia* for a bomb attack in Cairo and was identified as 'instigator' in the killing of 58 foreign tourists and four Egyptians at the Luxor temple complex in November 1997. In Texas, agents picked up Wadih Hage, formerly bin-Ladin's personal secretary in Sudan, who was also a friend of the Nairobi suspect, Mohammad Saddiq Odeh, and currently managed a Fort Worth tyre shop. He was charged on 11 counts with lying during an investigation into *Qa'ida*'s attempts to procure chemical weapons, and for providing logistical support and training to 'the persons who attacked the US and UN forces in Somalia in 1993 and the early part of 1994'.[33] Hage's former housemate, furthermore, was said to have been Haroun Fazil, a native of the Comoros Islands suspected of playing a key role in the Nairobi bombing, who disappeared in the aftermath and now carried a $2 million bounty on his head.[34]

While the Taliban leadership weighed the contradictory demands of friendship and financial advantage, the Iranian crisis rumbled on across the western frontier, rising in tenor as the bodies of the diplomats finally surfaced. Sixteen thousand five hundred troops were airlifted to the border in early September to repel an anticipated incursion and there were suggestions that Iranian air attacks were only averted in mid-August through back-channel contacts between Washington and Tehran concerning the US's imminent plans for Khost.[35] If true, it pointed to a flattering degree of consultation between capitals at loggerheads since the overthrow of the Shah 20 years earlier and casts an intriguing light on the State Department's reluctance to brand the East African bombings as acts of the state-sponsored terrorism pioneered by Tehran. As late as 12 September, the state-owned daily *Jomhouri Eslami* was continuing to play it straight: 'The end is still not clear in the savage genocide which the evil triangle of America, Saudi Arabia and Pakistan have launched, but all indications are that the Taliban and their bloodthirsty backers have sharpened their swords for further crimes against Afghanistan's oppressed peoples.'[36] On 16 September, UK Foreign Office Minister Derek Fatchett applied soothing balm from Qatar: 'We do understand Iranian anguish and frustration, but the best way to resolve that would be through diplomatic, and not military, action.'[37] Five days later, US Secretary of State Madeleine Albright and Iranian Foreign Minister Kamal Kharazi took tea together in New York in the two states' highest level meeting in 20 years and, possibly, the most surprising rapprochement of the decade.

Whatever the US and Iranian intentions, their missiles and threats had bought time for Massoud, a 'caged animal' hemmed in on three sides, who was using one of his last Mil-17 helicopters to ferry personal possessions to Tajikistan in readiness for exile, according one Taliban commander.[38] A visiting French journalist – the French were always his most fervent admirers – painted a sombre portrait in October of the Lion of Panjshir and his 'Christlike thinness', a Napoleon stripped of power gazing silently down through the chopper's windows at the fleeting northern valleys he had fought over for 20 years while clearing his mind for the grinding haggle with avaricious Russians at the airport in Dushanbe.[39] This was Massoud the Last *Mujahid*: his allies and enemies alike – Rabbani, Dostum, Khalili, Ismail Khan, Hekmatyar, Abdul Malik, Haqqani, Khalis and the rest – had all died, defected or fled the field.

He alone – and the 200–300 Tajik and Pashtun commanders who piled into a mosque in the Panjshir valley to hear him speak – retained the right to wear the *kolas*, the emblem not solely of the successful *jihad* against the Soviets, but of an Afghan nationalism overtaken by a modern obscurantism. He mocked the 'Ubuesque' regime in Kabul, but talked to his followers as comrades not as a demagogue, and remained convinced, even after two decades of combat and intrigue, that they were still fighting a war of resistance against Pakistani colonialism. 'We have lost Mazar-i Sharif,' he explained wearily. 'The commander did what the officers of Basir Salangi did here at the Salang Tunnel, when they went over to the Taliban, or Abdul Malik in the province of Faryab. He betrayed, sold out. He delivered his city for a fistful of dollars.' Massoud regretted not becoming the engineer for which he initially studied – a luxury, ironically, enjoyed throughout the *jihad* by Osama bin-Ladin.[40] This was a leader enfeebled, with his back to the rocks after 20 years of fighting and now reverting to the same whispered appeal he had employed in the corridors of his youthful rebelliousness. But he was not yet at the end of his charm, or the unique traits which made him Massoud, a general conjuring confidence from the cruellest emptiness in the world. A rare personal photograph, about one year earlier, had captured the love-light streaming in both directions between his eyes and those of his son, then seven and obviously as spoilt as a *khan*. Exile was as unconscionable as breaking that beam.

The loss on 11 August of Massoud's supply base in Taloqan had been serious, but it was not a fatal blow to a man used to eluding the Soviets' far superior armoury, while the Taliban faced the enormous task of imposing their will upon the great swathe of territory which had fallen under their rule since the collapse of resistance in Mazar-i Sharif. Manpower was their immediate problem. In spite of the Taliban's ethnic ties, the northern Pashtun minorities, out of convenience, had previously sided with either Dostum or *Hizb-i Wahdat* on their terms, and were largely untrustworthy. Massoud's goal was to open fresh supply lines for food and weapons to the Panjshir valley before the snows came. He retained Shomali plain 50 km northeast of Kabul, a position which allowed him to pin down troops in the capital as well as ensure a trickle of munitions through Bagram air base. Heavier weapons, it was hoped, would arrive from outside. In early autumn, an entire train carrying 700 tonnes of Iranian ordnance for Massoud was intercepted in Osh, Kyrgyzstan, providing an insight into the scale of regional gun-running.[41]

What Massoud did lack and badly needed were allies, not only for the counter-attack – if he could put one together – but to persuade the UN that a multi-ethnic, broad-based resistance to Taliban rule had survived the defeat at Mazar. Dostum was again out of the picture and Abdul Malik made a less reliable successor. Karim Khalili, the *Hizb-i Wahdat* chief, fled after losing Bamian, leaving three factions arguing over leadership while Tehran, founder of the unified Shia movement in Afghanistan, favoured its own candidate, Qurban Ali Turkemeni.[42] Other Shia chiefs, like Ustad Mohammad Akbari, had defected and were later rewarded with appointments in a parallel campaign by the Taliban to convince the UN that their government was also broad-based before the Credential Committee met in mid-October.[43]

Massoud's comeback commenced on 4 September with a two-pronged, pre-dawn attack from Bagram along the New and Old Roads, and a barrage of 15 Luna rockets on Kabul to knock out the runways. To the west, *Hizb-i Wahdat* launched a linked attack into Wardak Province, backed with artillery and tanks. On the 13 and 14 September, 70 more civilians died in rocket attacks on the capital, though Massoud denied responsibility and it was reported that the casualties occurred in the very Tajik districts which were his own constituency.[44] A pause ensued as Kabul braced itself for a repeat of the sieges suffered from Hekmatyar and the Taliban. On 8 October, Massoud wrote to the US Senate Committee on Foreign Relations, then holding a hearing on events in Afghanistan.

> Against all odds, we, meaning the free world and Afghans, halted and checkmated Soviet expansionism a decade ago. But the embattled people of my country did not savour the fruits of victory. Instead, they were thrust in a whirlwind of foreign intrigue, deception, great-gamesmanship and internal strife ... We Afghans erred too. Our shortcomings were as a result of political innocence, inexperience, vulnerability, victimisation, bickering and inflated egos. But by no means does this justify what some of our so-called Cold War allies did to undermine this just victory and unleash their diabolical plans to destroy and subjugate Afghanistan.

He wrote of the 'dark accomplishment' which had handed his country over to 'fanatics, extremists, terrorists, mercenaries, drug mafias and professional murderers'. He blamed Pakistan for this state of affairs, accusing it of fielding 28,000 paramilitary and military staff to stiffen the 'Taliban occupation'. 'Three major concerns,' he concluded, ' – namely terrorism, drugs and human rights – originate from Taliban areas but are instigated from Pakistan, thus forming the inter-connecting angles of an evil triangle. For many Afghans, regardless of ethnicity or religion, Afghanistan, for the second time in one decade, is once again an occupied country.'[45] 'Evil triangles' recur often in the region's rhetoric, but this one emitted the faint chimes of Najibullah's prophecy.

Four days later, after the meeting in the mosque recorded by the Frenchman, the formation was announced of a new alliance, composed of the same 200–300 commanders and headed by Massoud. Unlike the UIFLA and CDA it replaced, the new arrangement adopted a centralised structure of command and, on 19 October, it celebrated its first boost to morale with the recapture of Taloqan.[46] According to Taliban sources, the commanders who defected in August, handing them the keys to the town, had tricked them. Massoud's fighters had been issued with three guns each and instructed to surrender one to their overlords and bury the other two for a future uprising. The Taliban were taken unawares as they slept.[47] Similar localised rebellions were reported from Baghlan, Faryab, Jawzjan, Samangan, Kunduz and Balkh the following month, particularly among disaffected former *Hizb-i Islami* Pashtuns and usually over Taliban attempts to disarm them.[48] Massoud's spokesman claimed this reduced the movement's share of the country from 90 to 70 per cent.[49] On 21 October, the UN again deferred a decision by the Credentials Committee.

Resistance was visibly gathering as well in the 'settled' zones, conquered by the Taliban in 1996. In October, Justice Minister Mullah Mohammad Turabi launched a three-week purge in Jalalabad which scooped up 400 *Khalq* officers and 21 generals, once part of the Afghan army, but allied for the past two years with the local Taliban.[50] Among the 2,000 people finally arrested were tribal leaders, men with links to the peace movement or loyal to the Taliban's number two, Mullah Rabbani and even children, who were held hostage to force their parents out of hiding. By 1 November, the jails were so full that detainees were transferred to Kandahar where some died in detention.[51] The reasons for the crackdown remain obscure. Massoud had claimed in his October interview that commanders in Jalalabad, Kunar, Nooristan, Laghman and Nangarhar – many formerly loyal to Haji Qadir, Hekmatyar and al-Sayyaf – were still with him and ready to rise at any moment.[52] But rumours also flew that a rift had occurred between Mohammad Omar and Mullah Rabbani, with the latter pressing for an accommodation with Massoud, a policy allegedly endorsed by the remnants of the Afghan officer class. Even General Tanai, Najibullah's former defence minister and a crucial sponsor of the

Taliban in its early months, was reportedly detained, while Rabbani vanished to Dubai for the next two months.[53] The deputy governor of Jalalabad did little to calm things with an announcement that a plot to 'destabilise' the country had been smashed. 'They were backed by a foreign power,' he said, 'and were aiming to explode bombs and fuel lawlessness before taking control.'[54] In December, Mullah Rabbani was forced by articles in the Pakistani press to deny he had resigned: he had been absent from Kabul, he said, merely for reasons of 'stress'.[55]

14 Satellites and Stars

> If you look at the past, we don't think it strange that America will attack us. Unfortunately it is our fate that everyone attacks us.
> Mullah Wakil Ahmad Mutawakil, personal secretary to Mullah Mohammad Omar[1]

The US kept up the pressure on Kandahar to yield up bin-Ladin, as much out of respect for consistency as for any great wealth of evidence. On 4 November, the Manhattan Federal Court issued a sealed indictment – the usual procedure for a fugitive from justice – chronicling 238 separate charges against the Saudi, from participating in the 1993 World Trade Centre bombing and funding Islamist groups in New Jersey to conspiring with Sudan, Iran and Iraq to attack US installations. Informed sources said the indictment contained little hard evidential detail on bin-Ladin's involvement in the East African bombings, for which he denied any responsibility the following December, while still condoning the actions of the 'real' perpetrators.[2]

In a press conference around the same time, at a tent in the desert near Kandahar, he was his usual equivocal self in response to queries as to whether he had acquired yet more terrifying weapons in the struggle to 'liberate' Saudi Arabia, as the CIA had alleged after the destruction of the Al-Shifa plant. 'We don't consider it a crime if we have tried to have nuclear, chemical or biological weapons,' he opined sniffily, adding 'we have a right to defend ourselves and to liberate our holy land.'[3] This was three months after Mullah Mohammad Omar had banned the Saudi from media comment and two months after the Manhattan indictment, much of which was based upon the confession of the former tyre store manager Wadih Hage, the friend of the chief suspect in the Nairobi conflagration, Mohammad Saddiq Odeh.[4] Hage had been charged by the same court with attempting to solicit bio-chemical weapons for *Qa'ida*, putting bin-Ladin squarely in the frame. The Saudi admitted to an acquaintance with his accuser, though he claimed they had not met in several years.[5]

Four days after the indictment, on 8 November, the CIA's Counter-Terrorism Reward Programme dangled a $5 million bounty apiece for information leading to the arrest of bin-Ladin and 'another man', each of which was more than double the previous reward ceiling of $2 million. 'It might tempt some of these groups to deliver him,' observed a perceptive US official, 'they are very poor people.' The 'other man', bin-Ladin's apparent equal in the hit parade of terror, was Sheikh Tayseer Abdullah, a former Egyptian police officer who had been the right-hand man of the Saudi since 1983. There is little on file about the expertise of Sheikh Abdullah – whom US intelligence knew only by the name Mohammad Atef – save that he lived in Kandahar and acted as bin-Ladin's 'military commander' and head of personal security. The CIA insisted that Abdullah/Atef was the logistical engineer of the East African bombings, a charge which the Egyptian denied, saying that Washington's failure to apprehend the real perpetrators had led it to blame everything on him and his master.[6] Bin-Ladin took a very different view of the cupidity of his nearest companions: 'I did not even change one of my bodyguards as a result. None of the 'Arab Afghans' are so cheap as to be purchased by the Americans.'[7]

If bin-Ladin sounded relaxed at this point, the strain was definitely telling on the Taliban. Karl Inderfurth, the assistant secretary of state for south Asia, had let it be known that there were no alternatives: give up bin-Ladin or face further bombardment.[8] The day after Washington posted the rewards, on 9 November, Mullah Mohammad Omar approved the creation of a judicial inquiry to examine Western allegations against bin-Ladin according to principles of *sharia*, fixing a deadline of 20 November for the submission of evidence implicating the Saudi in acts of terrorism, subversion or sabotage. There was no public response from Washington, which was in no position to negotiate an extradition case with a government that it did not recognise, and in no mood either to have its own exhaustive investigations, however flawed, dismissed by a cabinet of illiterate and compliant mullahs. The emir was bound to protect the defendant by ties of friendship, the law of Pashtun hospitality and the Taliban's only vaguely defined sense of solidarity with the widespread Islamist crusade to liberate the holy places of Saudi Arabia. But he was also of the view that surrendering the Saudi would lead quickly to reconciliation with the US and, quite possibly, a fast track to diplomatic recognition, the return of the UN and an avalanche of donor investment. If so assured, Omar's next moves were either deeply confused, or suicidally honourable.

On 11 November, Chief Justice Noor Mohammad Saqib, the judge in charge of the case, said: 'America is looking for an excuse to fire more rockets on our dear Afghanistan and that excuse is bin-Ladin.'[9] If the comment gave an inkling of the state of heightened expectancy in Kandahar, it also underlined the one probable outcome if the court decided to acquit. One day later, the Taliban leader flirted with that prospect by ruling that the 238-point indictment against bin-Ladin was inadmissible evidence, because it was 'old material which was not convincing enough', effectively pre-empting the court's decision.[10] By the evening of 19 November, not a single scrap of testimony had crossed the chief justice's desk, prompting him to extend the deadline a further 10 days. On 30 November, Saqib officially closed the case against the Saudi for lack of evidence, declaring the defendant a 'man without sin' and free to go. Mohammad Omar's attempt to solve his bin-Ladin problem had been a game of legal and political solitaire.

The advancing winter was accompanied by squalls of further bad news. The Taliban's only corporate friend, UNOCAL, had suspended work on the Afghan pipeline immediately after the missile attacks near Khost. But more grievous than this blow to relations with Afghanistan, it announced, was the slide in world prices to below $12 a barrel, which had already forced the closure of three of its four Caspian Sea offices. On 4 December, the company formally wound up the Afghan venture amid speculation that the Argentinian rival, Bridas, would pick up its share in the Centgas consortium.[11] Two days later, Saudi Arabia held secret talks with Burhanuddin Rabbani, head of *Jamiat-i Islami*, amid rumours that Riyadh had now swung its support behind Massoud, because of the emir's protection of bin-Ladin.[12] The same day, on 6 December, an assassination squad of four Afghans was intercepted and liquidated one kilometre from the Saudi's house in Kandahar.[13] Saudi interest in eliminating the renegade was confirmed in the new year, when a second murder bid was reported, this time on the orders of Prince Salman bin-Abdel-Aziz, the governor of Riyadh, reportedly for a fee of $250,000. Prince Salman, one of the most influential full-brothers of King Fahd, had worked as deputy minister of petroleum affairs since July 1995.[14] In January, the Taliban accused Massoud of conniving at bin-Ladin's death with US officials. Even more intriguing than the prospect that Massoud was negotiating a $5 million contract killing with the CIA was the notion – in Taliban eyes, at least – that, after more than a decade, Washington had come to see some virtue in Afghanistan's most resilient military commander.[15]

On 8 December, the UN Security Council passed a motion of censure on the Taliban for its failure to conclude a ceasefire with the alliance; for killing the Iranian diplomats the previous August; the slaughter in Mazar-i Sharif; profiting from the narcotics trade; and harbouring terrorists. The only dissenting voice in the chamber was that of Ahmad Khan, Pakistan's UN ambassador, who called the resolution 'one-sided'. Four days later, Prime Minister Nawaz Sharif arrived in Washington to receive what was described as a personal dressing down from President Clinton, both for supporting the Taliban and for providing hospitality to other terrorist groups. By February, reports in the local press alleged the existence of a photograph taken in Lahore of Sharif, then the governor of Punjab, in affable converse with bin-Ladin himself.[16] It never came to light.

In US eyes, the case against bin-Ladin was rock solid. Some 80 alleged confederates had been picked up as far apart as Malaysia and Montevideo, and Washington claimed that the *Qa'ida* network had penetrated over 25 countries, including the US. Officials claimed that, since the August bombings, seven planned attacks on embassies in Albania, Azerbaijan, Cote d'Ivoire, Tajikistan, Uganda and Uruguay had been averted, as well as another on the Prince Sultan air base in Saudi Arabia.[17] Efforts to freeze bin-Ladin's fortune – officially revised downwards to a more manageable $250 million – had come to nothing: the funds were disguised behind 80 front companies, while transfers were conducted by unknown intermediaries briefed by satellite phone – in true Afghan style.[18] But a backlash against the theory of a global bin-Ladin conspiracy was gathering pace. Former CIA official Milton Bearden, with more than a passing involvement in the anti-Soviet *jihad*, warned that Washington had turned bin-Ladin into a 'North star' for the entire Muslim world. The evidence against Saleh Idris, owner of the Al-Shifa pharmaceutical plant in Khartoum, was soon to evaporate, leaving him free to take out a $30 million legal suit for damages.[19] In Kandahar, a different story was rehearsed about the wealth of its guest. Bin-Ladin was impoverished, living on remittances from an elder brother and unable to fulfil his own personal pledge of building in the Taliban capital the second largest mosque in the world. To visiting journalists, the Saudi played the family card: he passed the time playing football, riding horses deep into the desert or with his three wives and many children.[20]

In early February 1999, Mullah Mohammad Omar sent envoys to Washington and Riyadh, asking the former for advice in dealing with their guest, and the latter for guarantees that it would take care of his dependants in the event of his being handed over to the authorities. Deputy Foreign Minister Mulawi Abdul Jalil Akhund, meeting Inderfurth face to face in Islamabad for the first time since the Khost raid, reiterated his master's position: 'We cannot expel the Saudi national as he is a guest of the Afghan nation since the *jihad* days.' Inderfurth responded with his sternest warning yet of the consequences if bin-Ladin were not expelled, a message turned into hard-and-fast policy a few days earlier by Richard Clarke, the newly-appointed anti-terrorism tsar, who said the US reserved the right to retaliate against any country which knowingly harboured terrorists.[21] Deputy Secretary of State Strobe Talbott had accompanied Inderfurth to Islamabad for the nuclear reduction talks between Pakistan and India. In a speech to the Islamabad Institute of Strategic Studies in February, he called Afghanistan 'the focus of one of the first, most severe and ominous battles of the post-Cold War world – the battle against the forces of terrorism, extremism and intolerance'.

On 13 February – less than two weeks after the Inderfurth threat – bin-Ladin vanished. 'He left his residence in Kandahar some days ago without telling us where was going,' the one-eyed Mullah related. 'Contact with him has been broken. We think he is hiding somewhere, perhaps inside Afghan territory.'[22] The Taliban had 'confiscated' his satellite phone four days earlier, stripping him of any further room for financial or defensive manoeuvre, but other motives for the Saudi's evasion emerged as speculation and rumour fused to produce a riddle at once mythic and disingenuous. There had been a shoot-out in February between bin-Ladin's personal bodyguards and the Taliban squad assigned to protect, or restrain, him.[23] The emir had snubbed his old comrade at the *Eid al-Fitr* feast: 'Bin Ladin was made to wait for about two hours outside and, when they met, [Mullah Mohammad Omar] was very cold. Bin Ladin understood that he is not wanted anymore.'[24]

But what other havens were accessible? The Taliban's sole diplomatic coup in the preceding three months was the promise of recognition by the breakaway republic of Chechnya, although Yemeni notables paid court to the fugitive in late November to 'discuss future anti-US operations'.[25] Some appropriate asylum might be arranged in either location, but each required a dangerous transit across exposed terrain, as did other mooted bolt-holes in Iraq and

Somalia. In the third week of February, the absconder was reported to have crossed the Iranian border, north of Herat; to be in Hekmatyar's reduced strongholds in Kunduz and Baghlan; in Jalalabad, where he needed hospital access for his kidney complaint; or about to join forces with Saddam Hussein, a prospect that sent a delicious – but improbable – shiver down the spine of a suggestible Western press. The two men were the fangs of hugely different snakes. The sightings were denied by spokesmen in the various destinations. Mullah Ismail Haqq, leader of the Muslim Ulama Society of Pakistan, brought some common sense to the rescue in February: 'Bin-Ladin is neither weak nor stupid [enough] to leave Afghanistan and the Taliban is not that ruthless [as] to ask him to leave.'[26] On 24 February, the Taliban said they had sent an envoy to Jalalabad, where bin-Ladin was holed up in an old *Hizb-i Islami* base, appealing for him to return to Kandahar. He had demurred, saying 'he felt freer there'.[27] Taliban claims to ignorance of bin-Ladin's final whereabouts were incessantly undermined by chattering within the movement.

But was bin-Ladin even alive? Several witnesses – most notably the emir's secretary, Mullah Wakil Ahmad Mutawakil – claimed in garrulous moments that the Saudi had left Kandahar by night in a convoy of 20 Land Cruisers, accompanied by his teenage sons Ali and Abdullah, the military commander, Sheikh Tayseer Abdullah, Ayman al-Zawahiri of Egypt's *Jihad*, the sons of the blind Sheikh Omar Abdel Rahman, 10 Taliban guards and his personal security cordon of Arab Afghans, armed with Stingers to ward off pursuit by helicopter. The last was an old drug smugglers' trick. Swathed in road dust and a halo of satellites and stars, the party headed north to a derelict *Hizb-i Islami* base at Khagrel in the Sheikh Hazrat mountains, 50 km from Kandahar. Mutawakil insisted he knew nothing of their ultimate destination.[28] By such Pimpernel tactics – and in such august company – bin-Ladin dissolved into an Islamist mirror image of the Arthurian legend of the wounded king ready to arise with his comrades and sons when the call to battle once again resounded.

A different scenario was suggested by state radio in Tehran, a well-sourced – if little-believed – voice in the region.[29] Bin-Ladin had been murdered by the moderate faction of the Taliban and disposed of in the *dasht* to rid the emir of his unwelcome guest and, quite as credibly, to claim the $10 million reward and so relieve Washington of what had become a humiliating and dreary manhunt. The *New York Times* reluctantly agreed with Chief Justice Noor Mohammad Saqib that the evidence against bin-Ladin was skimpy in the extreme. 'Capturing bin-Ladin alive,' it reported, 'could deepen complications. American officials say that, so far, first-hand evidence that could be used in court to prove that he commanded the bombings has proven difficult to obtain. According to the public record, none of the informants involved in the case have direct knowledge of bin-Ladin's involvement.'[30] Trying him, it was inferred, would prove more embarrassing than allowing him to melt away from the scene. He was culpable only of using words to incite violence by sympathisers thousands of miles away.

A rigorous radio silence was imposed as his convoy slunk away between the sands.

* * *

After the blaze of UNOCAL's gas ambitions at Khost in August 1998, the US, in principle, had no further interest in the fate of Afghanistan, beyond a burning desire to see bin-Ladin behind bars and the honour of its intelligence services vindicated. But even as Karl Inderfurth threatened blue murder from the wings, on-the-ground relations with the Taliban over bin-Ladin displayed a remarkable reticence by the Goliath of the post-Cold War world. Yes, a reward had been posted and, yes, the assistant secretary of state made it abundantly clear that diplomatic recognition would depend upon Mullah Mohammad Omar handing bin-Ladin over to the US, or a third country, like Saudi Arabia. Elsewhere, an international intelligence operation was rounding up scores of his associates. But there was a marked reluctance to take any more direct action in Afghanistan, whether by challenging the Taliban over the Saudi's current whereabouts, or launching a cross-border raid to take him forcibly into custody. Wherever bin-Ladin was hiding, the Afghan whispering gallery guaranteed it would not remain secret for long.

Why did Washington fail to press its undoubted advantages, preferring to genuflect to the unfathomable logic of 'Pashtun hospitality' rather than resort to the more dignified alternative of a snatch operation, followed by a high-profile trial in Manhattan? Certainly, there was the risk that US agents could be killed or captured and later presented to the world through the whetted lens of the media, but an operation was still feasible with cut-outs, perhaps Arabs affiliated with Israel's Mossad intelligence agency. Big money had been committed: a snatch was not beyond the realm of possibility. Admittedly, the pressure on President Clinton was not as sharp as in August 1998 when the Lewinsky affair made any foreign distraction desirable. The *New York Times* had divulged part of the answer: the evidence against the Saudi was insufficient to convict on, apparently, any of the 238 counts in the secret Manhattan indictment. But the newspaper held back on the balance of logic. If it were not bin-Ladin, who then had planned the Nairobi bombing and why was US intelligence so dilatory, first to admit that its initial theory had been wrong and, second, in advancing another hypothesis that might point to the real perpetrators? If there were no second hypothesis, of course, then the *extravaganza* that had become the hunt for bin-Ladin could as readily be construed as a cover-up, certainly of gross negligence by the US intelligence service when faced with a 'global' threat to US life and property but, possibly, of a more far-reaching scandal.

On 26 January, Congressman Benjamin Gilman of New York, chairman of the International Relations Committee in the House of Representatives, gave a speech at the Indian Consulate to mark the country's Republic Day. He warned the diplomats of Pakistan's and Afghanistan's active promotion of terrorism abroad – particularly in Kashmir – and accused the State Department of 'failing to distinguish between friends and foes'. Gilman, a Jewish Republican, had served under former UN ambassador Jeanne Kirkpatrick and headed various congressional committees on human rights, narcotics trafficking and government reform. Though a fairly mundane recitation to his Indian listeners, his speech ended with a notable inference. Gilman emphasised the importance of bolstering relations with India and the Central Asian states in order 'to minimise the role of the US Embassy in Islamabad in future policy decisions concerning Afghanistan'.[31]

However limited, it was the first public reference by a member of the legislature to the possible existence of a covert US plan to aid the Taliban's rise to power. No motive was forthcoming and whether the Islamabad embassy acted autonomously or followed Washington's orders was not clearly elaborated. But in Gilman's stated view, the probity of its regional influence was in question. Most specifically, his doubts applied to the conduct of US policy in Afghanistan but, in speaking of that country, it was impossible to exclude the embassy's chemistry with the ISI – its historic mediator on Afghan affairs – and the ISI's own diverse portfolio of subterfuges in the region. Gilman implied that a rogue US embassy was writing the regional script, contrary to national interests.

Dana Rohrabacher, a Democrat from Orange County, California, was also trying to discover the Taliban's secret sponsors. A colleague of Gilman on the House International Relations Committee, he had weaved in and out of the Afghan peace process since a visit to Islamabad in August 1996. Five days after the Khost bombings, on 25 August 1998, Rohrabacher wrote to the State Department requesting the release of cable traffic with Islamabad and Riyadh and all other documents pertinent to recent US policy on Afghanistan, a privilege due his committee. Three months later, Secretary of State Madeleine Albright promised the documents would soon arrive, but her department refused to comply. The following March, two months after Gilman's speech, Rohrabacher told Inderfurth: 'For the State Department to be stonewalling us does nothing but confirm to us who believe the worst that there is the possibility of some skullduggery going on.'[32] Inderfurth denied the existence of any secret plan, insisting that the US favoured no faction and sought only a 'broad-based' government in Afghanistan.

On 21 May, the committee's chairman, Gilman, wrote to Albright, insisting that the documents arrive by 21 June. 'On numerous occasions,' said an exasperated Rohrabacher one month after the deadline had passed, 'I have charged that the Clinton administration, despite statements to the contrary, has conducted a secret policy with Pakistan and Saudi Arabia to tolerate the creation, rise to power and ongoing tyranny [of] the Taliban.' It was now almost a year since Rohrabacher's original request and not a single page had been handed over. 'The urgent matters of terrorism, opium production and massive human rights violations in Afghanistan underscore the urgency of my request,' continued the congressman. 'In order to better protect US diplomatic missions and American personnel serving overseas, I ask the support of my colleagues to obtain US policy documents on Afghanistan.'[33] To this appeal from America's foremost foreign policy oversight committee, coming barely a year after the killings in Nairobi, there was a resounding silence from the State Department and in the US press.

For reasons best known in the Islamabad embassy, the US was pulling its punches in Afghanistan and keeping schtumm at home. Bin-Ladin was out of sight and, because there was no demonstrable urgency in running him to ground, one can speculate that his disappearence was as welcome in Washington as it was in Kandahar. Gilman and Rohrabacher suspected the existence of an understanding, or a secret treaty, between the Taliban and the US, which had made American taxpayers morally accountable for the suppression of Afghan women's rights, the heroin epidemic at home and, by extension, for the victims of bombings carried out by terrorists under Kandahar's protection. However, like any agreement – if indeed it existed – it was made to be broken when conditions were favourable. At what point it may have been 'broken' is impossible to guess for a number of bifurcations had emerged between US and Taliban interests in the previous two years: Richardson's aborted peace mission, the embassy bombings, the Khost attack, UNOCAL's withdrawal from the pipeline project and the refusal to surrender bin-Ladin.

What is clear is that the intensive diplomacy between Karl Inderfurth and Kandahar over the winter of 1998–99 did little to restrain either the Taliban or its supporters within the Pakistani government. In early October 1998, Mullah Mohammad Omar offered to shut down Afghanistan's entire opium production in exchange for diplomatic recognition, destroying 34 processing laboratories in Nangarhar as a token of his good intentions. No one took the offer seriously: the owners, all Afridis from the Khyber Pass, received advance warning and escaped across the border.[34] Within less than a year, local production soared to over 4,600 tonnes of dried opium, threatening a heroin price war on the streets of the UK and Europe. Taliban rule, meanwhile, was extending to the refugee camps in Pakistan with the government's apparent approval; in November, girls' schools and four refugee universities were closed down.[35] In December, a campaign of assassinations against Afghan dissidents at home expanded to include *mujahedin* exiles in Peshawar, culminating in attempts against the retired former Kabul commander, Abdul Haq, and Haji Qadir, ex-governor of Nangarhar and an ally of Ahmad Shah Massoud.[36] Soon it began to target former associates of ex-King Zahir Shah himself, men with track records in parliamentary or academic work who underpinned the peace movement.[37] At home, the Taliban demonstrated the same sure touch for public approval. Six members of the Gurbuz tribe were killed in January near Khost when they refused to halt the egg-breaking competition traditionally held to honour the *Eid*.[38] On 3 March, leather jackets were banned and, 12 days later, car dealers were ordered to re-paint their gaudy signs in white and blue.[39]

The peace trail had grown cold since a limited exchange of prisoners of war the previous November. In February 1999, UN expatriates moved cautiously back to their stations after eight months' absence. With contrived timing, representatives of the Taliban and Massoud's Northern Alliance met in Ashgabat on 11 March for talks supervised by the UN's 6 + 2 group, comprising China, Iran, Pakistan, Tajikistan, Turkmenistan and Uzbekistan with the US and Russia. Four days later, 'in a spirit of sincerity, mutual respect and frankness', the rivals announced the formation of a coalition to a less-than-excited planet, agreeing to meet a month later to hammer out the dilemma of who would head this compromise regime, if not the uncompromising Mullah Mohammad Omar? Within the fortnight, the two sides were locked in combat over Bamian, Massoud had resumed the rocketing of Kabul and Taliban officials pouted their utter refusal to negotiate with 'former communists'.[40] After yet another Central Asian summit failed to elicit the requisite outcome some months later, UN Secretary-General Kofi Annan criticised unnamed members of the 6 + 2 group for only 'paying lip service to their own stated intentions', pointing out that peace negotiations in Afghanistan somehow always prefaced a new escalation in the fighting.[41]

This latest battle for Bamian re-emphasised the Taliban's now-total indifference to the hearts and minds of the defeated. *Hizb-i Wahdat* launched its attack shortly after the Ashgabat agreement was announced, profiting from a civilian uprising to seize the Shia city on 21 April. The Taliban recaptured it three weeks later. Two hundred and fifty Shias supected of fighting with the rebel force were locked inside their homes with their families and set on fire,[42] leading Mullah Mohammad Omar unusually to appeal on the radio for an end to the 'revenge killings'.[43] The pattern was echoed in Herat where a reported 25 Shias were lynched after an allegedly Iran-backed civil insurrection.[44] But the Bamian uprising ended with something of a historical flourish, as news came that the Koochi – Pashtun nomads granted grazing rights in Hazara lands by King Abdul Rahman Khan a century earlier – had returned to demand 'back rent' for the grasses lost in the 20 years since the Soviets collectivised local agriculture in 1978. The Taliban had taken a leaf from the dead king's book, in which the Koochis functioned as a trusted but ruthless buffer between Kabul and the rebellious Shias. In those days, a camel's life had been set at six times that of a Hazara; a Pashtun's at 1,000 camels.[45]

In the following month, a covert incursion into Kashmir by 400 Pakistani-backed *mujahedin* provoked a two-month border dispute with India, which again brought to the fore the likelihood of a conflict in newly-nuclearised south Asia – while deflecting attention from the heavier concentration of Pakistani manpower now deployed alongside the Taliban. The force of Kashmiri freedom fighters, Afghan mercenaries and Pakistani irregulars sneaked into the snows overlooking the Srinagar-Kargil road in early May, transgressing the 720-km Line of Control, which had demarcated the Indian and Pakistani sectors of Kashmir since 1949, precisely half a century earlier. The US had imposed sanctions after the nuclear tests the previous year and Pakistan earned international repudiation after Khost and the revelation that it had consistently abetted the training of terrorists for bloodshed abroad. Prime Minister Nawaz Sharif, meanwhile, was steadfastly dismantling the civil liberties introduced since the death of President Zia ul-Haq a decade earlier. It was at this juncture, with international political and economic pressures on Islamabad arguably at their stiffest, that Pakistan chose to test the Line of Control's legitimacy – without the risk of embroiling troops in an operation tantamount to an act of war against a nuclear neighbour.

Ex-president Burhanuddin Rabbani, still nominally head of the Northern Alliance, was quick to point out similarities between Pakistan's dual strategies in Kashmir and Afghanistan. In both, a far-from-representative domestic movement was beefed up by foreign volunteers and hired 'terrorists', whipped into military shape by retired regular officers and provided with fighting equipment by Pakistan's logistical teams. Afghanistan's former London ambassador, Wali Massoud, the brother of the commander, went further: he said the ISI, the Taliban and refugees from bin-Ladin's old camps at Al-Badri met in Kabul three months earlier to coordinate both the Kargil expedition and the now habitual summer offensive against the Northern Alliance.[46] This could so easily have been propaganda, an attempt by Massoud to bask in the same air of outraged innocence displayed by New Delhi throughout the Kargil crisis, but for the intelligence leached out of the field, not by the national security agencies – they shared information with no one – but by independent reporters.

The US had never openly pondered the whereabouts of the hundreds, perhaps thousands of Arab and non-Afghan 'terrorists' who scattered like ants after the bombardment around Khost, but were no less dangerous after the flight of their mentor. The US was obsessed by bin-Ladin, to the neglect of threats more immediately to hand. He came eerily back into focus in a 90-minute profile in June on the UAE's Al-Jazeera, a liberal TV station for the Gulf, which gave the Saudi his first and only chance to speak to his constituency in Arabic.[47] News of his former disciples took one month more to emerge. In the third week of July, the subjugation of Bamian was claimed as the work not of Taliban, but Pakistani irregulars backed by 400 Arabs, loyal to bin-Ladin and incorporated as a new 'crack' 055 Brigade.[48] The Arabs had been spared any part in previous Taliban campaigns by reason of their operational value overseas.[49] Now, prior to moving up to the front, they were bivouacked with 3–5,000 Pakistani irregulars in 1,500 tents at Rishkor, a former barracks outside Kabul turned training camp by its new controller, Kashmir's *Harakat ul-Mujahedin*.[50] Transport planes flew in nightly from Pakistan in readiness for the final offensive, an attack that analysts – and even the UN's special envoy, Lakhdar Brahimi himself[51] – warned was commanded by Pakistani officers and used seasoned Arab fighters in the vanguard.[52] Miles above the tented plain, the satellites peered selectively.

On Sunday 4 July, journalist Jason Burke awoke with the knowledge that his life would never rise to the same exalted timbre of professional euphoria it had achieved at the moment he opened his eyes. That day's *Observer* had carried his exclusive, revealing that Osama bin-Ladin was alive, well – though very paranoid – and squatting in an abandoned processing plant at Farm Hadda, the site of a Soviet-era project to develop an olive oil plantation on land irrigated by the Kabul River.[53] Bin-Ladin was spotted the previous Tuesday in a convoy on the road to Farm Hadda, five kilometres south of Jalalabad. There might have been three convoys, for pursuit had made the Saudi edgy. He rode in one vehicle, transferring to a second when instinct dictated, relaying messages through an aide to a third, which carried his satellite phones and hung back for fear of orbital surveillance.[54] He had purged the Afghans and relied now for security on his trusty Arabs – though 10 Arab families immediately escaped from the compound after Burke went public.[55] He anchored his story with quotes from Islamabad diplomats and the Jalalabad authorities who, in the Taliban fashion, avidly volunteered that bin-Ladin had offered to buy Farm Hadda outright – while denying he had ever been anywhere in the vicinity.[56] Burke's day was complete before the morning started: he had discovered what US intelligence was unable – or afraid – to find, though Jalalabad lay barely 70 miles away from its listeners across the Khyber Pass.

Bin-Ladin's hiding place was the story of the moment; thousands of hours of journalistic replastering went to shore up the shambles erected after his February evasion. The US government was also busy. From Cairo, on 6 July, came the first of a stream of leaked 'reports' that bin-Ladin had been sustained in his months of need by some $50 million in donations from prominent families in the Gulf, notably the proprietor of Saudi Arabia's largest advertising agency.[57] 'There's government money being laundered in the interest of keeping bin-Ladin away from Saudi Arabia,' charged Yossef Bodansky, head of a counter-terrorism committee in Washington, who accused Riyadh of playing both ends against the middle in Afghanistan – while giving in to moral blackmail at home.[58] One man arrested in connection with the transfers was Khaled bin-Mahfouz, owner of Saudi Arabia's National Commercial Bank and, coincidentally, Nimir Petroleum, Delta's junior partner with UNOCAL in the Trans-Afghanistan pipeline.[59] On 8 July, another man was detained in Kuwait with a forged passport in bin-Ladin's name, suggesting that an elaborate plan had been hatched for the Saudi to escape his confines.[60] One day later, Mullah Ahmad Wakil Mutawakil admitted that bin-Ladin was in Afghanistan, but he conceded: 'We are ready to talk with America over Osama. We want the matter to be solved, but no one listens to us.'[61] Five months had passed since bin-Ladin's disappearence, months characterised by prevarication and disinformation on both sides but, within days of Burke's report, the trail of bin-Ladin was piping hot again.

Responding to the horrendous publicity generated by its black sheep boy – and, possibly, Osama's own traumatic experience of satellites – the family firm in Saudi Arabia decided on 28 July to change the name of its mobile phone company from bin-Ladin to *Ba'id* ('Remote'). 'With a new name and logo,' said the accompanying press release, 'we reveal our new identity and we define our mission for the future.'[62]

15 The Bicycle Thieves

In Pakistan, the Constitution has been violated more often than the honour of a woman who regularly walks the streets. Ayaz Amir[1]

Prime Minister Nawaz Sharif had some idea of what was in store when he flew into Washington for talks with President Clinton on 4 July, the very morning that Osama bin-Ladin was rediscovered to the world. Not until much later would it emerge what had transpired behind the closed doors of Blair House, for nothing leaked out and Sharif denied that bin-Ladin was ever discussed.[2] At home – in the best traditions of Pakistani policymaking – the Kargil incursion had briefly restored Sharif's star at the real risk of a nuclear confrontation, though what possible advantage might accrue from such a gamble remained obscure, as was the identity of the country's military organisation that had been responsible for the project. It could, after all, have been an ISI ploy to distract domestic attention abroad, much as Clinton was believed to have attempted at Khost and Khartoum, when the Lewinsky enquiry was snapping at his heels. Meanwhile, Indian forces at great cost were gradually winkling the '*mujahedin*' out of their positions above the Srinagar-Kargil road. Sharif had asked for the meeting with Clinton; it is unlikely he relished its outcome.[3]

Three hours after entering Blair House, the prime minister signed the Washington Agreement, committing Islamabad to the immediate withdrawal of its forces from beyond the Line of Control and the signing of the Comprehensive Test Ban Treaty by the end of the year. No such concessions were wrung from India, whose moral right to occupy Kashimir was thus consolidated, rather than held up to international condemnation, while the latter's first play of the nuclear card a year earlier entirely escaped US censure. With one stroke of the pen, Sharif inflicted lasting damage on the nation's prestige and his own ability to rule. He flew home to a country on the edge of mutiny, with army leaders threatening to withdraw support and the opposition united on the streets in their demands for his resignation. He did not return entirely empty-handed, however: in exchange for capitulating over Kargil, Sharif had won Pakistan's military a free hand for one last gambit in Afghanistan.

Two days after the Washington Agreement, President Clinton announced sanctions against the Taliban, freezing $400,000 in assets held by the national airline in US banks and a further $24 million in conventional trade.[4] The boycott was as symbolic for the one country, whose largest export was illegal opium, as it was for the other, whose chief import from Afghanistan was heroin. With no more forthright US condemnation of the thousands of Pakistani and Arab fighters mustering at Rishkor, the Taliban protectors of bin-Ladin and Brigade 055 received the go-ahead to unleash the campaign which, it was fervently hoped, would finally put paid to Massoud.

There had been sporadic fighting in Samangan, Kunduz, Balkh and the Shomali Plain since the collapse of the Ashgabat agreement in the spring, but this was little more than jockeying for advantage in the onslaught to come. The Northern Alliance still held four provinces – Parwan, Kapisa, Takhar and Badakhshan – and was well-supplied with weapons from across the Amu Darya. From his command post in the Panjshir valley in June, Massoud owned to 20,000 available troops and a journalist saw rows of recently-acquired tanks and multi-barrelled rocket launchers. 'We know they will come soon,' he said, 'but, with God's will, they will cause us few problems.'[5] Another traveller one month later remarked on the valley's 'well-nourished and carefree children ... living on a diet of peaches, apples, apricots, honey, *nan* bread and yoghurt'.[6] In mid-July, the UN summoned the 6 + 2 members to Tashkent in a last ditch attempt to avert the approaching battle, extracting 'firm assurances' from the Taliban that it would not attack and a joint agreement from neighbouring countries 'not to provide military support to any Afghan party and to prevent the use of their territories for such purposes'.[7] With utter predictability, the storm broke a week later.

At midnight on 28 July, the Taliban launched three simultaneous thrusts against the enemy at Tagab, east of Kabul; eastwards from Kunduz to Takhar; and into the 80-mile long expanse of wheatfields and orchards that make up the fruitful Shomali Plain. As in previous years, the objectives were to drive Massoud out of missile range of Kabul, to lock him in the Panjshir valley and knock out his supply lines from Tajikistan through Taloqan. But the strength and coordination of the 1999 campaign suprised analysts, who noted the Taliban's three-to-one numerical superiority and the fact that the shock tactic of a rapid advance in pick-ups – the Taliban's preferred mode of attack – had been replaced by stolid infantry movements, reinforced with tanks and artillery.[8] Tagab and Najrab in Kapisa fell swiftly. On 30 July, a force with 30 tanks captured Barikab Hill overlooking Bagram and the airbase fell after a fierce battle. 'It was loud, very hot fighting,' said a witness, 'particularly before dawn.'[9] After three days, the number of dead was set at 1,000 and the bodies of Massoud's men littered the road to Bagram.[10] The loss of the base, a thorn in the side of the Taliban since the fall of Kabul in 1996, was a massive boost to morale. Charikar, Jabal Saraj and Gulbahar all fell without resistance on 2 August, Massoud having withdrawn to the Panjshir valley after dynamiting the entrance to delay pursuit. From the north came other promising news. On 3 August, Taliban forces captured Sher Khan Bandar, the river port across from the Tajik border which underpinned the opposition supply line. Massoud was again boxed in his lair, but keeping him there, or eliminating him completely, would demand graver sacrifices. 'Two men with Kalashnikovs could hold the passes,' said a Western observer. 'So it really boils down to whether the Taliban can throw men at Massoud faster than he can kill them.'[11]

The Taliban had made an alternative plan to their soldiers dying in droves. On 4 August came the first report of what proved to be an exodus from the Shomali Plain with people heading for shelter either to Kabul or the Panjshir valley itself. According to agency estimates, 100,000 were on the move, though the opposition put the figure as high as 250,000.[12] At Bamian in 1998, the locals had fled out of fear of Taliban reprisals, but the Tajik inhabitants of Shomali were simply herded out en masse to prevent Massoud ever again relying on the fat of their land. Six thousand Taliban and their Pakistani allies were allotted the task of clearing the district of Massoud sympathisers, 'killing wantonly, emptying entire towns, machine-gunning livestock, sawing down fruit trees, blasting apart irrigation canals'. They shot anyone young enough to be a soldier.[13] A spokesman said the Taliban trucked 1,800 families to the grim Sar Shahi refugee camp outside Jalalabad for 'their own protection'; it was a 'temporary measure' to prevent civilians being caught in the crossfire during the anticipated counter-attack; they had only dynamited the canals to stop their use as trenches.[14] During 8–12 August, 55,000 refugees streamed down the Old Road to Kabul.[15] On 15 August, the UN accused the Taliban of waging a 'scorched earth war', without surrendering to the blunter, more candid description of 'ethnic cleansing'. 'Families speak of whole villages being burned to the ground,' said the UN, 'and crops set on fire to prevent them moving back to this once-fertile valley'.[16] Nor did they spare the mulberries, whose fruit had sustained Afghans through hard winter for centuries. The trauma of such losses became evident only in October. Among a group of displaced Tajiks in Bazarak, north of Jalalabad, a reporter stumbled across an old woman who had been sobbing inconsolably for two months, fingering a red flower embroidered on a pink cloth. No one was quite sure what her story had been.[17]

With the sound turned down, something stately could still be discerned in the local art of war. Barbarities aside – and, from the evidence, they were largely indulged in by the Taliban or their allies – war was as measured as a gavotte and it was ruled by a pattern of similarly ritual, and largely symbolic, thrusts and parries – much like the local brand of diplomacy. On 4 August, Massoud launched a counter-attack from the mouths of the Panjshir and Salang valleys, retaking Charikar in the early hours, literally as the Taliban slept.[18] He had announced early in the campaign that any captured non-Afghans would be executed and many 'Taliban' prisoners were slaughtered by the displaced men of Shomali, who had rallied to Massoud in an attempt to win back their homes.[19] An alliance spokesman put the number of Taliban dead at 500, including a 'large number of Pakistanis and Arabs', rising to 1,000 by the end of the two-week offensive.[20] On 6 August, Kabul was back within rocketing range and Bagram surrounded, its fall to Massoud all but inevitable. Two days later, allied troops were reported to be closing in on Tagab and Najrab, while fighting continued at the northern port of Sher Khan Bandar. On 8 August, Mullah Mohammad Omar appealed to the heads of Pakistani *madrassa* to declare a 10-day holiday so that students could cross the border to handle security in Kabul, freeing more seasoned troops to bolster the Taliban's collapsing frontlines. More than 2,000 started for the capital over the next two days.[21] Meanwhile, the Tajik population continued to stream out of the contested zones, with 200,000 leaving by 30 August, more than half of them bound for the relative sanctuary of the Panjshir valley.[22] With history at their backs, 12,000 also found temporary respite in the grounds of the old Soviet embassy in Kabul.[23]

The fighting soon subsided to its usual level of low intensity, mostly to Massoud's small advantage, but August remained a month of anxious anticipation elsewhere. Afghans searched the skies for signs either of a fresh US attack to commemorate the first anniversary of the East African embassy bombings, or a second Tomahawk strike, perhaps at Jalalabad, to eliminate the man who had escaped vengeance at Khost. In late July, US battleships moored outside Pakistani waters while, from Qatar, came reports of military transports, laden with US commandos, bound for Islamabad and Quetta in preparation for a raid inside Afghanistan.[24] The anniversaries came and passed unpunctuated – to an almost audible sigh of relief from Afghan and American alike.

Four days after the Khost anniversary, at 10 p.m. on 24 August, a broken-down fuel truck, parked close to Mullah Mohammad Omar's home in Kandahar, exploded, damaging buildings up to one kilometre away. The mullah miraculously survived, but among the 40 fatalities were two of his brothers, a brother-in-law, fourteen members of his bodyguard, six police, three civil servants and, interestingly, six Arab nationals. One of his sons was injured.[25] Most Afghans immediately suspected 'America', but the US denied any connection to the bombs, which were hidden in fuel drums by the perpetrators who escaped hours before the blast. Pakistan and the so-called moderate faction of the Taliban could equally have been to blame, for Mullah Mohammad Omar had demonstrated clearly in the preceding weeks both his inability to win the war and an absolute refusal to sue for peace. In public, the mullah accused no one, calling the assassination attempt an 'act of terrorism' but, privately, he suspected the hand of Iran, and 70 Shias were rounded up for 'interrogation'.[26]

Coming so soon after the Kargil fiasco, the spoiling of Pakistan's ambitions in Afghanistan by Massoud and his ragtag army of mountain fighters was as humbling, as it was public. Indeed, the scourging of the Shomali Plain seemed more the reaction of an injured conventional power than any domestic faction, for the latter were inured to the thin pickings of an Afghan 'victory' and in thrall to the *fiat* of destiny and the abiding consolation of patience. For the first time since the mysterious rise of the Taliban five years before, the UN finally came clean about the movement's foreign support. 'These thousands of young people are not fighting a foreign invasion force as it was when the Russians were there,' said Special Envoy Lakhdar Brahimi. 'They are taking sides in a local conflict.'[27] But he was silent as to whether these 'young people' had ever worn Pakistani uniforms. Switching to its civilian hat, Islamabad quickly offered in mid-August to mediate a fresh round of talks between the Afghans, and a mission was sent to meet Massoud's representatives in Dushanbe. It was led, impudently, by a middle-ranking official in Pakistan's Interior

Ministry, an office dealing with local law and order, not foreign relations. The alliance rejected its overtures on 24 August.[28]

Such incongruous alternations between the approaches of the military and diplomatic wings of government were not unique to Pakistan: what was really astonishing was the sheer disconnectedness in Pakistan's application of the policy of dual engagement. It was all very well – up to a point – to send to Afghanistan volunteers, advisers, weapons and fuel on a scale that was royal for a country that had travelled far beyond any orthodox definition of bankruptcy. To do so without preparing for the long series of possible geopolitical endgames – and, in Kargil, ones with nuclear consequences – raised worrying questions about the competence of an institution which, aloof from the Punch and Judy show of Pakistani politics, routinely aspired to be the natural arbiter in any serious discussion of the national interest. A military manoeuvre is implemented to secure gains which can be bartered later at the negotiating table for something more concrete – some critical alteration in the existing status quo, however minute. The Pakistani army staff seemed oblivious to the finer shadings of the region's nuclear balance, with the result that any gains from their military adventures were nervously frittered away by the civil government during the international panic that inevitably followed.

Little wonder if the army blamed the government for its loss of dignity, but the army had a tendency to shove its face in the path of incoming fists. Afghanistan was the exception: no one much cared what went on in that broken boneyard, though Pakistan had invested far more resources in the outcome of the Taliban adventure than in its recent foray into Kargil. 'The armed forces of Pakistan,' wrote retired Brigadier Usman Khaled on 29 September, 'have been steadfast in playing their role in safeguarding the security of the country. They have sought to safeguard the nuclear deterrent of Pakistan, resisted pressures to withdraw support from the *mujahedin* in Kashmir and have been steadfast in their support to the Taliban in Afghanistan.'[29] As the *mujahedin* were forced down from the heights in Kashmir after the signing of the Washington Agreement on 4 July, Afghanistan had become the only arena where the honour of the Pakistani army, its generals and rank-and-file, and the value of their contribution to the nation's 'wellbeing' could feasibly be redeemed.

Bin-Ladin remained silent after his rediscovery by the *Observer* in July, but news of his far-flung enterprises again began to surface after

7 August when Russia launched a full-scale military invasion of the rebel republic of Dagestan, Chechnya's restless neighbour in the Caucasus. *Wahhabi* rebels there, led by a Jordanian veteran of the Afghan *jihad* named Khattab, were financed by the Saudi, Moscow claimed, and he had also visited one of their training camps in Chechnya.[30] Yossef Bodansky, Washington's resident bin-Ladin 'expert', envisaged a 'multinational force of more than 10,000 disciplined and well-armed fighters' trained in Pakistan, Afghanistan and Sudan, whose single goal was to carve out an independent Islamic state in the sensitive Caucasus.[31] For two weeks beginning on 1 September, a bombing campaign claimed over 250 Russian lives in blasts at residential buildings in Moscow and Buinaksk, spurring Foreign Minister Igor Ivanov to order Islamabad to stop the use of its territory for the training and dispatch of terrorists to Russian soil. On 20 September, he said that such activities 'could pose a threat to the existence of the existing regime' in Pakistan.[32] Other voices pointed out – with reason – that the destabilisation of the Caucasus and the birth by Caesarean of a new sovereign state was particularly well suited to the vexed interests of US oil companies.

Whether prompted by Washington or to ensure his own survival, Sharif finally took steps to distance his government from the Taliban and bin-Ladin, but time was running out. In a move seen as giving more bite to the US sanctions announced on 6 July, Pakistan announced in mid-August new restrictions on the Transit Trade Agreement whereby luxuries, as well as basic commodities, were routinely imported duty-free to Afghanistan – only to end up on the Pakistani black market.[33] On 20 September, an unnamed Washington official – who could easily have been Assistant Secretary of State for South Asia Karl Inderfurth – 'intimated' US opposition to any 'interrupted democracy' in Pakistan, a comment that lit a bonfire of speculation around Sharif's future in office and which was interpreted in Pakistan as notice to the Chief of the Army Staff, General Parvez Musharraf, not to proceed in a direction which had clearly come to the attention of US intelligence already.[34]

At 56, General Musharraf was a soldier of the old school, a liberal Muslim who kept Pekinese, played golf and drank whisky in a White House-style mansion in the suburbs of Islamabad.[35] Trained at the Royal College of Defence Studies and Fort Bragg, he had failed in the 1980s to win a recommendation to become secretary for General Zia ul-Haq through his apparent lack of international polish. In 1993, however, he was appointed head of military operations, a post which required a weekly phone call to his Indian counterpart, as well as juggling Pakistan's contribution to the UN's peacekeeping operations elsewhere in the world. 'He is a little decisive, a little bold,' hazarded a former superior, Lieutenant-General Farrakh Khan. 'But I would say he is not impetuous, or jumpy.'[36] Khan had cause to be stinting in his praise. In October 1998, Musharraf had been promoted chairman of the Joint Chiefs of Staff Committee, the pinnacle of the military establishment, not in any way as a tribute to his generalship, but because he was perceived as a more malleable partner by Sharif, following his abrupt dismissal of General Jehangir Karamat some days earlier. Selig Harrison, one of the architects of the 1989 Soviet withdrawal, subsequently observed that Musharraf, along with a number of other high-ranking military staff, also had 'ties with many of the Islamic fundamentalist groups that have been supporting the Taliban'.[37] If so, it scarcely showed in the figure of the dapper general, but the allegation festered as the logic behind what happened next grew ever more obtuse.

The timing of the US warning was significant. Sharif planned to meet with Musharraf on 20 September to confirm him in office as full-time chairman of the Joint Chiefs of Staff Committee, an act equivalent to brokering a power-sharing arrangement with the military in a bid to hold on to personal office.[38] However the head of ISI intelligence, Lieutenant-General Khawaja Ziauddin, was in Washington that same day with Sharif's brother, Shahbaz, the head of the Punjab provincial government. Ziauddin either seized the moment to alert Inderfurth to Musharraf's imminent treason, or to build US support for Sharif's counter-ruse of using the bin-Ladin card – to which Washington attached so much importance – to justify a long-planned assault on the supreme heights of military power.[39] They were the last obstacle to Sharif's ambitions for absolute dictatorship. Of course, in order to play the bin-Ladin card effectively, you first had to own it.

Whatever deal was brokered, both Nawaz Sharif and Lieutenant-General Ziauddin experienced miraculous conversions on the latter's return to Islamabad. Two days after the 20 September meeting in Washington, the US partially reneged on its trade boycott of Pakistan the previous year by waiving a few minor sanctions and granting $330,000 for projects tied to the fight against narcotics. There were strong indications that President Clinton would commit to a long-awaited state visit in 2000 – the first by a US president in nearly three decades – though the security implications were frightening.[40] The inference was that, in spite of the democratic deficit in Sharif's bankrupt, but nuclearised Pakistan, Washington was giving a cautious vote of confidence to the prime minister as its preferred agent of change in a region where the US had amassed a horde of unfinished business. Local journalists listed US conditions for underwriting a continuation of Sharif's rule as: closing the Pakistani border with Afghanistan; ending the infiltration of fighters to Kashmir; disarming some 200,000 domestic Islamists; creating a peaceful environment with India; but, above all, settling with the Taliban terms for the surrender of bin-Ladin.[41] But implementing such a wish list would test Sharif's political support to the limit, while setting him on a collision course with the military.

On 7 October Mohammad Rizvi, a Shia controller of programmes at Pakistan TV, was gunned down on his way to work in Rawalpindi, bringing to 40 the number of civilians killed in sectarian violence over the preceding 10 days.[42] On the same day, coincidentally, Lieutenant-General Ziauddin flew to Kandahar to confront Mullah Mohammad Omar with 'concrete evidence' of a training camp in Afghanistan specifically set up to launch Sunni attacks against Pakistani Shias.[43] 'Who on earth can believe,' wondered a blasé Pakistani official out loud, 'that it was only last week [that] Islamabad came to know about Pakistanis being given military training in Afghanistan?'[44] Nawaz Sharif flew to Dubai shortly after to brief the Gulf states on his plans to withdraw support for the Taliban and push for the extradition of bin-Ladin.[45] 'Sharif said he insisted that the Taliban stop all activities in Pakistan, hand over Osama bin-Ladin, or ask him to leave Afghanistan, and shut down all training camps,' said an anonymous official.[46] On 10 October, four Afghans from Kandahar were arrested in Peshawar in connection with other sectarian killings in Karachi and Dera Ismail Khan, apparently following a CIA tipoff.[47] CIA agents were reported to have joined local army and police units in 'Search and Watch' operations inside Afghanistan. 'We have information of at least three teams having entered our country,' said an official in North West Frontier Province, 'whereas others are awaiting the go-ahead from powers that be.'[48] The Revolutionary Association of Afghan Women, a throwback to the Najibullah era, welcomed Pakistan's 'change of Afghan policy', while a Taliban spokesman denounced the US for trying to 'drive a wedge between Kabul and Islamabad'.

On 11 October, Mullah Mohammad Omar publicly decried terrorism in all its forms, adding with a tangible poignancy: 'It is beyond justice that today no distinction is drawn between terrorists and *mujahedin* in the world.'[49] That world had gone forever, alas.

* * *

Musharraf was on the golf links near Colombo in the early afternoon of 12 October when he received a satellite call from a senior officer who announced that Sharif had made his move.[50] Taking advantage of the general's absence at the 50th anniversary celebrations of the Sri Lankan army, the prime minister was reportedly conniving in Islamabad with his political ally, Lieutenant-General Khawaja Ziauddin of the ISI, in a manoeuvre which would see Ziauddin imposed as head of the armed forces and Musharraf forcibly retired. It was a desperate gamble on the face of it; the lines of military and civilian command had rarely been more polarised, chiefly as a result of the Kargil 'betrayal'. Three days before, Lieutenant-General Tariq Parvez, commander of the Quetta corps – one of nine making up the Pakistani army – was 'retired' by Musharraf for holding an unauthorised meeting with Sharif.[51] In any other semi-democracy, such a conference would have been routine but, after three years of Sharif's rule, the army's ears were as sharply pricked for signs of a putsch by the civilian government as they were to any military threat from India. Under such circumstances, it seems certain that the prime minister's meeting rooms were wired: they probably had been so for a decade.

But there was a slit of opportunity that could still bestow success upon Sharif's enterprise. The general was at least three and a half hours flying time from Karachi and five or more from Islamabad. Five hours was all the breathing space Sharif and Ziauddin believed they required to exploit the ambitions of the corps commanders, win their loyalty and eliminate Musharraf. As the general raced to Colombo's airport to catch the Pakistan International Airways 1515 flight back to Karachi, Sharif ordered the broadcast of a message on Pakistan Television to announce Musharraf's 'retirement' at 5 p.m. Instructions were sent to Karachi airport to deny landing permission to Musharraf's plane and redirect it to a remote airstrip in Sindh where, it was alleged, further orders had been given for his arrest by the provincial police.[52]

All nine commanders rejected Sharif's offers in the intervening hours, effectively dooming the 'civilian' coup before Musharraf landed, though whether it was out of loyalty to the general as an individual, or the army as Pakistan's ruling institution, remains obscure.[53] In reports afterward, Musharraf was portrayed in the heroic style, using the cockpit radio to summon loyal troops to take over the Karachi control tower, while the PIA jet and its 198 passengers clutched at the sky with only six minutes of fuel remaining. By that time, Musharraf had fallen into the hands of the myth-makers whose brief, amid the uncertainty which followed, was to redefine an essentially modest if unfathomed soldier as a dynamic commander of men – albeit a far from pefect democrat.

In fact Lieutenant-General Mahmoud Ahmad of the 10th Corps in Rawalpindi, whose proximity to the capital gives it life-and-death power over whoever governs there, had ordered his 111th Brigade out of barracks at least an hour before with orders to secure the prime minister's house and black out the PTV studios. It was to Ahmad that Musharraf, ultimately, owed his allegiance.[54] Programming was interrupted at 6.10 p.m, as the news announcer gave way to the familiar, almost Retro excitement of military parades and martial music, while the general's plane landed at Karachi 40 minutes later. Musharraf made his first television appearence as Pakistan's new ruler the following morning at 2.50 a.m, when he accused Sharif of having tried to 'politicise the army, destabilise it' and 'create dissension' within its ranks. This, along with accusations of criminal conspiracy, attempted murder and hijacking, would amount to capital charges when Sharif was arraigned before a special anti-terrorist court in Karachi on 20 November.[55]

It was left to a handful of Westerners the following day to mourn the passing of Pakistani democracy. The *Frontier Post*, whose chief editor had been held in prison since the previous April, spoke of a 'palpable sigh of relief among the citizens' while Ayaz Amir, columnist with *Dawn* newspaper, wrote scathingly of 'the dolt ... who had not the wit to understand that it is only so much incompetent audacity the Furies can stand'.[56] After an almost embarrassed silence lasting two days, Musharraf finally issued an emergency proclamation on 15 October in which he declared himself chief executive and suspended the constitution, the elected assemblies and the powers of the federal ministries. He committed his regime to rooting out corruption and tax avoidance among the ruling elite, but there would be no immediate return to the 'sham democracy' that had dogged Pakistan since Benazir Bhutto's first term.

'There is despondancy and hopelessness surrounding us,' he told Pakistanis in an extended policy address on 17 October.

> The slide has been gradual but has rapidly accelerated in the last many years. Today we have reached a stage where our economy has crumbled; our credibility is lost; state institutions lie demolished; provincial disharmony has caused cracks in the Federation; and people who were once brothers are now at each others' throats.[57]

The voices of Najibullah, Ghafoorzai and Massoud seemed to whisper in the soldier's ear-piece. In an attempt to pacify Washington and India, Musharraf pledged a policy of nuclear and missile restraint, a reduction of troop levels on the Indian border and a refusal to tolerate Islamist extremism. 'I urge them to curb elements which are exploiting religion for vested interests and bringing a bad name to our faith,' he said.[58]

By and large – and most particularly at home – Musharraf's performance earned a good press, but he was clearly playing for time. There was a country first to convince and it was crucial to that priority that no substantive inch be conceded on tricky issues of national or military interest. The initial US reaction, not surprisingly, was muted, largely because the new configuration of power was diametrically opposite to the one which the State Department had calculated and planned to achieve with Sharif in September – but also because a full-scale trade boycott had been in force since the nuclear tests of June 1998. Digging deep into a depleted barrel of sanctions, the Clinton administration suspended a $1.7 million health programme, while pressing ahead with a $2.5 million counter-narcotics initiative. Karl Inderfurth didn't think further sanctions would have much effect: 'We have lost touch with a generation of Pakistani military leaders,' he told a Senate Foreign Relations sub-committee on 14 October.[59]

Opinions varied as to what possible impact Musharraf's rise to power might have on US interests, particularly in regard to nuclear non-proliferation and the pursuit of bin-Ladin. On 4 November, former CIA chief Milton Bearden told a congressional committee that Musharraf represented 'the last good chance' for the US to influence Pakistan's direction in the new millennium. 'The once outward-looking officer corps ...,' he said, 'whose foundations were laid at Fort Benning and Fort Bragg..., [is] being replaced by inward-looking officers who have been trained only in religious fundamentalist *madrassah* schools.'[60] This was over-egging the pudding. Selig Harrison took a wholly contrary view. Far from being a 'safe pair of hands' in which to entrust the world's first Islamic bomb, as Bearden appeared to suggest, Musharraf was a very wolf in sheep's clothing. 'Sharif's recent call on the Taliban not to be a haven for terrorists, ' he said, 'was one of the precipitating factors in the crystallisation of the desire of the military to take over.'[61] In other words, by pressing Sharif, in pursuit of bin-Ladin, to shatter the glass wall which had always separated the military and civilian branches of Pakistani power, Washington had only succeeded in forcing a jagged shard deep into the prime minister's throat. A middle ground existed between these two positions that was equally alarming but quite as credible. Before Sharif's overthrow, it had been the fear of losing international legitimacy based upon what Musharraf dismissed as 'sham democracy' which stood between Pakistan and the Islamist bomb. Now it was a general of the old school, whose example had merely mapped out a more direct course for his Islamist young Turks to follow.

News of the coup was greeted stoically by the Taliban, still reeling from the Sharif crackdown in his dying days of power. It was a purely internal matter, sniffed Mullah Mohammad Omar, 'in reaction to certain moves by foreign powers against the Pakistani nation'.[62] He was not far wrong at that. In compliance with the now-departed Sharif's demands, troops were instructed on 13 October to disarm non-Afghan volunteers in Jalalabad, confining them to their training camps.[63] On the other side of the Khyber Pass, Musharraf took the momentous leap of banning exports of wheat flour, driving up Afghan bread prices by a fifth. The move was construed as a sign that the general wished to remind the Taliban of who was actually boss, but no further demands were made and the ban was quietly dropped on 17 November.[64]

The Taliban leadership was far more exercised by UN moves in New York to impose deeper sanctions on Afghanistan, than any change of government in Islamabad. On 15 October, the Security Council met to debate a US-drafted resolution to freeze the Taliban's assets in foreign banks and to ban Ariana Airways jets from landing anywhere but Mecca until bin-Ladin was extradited. Torn between its staff's reliance on security in the field and New York's need for the release of the US long-delayed funding contributions, the UN appeared to have taken to the political road by prioritising bin-Ladin's threats to US territory, over the Taliban's maltreatment of Afghan women and children. In a statement on 25 October, the 15-member Security Council – with Muslim Brunei and Malaysia abstaining – roundly condemned the Taliban's offensive of July 1999, the slaughter in Mazar-i Sharif, its provision of shelter and training to terrorists, its reliance on opium revenues, the use of child soldiers, discrimination against women and children, indiscriminate bombing, the burning of crops, the forced displacement of civilians, the separation of men from their families, the murder of the Iranian diplomats, as well as castigating neighbouring countries for fuelling the war with fresh ammunition and weaponry. However, the statement implied, all of the above could be overlooked or airbrushed out if – but only if – Osama bin-Ladin were handed over the the appropriate legal authorities before 14 November.[65] In the meantime, the Credentials Committee had once again allotted the Afghanistan seat at the UN to representatives of the Rabbani government with no objection on this occasion from the Pakistani delegation.[66] The UN sanctions came into force one month later, to the accompaniment of Taliban-organised riots in Kabul. Commented Erick de Mul, then UN coordinator for Afghanistan: 'They are saying: "We are at a low level, so it's very difficult for us to have a situation much worse than we already have, so we will be able to get through this period".'[67] A similar logic had prevailed in Afghanistan since the overthrow of Najibullah, but history had a tendency to demonstrate that the worst was always yet to come.

Three days after the coup, and on the same day that the UN Security Council met to finalise its programme of sanctions, four convicted thieves were led into Kabul football stadium to have their hands amputated for the theft of $50, a tape recorder, 15 teapots and 18 fruit bowls. Attendances had plummeted since the fall of the capital just over three years earlier, with barely 500 spectators taking their seats for the gory, weekly spectacle. A Taliban guard said that security had been stepped up outside after spectators complained that their bicycles had been stolen while they were inside watching the punishments meted out for theft, rape and murder.[68] It was a keen, if unintended, tribute to the Afghan's ability to survive and to profit even in the bleakest of times.

16 Mr Sam & the Food and Beverage Industry

For the first time since the Taliban seized the capital three years earlier, the sound of music echoed eerily through the homes of Kabul on 15 November 1999. In response to the declaration of UN sanctions, Radio *Sharia* allowed the unique broadcast of a male singer, accompanied by traditional musical instruments. He chanted: 'Oh America, you are an enemy of Islam ... but you haven't heard the roar of Islam.'[1]

For most Afghans, that 'roar' was experienced as a low, dull keening throughout Millennium year as the catalogue of usual misery was supplemented by the worst drought in a generation and a further torquing of the duel over Osama bin-Ladin. Once the song was over, the silence grew denser with the signals of impending disaster. So much so that, by the end of 2000, Kabulis had fallen under the influence of a craze for the *Titanic*, triggered by underground showings of the Hollywood blockbuster on videos smuggled from Pakistan. Popular resistance may take strange, syncretic forms, as the emergence of the Taliban itself had proven. In spite of – or, perhaps, because of – official attempts to cool *Titanic* fever, the liner became a ploy for marketing cosmetics, clothes, footwear, men's hairstyles, wedding cakes, vehicles, even rice. Bakers in Chicken Street were 'seriously advised' by Taliban newspapers to stop making sponge and icing replicas of the doomed boat and to model their creations on what remained of Afghanistan's cultural heritage, but the course was set – and the prospect for collision growing.[2]

The declaration of US sanctions was answered on 12 November with a volley of seven rocket attacks against the US Embassy, the UN building, the US Information Centre and various government buildings in Islamabad. Pakistani officials said they suspected 'commandos' associated with bin-Ladin of involvement.[3] Like clockwork, two days later, a man with an Arabic accent telephoned to claim that the *Al-Jihad* group, based in Kandahar, had carried out the explosions – but wouldn't do it again – and he hung up.[4] On the same day as the Islamabad attacks, three people were injured when a bomb exploded outside a mosque in Wazir Akbar Khan favoured by members of the Kabul *shura*.[5] The UN sanctions, in their turn, led to a wave of attacks on UN property in Kandahar, Farah, Mazar-i Sharif, Jalalabad and Herat, while tens of thousands of protesters streamed through the streets of Kabul chanting 'long live Osama' and 'death to America', as Taliban guards fired rifles in the air to control them.[6] Much of the noise in Kabul was orchestrated cabaret – though of a hugely different order to the public execution of a murderess in Kandahar football stadium, which took place on the same day that Mullah Mohammad Omar apologised to the UN for the damage, and normal business was resumed.[7]

But how normal could the business of aid actually be under the combined conditions of global sanctions, a massive food shortfall in the drought-hit south, 20 years of war, a crack-down on the cross-border trade by Pakistan's new military rulers and a winter that was soon to hit its stride? The US State Department called its boycott 'smart sanctions', using the same deceptive word applied to the fallible bombs dropped on Baghdad during the Gulf War: they were crafted toward forcing the Taliban to recognise its responsibilities in regard to international terrorism and narco-trafficking, and were not targeted against ordinary Afghans.[8] There would be no 'collateral damage'. But the cancellation of Ariana's landing rights in Dubai immediately disrupted the inflow of $4.5 million a week in hard currency, whether for commodity purchases or remittances to cash-strapped families for whom it was the sole means of support.[9]

Médecins Sans Frontières initially discovered that it was unable to fly medicine and other relief from Dubai because no Security Council member wanted to chair the committee set up to oversee exemptions to the UN prohibition on international landings.[10] Afghanistan's inventive merchants, expected to provide 800,000 tonnes of wheat-flour to relieve the shortage, found peremptory curbs on supply due to Islamabad's fears for its own food security, its determination to reduce smuggling and a genuine confusion as to whether trading anything across the border was still legal under the UN sanctions. A balance was eventually found – thanks to a most unexpected helper – but it seemed that distinguishing between what was relief, private trade, smuggling and sanctions-busting could soon erupt into same poisoned dilemma faced by the UN in 1997, when it was compelled to choose between defending women's rights in general, or feeding widows. That helper was the Islamic Republic of Iran. One year after the killing of its diplomats in Mazar-i Sharif, Tehran reopened the border on 21 November, restoring the traditional road link from Dubai.

Perhaps Tehran brought down the barriers in order to prod the Taliban into surrendering the killers, but it also sought a more articulate conversation with its unruly neighbour on a variety of border issues, notably the high-intensity war on Afghan drug-trafficking which, allegedly, cost the Iranian exchequer $800 million in 1999.[11] This was only the first in a series of new diplomatic shuffles that followed the imposition of sanctions. Russia and the FBI agreed to pool their intelligence on bin-Ladin, which the former held responsible for helping the Islamist rebels in Chechnya; the Islamophobe government of Uzbekistan, a former sponsor of Dostum, reluctantly opened talks with the Taliban. General Musharraf visited Tehran in December for the first time, returning two days later with a pledge that Iran and Pakistan would henceforth coordinate policy on Afghanistan and 'work towards the formation of a broadly-based government consisting of all Afghan factions'.[12] Afghan specialist and former US ambassador Peter Tomsen commented acidly: 'Whereas Pakistan and Iran before separately tried to manipulate the Afghan scene ... now, Musharraf's visit to Tehran indicates that they are going to cooperate together to manipulate the Afghan scene, which is even worse.'[13] But Tehran continued to offer open house to the anti-Taliban opposition, and ousted President Burhanuddin Rabbani visited the same month for a war conference with Rashid Dostum, Abdul Malik and *Hezb-i Wahdat* leader Karim Khalili in a bid to assemble a functioning alliance.

Any hope that Mullah Mohammad Omar would adopt a more submissive profile in the face of the combined censure of Washington and the UN evaporated as the world armed itself for a party at the end of the Millennium, a party cursed by a reckoning that seemed to be daily closing in. Y2K specialists had long warned of a catastrophe as the clock struck midnight with airliners, shorn of their flight systems, curving like tracer fire through blossoms of valetudinarian fireworks; men on their knees before the mechanisms that once nurtured them. In truth, neither Mullah Mohammad Omar – nor bin-Ladin – retained manual control of the loosely-knit *Qa'ida* network that US intelligence accused the latter of building in his 22-year exile in Sudan and Afghanistan. If the grand conspiracy existed, it existed either at the frontiers of the American mind, or in an archipelago of autonomous colonies of conviction that flourished between the paving stones of US immigration policy. The colonists looked to Kandahar, to bin-Ladin's probity and the shining fact of the Taliban hegemony for inspiration but, as new Americans, they were also saturated with the portents and imagery that surrounded that ultimate year.

With Christmas approaching, police on 14 December intercepted a lone Algerian, 32-year-old Ahmad Ressam, at a remote crossing on the border between Canada and Washington state. In the boot of his rented car were found 54 kg of nitroglycerine, several bags of urea and four Casio watches, 'enough to bomb four city blocks into rubble'.[14] Similar timers and ingredients were used in the World Trade Centre bombing, an apartment bombing in Moscow and the embassy bombings in Kenya and Tanzania. US intelligence said the components bore the unmistakable signature of the simple, but deadly bomb-making techniques taught at bin-Ladin's training camp outside Khost. But what on earth was the target? Ressam carried a second passport, used to reserve a getaway flight through Chicago and New York to London one day later. He planned, said the investigators, to spend a single night at a motel a short ride away from the Seattle Space Needle and the Seattle Centre, scenes of a grand end-of-Millennium spectacle in the home town of Boeing and Microsoft. Some days later the Royal Canadian Mounted Police reported the discovery of an Algerian 'cell' in Montreal, with links to the GIA in Algeria and, on 30 December, Abdel Ghani Meskin, also from Algeria, was arrested in Brooklyn, and charged with conspiring with Ressam.[15]

Simultaneously, in Amman, Jordan, police announced the arrest of 13 Jordanians of Palestinian descent with elaborate ties to bin-Ladin, this time through another alleged training facility high in the mountains above Kunar province on the Pakistani border. It emerged at their jury-less trial in April that they had intended to attack sites of Christian tourism, including Mount Nebom where Moses first gazed upon the Promised Land of Palestine, and a Christian settlement on the river Jordan where Jesus is said to have baptised John the Baptist. One of the defendants, Khalil Deek, was a naturalised US citizen, army veteran and a computer technician. He called the charges against him 'all this hocus pocus'[16], and, despite the ever-escalating evidence, the voice of another defendant in the dock, Issam Baqawi, had the particular ring of sincerity: 'So what if (police) seized two machine-guns and two pistols from young men who thought of fighting Jews. Is that terrorism?'[17]

The suspicion that the Taliban and Afghanistan were situated in the eye of an impending storm of terrorist violence was reinforced when five Pakistani hijackers, armed with knives and obsolete guns, seized control of Air India's flight 814 from Katmandu to New Delhi on Christmas Eve, forcing its 155 passengers to fly to Lahore, Amritsar and Dubai before finally setting down in baking temperatures in the derelict civil airport in Kandahar in the middle of *Ramadan*. One passenger, homeward bound after a honeymoon in Nepal, was unceremoniously killed and dumped on the tarmac, unbeknown to his wife in the rear of the plane, but the hijack was seen as a heaven-sent invitation to the Taliban authorities to demonstrate that they were tough on terrorism. Drained by fasting, they nevertheless threatened to storm the plane if any other passenger were harmed – although three French hostages from Nice later testified that they were convinced the hijackers had been given more effective weapons upon landing in the Taliban capital.[18]

Pakistan clearly enjoyed the discomfort of Indian mediators shuttling to Kandahar throughout the crisis, and the eventual surrender of the imprisoned Kashmiri militants, whose liberation had been the object of the mission. The Taliban, basking by now in the applause of the world's Christmas TV audience, gave the hijackers and their quarry ten hours to leave the country and they evaporated, bin-Laden-style, in a blizzard of road dust toward the Pakistani border, never again to come to light. Inspired, perhaps, by the Air India incident – though of far less global account – was the hijacking in February of an Ariana Airways flight from Kabul to Mazar-i Sharif by hijackers claiming to seek the release of Ismail Khan, the former emir of Herat, captured by the Taliban after the mutiny by Abdul Malik which had led to the capture of the northern capital in 1998. While hijackers and hijacked stewed in a long-drawn-out siege at Stansted – and the even longer bureaucratic stand-off that constitutes the asylum process in London – one month later Ismail Khan managed to escape after three years in fetters in a windowless cell in Kandahar, along with the son of former Nangarhar governor Haji Qadir. They later gave 'harrowing accounts of torture' to the UN Special Rapporteur on Human Rights in Afghanistan.[19]

With the suspicion of a worldwide Islamist conspiracy mounting higher by the day, US prosecutors began in late January to divulge some of the evidence they held against Osama bin-Ladin, chiefly in response to bail demands by lawyers for Wadih Hage, the Texas-based chief suspect in the Nairobi embassy bombing who had spent 15 months in prison awaiting trial. It emerged that US intelligence had known of Hage more than a year before the blast; that he had gone to live in Nairobi on 22 February 1997, over a year before the bombing; that his house had been searched by federal agents working with the Kenyan police; and that he was later interviewed by the FBI in Texas, still a full year before the embassy was destroyed. Prosecutors described him as 'one of bin-Ladin's most trusted and dangerous aides, privy to his secrets and a personal courier of his instructions', who had 'militarised' a pre-existing Kenyan 'cell', using the local NGO, Mercy International Relief Agency, as a conduit for the financial and logistical assistance required to conduct a major terrorist operation.[20]

The interception of email, fax and satellite telephone communications between bin-Ladin and his overseas associates revealed an astonishingly naive grasp of spy-craft, the prosecutors revealed. In one letter, the Saudi was referred to as 'Mr Sam' or 'Mr O'Sam' and repeatedly warned to beware of 'an opposition company called the Food and Beverage Industry, based in the US'. Hage had followed this warning up with a further letter, in which he wrote: 'Give my regards to Sam and tell him to take extra precautions because business competition is very fierce.'[21]

It was about to get much fiercer.

* * *

General Musharraf showed few signs of actively pursuing his 17 October pledge to combat Islamist terrorism, despite the diplomatic woes arising from his dismissal of the Sharif government and the network of *jihadi* cells spreading through the Middle East, the Caucasus and Central Asia allegedly nurtured by the Taliban/bin-Ladin axis. After the Air India hijack, which Indian analysts claimed bore the hallmarks of an ISI-backed operation, no ostensible attempt was made to capture either the hijackers themselves or the three prisoners freed by India to end the crisis, all safely ensconced on Pakistani soil, or transiting through to sanctuary in Pakistani Kashmir. New Delhi, as a result, called on Washington to declare Pakistan a sponsor of terrorism – as the US had been inclined to do earlier in the decade.[22]

Nor, despite the negotiating muscle acquired by the disruption of Afghanistan's supply of food, was there a significant reduction in the number of training camps on Afghan soil, although much of their graduate output was, by most accounts, fighting alongside Taliban and Pakistani irregular forces at the various front lines. In early February, Musharraf flew to Kandahar for his first official talks with Mullah Mohammad Omar, a potentially disciplinary meeting that ended with rosy expressions of mutual esteem and hopes for future collaboration. He subsequently told Washington that it would have to deal directly with Kandahar over bin-Ladin. In fact, the only progress he justly could claim in regard to the terrorism issue was the appearance before an Anti-Terrorism Court in mid-February of former Prime Minister Nawaz Sharif, charged with conspiracy to murder and kidnap. The prosecutors immediately demanded a complete reporting ban on the accused's statements on the grounds of national security and that they were 'likely to be scandalous, aimed at tarnishing the image of the present system'.[23]

Yet Washington felt it had little alternative to 'keeping the channels open' with the new masters of Islamabad,[24] though the diplomatic aperture was constrictive. His presidency crippled by the Lewinsky investigation, Bill Clinton had turned from the ruins of his domestic ambitions to attempts at mediation in long-running conflicts abroad – Northern Ireland, the Middle East, Kashmir – in a bid to preserve his presidency for history. Clinton profited politically, at a crucial moment in the Lewinsky saga, from the imminence of the bin-Ladin menace but, in the brutally precise calculus of presidential accountability, it was neither the product nor consequence of his watch, but of another's – whether Jimmy Carter's or Ronald Reagan's – and the intelligence services which had been granted such licence during the most apocalyptic of the Cold War's proxy conflicts. Given the limited time left to his term, the Islamist conspiracy was irremediable. But, however unhelpfully Pakistan behaved in the convoluted business of exporting Islamist militancy, the latter was, in US eyes, a minor sub-plot to, or secondary infection of, the far graver drama of the two regional nuclear powers at odds over Kashmir.

The primary purpose of the visit that Clinton made to South Asia in late March was to persuade India and Pakistan to deepen the proximity between them that emerged after the Kargil escapade, and Musharraf's later decision to scale down Pakistan's military presence on the Line of Control. At best, there was the possibility of some progress toward ratifying the nuclear Comprehensive Test Ban Treaty, and encouraging military chiefs in both countries to collaborate on building the vital decision-making mechanisms that limit the danger of 'accidental' war between more mature nuclear powers. But Washington had also expected that his host in Pakistan would be the pliable Nawaz Sharif, rather than the usurping general who now had him on trial for his life. There was justifiable concern on the US side that the visit would be seen to confer legitimacy on Musharraf's regime, while Islamabad was keeping a keen eye out for evidence of favouritism in Clinton's dealings with New Delhi.

In the event, after a five-day visit to India, the US president spent less than six hours in Pakistani territory in what was described as a 'stopover', rather than a full state visit. After 80 minutes of talks – in which Musharraf was reported to have conceded nothing – Clinton delivered a brief speech on Pakistani television calling for a return to civilian rule and the end of the wasteful rivalry over Kashmir, in which Afghanistan was mentioned once and bin-Ladin not at all. However, by August the US and India had agreed to establish a joint working group on Islamist terrorist intelligence and a CD-Rom copy of *The Encyclopaedia*, a six-volume manual of terrorism allegedly used as a text book at bin-Ladin's training camps, had been delivered to New Delhi for its perusal.[25]

The former US ambassador, Peter Tomsen, who had lobbied hard for Clinton to spearhead a new US-led peace process in Afghanistan and announce an arms embargo on all combatants, considered the visit a missed opportunity. He concluded: 'We cannot expect an effective foreign policy on Afghanistan before this administration ends. Whichever party wins in November, it will take at least a year for the next administration to establish the essential analytical framework and policy approach needed to satisfy US interests in Afghanistan and the region.'[26] As first steps towards a more committed US approach, he recommended the appointment of a special US envoy to Afghanistan – to compensate for the absence of a US ambassador in Kabul – and the resumption of a direct US aid effort to non-Taliban areas.

Living conditions in Afghanistan continued their relentless deterioration, accentuated by donor distaste for Taliban policies. The drought dried wells and killed crops across the south and centre, causing a massive destruction of the livestock on which so many relied and a consequent exodus to the cities. In addition to one of the world's largest refugee populations – three million distributed between Pakistan and Iran – Afghanistan could also lay claim to one of the largest populations of internally displaced: a quarter of a million people were driven from their homes in the 1999 fighting in the Shomali Plain and still had not returned.[27] By the end of 2000, the World Food Programme (WFP) was providing emergency rations for some three million people, twice the number it had fed before the drought, while a UN appeal for emergency funding to cope was only 60 per cent-subscribed. Contributions to the UN's consolidated funding appeal, meanwhile, were so low that by September mine-clearance work was cut by half.[28] Even the good news was bad. With the drought threatening to cut opium output by a third to 3,275 tonnes, Afghans' supply of foreign exchange was expected to shrink from $230m to $160m.[29]

Some aid workers believed that the Taliban were finally preparing to relax some of their fiercer strictures, particularly after a formal celebration on 8 March of International Women's Day, an event attended by 700 women, including former university professors, engineers, teachers, doctors, nurses and school principals.[30] But a series of incidents and decisions in early July quickly put paid to the illusion. A team of Pakistani footballers, visiting for the first international 'friendly' match in over 20 years, was arrested in Kandahar football stadium for wearing shorts in defiance of the Islamic dress code; their heads were shaved and they were expelled. An edict was issued once again banning women from working for the UN or NGOs, forcing the WFP to shut down a training programme for 600 female relief workers.[31] And on 8 July, 71-year-old Mary MacMakin, an American who had devoted over 20 years running a physiotherapy and rehabilitation centre in Kabul, was arrested and charged with 'spying and spreading anti-Taliban propaganda'. She was released and forced to leave the country.[32]

Other star-gazers were similarly, simply, though far more dramatically, wrong. In the same month came a flock of forecasts from a variety of well-informed sources of the scattering and imminent demise of the entire Taliban project. 'We believe the Taliban now have little prospect of completing their goal of gaining control over the 15 per cent held by the opposition,' Assistant Secretary of State Karl Inderfurth told the Senate Foreign Relations Committee on 20 July. 'In short ... we believe the Taliban have reached their highwater mark.' Citing as indicators the recent assassination of the governor of Kunduz, continuing sabotage at Kabul airport, the growing refusal of Afghans to be recruited to fight Taliban battles, equipment shortages and splits within the movement, he predicted their expulsion from Kabul 'by the end of the year'.[33] In anticipation, Congress had provided $100,000 to foster the Zahir Shah peace initiative, a figure expected to rise to $500,000 by December. Inderfurth's opinion, informed by the best US intelligence and spies inside the Taliban and Pakistani administrations, was shared by Peter Tomsen,[34] who testified before the same hearing, and by Wali Massoud, the Afghan ambassador in London and brother of Ahmad Shah Massoud.[35]

Why were they so confident? A massive airlift of heavy weaponry and hard currency to Massoud could only instigate the beginning of a reversal on the scale predicted in Washington; and, if such a breakthrough were to occur, Kabul could not be delivered with any certainty within the five-month timetable, such are the imponderables of the Afghan battlefield. Inderfurth's conviction, therefore, was based on a different mark of surety: inside knowledge, perhaps, of a second plot to assassinate Mullah Mohammad Omar with the goal of splintering the Taliban into factions; knowledge of a US-assisted mutiny by the so-called moderate wing, led by Mullah Rabbani, with the aim of opening a second front to the rear of the main Taliban force; or – and equally beyond the realm of verification – knowledge of a secret agreement with General Musharraf to discontinue absolutely his support and withdraw before the deadline all Pakistani military personnel fighting with the Taliban. Whatever he thought he knew then, Inderfurth was now to learn the Afghan punishment for counting chickens.

The Taliban opened their summer campaign on the eastern border of Baghlan, cutting Massoud's link with the Panjshir valley on 1 August when, after heavy air attacks, Ishkamish fell. One week later, they seized Bangi, opening the western road to reinforcements from Kunduz for a combined attack on Massoud's northern headquarters in Taloqan city. According to a report in *Jane's Defence Weekly*, later confirmed by NGO staff in the district, around one-third of the 20,000 Taliban mustered for the Taloqan campaign were of Pakistani origin, while a further 1,000 Arab fighters were identified as members of Brigade 055, the cohort trained and paid for by Osama bin-Ladin.[36] 'Some 40 per cent of the Taliban force is made up of non-Afghans,' said Massoud, a claim also backed by Western officials.[37] After a bitter offensive lasting three weeks, the Taliban finally captured Taloqan for the third time on 5 September, choking off Massoud's main river supply routes at Dasht-i Arshi, Imam Sahib and Sher Khan Bandar, as well as airstrips at Taloqan and Khawaja-garh. Some 90,000 inhabitants of the district, mostly Tajiks, sought refuge in the caves, valleys and mountains surrounding their villages to avoid the same Taliban purges carried out after Mazar, Bamian and Shomali Plain had fallen in previous years.[38]

Massoud said his retreat was tactical, that his forces left with their weaponry mostly intact. Over the next two weeks, as if in confirmation, he laid vigorous siege to Taloqan from three sides from positions high on the surrounding peaks, even cutting the Bangi approach road to prevent resupply from Kunduz.[39] Morale remained high among the troops of the Northern Alliance,[40] but the Taliban clung to their prize with an uncharacteristic tenacity, in the light of previous altercations when defeat or, at the very least, a semblance of the *status quo*, had always been snatched from the jaws of what had first seemed like a crushing victory over Massoud. Despite the loss of 1,000 lives and 1,500 other casualties,[41] the Taliban consolidated control of the district, aided by a wave of defections that included the commander at Farkhar Gorge southeast of the city.[42] Both Massoud and President Rabbani insisted that Taloqan would be recaptured before the first snows of November, and Russian ammunition planes buzzed into Faizabad, 110 km east of the fighting, to bolster the coming fusillade.[43] But Massoud decided to cut his losses and quit, probably for fear that the demoralised commanders in his Badakhshan hinterland should choose the very same moment that he faced his greatest military challenge to forget their loyalties and seek God. When the first snow fell, Taloqan was still in Taliban hands: the Lion of Panjshir had suffered the most far-reaching defeat since his loss of Kabul four years before.

A Pakistani defence expert, writing one month later, estimated his chance of a serious comeback as slim. The loss of Taloqan had brought the Taliban within shooting range of Tajikistan, sowing panic in the frontline states of Central Asia, but there was no indication of any more aggressive supply of heavy weaponry from Russia, Iran or India on a scale and of the quantity necessary to rescue their protege and drive back the invading forces. Massoud continued to hold Farkhar, parts of Taloqan province and all of Badakhshan, including Faizabad where the court of President Rabbani was now housed in a two-storey home that formerly belonged to the governor. The Taliban took their time, moving slowly along the demolished roads and blown-up bridges, advancing to a final reckoning that would determine who controlled the last 5 per cent of Afghanistan and the 600-km frontier with Tajikistan, from Darwaz to the tip of the serpentine Wakhan Corridor. After failing to retake Taloqan, Massoud had no option left but to wage guerrilla warfare, assisted by a loose organisation of 1,500 'freelance saboteurs' to carry out bombings and assassinations behind Taliban lines.[44] The snow, mercifully, intervened, but how had Inderfurth come to be so misled?

Massoud's popular base began to evaporate shortly before the fall of Taloqan. On 14 September Tajikistan closed its border to thousands of Afghans teeming to get across the river Pyandj, which constitutes the frontier, in spite of the shelter offered to Tajik escapees from the civil war in 1992. By early October, 100,000 more had found their way to Faizabad and Kisham districts,[45] while 23,000 trudged down the mountains to cross the Pakistani border at a rate of 500 families each day.[46] In November, Islamabad closed the frontier entirely, ignoring Taliban pleas, saying it had insufficient resources to offer further hospitality. All that was now left to the Tajik in his marginalised mountain domain was the friable loyalty of his Central Asian backers and an unholy alliance with the belligerent successor to the Soviet Union. In August, after a withering denunciation of the Taliban at the G-7 Summit in Okinawa, Russian President Vladimir Putin's spokesman, Sergei Yastrzhembsky, had announced Moscow's intention to launch 'preventive and aggressive' air strikes inside Afghanistan, a move which so alarmed Uzbekistan, always sensitive to signs of Russia's post-imperial designs, that it begged off from signing a collective security agreement in October. On 6 October, soldiers of Russia's 15,000-strong 201 Motorised Division in Tajikistan, widely regarded in the region as a Russian protectorate, closed border checkpoints after the Taliban seized districts close to the river Pyandj, and a further 135,000 refugees arrived pleading for sanctuary.

All this Russian activity, and a budding new defence and arms pact signed with India on 4 October, rankled with Tashkent which had signed a collective security agreement the previous April with Kazakhstan, Kyrgyzstan and Tajikistan to engage in joint military activity if the Taliban attacked any one of them. But the greater fear of Russian aggrandisement, in response to the still vaguely defined Taliban threat to his borders, led Uzbek President Islam Karimov to stay his hand and, on 12 October, he pulled out of another pact, which had amounted to setting up a legal framework for the rapid deployment of Russian forces through Uzbek territory to counter further Taliban aggression.[47] Karimov had met Taliban leaders earlier in the year to discuss the movement's protection of a 70–100-strong group of militants belonging to the Islamic Movement of Uzbekistan (IMU), which it held responsible for a spate of bombings of government buildings in February 1999. 'Uzbekistan is hostile to the IMU,' said an Uzbek military journalist, 'but it doesn't want to make an enemy of the Taliban'.[48] After Taloqan, the Taliban were transformed in Karimov's speeches from the 'main source of fanaticism and extremism in the region' to a 'partner in the struggle for regional peace'.[49] On 19 October, Tashkent reopened Friendship Bridge, linking its river city of Termez with Hairatan, in a gesture which suggested that it feared Kabul far less than Vladimir Putin, and the scare tactics he had devised to increase Russian influence in Chechnya and Central Asia.[50] The decision triggered speculation that Uzbek recognition of the Taliban might also be in the pipeline, a prospect guaranteed to give Mullah Mohammad Omar pause for thought before acting.

One week earlier, and several thousand miles away, the US destroyer *Cole* pulled into Aden harbour in Yemen on 12 October for refuelling where it was rammed by an explosives-laden skiff which blew up, killing 17 sailors, wounding 39 others and crippling the vessel. The two perpetrators – whose remains were later described as 'confetti-sized'[51] – were subsequently identified as Saudi-born Yemeni veterans of the Afghan war. Uncomfortably for Yemeni President Ali Abdullah Salih, they had been recruited, with several hundred more former *mujahedin*, to fight with the army during the bloody war of secession by leaders of the former Marxist republic of South Yemen, that broke out in the early 1990s following the over-hasty unification which followed on the collapse of the Soviet Union. Throughout the investigation, FBI officials were denied direct access to witnesses and suspects; access to unedited transcripts of interviews or videos; and barred from talking directly to neighbours of the safe houses where the bombers had planned their escapade, in spite of President Clinton's written request for 'a genuine joint investigation'. The suspicion lingered of an official cover-up of involvement in the bombing by high-ranking members of a government whose policy over the previous decade had been to include radical Islamist elements of its society, rather than criminalise them.

More compelling still, were the similarities in origin, conviction and, ultimately, in target, between the dead bombers and another

Saudi-born Yemeni with strong ties to Sana'a, and a burning hatred of the US military – Osama bin-Ladin. They had, moreover, sufficient funds at their disposal to obtain false identity documents, a four-wheel-drive vehicle, the boat and three safe houses in Aden, in addition to the explosives used to such devastating effect.[52] Bin-Ladin denied any involvement during a telephone conversation to Kuwait's *Al-Rai al-Aam* newspaper[53] but, as the investigation continued, he left his Kandahar home in a convoy of 15 vehicles on 22 October and was last seen heading north towards a base in the Parapamizad Mountains, Oruzgan,[54] where there were Stingers, anti-aircaft guns and 2,700 Arab Afghans to protect him.[55] With US elections due in November, a strike was expected at any time. On 25 October a CNN news crew was expelled from Kandahar because its presence 'increased fears' of a US missile attack[56] while, a week before, Pakistan officially denied Washington the use of its airspace for any such raid. But the Arab press reported US jets hovering over Kandahar[57] amid rumours that a US-backed mercenary force was already inside Afghanistan. On 1 November, mosques in Pakistan and Afghanistan held special prayers for God's protection of bin-Ladin.[58]

Principal Characters

BURHANUDDIN RABBANI

A theologian and former professor of religion at the University of Kabul, he founded *Jamiat-i Islami* in 1973. A Tajik from Badakhshan, he is a moderate Islamist. *Jamiat*'s military wing dominated the north during the Soviet war, and had a strong showing in some areas of the west and south. Under the Peshawar Accord, he took over as president in June 1992 for a four-month period. This term was extended twice: to June 1994, under the terms of the Islamabad Accord; and to December 1994 by his unilateral decision. Frequent offers to step down were never realised due to the absence of an acceptable mechanism for the transfer of power. His regime at varying times received support from Saudi Arabia, Iran, Russia and India. On the fall of Kabul, he fled to Takhar province and thence to Iran.

AHMAD SHAH MASSOUD

Son of a Tajik military officer and a former student at the French Lycée in Kabul, he was *Jamiat-i Islami*'s senior commander during the Soviet war and a minister of defence in the first *mujahedin* government. He forged an alliance with General Rashid Dostum and other generals from the Najibullah regime to capture Kabul in April 1992. Forced to step down following the Islamabad Accord, he retained control of the largest *mujahedin* army. Between January 1994 and February 1995, he withstood a joint attack on Kabul by the forces of Dostum, Hekmatyar and Mazari, supported variously by Pakistan and Iran. After the loss of Kabul, he retreated to his base in the Panjshir valley, forming a mutual defence pact with Dostum and the Shia leader, Karim Khalili, to resist the Taliban. Widely acclaimed for his skills as a tactician, he has subsequently enjoyed the covert backing of Russia. His links with France and the UK, where his brother is Afghan ambassador, suggest a future exile in one of those countries.

GULBUDDIN HEKMATYAR

A Pashtun from the northern province of Kunduz, former military cadet and engineering student, he founded the radical Islamist *Hizb-i Islami* while exiled in Pakistan. During the *jihad*, he received the largest share of the US and Gulf military aid distributed by Pakistan and continued to receive military and tactical support from Pakistan's military intelligence service, the ISI, well after the collapse of the Najibullah regime. Despite a well-organised party structure, his domestic power base was limited to two provinces, Logar and Laghman, and strategic positions around the capital. His attack on Kabul in 1992–93 led to the Islamabad Accord, under which he became prime minister. A second siege, in collaboration with Dostum and Shia forces, lasted 13 months until February 1995 when *Hizb-i Islami* was driven back by the Taliban. After rejoining the Rabbani government in March 1996, he was reappointed prime minister but remained outside the anti-Taliban pact which was formed after the capture of Kabul. Hekmatyar is widely reported to have links with both the narcotics trade and international Islamist terrorist movements.

RASHID DOSTUM

A general in the northern Uzbek militia under Najibullah, his mutiny and later alliance with Massoud in April 1992 was decisive in bringing the *mujahedin* to power but he was excluded from the Jalalabad and Islamabad conferences which attempted to create the post-communist political order. During 1992–97, his *Junbish-i Milli-i Islami*, or National Islamic Movement, ruled over a semi-independent state of seven northern provinces, largely populated by Uzbeks, Turkmens, Tajiks and Ismaili Shias. Dostum controlled Afghanistan's best-equipped forces, its gas supplies and received aid from Russia, Uzbekistan, Turkmenistan, Turkey and Iran. His switch to Hekmatyar's side in January 1994 led to improved relations with Pakistan and Saudi Arabia. His refusal to mend fences with Rabbani after Hekmatyar's defeat was instrumental in the loss of Kabul to the Taliban and directly contributed to his own overthrow following the mutiny of General Abdul Malik, the Uzbek commander of Faryab Province. Dostum flew into exile in Turkey from Uzbekistan in late May 1997 but returned to his Shiburghan power base the following August.

ABDUL ALI MAZARI

Until his murder by the Taliban in 1995, Mazari headed *Hizb-i Wahdat*, an alliance of eight Shia resistance groups created in 1990 by Iran to counter the influence of the Sunni-dominated, seven-party *mujahedin* alliance created by the ISI in Peshawar. Iran continued to be a crucial supplier of military aid, both to *Wahdat*'s popular base in Bamian province and to its urban strongholds in southwest Kabul. An ally of Massoud and Dostum in the 1992 capture of Kabul, it switched to the side of Hekmatyar's *Hizb-i Islami* following attacks on its positions in the city in the following year, although a Shia splinter group, *Harakat-i Islami*, remained loyal to the Rabbani government. In March 1995, *Wahdat* surrendered its Kabul positions to the Taliban, resulting in Mazari's death. He was replaced as leader by Karim Khalili, who switched the *Wahdat* headquarters to Bamian and joined the anti-Taliban pact following the ouster of Massoud's forces from Kabul. *Wahdat* resistance both at Shibar Pass and in Mazar-i Sharif delivered the Taliban's two most crushing defeats.

ABDUL RASUL SAYYAF

A Sunni religious scholar of Pashtun origin, Sayyaf co-founded *Jamiat-i Islami*, for which he served as deputy leader in the early 1970s. From 1980, he headed *Ittehad-i Islami*, a marginal faction with a following in Paghman and Kabul provinces, and which won disproportionate political influence as a result of lavish funding from Saudi Arabia and Pakistan's *Jamaat-i Islami* political party. This was chiefly due to Sayyaf's ability to speak Arabic and his vehement anti-Shiism. Sayyaf was the sole Pashtun leader to join the Rabbani administration, in which he was responsible for drafting a new constitution. His whereabouts following the defeat of the government are unknown.

MAULAWI YUNIS KHALIS

Anti-Shia, Pashtun religious leader from Nangarhar Province, he fled to Pakistan in 1974 and created his own faction, *Hizb-i Islami (Khalis)*. Highly effective in the field during the *jihad*, Khalis refused to join or recognise the *mujahedin* governments and did not participate in the Jalalabad or Islamabad conferences. He retained considerable influence, both as 'honest broker' during the first siege of Kabul when he recruited a peacekeeping force of neutral *mujahedin*, and through his influence with Haji Qadir, governor of the Nangarhar *shura*. Khalis lives in Peshawar.

MAULAWI MOHAMMAD NABI MOHAMMADI

An Amadzhai Pashtun from Logar and a pre-communist MP, Mohammadi founded *Harakat Inqilab-i Islami*, the largest of the three 'traditionalist' resistance groups, so-called to distinguish them from the four 'Islamist' formations. *Harakat* combined elements from both the urban intelligentsia and the *madrassa* system and controlled several southern provinces. He endorsed both the Jalalabad and Islamabad accords, served as vice-president under Rabbani who was rumoured to favour him as a successor in the event that he would step down. A number of former *Harakat* commanders, including Mullah Mohammad Omar, joined the Taliban and currently sit in its *shura*. Mohammadi lives in Peshawar.

SIBGHATOLLAH MOJADEDDI

'Traditionalist' religious leader from a prestigious Sufi family, Mojadeddi's Afghanistan National Liberation Front was predominantly Pashtun but lacked significant external funding. He was appointed first interim president after the fall of Najibullah, handing power to Rabbani whom he subsequently condemned, without committing his small group of fighters to Hekmatyar's military effort.

PIR SAYED AHMAD GAILANI

Western-educated Pashtun of Arab origin and spiritual head of the Sufi Qadiryya sect, Gailani was regarded as one of the most moderate of the *mujahedin* leaders during the Soviet war. His military force remained small, due to lack of external patronage and, possibly, his blood connections with the former royal family.

ISMAIL KHAN

Born in Farah and a military captain in Herat, he commanded the 1979 mutiny against the 'Saur Revolution' of President Taraki which led to the Soviet invasion. A high-ranking member of *Jamiat-i Islami*'s western command, he diversified his alliances after becoming *emir* of Herat in April 1992 to accommodate Iranian and Turkmen demands and stabilise the province's large Pashtun minority. After the fall of Herat to the Taliban in September 1995, he fled with 8,000 men to Mashad in Iran, only returning in October 1996 to join forces with Dostum's troops in Badghis Province. He was arrested in May 1997 by the mutinous General Abdul Malik of Faryab province and handed over to Taliban forces in Mazar-i Sharif, before being flown to Kandahar. He escaped in early 2000.

Notes

CHAPTER 1

1. Nancy Hatch Dupree, *Afghanistan through the eyes of Pakistani cartoonists*, Baba, 1994
2. *Sunday Times*, 29 September 1996; *Guardian*, 12 October 1996
3. *Guardian*, 12 October 1996
4. Ibid.
5. *Sunday Times*, 29 September 1996; *Guardian*, 12 October 1996
6. *Daily Telegraph*, 28 September 1996; *Guardian*, 12 October 1996; interview with Terry Pfizer, UNHCR, January 1997
7. *Sunday Times*, 29 September 1996; *Guardian*, 12 October 1996
8. *Guardian*, 12 October 1996; personal interview, January 1997
9. *Sunday Times*, 29 September 1996
10. *Guardian*, 2 October 1996
11. Personal interview, January 1997
12. *International Herald Tribune*, 11 March 1992
13. *UNICEF Country Programme Management Plan, Strategic Review*, 1996
14. Franz Fanon, *A Dying Colonialism*, Pelican Books, 1970
15. *Guardian*, 21 October 1996
16. Taliban decree, translated by Acbar, 6 January 1997
17. Amnesty International, *Grave Abuses in the Name of Religion, November 1996*; personal interview, January 1997
18. *Grave Abuses*, November 1996
19. Personal interview, January 1997
20. *Guardian*, 24 December 1997
21. *The Nation*, 11 May 1996
22. *The Nation*, 19 October 1996
23. Personal interview, January 1997
24. *New York Times International*, 31 December 1996
25. *Jane's Intelligence Review*, Vol. 7, No. 7
26. Ibid.
27. Personal interview
28. *The World Today*, March 1996
29. *The Muslim*, 9 September 1996
30. *The Muslim*, 12 September 1996; *Frontier Post*, 12 September 1996
31. *The Muslim*, 12 September 1996
32. Economist Intelligence Unit, 4/1996; personal interview, January 1997
33. *Frontier Post*, 2 December 1996

CHAPTER 2

1. John Fullerton, 'The Soviet Occupation of Afghanistan', *Far Eastern Economic Review*, 1983

2. *Asiaweek*, 12 February 1996
3. Barnett R. Rubin, *The Search for Peace in Afghanistan*, Yale University Press, 1995
4. Ibid.
5. *The Soviet Occupation*
6. Amnesty International, *Human rights defenders in Afghanistan*, November 1996
7. *BAAG*, 10 October 1994
8. *Jane's Intelligence Review*, April 1996
9. *The Search for Peace*
10. Ibid.
11. Ibid.
12. Ibid.
13. *Jane's Intelligence Review*, Vol. 7, No. 7
14. *The Search for Peace*
15. *Jane's Intelligence Review*, March 1993
16. *BAAG*, 24 August 1992
17. Robert Byron, *The Road to Oxiana*, Macmillan and Co., 1937
18. *BAAG*, 15 April 1994
19. Ibid., 24 August 1992
20. Economist Intelligence Unit, *Country Profile*, 1993–94
21. Personal interview, UNICEF, 1995
22. *BAAG*, 24 August 1992
23. *The Search for Peace*
24. Personal interview, December 1997
25. Amnesty International, *Women in Afghanistan: a human rights disaster*, May 1992
26. UNHCR Repatriation Statistics 1992, (published May 1997); *BAAG*, 30 September 1992
27. *BAAG*, 15 April 1994; *BAAG*, 10 October 1994
28. Ibid., 10 October 1994
29. Ibid., 10 October 1994
30. Ibid., 10 October 1994

CHAPTER 3

1. *Time*, 31 March 1997; *New York Times International*, 31 December 1996
2. Barnett R. Rubin, *The Search for Peace in Afghanistan*, Yale University Press, 1995
3. UN document, *Profile of Afghan leaders and personalities*, (undated)
4. *New York Times International*, 31 December 1996
5. Ibid.
6. *BAAG*, 10 October 1994
7. Economist Intelligence Unit, 4/1994
8. Ibid., 1/1995
9. *Jane's Defence Weekly*, Vol. 7, No. 7
10. Economist Intelligence Unit, 4/1994
11. *Time*, 27 February 1995

12. Rubin, *The Search for Peace*; UN Special Mission to Afghanistan, July 1994
13. Amnesty International, *Responsibility for Human Rights Disaster*, September 1995
14. Ibid.
15. *Time*, 27 February 1995
16. Agence France-Presse, 18 November 1996
17. *Jane's Defence Weekly*, 9 October 1996
18. *BAAG*, 16 February 1995
19. Economist Intelligence Unit, 2/1996
20. UNICEF's Marc Powe in a letter on 3 February 1997; *Daily Telegraph*, 22 February 1997
21. *Jane's Defence Weekly*, Vol.7, No. 7
22. *Time*, 27 October 1995
23. Personal interview, January 1997
24. Economist Intelligence Unit, 3/1995
25. Agence France-Presse, 24 December 1995; UN *Weekly Update*, 2 January 1996
26. *Sunday Times*, 24 March 1996
27. *UN Weekly Update*, 19 February 1996
28. Economist Intelligence Unit, 3/1996
29. Ibid., 4/1996
30. Ibid.
31. *New York Times Service*, 17 February 1997
32. *Jane's Defence Weekly*, 27 November 1996
33. *Independent*, 10 October 1996
34. *Jane's Intelligence Review*, August 1997
35. *BAAG*, 24 July 1996; *Jane's Intelligence Review*, August 1997
36. *The Nation*, 8 October 1996
37. UNICEF's Marc Powe in a letter on 3 February 1997
38. Economist Intelligence Unit, 1/1997
39. Ibid.
40. Ibid.
41. UNICEF's Marc Powe in a letter on 3 February 1997

CHAPTER 4

1. *Guardian*, 4 January 1997
2. *Time*, 31 March 1997
3. *Observer*, 9 March 1997
4. Ibid.
5. *Guardian*, 4 January 1997
6. *New York Times International*, 31 December 1996
7. *Le Monde Diplomatique*, February 1997; private interview, Kabul, February 1997
8. *The Nation*, 19 November 1996

9. Louis Dupree 'Tribal warfare in Afghanistan and Pakistan', in Akbar S. Ahmed and David M. Hart (eds), *Islamic Tribal Societies*, Routledge and Kegan Paul, London, 1994
10. *The Muslim*, 10 September 1996
11. *Frontier Post*, 20 October 1996
12. *New York Times International*, 31 December 1996
13. V. Gregorian, *The Emergence of Modern Afghanistan: Politics of Reform and Modernisation 1880–1946*, Stanford, California 1969. Cited in Asgar Christiansen 'Aiding Afghanistan: the background and prospects for reconstruction in a fragmented society', SIDA, Stockholm, 1994
14. Amnesty International, *Afghanistan: grave abuses in the name of religion*, November 1996
15. *Frontier Post*, 11 February 1996
16. Amnesty International, *Afghanistan*, November 1996; Amnesty appeal, *Fear of further amputations*, 24 April 1997; *Guardian* 24 October 1996
17. *Daily Telegraph*, 27 July 1997
18. *BAAG*, 15 November 1996
19. *Guardian*, 21 December 1996
20. Personal interview, Kabul, February 1997
21. *Guardian*, 7 November 1996
22. Amnesty International, *Women in Afghanistan: The violations continue*, June 1997
23. *Guardian*, 6 January 1997
24. *The Nation*, 19 November 1996
25. *Guardian*, 4 January 1996
26. *Le Monde Diplomatique*, February 1997
27. *News*, 4 October 1996
28. *The Nation*, 19 November 1996; *News*, 4 October 1996
29. Private interview, Kabul, January 1997
30. *Pakistan Times*, 11 January 1997
31. *UN Weekly Update*, 2 January 1997
32. Personal interview, January 1997
33. *BAAG*, 24 April 1996
34. Ibid., 1 October 1996, *Guardian*, 4 January 1997, *Time* 31 March 1997
35. *Jane's Defence Weekly*, 27 November 1996
36. *Economist Intelligence Quarterly*, March 1995
37. *BAAG*, 24 April 1996
38. *Economist Intelligence Quarterly*, March 1995
39. *Guardian*, 24 December 1996
40. *The Nation*, 11 May 1996
41. Reuters, 10 June 1997
42. Taliban prohibition, No. 6240, 26 September 1996
43. *Guardian*, 12 December 1996
44. Taliban edict, 15 December 1996
45. Interview, Kabul, February 1996
46. Interview, Kabul, February 1996
47. *The Muslim*, 7 October 1996
48. *Al-Majallah*, 23 October 1996

CHAPTER 5

1. *Los Angeles Times*, 23 November 1995
2. *Washington Post*, 19–20 July 1992
3. Barnett R. Rubin, *The Search for Peace in Afghanistan*, Yale University Press, 1995
4. *The News*, 25 August 1996
5. Economist Intelligence Unit, 1/1995
6. *Frontier Post*, 22 August 1996
7. *The Nation*, 6 May 1996
8. *Ibid.*, 19 October 1996
9. *Ibid.*, 2 October 1996
10. *The News*, 2 September 1996
11. *Frontier Post*, 7 October 1996
12. *Time*, 4 November 1996
13. Economist Intelligence Unit, 4/1994
14. *Jane's Intelligence Review*, Vol. 7, No. 7; *Le Monde Diplomatique*, February 1997
15. *Jane's Intelligence Review*, December 1996
16. Personal interview, January 1997
17. *Speech to the UN General Assembly*, 4 October 1995
18. *The News*, 20 December 1995
19. Economist Intelligence Unit, 3/1995; *The World Today*, March 1996
20. *The News*, 12 March 1996
21. *BAAG*, 15 October 1995; Economist Intelligence Unit, 3/1995
22. *The World Today*, March 1996
23. *BAAG*, 28 March 1996
24. Economist Intelligence Unit, 2/1996
25. *BAAG*, 30 January 1996
26. *The News*, 12 March 1996
27. Economist Intelligence Unit, 2/1996
28. *The Muslim*, 23 May 1996; *BAAG*, 1 October 1996
29. Agence France-Presse, 25 May 1996
30. *The Nation*, 11 May 1996
31. *The News*, 2 September 1996
32. *Frontier Post*, 12 May 1996
33. *The Muslim*, 5 May 1996
34. *BAAG*, 1 October 1996
35. Agence France-Presse, 11 January 1997

CHAPTER 6

1. Barnett R. Rubin, *The Search for Peace in Afghanistan*, Yale University Press, 1995
2. Agence France-Presse, 25 May 1996
3. *UN Special Mission to Afghanistan*, July 1994
4. Ibid.
5. Private interview, February 1997

6. Rubin, *The Search for Peace*
7. Economist Intelligence Unit, 3/1995
8. *The Muslim*, 6 November 1996
9. Economist Intelligence Unit, 3/1995
10. Ibid.
11. *The News*, 20 December 1995
12. *BAAG*, 1 October 1996; *Guardian*, 4 January 1997
13. *Guardian*, 17 October 1996, *The Muslim*, 23 October 1996, *The Nation*, 25 October 1996
14. <http://www.rediff.com>
15. <http://www.rediff.com>
16. *Guardian*, 12 February 1997
17. *BAAG*, 15 June 1994, *The Nation*, 11 May 1996
18. Economist Intelligence Unit, 3/1997
19. *Guardian*, 12 February 1997
20. Economist Intelligence Unit, 4/1996
21. UNICEF's Marc Powe in a letter on 3 February 1997; *Daily Telegraph*, 22 September 1997
22. *Jane's Intelligence Review*, Anthony Davies, August 1997
23. *Time*, 9 June 1997
24. *Jane's Intelligence Review*, Anthony Davies, August 1997
25. <http://www.rediff.com>
26. *Jane's Intelligence Review*, Anthony Davies, August 1997
27. *The Times*, 26 May 1997, *Time*, 9 June 1997
28. *Daily Telegraph*, 26 May 1997
29. *Jane's Intelligence Review*, Anthony Davies, August 1997
30. *Jane's Intelligence Review*, Anthony Davies, August 1997; *Time*, 9 June 1997
31. *Daily Telegraph*, 27 May 1997
32. *Time*, 9 June 1997; *Daily Telegraph*, 27 May 1997
33. *Daily Telegraph*, 27 May 1997
34. *Guardian*, 11 June 1997
35. *New York Times*, 25 August 1997; *Jane's Intelligence Review*, August 1997
36. *Economist Intelligence Unit*, 3/1997
37. *Middle East International*, 13 June 1997;
38. *Amnesty International*, November 1997
39. Reuters, 10 June 1997
40. *Time*, 9 June 1997

CHAPTER 7

1. <http://www.gov.uz>
2. *Jane's Intelligence Review*, 'Drugs war in Central Asa', October 1994
3. *BAAG*, 1 October 1993
4. *Ibid.*, 15 June 1994, passim
5. *The World Today*, March 1996
6. *The News*, 28 October 1994
7. *The World Today*, March 1996

8. Amnesty International, *Responsibilities for human rights disasters*, September 1995
9. *The News*, 18 August 1996
10. *The World Today*, March 1996
11. Ibid.
12. Ibid.
13. Ibid.
14. Ibid.
15. Ibid.
16. *Guardian*, 26 May 1997
17. *Far East Economic Review*, 24 October 1996

CHAPTER 8

1. *Jane's Intelligence Review*, February 1996
2. Bridas Corporation, *Corporate Profile,* 1996
3. Economist Intelligence Unit, *Country Profile, Afghanistan, 1994–1995*
4. Ibid.
5. World of Information, *Turkmenistan*, 1995
6. World of Information, *Azerbaijan*, 1995
7. *Oil and Gas Journal*, 20 June 1994
8. *Jane's Intelligence Review*, February 1996
9. World of Information, Azerbaijan 1995
10. 'Russia, the West and the Caspian energy hub', *Middle East Journal*, Vol. 49, No. 2, 1995
11. *Jane's Intelligence Review*, February 1996
12. *Houston Chronicle*, 27 June 1996
13. Carlos Bulgheroni, keynote address, 13 March 1996, TIOGE '96
14. *Transitions*, October 1998
15. *Saudi Arabia Petroleum Industry*, Arab Press Service, 23–30 October, Sunningdale Publications, 1996
16. Ibid.
17. *Houston Chronicle* 27 June 1996
18. Ibid.
19. *Transitions*, October 1998
20. *New York Times International*, 31 December 1996
21. Frédéric Grare, 'La nouvelle donné énergetique autour de la Mer Caspienne', CERI (Centre for International Studies and Research), No. 23, June 1997
22. *The News*, 16 March 1996
23. Economist Intelligence Unit, 4/1996
24. Reuters, 1 October 1996
25. *Transitions*, October 1998

CHAPTER 9

1. Yossef Bodansky, 'Rise of HizbAllah International', *Strategic Policy*, Vol XXIV, No. 8, 3 August 1996

2. Ibid.
3. *The Muslim*, 23 May 1996
4. *New York Herald Tribune,* 11 March 1992
5. Anthony Hyman, 'Arab involvement in the Afghan war', *Beirut Review*, spring 1994
6. Barnett R. Rubin, *The Search for Peace in Afghanistan*, Yale University Press, 1995
7. Ibid.
8. James Bruce, 'Arab veterans of the Afghan War, *Jane's Intelligence Review*, Vol. 7, No. 4; *Beirut Review*
9. *Beirut Review*; private interview, Kunar valley, December 1994
10. *BAAG*, 1 October 1993; Economist Intelligence Unit, 1/1996
11. *Jane's Intelligence Review*
12. Ibid.
13. *Guardian*, 17 July 1997; *Joint CIA/FBI statement*, 17 June 1997; <http://www.odci.gov/cia/public_affairs/press_release/>
14. *BAAG*, 1 October 1993
15. Agence France-Presse, 17 February 1997
16. *Beirut Review*
17. *Intelligence Newsletter*, No. 300, 28 October 1996
18. *Boston Globe*, 27 August 1998
19. *Nida' ul-Islam* October-November 1996; http://www.cia.com.au/islam/articles/15/LADIN>; *Intelligence Newsletter*
20. *The Times*, 10 May 1997; *Intelligence Newsletter* No. 239, 20 April 1994; <http://www.indigo-net.com/dossiers/>
21. *Intelligence Newsletter*, No. 331, 19 March 1997; *Independent* 22 March 1997
22. *Newsweek* (International Edition), 13 October 1997
23. State Department press release, February 1996; *Sunday Times*, 27 October 1996
24. Chris Kozlow, 'The Bombing of Khobar Towers: who did it and who funded it', *Jane's Intelligence Review*, December 1997; *Sunday Times*, 27 October 1996
25. *Jane's Intelligence Review*, December 1997
26. Ibid.
27. *Strategic Policy*, Vol XXIV, No. 8, 3 August 1996
28. Ibid.
29. Ibid.
30. Ibid.
31. Ibid.
32. Thomas Hunter, 'Bomb School: International terrorist training camps', *Jane's Intelligence Review*, March 1997
33. *Intelligence Newsletter* No. 312, 29 May 1997; *Jane's Intelligence Review,* March 1997
34. *Intelligence Newsletter* No. 312, 29 May 1997
35. Ibid.
36. *Independent*, 22 March 1997; *Guardian 17 July 1997*
37. *Al-Quds Al-Arabi*, 27 November 1996
38. Ibid.

39. *Independent*, 22 March 1997
40. *Al-Quds Al-Arabi*
41. *CNN Impact*, 12 May 1997, 'Osama Bin-Ladin: Holy Terror?'
42. *The Times*, 10 May 1997
43. *Sunday Times*, 27 October 1996
44. Private interview, Jalalabad, February 1997
45. *Sunday Times*, 27 October 1996
46. *Guardian*, 28 November 1996
47. Agence France-Presse, 10 December 1996
48. Roger Howard, 'Wrath of Islam: HUA analysed', *Jane's Intelligence Review*, October 1997
49. <http://www.afghan-government.com/news/97_11_02.html>
50. <http://www.rediff.com>
51. *Jane's Intelligence Review*, October 1997
52. International Institute of Strategic Studies, Vol 4, Issue 8, October 1998
53. *The Nation*, 17 February 1997
54. *Jane's Intelligence Review*, October 1997
55. *Intelligence Newsletter*, No, 331, 19 March 1997
56. Reuters 17 April 1998; <http://www.afghanistan-center.com/news>

CHAPTER 10

1. *Middle East Intelligence*, 17 February 1995
2. Reuters, 10 June 1997
3. Interview, Jalalabad, February 1997
4. *The Nation*, 25 September 1996
5. Interview, Kabul, February 1997
6. United Nations Drug Control Programme (UNDCP), *Afghanistan Opium Poppy Survey*, 1994
7. Alfred W. McCoy, *The Politics of Heroin: CIA Complicity in the Global Drug Trade*, second edition, Lawrence Hill Books, 1992
8. Sumita Kumar, 'Drug Trafficking in Pakistan', New Delhi Institute for Defence Studies and Analyses, 1995
9. McCoy, *The Politics of Heroin*
10. Ibid.
11. Ibid.
12. UNDCP *Afghanistan Opium*
13. Amnesty International, 'Afghanistan', November 1995
14. Thomas Hunter, 'Manportable SAMs: the airline anathema', *Jane's Intelligence Review*, October 1996
15. *Pakistan Times*, 30 September 1996
16. McCoy, *The Politics of Heroin*
17. Barnett R. Rubin, *The Search for Peace in Afghanistan*, Yale University Press, 1995, p. 118–19; McCoy, *The Politics of Heroin*
18. McCoy, *The Politics of Heroin*; Anon, 'Afghanistan: The Taliban face an opium dilemma', *Geopolitical Drug Dispatch*, No. 63, January 1997
19. *Washington Post*, 12 September 1994

20. CIA Report, 'Heroin in Pakistan: Sowing the wind', reproduced in *Friday Times*, 3 September 1993
21. Anon, 'Tajikistan: Three borders for the labs', *Geopolitical Drug Dispatch*, No. 63, (January 1997)
22. UNDCP, 1996 *Afghanistan Opium*
23. *Geopolitical Drug Dispatch*, No. 63, January 1997
24. Ibid.
25. Ibid.
26. Ibid.
27. Amnesty International, *Grave abuses in the name of religion*, November 1996
28. *Geopolitical Drug Dispatch*
29. Interview, Islamabad, February 1997
30. *Geopolitical Drug Dispatch*

CHAPTER 11

1. *Independent*, 8 October 1996
2. *The News*, 30 September 1996
3. *The News*, 6 October; 30 November 1996
4. UNICEF *Country Programme Management Plan, Strategy Review Exercise*, 1996
5. *Guardian*, 27 December 1996
6. *Guardian*, 27 December 1996
7. Amnesty International, *Grave Abuses in the Name of Religion*, November 1996; *Women in Afghanistan: The Violations Continue*, June 1997
8. Agence France-Presse, 6 October and 13 November 1996
9. *BAAG*, 15 November 1996
10. Personal interview, January 1997
11. Personal interview, January 1997
12. Personal interview, January 1997
13. Personal interview, December 1995
14. Agence France-Presse, 20 October 1996
15. Personal interview, January 1997
16. Personal interview, January 1997
17. Economist Intelligence Unit, 4/1996
18. Email, February 1998
19. Carol A. Le Duc and Homa Sabri, *Room to Manoeuvre: Study on Women's Programming*, UN Development Programme, July–September 1996
20. Email, February 1998
21. *Guardian*, 11 November 1995
22. UNHCR fax, 20 May 1998, *Refugee Statistics* 1997
23. Personal interview, January 1997
24. Email, February 1998
25. Personal interview, April 1996
26. Memo by Michael Scott, *In lieu of a conclusions and recommendations section – some questions*, 12 November 1996

27. Kabul Information Forum, *Position statement of international agencies working in Kabul*, 5 October 1996
28. *The News*, 6 October 1996; UN Assistance to Afghanistan, *Weekly Update*, No 187; edict by *Amr Bil Marof Wa Nai An Munkir*, late November 1996
29. Agence France-Presse, 5 November 1996
30. *The News*, 30 September 1996
31. *Frontier Post*, 2 October 1996; *The News*, 23 December 1996
32. Reuters, 3 December 1996
33. Jim Mohan, UNICEF, personal interview, January 1997
34. Paul Barker, CARE, personal interview, January 1996
35. David Bellamy's memo to Qazi Shaukat Fareed, UN Department of Humanitarian Affairs, 18 November 1996
36. Letter to Benon Sevan from Qazi Shaukat Fareed, UN Department of Humanitarian Affairs, 18 November 1996
37. Agence France-Presse, 10 October 1996, *BAAG*, 15 November 1996
38. Personal interview, February 1997
39. Amnesty International, 21 March 1997
40. Nancy Dupree, interview, December 1995
41. ACBAR *Annual Report* 1993/94; David Lockhart, UNDP, personal interview, December 1995
42. Personal interview, December 1995
43. Personal interview, January 1997
44. *Guardian*, 27 May 1997
45. Personal interviews, February 1997; International Forum of Assistance to Afghanistan, Working Paper 14; Le Duc and Sabri *Room to Manoeuvre*
46. International Forum of Assistance to Afghanistan, *Summary of Proceedings*
47. Internal UNICEF memo, undated, cited January 1997
48. Internal UNICEF memo, undated, cited January 1997
49. UNICEF press release, 1 April 1997

CHAPTER 12

1. <http://www.taleban.com/comment.html> *Massacre of prisoners in Northern Afghanistan*, note handed to UNDP, 22 December 1997
2. Ibid.
3. Ibid.
4. John F. Burns, *New York Times Service*, 25 August 1997
5. Al Santoli, *US Veteran Dispatch*, June/July/August 1997
6. Ibid.
7. *OMRI*, 14 October 1996; <http://www.eia.doe.gov/emeu/cabs/turkmen.html>
8. *Washington Post Service*, 12 January 1998; 'Pipeline to power', *Transitions*, October 1998
9. 'Afghans' treatment of women leaks into pipeline deal', *Washington Post Service*, 12 January 1998

10. *Jane's Intelligence Review*, August 1997
11. Amnesty International, *Concerned about the safety of opposition general*, 23 May 1997
12. UNDP email
13. Anthony Davies, *Jane's Intelligence Review*, August 1997
14. <http://www.afghan-government.com/news/97_10_10.html>
15. Association for Peace and Democracy for Afghanistan, 24 September 1997
16. Reuters, 15 October 1997
17. RFE/RL, 12 September 1997
18. UNDP email
19. Reuters, 15 October 1997; UNDP email
20. UNDP email
21. Ibid.
22. Reuters, 8 November 1997; IPS, 26 November 1997
23. Reuters, 8 November 1997
24. Reuters, 13 November 1997
25. UNDP email
26. *Private Eye*, 2 October 1998
27. *Journal of the American Medical Association*, 5 August 1998
28. Sarah Horner, *IPI Report*, Fourth Quarter 1997
29. Amnesty International USA, 24 June 1997
30. Reuters, 10 November 1997
31. *Index on Censorship,* Interview with Emma Bonino, 2/1998
32. Sarah Horner, *IPI Report*, Fourth Quarter 1997:
33. *Washington Post Service*, 12 January 1998
34. Ibid.
35. Editorial, *New York Times*, 5 November 1997
36. Reuters, 18 November;
37. *Transitions*, October 1998
38. Ibid., October 1998
39. *Washington Post Service*, 12 January 1998
40. Reuters, 22 July 1997; *Washington Post Service*, 12 January 1998
41. Press release, *Agencia Efe*, 8 March 1997
42. *Transitions,* October 1998
43. *UNOCAL and slave trade in Burma*, <http://www.sf-frontlines.com/mar98/columns/burma.html>
44. News Service Amnesty International, 133/97, 25 July 1997
45. Reuters, 13 July 97
46. Economist Intelligence Unit, 2/1997
47. Reuters, 11 October 1997
48. Ibid.
49. Ibid., 11 November 1997
50. UN Department of Public Information, *Reporting human rights violations in Afghanistan*, 10 November 1997
51. Reuters, 13 November 1997
52. Amnesty International, *Flagrant abuse of the right to life and dignity*, April 1998; <http://www.afghanistan-center.com/news_98_03.html>
53. Amnesty International, April 1998

54. Ibid.
55. *The Nation*, 16 April 1998; <http://www.afghan-web.com/aop/yest.html>
56. *The Nation*, 16 April 1998
57. Network, *Vision of Islamic Republic of Iran* 12 September 1998; Reuters, 17 September 1998
58. Afghan Islamic Press, 13 February 1998
59. Ibid.
60. *ICRC newsletter*, March 1998
61. *International Herald Tribune*, 26 March 1998
62. Reuters, 16 April 1998
63. Ibid.
64. *Intelligence Newsletter*, No. 331, 19 March 1998; *International Herald Tribune*, 1 September, 1998
65. *Al-Quds al-Arabi*, 'Text of *fatwah* urging *jihad* against Americans', 23 February 1998
66. Agence France-Presse, 6 September 1998
67. Reuters, 17 April 1998
68. *Jane's Defence Weekly*, 13 May 1998; Reuters, 17 April 1998
69. *Jane's Defence Weekly*, 13 May 1998
70. Ibid.
71. *International Institute for Strategic Studies*, Vol. 4/8, October 1998
72. Reuters 2 June 1998; 5 June 1998
73. Ibid.; *The Scotsman*, 31 July 1998
74. Ibid.
75. Ibid.
76. Ibid., Reuters 4 June 1998
77. Reuters 4 June 1998, Reuters, 6 July 1998
78. Ibid., 6 July 1998
79. Ibid., 20 July 1998; 23 July 1998
80. Ibid., 19 July 1998; 20 July 1998
81. Reuters, 6 July 1998
82. Ibid.
83. Ibid., 22 July 1998
84. Ibid., 22 July 1998
85. Ibid., 23 July 1998
86. Ibid., Agence Europe, 23 July 1998
87. *Janes's Defence Weekly*, 26 August 1998
88. Ibid.
89. Iran Network 1 TV, 4 August 1998; *ITAR-TASS* news agency, 5 August 1998; *Reuters*, 17 August 1998
90. Human Rights Watch, November 1998, Vol. 10, No. X; *Middle East International*, 13 November 1998
91. Human Rights Watch, November 1998, Vol. 10, No. X; *Middle East International* 13 November 1998
92. Ibid.
93. Human Rights Watch, November 1998, Vol. 10, No. X
94. Ibid.; *Middle East International*, 13 November 1998
95. Human Rights Watch, November 1998, Vol. 10, No. X

96. Ibid.
97. Ibid.
98. *The News*, 3 November 1998
99. Amnesty International, *Flagrant abuse of the right to life and dignity*, April 1998
100. Human Rights Watch, November 1998, Vol. 10, No. X
101. Ibid; *Middle East International*, 13 November 1998
102. Human Rights Watch
103. Ibid.
104. Ibid.
105. Ibid.
106. Ibid.
107. Ibid.
108. Ibid.
109. Agence France-Presse, 15 August 1998
110. *Middle East International*, 13 November 1998
111. Ibid.
112. Ibid.

CHAPTER 13

1. *Washington Post*, 21 September 1998
2. *New York Times*, 10 August 1998
3. *The Nation*, 21 September 1998
4. *New York Times*, 22 September 1998
5. *Independent*, 21 August 1998
6. Reuters, 8 August 1998
7. *Jang*, 5 September 1998
8. *Observer*, 21 August 1998
9. *Time*, 4 January 1999; *Newsweek*, 4 January 1999
10. *Observer*, 23 August 1998; *Sunday Times*, 23 August 1998
11. *Ettela'at*, 17 September 1998
12. *Frontier Post*, 31 October 1998
13. *Time*, 31 August 1998
14. *Jane's Defence Weekly*, 2 September 1998; RFE/RL, 12 September 1997; *Independent on Sunday*, 1 November 1998
15. *Time*, 31 August 1998
16. Ibid.
17. *Sunday Times*, 23 August 1998
18. Al-Jazeera TV, 12 September 1998, cited by Reuters, 14 September 1998
19. *Time*, 4 January 1999; Electronic Telegraph, 21 February 1999
20. *Guardian*, 22 August 1998
21. Ibid., 25 August 1998; *Jane's Defence Weekly*, 2 September 1998
22. *Guardian*, 22 August 1998
23. *Jane's Defence Weekly*, 2 September 1998
24. *The News International*, 5 September 1998
25. BBC World Service, 17 November 1998; Reuters, 17 November 1998
26. Reuters, 17 November 1998

27. *Guardian*, 21 August 1998
28. *Frontier Post*, 4 September 1998
29. *Hindu Online*, 11 November 1998
30. *Jane's Defence Weekly*, 2 September 1998
31. Al-Jazeera TV, 12 September 1998, cited by Reuters, 14 September 1998; *Sunday Times*, 13 September 1998
32. *Sunday Times*, 13 September 1998
33. *Washington Post*, 23 September 1999
34. Ibid., 21 September 1998
35. Ibid., pA27, 6 September 1998; *Guardian*, 5 October 1998
36. Reuters, 14 September 1998
37. Ibid., 16 September 1998
38. *New York Times Service*, 5 October 1998
39. *Le Monde*, 31 October 1998
40. Ibid.
41. *The Nation*, 16 April 1998; *The News*, 3 November 1998
42. *Frontier Post*, 31 October 1998
43. *The News*, 30 November 1998
44. Agence France-Presse, 1 October 1998
45. *A Message to the People of the USA*, 8 October 1998, via the Senate Commission on Foreign Relations
46. *Le Monde*, 31 October 1998
47. *The News*, 3 November 1998
48. *The News*, 12 May 1998
49. Agence France-Presse, 5 December 1998
50. *Fox Research*, 19 October 1998; *Observer*, 1 November 1998
51. Amnesty International, *Detention and killing of political prisoners*, March 1999
52. *Le Monde*, 31 October 1998
53. *Fox Research*, 19 October 1998; *The News*, 10 December 1998
54. *Observer*, 1 November 1998
55. *The News*, 10 December 1998

CHAPTER 14

1. *Guardian*, 1 March 1999
2. *New York Times Service*, 9 November 1998
3. *Time*, 4 January 1999; *Newsweek*, 4 January 1999
4. *Washington Post Service*, 23 September 1998; *Time*, 4 January 1999
5. *Time*, 4 January 1999
6. *The News*, 26 January 1999
7. *Newsweek*, 4 January 1999
8. *The News*, 4 February 1999
9. Associated Press, 11 November 1998
10. *The Nation*, 12 December 1999
11. *New York Times*, 5 December 1998; *Business Recorder*, 4 February 1999
12. *The News*, 6 December 1998
13. Reuters, 6 December 1998

14. *International Herald Tribune*, 1 September 1998; Electronic Telegraph, 21 February 1999
15. News Network International (NNI), 1 April 1999 <http://www.afghan-web.com/aop/today.html> (5 April 1999)
16. *Frontier Post*, 5 February 1999
17. *USA Today*, 11 December 1998; Associated Press, 24 February 1999; *Guardian*, 25 February 1999
18. *Middle East International*, 26 February 1999, *USA Today*, 11 March 1999
19. *New York Times*, 13 April 1999; *Boston Globe*, 15 May 1999
20. Agence France-Presse, 2 January 1999; Reuters, 3 January 1999; *Time* 4 January 1999
21. *Middle East International*, 26 February 1999, *Far East Economic Review*, 11 March 1999
22. *Newsweek*, 22 February 1999
23. Reuters, 4 March 1999
24. *Middle East International*, 26 February 1999; Agence France-Presse, 30 November 1998
25. *Frontier Post*, 22 November 1998
26. *Global Intelligence Update*, 'Where's Osama?', 18 February 1998
27. *Al-Hayat*, 24 February 1999
28. *Guardian*, 1 March 1999
29. *Global Intelligence Update*, citing Voice of the Islamic Republic of Iran, 18 February 1999
30. *New York Times*, 13 April 1999
31. NNI, 28 January 1999
32. AAR, 6 March 1999
33. AAR, 20 July 1999
34. *Guardian*, 7 October 1999; *The News*, 15 March 1999
35. *Dawn*, 17 November 1998
36. *Guardian*, 24 February 1999; Amnesty International, *Detention and killing of political personalities*, March 1999
37. *The News*, 15 July 1999
38. NNI, 26 January 1999
39. Associated Press, 3 March 1999
40. *Guardian*, 13 April 1999
41. Reuters, 27 September 1999
42. Agence France-Presse, 25 May 1999
43. Associated Press, 25 May 1999
44. Agence France-Presse, 22 May 1999
45. Ibid., 19 June 1999
46. *Times of India*, 14 July 1999
47. Associated Press, 10 June 1999
48. Agence France-Presse, 26 July 1999
49. <http://www.rediff.com>
50. *Electronic Telegraph*, 22 July 1999
51. Reuters, 30 July 1999
52. *Electronic Telegraph*, 22 July 1999
53. *Observer*, 4 July 1999
54. Ibid.

55. NNI, 21 July 1999
56. *Observer*, 4 July 1999
57. Associated Press, 6 July 1999
58. *ABC News*, 9 July 1999
59. *Ibid.*
60. *Al-Rai al-Aam,* 8 July 1999, cited in *Dawn*, 8 July 1999
61. Reuters, 9 July 1999
62. *The News*, 28 July 1999

CHAPTER 15

1. *Dawn*, 15 October 1999
2. <http://www.stratfor.com> *Special Report*, 9 July 1999; *The Nation*, 1 August 1999
3. <http://www.stratfor.com> *Special Report*, 9 July 1999
4. United Press InternationaI, 6 July 1999; Agence France-Presse, 20 September 1999
5. *Observer*, 27 June 1999
6. *Middle East International*, 15 October 1999
7. *The News*, 30 August 1999
8. Agence France-Presse, 3 August 1999
9. Ibid.,1 August 1999
10. *Guardian*, 30 July 1999; Agence France-Presse, 1 August 1999
11. Agence France-Presse, 3 August 1999
12. Ibid.
13. *New York Times*, 19 October 1999
14. Agence France-Presse, 4 August 1999; *Guardian*, 6 August 1999
15. *UN Weekly Update* 330, 14 September 1999
16. *International Herald Tribune*, 16 August 1999
17. *New York Times*, 19 October 1999
18. Agence France-Presse, 5 August 1999
19. Ibid., 26 July 1999
20. *The News*, 6 August 1999
21. BBC News, 9 August 1999; Agence France-Presse, 14 August 1999
22. Agence France-Presse, 30 August 1999
23. *New York Times*, 19 October 1999
24. *Frontier Post*, 6 August 1999; Reuters, 9 August 1999
25. *The News*, 11 September 1999
26. Ibid.
27. Reuters, 1 August 1999
28. *The News*, 24 August 1999
29. *Frontier Post*, 29 September 1999
30. *San José Mercury News*, 10 September 1999
31. Ibid.
32. *Times of India*, 20 September 1999
33. NNI, 27 August 1999
34. <http://www.stratfor.com/asia/specialreports/special81.htm>
35. *Guardian*, 19 October 1999

36. Ibid., 18 October 1999
37. AAR, 13 October 1999
38. <http://www.stratfor.com/asia/specialreports/special81.htm>
39. *Friday Times*, 1–7 October 1999
40. Ibid.
41. Ibid.
42. BBC News, 8 October 1999
43. NNI, 8 October 1999
44. *The News*, 8 October 1999
45. Reuters, 13 October 1999
46. Ibid.
47. *Frontier Post*, 10 October 1999
48. Ibid.
49. Agence France-Presse, 11 October 1999
50. *Observer*, 17 October 1999
51. *Frontline*, 19 November 1999
52. *Observer*, 17 October 1999; *Frontline*, 19 November 1999
53. *Frontline*, 19 November 1999
54. Ibid.
55. *Guardian*, 18 October 1999
56. *Frontier Post*, 14 October 1999; *Dawn*, 15 October 1999
57. *Frontline*, 19 November 1999
58. *Guardian*, 18 October 1999
59. Associated Press, 15 October 1999
60. *Dawn*, 4 November 1999
61. AAR, 13 October 1999
62. BBC News, 13 October 1999
63. *Frontier Post*, 13 October 1999
64. <http://www.stratfor.com> 19 November 1999
65. *M2 Communications*, 25 October 1999; UN Document S/PRST/1999/29
66. NNI, 28 October 1999
67. CNN, 15 November 1999
68. Agence France-Presse, 15 October 1999

CHAPTER 16

1. <http://www.realworldrescue.com>
2. Agence France-Presse, 16 November 2000
3. Associated Press, 12 November 1999
4. Agence France-Presse, 14 November 1999
5. Reuters, 12 November 1999
6. *UN Weekly Update*, 17 November 1999: NNI, 15 November 1999
7. Associated Press, 16 November 1999
8. <http://usinfo.state.gov/topical/pol/terror/00120502.htm>
9. *Friday Times*, 17–23 December 1999
10. *New York Times Service*, 17 December 2000
11. *Los Angeles Times*, 21 March 2000
12. *Asiaweek*, Vol.25, No.51, 24 December 1999

13. Interview with Peter Tomsen, Azadi Afghan Radio, 29 January 2000
14. Agence France-Presse, 18 December 1999
15. *Washington Post*, 22 February 2000
16. Agence France-Presse, 5 March 2000
17. *Washington Post*, 24 April 2000
18. Agence France-Presse, 2 January 2000
19. *Statement of the Special Rapporteur on the situation of human rights in Afghanistan*, UN General Assembly, 24 October 2000
20. *New York Times*, 24 January 2000
21. Ibid.
22. BBC News, 3 January 2000
23. *Dawn*, 24 February 2000
24. *New York Times*, 9 March 2000
25. *Times of India*, 10 August 2000
26. Senate Foreign Relations Committee, testimony by Peter Tomsen, 20 July 2000
27. UN Office of the Coordinator for Afghanistan, *Afghanistan Outlook*, December 1999
28. *Statement of the Special Rapporteur*, 24 October 2000
29. *Times of India*, 21 October 2000
30. *Statement of the Special Rapporteur*, 24 October 2000
31. *Statement of the Special Rapporteur*, 24 October 2000
32. *Guardian*, 9 July 2000
33. Senate Foreign Relations Committee, testimony by Assistant Secretary of State Karl F. Inderfurth, 20 July 2000
34. Senate Foreign Relations Committee, testimony by Peter Tomsen, 20 July 2000
35. Personal interview with Wali Massoud, July 2000
36. Azadi Afghan News, 9 October 2000
37. *Daily Telegraph*, 3 October 2000
38. Ibid.
39. *Business Recorder*, 24 October 2000
40. *The Times*, 28 October 2000
41. *Daily Telegraph*, 3 October 2000
42. BBC News, 30 September 2000
43. CNN World News, 23 October 2000; *Business Recorder*, 24 October 2000
44. <http://www.defencejournal.com/2000/nov/talibaan.htm>
45. NNI, 8 October 2000
46. *The News*, 19 and 21 October 2000
47. Associated Press, 12 October 2000
48. *Program on New Approaches to Russian Security Policy*, memo 1555, 'A Dangerous Balancing Act', Yale University, November 2000
49. *Program on New Approaches* 1555, 'A Dangerous Balancing Act'
50. *The News*, 19 October 2000
51. *New York Times*, 24 November 2000
52. *New York Times*, 24 and 27 November 2000
53. BBC News, 13 November 2000
54. *Guardian*, 7 November 2000; Reuters, 13 November 2000

55. Reuters, 13 November 2000
56. Agence France-Presse, 25 October 2000
57. *Al Hayat*, 1 November 2000
58. United Press International, 1 November 2000

Index

Compiled by Syra Morley